A History of the Orchid

Old print illustrating two varieties of *Cattleya labiata*.

A History
of the Orchid

by Merle A. Reinikka
with a Nomenclatural Update by Gustavo A. Romero

Timber Press
Portland • London

Cover illustration: *Barkeria lindleyana*, photo by Kerry A. Dressler.
Photograph credits: courtesy of American Orchid Society, Inc., pp. 4, 7, 14, 19, 21, 22, 26, 27, 32, 42, 51, 54, 59, 71, 72, 87, 89, 124, 139, 153, 156, 171, 191, 196, 206, 212, 215, 221, 228, 255, 272, 287, 293, 297, 302; Flora Malesiana Foundation, pp. 130, 141, 145; Montreal Botanical Gardens, pp. 202, 248; Royal Botanic Gardens, Kew, p. 122; Royal Horticultural Society, London, pp. 149, 169, 174; Royal Swedish Academy of Science, p. 113; and Sidney Botanic Library, p. 236.
Frontispiece courtesy of George Rosner; photographs on p. 28 by Alan Kapuler, courtesy of American Orchid Society, Inc.; on p. 226 courtesy of Miss Eileen Low; and on p. 260 courtesy of David Sander.
Photographs on p. 9 from *Theatrum Botanicum* by John Parkinson; on p. 116 from *The Botanical Explorers of New Zealand* by Rewa Glenn; on p. 127 from *Journal of Botany*; on pp. 136, 184, 199, 211, 246, 279 from *Curtis's Botanical Magazine—Dedications and Portraits*; on p. 160 from *British Botanists* by John Gilmour; on p. 164 from *Paxton and the Bachelor Duke* by Violet R. Markham; on p. 179 from *The Garden*; on p. 189 drawn from a photographic portrait in *Ogrodnictwo*; on p. 250 from *La Tribune Horticole*; on pp. 193, 204, 219, 223, 230 courtesy of *Gardeners' Chronicle*; and on p. 275 courtesy of *Orchid Review*.

The Haseltine Building
133 S.W. Second Avenue, Suite 450
Portland, Oregon 97204-3527
www.timberpress.com

2 The Quadrant
135 Salusbury Road
London NW6 6RJ
www.timberpress.co.uk

First published in 1972 by University of Miami Press

Printed in the United States of America

Library of Congress Cataloging-in-Publication Data

Reinikka, Merle A.
    A history of the orchid / by Merle A. Reinikka ; with a nomenclatural
update by Gustavo A. Romero.
        p.   cm.
    Includes bibliographical references and index.
    ISBN-13: 978-1-60469-047-7 (pbk.)
    1. Orchid culture—History. 2. Orchids. 3. Plant collectors—Biography. 4.
Botanists—Biography.   I. Romero, Gustavo A., 1995–   . II. Title.
SB409.R37 1995
635.9'3415'09—dc20   95-10784
                                                                     CIP

A catalog record for this book is also available from the British Library.

Contents

Illustrations

Foreword

IT IS A UNIQUE PLEASURE TO HAVE A SHARE IN INTRODUCING THIS BOOK TO my fellow orchid growers, for it covers a subject long dear to my heart. In *A History of the Orchid* Merle Reinikka enables us to meet the pioneers, the explorers who collected orchids in the wilds of little-known parts of the world, the scholars who classified and named the myriad kinds, and the horticulturists, the scientists, the growers, and the experimenters who have literally given orchids to the world.

Orchids have always been exciting. No amateur today would concede any thrill much greater than flowering his first orchid plant. No one today, fortunate enough to go to the tropical forests, would exchange for any other experience his first sight of orchid plants growing on the branches amid the lush greenery of those forests. Yet if this is exciting to us, think how wonderful it must have been in the early days—100, 150, 200 years ago—during the fever of the great botanical explorations, when hundreds of new species were discovered each year under conditions of travel that we can scarcely imagine, when those who received them back home were challenged to find out what they were and how to grow these strangers! Knowing what we do today of the never-ending variety among orchids, think what a stir it must have created as one after another revealed mysteries never before seen in horticultural or scientific circles!

Until now there has been no way for the ordinary person to find out about the people who made orchid history without doing a large amount of searching. Through occasional biographies in current literature, and through brief references, we have come to know that this person or that was an orchidologist or a horticulturist of renown. Among our plants we find such names as *lindleyana, reichenbachiana, roezlii, loddigesii, boxalii, hookeri, lowii,* and so forth, and we realize that these plant names are coined from the names of people who were important in some way in the orchid world. But such snatches of knowledge do not reveal who they were, what kind of lives they led, what they were like as persons, what events gave the spark that set them going in their particular fields, or just what contributions they made that caused their names to be so honored. For the most part, their life stories are scattered in old journals, in comments by their contemporaries, even in obituaries. About some, very little was written, about others, a great deal, but few had anything like a complete biography.

Mr. Reinikka has had the patience and determination to ferret out the information and the stories. It was often tedious, I know, but I am sure that what kept him going was the fascination of the detective work involved. The cooperation he found among people all over the world was testimony of their assurance of the worth of the book to come. Gaining the information was only half the work, however, for it took perception and skill to sort out the bits and pieces and put them together into a whole. In addition to the history that comes close to our time, Mr. Reinikka gives us that from the dim past, going back even into ancient literature to the early recognition of orchids and legends about their powers. It is fascinating to learn that orchids were considered special from the very first. Of great value are the references at the end of each section and each biography, which not only set down permanently where the information was found but will save those interested from going through the painful hours of research spent by Mr. Reinikka.

The lore about orchids and the people behind them will take you through this book at a fast pace. When you finish it you will feel that you have personally experienced the exciting events and met the great people revealed between its covers. But one reading will not suffice. You will return to it again and again through the years for specific pieces of information. Thus, *A History of the Orchid* will find its place as an enduring contribution to orchid literature.

REBECCA T. NORTHEN

Acknowledgments

I SUPPOSE THAT MOST NEW AUTHORS PLUNGE INTO THE DEVELOPMENT OF their first books, full of confidence and expectations of single-handedly seeing their works through to the conclusion. I think I did. Little did I realize how essential would be the advice and assistance of orchid friends, acquaintances, and authorities throughout the world. Fortunately, a great deal of encouragement and support was given from every quarter, for which I am extremely grateful. Without that interest, it is certain that the *History* couldn't have been completed—by this author, at least. A major asset during the *History*'s development was the host of contacts and acquaintances made, primarily through correspondence, by whose selfless aid it was brought to a fruitful conclusion.

At the inception of this work, one of its most enthusiasic proponents was Mrs. Rebecca T. Northen, of Laramie, Wyoming. Her own successes in orchid book publication were inspiring factors alone, but her confidence in my ability to do such a work was the one element which nurtured my own determination. Her sincere interest and counsel are deeply appreciated.

I am particularly indebted to a great number of botanical and horticultural institutions, libraries, and individuals who were so necessary and instrumental in providing difficult-to-find references. I extend heartfelt thanks to: Dr. Leslie A. Garay, curator of the Oakes Ames Orchid Herbarium at Harvard University, for his assistance in determining a suitable outline of data necessary to such a specialized history and for his reference suggestions; Dr. Herman R. Sweet, associate professor of biology at Tufts University, for the often extended loan of reference material from his personal library; Dr. Wilhelm Odelberg, chief librarian of the Library of the Royal Swedish Academy of Science, Stockholm, Sweden; Mr. Glauco Pinto Viegas, director general of the Instituto Agronômico, São Paulo, Brazil; Sir George Taylor, director of the Royal Botanic Gardens, Kew, Surrey, England; Mr. John W. Blowers, editor of *The Orchid Review*, Maidstone, Kent, England; Dr. George H. M. Lawrence, director of the Hunt Botanical Library, Pittsburgh, Pennsylvania; Mr. John G. Scott Marshall, editor of the *Gardeners' Chronicle*, London; Dr. C. G. G. J. van Steenis, director of the Flora Malesiana Foundation, Leyden, Netherlands; Dr. George C. Kent, head of the Department of Botany, Cornell University, Ithaca, New York; Mr. Ronald Kerr, editor of the *Australian Orchid Review*, Normanhurst, New South Wales, Australia; Miss Maureen Sloan, of the National Portrait Gallery, London; H. M. Burkill, director of the Botanical Gardens Library, Singapore; Mr. Ray Clark, acting librarian of the California Academy of Sciences, San Francisco, California; Mrs. P. Gonda, Library of the Royal Botanic Gardens and National Herbarium, Sydney, Australia.

I wish also to express my appreciation to The Linnean Society of London; the Mitchell Library, Sydney, Australia; the Massachusetts Horticultural Society, Boston, Massachusetts; Harvard University Herbarium Library, Cambridge, Massachusetts; and the Lindley Library, London, for the willingness with which their staff members unhesitatingly labored to search out references, had them duplicated, and sent them on to me.

Much valuable reference material was provided by interested individuals. I am especially obligated to: Mr. Marcel Lecoufle, Paris; Mr. Jerzy Sampolinski, Warsaw, Poland; Dr. R. E. Holttum, Surrey, England; Miss W. Eileen Low, Sussex, England; Mr. Thomas Fennell, Sr., and Mr. Thomas Fennell, Jr., Homestead, Florida; Mrs. E. W. Menninger, Arcadia, California; Mr. Victor S. Summerhayes, Surrey, England; Mr. David F. Sander, Sussex, England; Lt. Col. C. F. Cowan, Berkhamsted, Herts., England; and Dr. Calaway H. Dodson, University of Miami at Coral Gables, Florida.

In the procurement of illustrations and photographs, for their assistance I sincerely thank Dr. Richard G. Domey, Boca Raton, Florida; Mr. J. E. Downward, Essex, England; the National Portrait Archives, Stockholm, Sweden; and the American Orchid Society, Inc., Cambridge, Massachusetts.

Assistance in the translation of French and German biographical material was freely given by Mrs. Charles H. Thomas of Lexington, Massachusetts, and Mrs. Victor Ruta of Salem, New Hampshire, for which I am profoundly appreciative.

Finally, I am indebted for valuable advice and constructive criticism to Mr. Gordon W. Dillon, executive secretary of the American Orchid Society, Inc. His knowledge of orchid history plus his understanding of the difficulty involved with historical compilation were invaluable determinants in all phases of the *History*. On the journalistic level, his broad experience has provided a reservoir of kindly and charitable guidance. His benevolent advice has proved to be of immeasurable value, for which I am exceedingly grateful.

Introduction

IT WAS OBSERVED IN THE TWELFTH CENTURY BY A REMARKABLE CHRONI-cler, Henry of Huntington, that an interest in the past was one of the distinguishing characteristics of man as compared with the other animals. Certainly, in nearly any worthwhile endeavor, the acquisition of past knowledge endows further meaning to previous accomplishments; former studies and experiences are invaluable aids in any channel of interest.

Many orchid names themselves imply historically fascinating origins. Specific epithets—names such as *loddigesii, warscewiczii, lindleyana, cavendishianum, lobbii, parishii, lowianum, micholitzii, sanderiana,* and hundreds more—are often based on those individuals who discovered or introduced the orchid genera and species that bear the latinized counterparts of their own names. But not only do these particular names involve true-to-life tales of adventure and intrigue; *each* known orchid, regardless of terminology, holds its own story. In nearly every case the story can be discovered by a search through the published works about this large and magnificent plant family. The references are not invariably easy to come by, and many of the observations recorded may seem faulty, unreasonable, or puzzling. Nevertheless, searching out the complete history of nearly any orchid involves a certain degree of challenge and a subsequent enlightenment. The thousand-and-one tales of the *Arabian Nights* are extremely limited by comparison, for in the Orchid Family there are easily twenty times that number of stories and legends to be unfolded to the student of orchidology. A quote by Professor Oakes Ames, Harvard University's late "Dean of American Orchidology," adequately conveys this concept:

The concentrated romance, mystery and tragedy built into the story of orchid collecting are rarely considered when we enter a greenhouse to admire for a few fleeting minutes the strange beauty of orchid flowers. And yet, there are many species which, whenever seen, suggest to the student of orchid history events full of fascinating associations and uncanny experiences.

Though orchids, as cultivated plants, have commonly been known for only a few hundred years, volume upon volume could be compiled on the occasions of their discovery, personalities instrumental in their popularization, and progressive development in their culture. This small book could not possibly contain all that information. Instead, it relates to the reader a sketch, at most, of the important dates, names, and incidents relevant to the historical role of orchids and their effect on the interests of man. The intent, therefore, is to stimulate a more profound appreciation of the orchidological efforts put forth by orchid devotees of years past.

The history of the Orchid Family is so closely associated with drama, adventure, and world history in general that it is very nearly impossible for the serious student of orchid history *not* to become involved with more general historical knowledge than he may have perhaps intended. The lives and pursuits of those persons who have contributed largely to progress in the field of orchidology were often filled with a variety of interests, a characteristic which seems perpetuated in today's orchidists, as well. This, perhaps, is the mark which identifies orchid enthusiasts—and that which provides the incentive for their abundantly active lives.

Orchid history is so closely related to all the other important botanical and horticultural fields—overlapping, intermingling, joining—that it is difficult to speak of the Orchid Family, historically, as an entity distinct. Yet the Orchid Family is distinctively set apart from the rest of the plant kingdom, and, because no very comprehensive survey of its history has yet been prepared, a few years ago I set myself to this pleasurable (but naive) task. What an undertaking it turned out to be! The blithe assumption that references might readily be gathered into an easily absorbable chronology was abandoned at an early date during the initial research. The spread of historical information was simply too complex. After much trial and error, the most sensible approach, it seemed, was to segregate each major field of development within orchidology, chronicling the important historical happenings within that field. A vast ocean of reference material existed both at home and abroad—in early herbals, journals, periodicals, pamphlets, and papers. Unnumbered hours were involved merely in cross-referencing bibliographies. Obscure volumes, located in the acrid and dusty shelves of botanical library archives, were systematically pored over one title after another, index by index, page by page.

Plans called for the use of illustrations depicting the famous botanists, naturalists, professional orchid hunters, hobbyists, and gardeners who contributed most significantly in their respective fields to the overall development of orchid cultivation and study. The search for these illustrations was itself an exhaustive undertaking. Clues turned up gradually through lengthy correspondence with botanical libraries, universities, and foundations throughout the world—in Australia, England, Poland, Sweden, Singapore, the United States, France, and Germany. In time, all but a few of the needed illustrations were almost incredibly obtained. In the case of a few "missing persons," authoritative sources confirmed that no portraits, photographs, or similar depictions of the individuals in question were known to exist, and so I was gratified in the knowledge that my diligence and persistence were not all in vain.

Gradually, as material was gathered and bibliographical leads were followed, it became apparent that several fields of endeavor were involved in the development of orchid history and that it would be practically impossible to delineate them in order of sequence and still maintain literary digestibility. The course ultimately worked out, then, was to treat one field at a time, sequentially, as in Part I of this *History*. Still, there remained such a myriad of interesting facts and events surrounding the lives of each of the important world figures mentioned in each section of Part I that it somehow seemed unfair merely to list their names in connection with their roles in the panorama of orchid history. Their personalities mattered too. The solution rested in the organization of Part II, a biographical section which presents these eminent orchid men and their accomplishments in the order of their birth. Thus, in either part the saga of orchid history is unfolded, with fields of specialization in the first part and specific biographical records in the second.

Regrettably, as much data as were used in this *History* were also omitted. Nearly any written history can be treated with more lateral than vertical expansion, depending upon how far the author wants to go. This, I am sure, must be a dilemma to every author-historian. In order to avoid going to incalculable lengths, it was thus necessary to limit the *History* to those events and works which contributed more significantly to the total picture of orchids and their history than others which seemed of less consequence. The omission of certain facts, events, and personalities was regrettable, for while they may not have seemed as consequent as the information that was used, they held great historical interest nonetheless. Boundaries had to be drawn, however; else, instead of calling the work "A History of the Orchid," it might easily have evolved into a lifelong work of several volumes speculatively entitled "An *Encyclopaedia* of Orchid History." Such are the limits of the writer. If proper credit is not given in regard to particular individuals and their work, therefore, it is due to fallible interpretation rather than intent.

As a branch of science, orchidology is concerned largely with the myriad diversification within the Orchidaceae, but those individuals who have developed it have proven as versatile and diverse in their abilities. Their exceptional talents brought us to our present level of knowledge concerning these plants. The *History*, therefore, is hopefully intended not only to chronicle the principal achievements of orchid discovery and development but to offer in addition a personal acquaintance with those individuals who provided the basic framework of this rapidly growing and provocative area of plant study.

Part I:
Historical Development

The Emergence of Orchids as Botanical Entities

CHANGES IN BIOLOGICAL SYSTEMS OF CLASSIFICATION OFTEN DICTATE THE revision of genera and species; it is therefore somewhat remarkable that the original name given to the Orchid Family should have retained the same general designation for well over 2000 years. The term *orchis*, the root on which the Orchid Family's nomenclature is based, came into being between 370 and 285 B.C., when it was first used in a Greek manuscript, *Enquiry into Plants*, written by the philosopher Theophrastus, a pupil of Plato and Aristotle who became known as the "Father of Botany."

The word "orchid" is a derivation of the Greek *orchis*, meaning *testis*, in reference to the testiculate bulbs or tubers with which the particular plants of those Mediterranean regions were furnished. Theophrastus established his nomenclature on the basis of the one orchid he described, probably of the genus *Orchis*, for these plants are common in the Mediterranean Archipelago and possess paired, testiculate tubers. Because of the medicinal properties orchids supposedly possessed, they were given a prominent place in the fifteenth, sixteenth, and seventeenth centuries. Herbalists gathered them for their roots because these underground organs, packed with carbohydrates and alkaloids, were prized for their curative powers. There was little interest in the flowers, however, beyond the fact that they indicated the locations of certain kinds of roots. The earliest drawings and descriptions of orchids were those which appeared in the herbals of the times, and it is through these often immense volumes that the foundations of early orchidology are revealed.

Dioscorides, a Greek botanist of Anazarba in Asia Minor, wrote a treatise on materia medica in the first century A.D. in which were de-

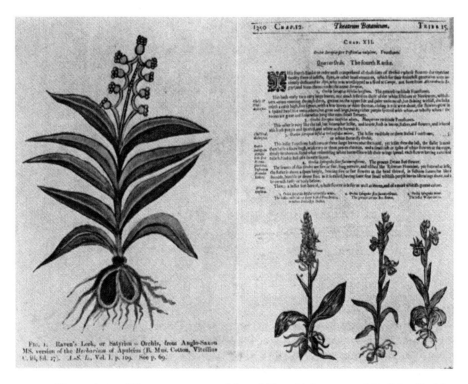

Illustrations of European terrestrial orchids which appeared in John Parkinson's *Theatricum Botanicum* in 1640.

scribed two species of orchids. Because he presumably based at least one of his identifications on the singular species described by Theophrastus, he also used the term *orchis* for the descriptions of the two species he discovered in eastern Greece. Dioscorides influenced botany and medicine greatly for he adopted and promoted the spread of the peculiar Doctrine of Signatures. This "doctrine," which endured through the sixteenth and seventeenth centuries, was a set of beliefs that taught of the treatment and cure of human ailments by the various uses and applications of the plants and plant parts that resembled parts of the human anatomy in aspect of shape, color, or structure. And because the writings of the scholarly Greeks were looked upon as almost divine, the Dioscoridean works and ideas reigned supreme for hundreds of years.

Because the majority of European orchids had testiculate "bulbs" or tubers, the Doctrine of Signatures implied that they were capable of influencing sexual manifestations. Through their resemblance to human and animal sexual organs, orchids were thought to heal such affected parts or to stimulate lust—or "venery," as described in the early herbals.

Physicians and herbalists thought the curative powers of the plants were revealed through these resemblances, e.g., the walnut was supposed to be good for the brain, bloodroot for anemia, and boneset for fractures. Dioscorides wrote, as reported later, "that if men do eat of the great full or fat roots of these kinds of Dogs Stones, they cause them to beget male children; and if women eat of the lesser dry or barren root which is withered or shriveled, they shall bring forth females." The occurrence of the term "Dogs Stones" is concurrent with the sexual significance attached to the testiculate terrestrial orchids. Goat Stones, Fox Stones, Fenney Stones, Fool's Stones, etc., were other common appellations.

The search for orchids of medical value extended into Europe, though a distinction between the Mediterranean and European species was not even considered. The quest, however, brought the total number of orchids known to civilized Europe to thirteen by 1561.

At a time when as much superstition as practical knowledge was used in medical treatment, the spontaneous generation of plants and animals was a common belief. Such conjecture and superstition is typified in the writings of Bock (1498–1554), or Hieronymus Tragus, as he was called. Bock was the first to point out the natural similarity of orchids to certain birds and animals. He speculated that orchids did not produce seeds; instead, a fine dust eventually emanated from where the flower had been. The Doctrine of Signatures had long held that orchids were associated with sexual intercourse, and Bock believed that they arose in fields and meadows where the seminal secretions of birds and beasts had fallen to the ground. These beliefs were later supported by Athanasius Kircher (1601–1680), a German Jesuit who published *Mundus Subterraneus* in 1665. In regard to orchids, he mentioned that shepherds and farmers noticed the occurrence of orchids in those places where livestock had been brought together for breeding. Kircher further attempted to add to the beliefs of Virgil's time, when bees and wasps were believed to be generated from the carcasses of bulls and horses. Kircher reasoned that if these insects were generated from the bodies of animals, then the orchids which resembled those particular insects must certainly be of spontaneous generation through the fallen semen of said animals. Those orchids which resembled bees were thought to have sprung from the semen of the bull, while those similar to wasps were thought to have sprung from the semen of horses, since wasps were believed to generate from horses. Kircher stated:

It has been proved by the authority of all recent as well as ancient writers that bees are produced by Cattle. Varro, Pliny and Virgil agree that bees originate not only from the excrements of the bull but also from its decaying carcass.

Francesco Redi (1626–1695) attempted by actual experimentation to disprove the theory of spontaneous generation, but the biblical account of Samson killing a lion and the subsequent issue from the carcass of a swarm of bees (Judges 14:8) was conclusive evidence for the savants of the age. To further augment the superstitious idolatry of these theories, Pierre Pomet included a plate in his *Histoire Générale des Drogues* (1694) which showed the spontaneous generation of bees from the dead bodies of both a lion and a bull.

At a time when man's needs were of prime importance, we likewise find him searching for the economic values and uses of orchids rather than for esthetic appreciation. In the first English herbal (1568) by Turner, the "Father of English Botany," the "virtues" of the orchis—also called Adder Grass—were described:

The roote of it, when it is sodden inough, is eatable as bulbus is. They write of this herbe that if the greater roots be eaten of men it maketh men chyldren, and if the roote be eaten of women it maketh weomen chyldren. And moreover this is also told of it—that weomen of Thessalia geve it wyth gote's milk to provoke the pleasure of the bodye whylse it is tender, but they geue the dry one to hinder and stop the pleasure of the bodye. And it groweth in stony places and in sandy groundes. There is another kynde whych is called Serapias as Andreas sayth for the manyfolde use of the roote, it hath leaves lyke unto a leke, long but broder and fat, bowynge inward about the setting on of the leaves, and little stalks a span hygh, and floures somthyng purple; there is a roote in under like unto stones.

Turner further described the virtues of a second group of orchids called Testiculus:

Thys layed to hath the propertye of drying awaye swellinge and scouring of sores, and to stay running tetters. It putteth away fistules, and if it be layed to, it swageth places that are inflamed and set afyre. The same drye, stoppeth eating sores and rotting sores and it healeth the grevous sores that are in the mouth. It stoppeth also the bellye if it be dronken wyth wyne.

William Langham discussed the power of the orchis in *The Garden of Health*, printed in London in 1579. *Orchis odorata* is especially mentioned in application to conception, consumption, fever hectique, fistula, flux, generating maleness and femaleness, inflammation, causing and avoiding lust, and curing mouth sores and general sores and swellings.

The study of history is itself most complex and sometimes confusing because of the difficulty involved in relating a particular event with other occurrences of the same period. In a singular study of the history of the orchids, therefore, it is not strange that other endeavors might seem trivial and unrelated. Classic literature, for example, would seem to have little bearing on the matter; however, at a time when numerous of the herbals were in common use, William Shakespeare was the bard of literature and drama. Shakespeare was a keen observer of nature, and

Orchis spectabilis, a showy North American counterpart of the genus on which the nomenclature of the Orchid Family is based.

plants were among the many entities mentioned in his plays. Though mentioned only once in all his works, orchids make their debut in *Hamlet* (about 1602) in act 4, scene 7, where the queen, in her description of the death of Ophelia, says:

> There is a willow grows aslant a brook,
> That shows his hoar leaves on the glassy stream;
> There, with fantastic garlands did she come,
> Of crow-flowers, nettles, daisies, and *long purples,*
> That liberal shepherds give a grosser name,
> But our cold maids do *dead men's fingers* call them:

The term "long purples" is most often associated with *Orchis mascula*, which possesses twin underground tubers. Shakespeare apparently erred in likening this species to "dead men's fingers," for the plants known by this name were *Orchis latifolia* and *Orchis maculata*, species having digitate or palmate tubers. In *The Plant-Lore and Garden-Craft of Shakespeare* (1884) the Rev. Henry N. Ellacombe concluded that the "grosser name" given by the shepherds referred to Fool's Stones—the common name given to *Orchis mascula*—and that Shakespeare had really made reference to that species as being woven into Ophelia's garlands. Opinions vary that Shakespeare was either inexact in his use of plant names or that the common names of the various species of *Orchis* were loosely designated in his day. It is possible, also, that poetic license was taken simply for the sake of meter. In any case, though Shakespeare was in error, his reference is another worthwhile glimpse of the orchids as known in the times of the herbalists.

A study of the several Medieval herbals indicates that very little fresh information was introduced—each succeeding writer seemed only to compile the works of his predecessors. Most of the herbalists quoted Dioscorides directly. John Gerard's *Herball or Generall Historie of Plantes*, printed in London in 1633, was one of those which clung to superstition and lack of independent thought—so typical of those who depended upon the "divination" of Greek philosophy. Science, as such, was still unknown; it was merged with philosophy—an inquiry into the nature of things. The monotonous repetition of one author after another illustrates how prima facie authority can independently maintain its influence in the absence of reason and inquiry. Gerard's descriptions of the plants, however, are most intriguing. Lacking the technical language and refinements of true science, he likened his plants and flowers to other things. His description of *Cynosorchis major* is typical:

The small floures are like an open hood or helmet, having hanging out of every one as it were the body of a little man without a head, with arms stretched out, and thighs stradling abroad, after the same manner almost that little boys are wont to be pictured hanging out of Saturnes mouth.

Even though Gerard adhered to much of the earlier superstition of Dioscorides and the Doctrine of Signatures, he independently attempted a serious classification of the orchids.

In 1640 John Parkinson, an apothecary of London and royal herbalist to King Charles I, finished the *Theatricum Botanicum* (Theatre of Plants). This work is also quite repetitious, but, in reference to the virtues of the greater and lesser roots of cynosorchis in determining the sex of the unborn child, he wrote "that the vertue of the one is extinguished by the taking of the other," thus introducing the Doctrine of Contraries by this and other examples. He further revealed the fact that orchids were among the drugs dispensed in London during Oliver Cromwell's time.

Parkinson disclosed some interesting data concerning the occurrence of a native North American cypripedium in England. On page 217 of the *Theatricum* is shown an illustration of the plant and flower. The plant, classified among the helleborines, is referred to as the "great wilde Hellebor" and "our Ladyes Slipper." The botanical caption, *Calceolus Mariae Americanus*, though in error generically, seems a reasonable attempt at classification. Parkinson wrote:

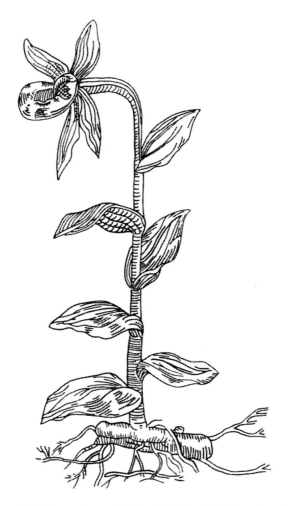

The early woodblock cut shown in John Parkinson's *Theatricum Botanicum* (1640) illustrating a North American species of *Cypripedium*.

... a sort thereof hath been brought from the North parts of America, differing onely in being greater both in stalkes, leaves and flowers, which are not yellow but white, with reddish strakes through the bellies of them.

Here, then, is reported the occurrence of a native North American orchid in Europe sixty years prior to the introduction of tropical species. The description given indicates *Cypripedium acaule*, and since *Cypripedium calceolus* was common in England, it is understandable that a specific affinity to *Cypripedium calceolus* was intended. The plants were very likely collected and dispatched by British colonists, for it is known that English navigators returning from North American settlements took botanical specimens back to England with them.

The 1600s heralded an enlightening and significant reversal of man's interest in orchids. The utilization of orchids as elixirs, medicants, and aphrodisiacs gradually diminished, for as travel increased between Europe and the rest of the world, knowledge and understanding of botanical phenomena were likewise augmented. Colonial representatives, physicians, merchants, and tradesmen were all instrumental in the introduction of tropical orchids to European gardens, and as foreign trading stations were established, increasing numbers of the orchids indigenous to those tropical regions were collected, returned to Europe, and described.

References

Ames, Oakes. 1944. Orchidaceae versus Orchiaceae. *Amer. Orch. Soc. Bull.* 13, no. 3.

Ames, Oakes. 1942. Orchids in Retrospect. *Amer. Orch. Soc. Bull.* 11, no. 4.

Ames, Oakes. 1942. The Origin of the Term Orchis. *Amer. Orch. Soc. Bull.* 2, no. 5.

Miller, Morrison A. 1959. Orchids of Economic Use. *Amer. Orch. Soc. Bull.* 28, no. 3.

Stearn, William T. 1960. Two Thousand Years of Orchidology. *Proceedings of the Third World Orchid Conference.* Historical Session. Staples Printers Ltd. Rochester, Kent, England.

Expanded Interest and Introductions

CONTRARY TO THE POPULAR BELIEF THAT INITIAL INTEREST IN ORCHIDS originated in Europe, early manuscripts indicate that mankind's attention to the study and cultivation of these plants began in the Orient. A Chinese legend holds that, in the twenty-eighth century B.C., the Emperor Shen Nung described *Bletilla hyacinthina* and a dendrobium in *Materia Medica*, a work which reputedly is the first to advise on the use of plants and animals for human needs.

Among the peoples of the Orient, a great share of interest in orchids has derived from the fragrance of the flowers, for, again contrary to popular belief, many members of the Orchid Family are highly scented. The noted Chinese philosopher Confucius (551–479 B.C.) called the *lan* (the Chinese term for orchid) the "King of Fragrant Plants." In his early books, Confucius made numerous reference to the "supreme fragrance of *lan*," and the oldest book of philosophy in China, *I-ching*, or Book of Changes, of which Confucius is believed to be joint author, contains these lines:

> Words by friends with one and the same heart
> are just as sweet as the aroma of *lan*.

Ornamental plants have long been of important symbolic significance in Oriental culture. Plum and chrysanthemum blossoms signify constant friendship and devotion to study; bamboo, with its evenly spaced nodes, straight stems, and persistence of foliage, symbolizes the inviolability of moral law; the orchids, enjoyed for their beauty and fragrance, stand for refinement, friendship, perfection, numerous progeny, all things feminine, noble, and elegant. In *Shih-ching* (Book of Poems), which is also supposedly edited by Confucius, these lines appear:

> Shin and Yu* are full of water now,
> For spring has come to melt the snow,
> And men and women of the state wear *lan* now,
> She says to him: There let us go
> To see the places. He says: No,
> For I have seen the places years ago.
> She says again: There let us go;
> There is a place beyond the river Yu
> Where we can our love do . . .

The earliest Chinese manuscript given entirely to botany, *Nan-fang Ts'ao-mu Chuang*, was written by Ki Han, minister of state under the Emperor Hui Ti, during the Chin Dynasty (290–307 A.D.). In this manuscript both *Cymbidium ensifolium* and *Dendrobium moniliforme* were treated in a section under herbs. *Lan Pu*, a book written by Wang Kuei-lüeh during the Sung Dynasty (960–1279), contained a treatise on orchids by Mao Hsiang entitled Lan-yen, which was reprinted in the *Chao-tai ts'ung-shu*. According to the late Dr. Yoshio Nagano, a Japanese orchidist and philosopher, a Chinese scholar named Kin-shō wrote, also during the tenth century, a work known as *Kin-shō's Orchid Book*. In it, a history was given of Oriental cymbidiums, with the names of the first growers, geographical locations, cultural methods and the degrees of superiority of the many varieties of *Cymbidium gyokuchin*, also known by the names *makino* and *soshin*. Regrettably, none of these early Oriental books are available today; only references exist in encyclopedic histories or compilations. Known reference has been made to the following:

Orchid Guide for Kuei-men and Chang-chou, by Chao Shih-ken, published in 1228 A.D.
Wang's Orchid Guide, by Wang Kuei-hsüeh, published in 1247 A.D.
Secrets in Orchid Culture, by Chou Lu-ching, published about 1590 A.D.
A Monthly Cultivation Book for Orchids, author unknown, published about 1600 A.D.
An Orchid Guide for Fukien, author unknown, published about 1600 A.D.
Orchid Talks, by Mao Hsiang, published between 1611-1693 A.D.

Orchids had become a favorite subject matter of Chinese painting by the end of the Yüan Dynasty (1279–1368), and the same dexterity shown in Oriental handwriting is shown also in their orchid paintings, particularly with the genus *Cymbidium*, for the tapering grass-like leaves and delicate flowers were ideal for illustration.

---

* Shin and Yu were rivers of the state.

The growing of orchids is also known as an ancient practice in Japan, even though that island nation was still highly warlike and uncivilized before the seventeenth and eighteenth centuries. Many of the early accounts and descriptions of orchids are attributed to individuals employed in foreign trade—and not primarily concerned with the Orchid Family. One such was Engelbert Kaempfer, a German physician working for the Dutch Trading Company. After Japan discontinued trade relations with the West in 1639, the Dutch Trading Company had sole access to Japanese trade, and through this association Kaempfer was enabled to visit Japan on occasion, keeping an account of the fruits and drugs found there. In his accounts, *Amoenitatum exoticarum . . . Fasciculi* (1712), *Dendrobium moniliforme* is mentioned as a curiosity.

Though references point to the existence of orchid books in Japan at earlier dates, it was not until 1728 that a book of orchids was truly known to be produced there. This work, ordered written in the reign of Cheng-te by the then ex-Emperor Higashiyama, was undertaken by Jo-an Matsuoka, who wrote under the pseudonym Igansai, and the book was entitled *Igansai-ranpin*. Rewritten in Chinese and published in 1772, after the author's death, it contained numerous wood-block illustrations and described various genera such as *Cymbidium, Neofinetia, Aerides, Dendrobium, Bletilla,* and many other plants possessing fragrant blooms. Though the book was dedicated to the description of *ran,** the tendency to call all plants with strange fragrance *ran* (hereafter referred to as *lan,* in the Chinese translation) had indiscriminately spread, with little difference recognized between certain plant families. Fortunately, the true orchids were more properly designated as *lan hua* or *lan-ts'ao hua,* the specific epithets being important in order to avoid descriptive confusion. Under each of the valid orchid names given in Matsuoka's book, six major categories were enumerated and illustrated, with many varieties of each also evaluated: *Cymbidium ensifolium, Cymbidium virescens, Aerides japonicum, Neofinetia falcata, Bletilla hyacinthina,* and *Dendrobium moniliforme.*

Social distinctions during the dynasty seemed to distinguish the affinity to certain genera, and while merchants and other wealthy persons were fond of all the endemic orchids of their country, they particularly delighted in cymbidiums. These were appreciated first because of their fine, sweet fragrance and because of the beautiful variegated patterns found in the several interspecific varieties. Concerning cymbidiums particularly, Matsuoka is popularly renowned for his four simple "commandments" on their culture:

> In spring don't put them out-of-doors.
> In summer don't expose to too much sun.

* The pronunciation of the Japanese word *ran,* meaning orchid, is derived from the Chinese word *lan,* which is written with the same character.

In autumn don't keep too dry.
In winter don't keep too wet.

Samurai warriors grew *Neofinetia falcata*, known eulogistically as "an orchid of wealth and nobility." Many of the feudal lords were also very attached to this species, and the tale is told that they carried the plants with them on journeys between Edo (now Tokyo) and their own dominions.

Friends of the imperial aristocracy of Kyoto grew *Dendrobium moniliforme*, called *sekkoku* in Japanese, a literal translation meaning "an orchid that makes men live a long life." During centuries of cultivation this species had varied into more than a hundred forms.

The first reference to orchids in the Western Hemisphere appears in

Neofinetia falcata, as grown for centuries by the noble and aristocratic members of Japanese society.

the *Badianus Manuscript*, an Aztec herbal of 1552. The *Badianus Manuscript*, for years cached away in the Vatican Library, depicts *Vanilla* in plate 104.

As well as a flavoring for cocoa and its use as perfume, vanilla, or *tlilxochitl*, as it was called in the Aztec tongue, was used in the making of a "lotion to be used against fatigue of those holding public office." The use of the lotion was thought to "bestow the bodily strength of a gladiator, drive weariness far away, and finally drive out fear and fortify the human heart." Hernán Cortés noted the use of *tlilxochitl* when he conquered Mexico in 1519, which account is given in the *Manuscript*. One of Cortés' officers, Bernal Díaz, first noticed the Aztec ruler Montezuma drink *chocolatl*, a beverage made from the ground *tlilxochitl* fruits and cacao seeds. The early Mayans of Mexico were also familiar with vanilla and its uses, their name for it being *sisbic*.

About the year 1510 vanilla is reported to have been brought to Europe as a perfume, along with indigo, cochineal, and cacao—nine years before the Spanish Conquest. This presumably referred to the seed pods, not plants.

Botanical notice of vanilla was first given by the Flemish botanist Carolus Clusius in 1605 in his *Exoticum Libri Decem*. The dried fruits were the basis of Clusius' description and name, *Lobus oblongus aromaticus*. The pods had been obtained three years earlier from Queen Elizabeth's apothecary, Hugh Morgan, who subsequently introduced and advocated the use of vanilla as a distinctive flavoring agent apart from its use in chocolate. Prior to this time, certain healing properties were attributed to the fruits.

Francisco Hernández, on order of King Philip II of Spain to establish an expedition to study the plants and animals of New Spain (Mexico) in 1571–1577, published a manuscript in which was figured a woodcut of two fruits and a portion of the vine of vanilla, under the name *Arico aromatico*, with the native appellation *tlilxochitl*. This work was first published in Rome in 1651, but only the plant's use as a drug was given.

In 1658 the term *vaynilla* appeared in a work by William Piso, who added that this name was given by the Spaniards. The Indian name *tlilxochitl* very probably caused some linguistic difficulty, so the name vanilla was adopted, a diminutive of the Spanish *vaina*, meaning "a little pod" or capsule.

William Dampier observed vanilla plants growing in Southern Mexico at the Bay of Campeche in 1676 and at Boca-toro in Costa Rica in 1681. In his *A New Voyage Round the World* he mentioned that the Indians sold the vanilla beans to the Spaniards, also describing the method by which the fruits were cured:

We found a small Indian village, and in it a great quantity of Vinello's drying in the sun. The Vinello is a little Cod full of black seeds; it is 4 or 5 inches long, about the bigness of the stem of a Tobacco leaf, and when dried much resembling it: so that our Privateers at first have often thrown them away when they took any, wondering why the Spaniards should lay up Tobacco stems. This Cod grows on a small Vine, which climbs about and supports itself by the neighboring trees; it first bears a yellow Flower, from whence the Cod afterwards proceeds. It is first green, but when ripe it turns yellow; then the Indians (whose manufacture it is, and who sell it cheap to the Spaniards) gather it, and lay it in the sun, which makes it soft; then it changes to a Chestnut colour. Then they frequently pass it between their fingers, which makes it flat. If the Indians do anything to them besides, I know not, but I have seen the Spaniards sleek them with Oyl.

This and later reports of the plant and the use of its pods for flavoring, in medications, and as perfume attracted considerable notice, and other similar plants were soon confused with it. Sloane and Plunkenet were among those who mistook other nonaromatic species of vanilla with the *Arico aromatico* described by Hernández.

Plumier enumerated three West Indies species of vanilla in 1703, but failed to include the Mexican species (*Vanilla planifolia*).

Pierre Pomet, in his *Compleat History of Drugs* (1712), wrote of vanillas, describing the plants as being found in Mexico, Guatemala, and Santo Domingo. With their description, Pomet enumerated the properties supposedly attributed to the pods: "cordial, cephalick, stamachick, carminative apertive; it alternates vicious humors, provokes urine and womens courses; is mixed in chocolate."

H. A. Rheede tot Draakenstein (1636–1691), Dutch governor of Malabar in southern India, was the first botanist to write of the abundance of native orchids in tropical Asia. His *Hortus Indicus Malabaricus*, published after his death (1703), enumerated six species of orchids under their vernacular names:

Rhynchostylis retusa (*Angeli-Maravara, Biti-Maram-Maravara*)
Vanda spathulata (*Ponnampou-Maravara*)
Acampe wightiana (*Thalia-Maravara*)
Sarcanthus peninsularis (*Tsjerou-Mau-Maravara, Kolli Tsjerou-Mau-Mara-vara*)
Dendrobium ovatum (*Anantali-Maravara*)
Cymbidium aloifolium (*Kans jiram-Maravara*)

He explained that "on one tree ten or twelve different sorts of leaves, flowers and fruits might be met with," and that the name *Maravara* was a term used to designate any of these tree-dwelling plants.

Epiphytic orchids were discovered by Hans Sloane (1660–1720) in Jamaica during a two-year stay there, 1687–1689. Because he was unfamiliar with orchids as botanical entities, he joined the representative species he found with other plant families. *Stenorrhynchus speciosus* was classified as a cardamomum; *Erythrodes plantaginea* was recorded as the previously known *Orchis elatior*; *Vanilla claviculata* was thought to be a kind of cactus; and because they grew on trees, *Brassavola cordata*, *Oncidium guttatum*, *Oncidium luridum*, and *Broughtonia sanguinea* were thought to be species of mistletoe and recorded in his *Voyage to the Islands Madera . . . and Jamaica* (1707–1725) under the generic title *Viscum*.

At nearly the same time, the German physician Engelbert Kaempfer (1651–1716) was traveling in Japan and Java. The Dutch East India Company, by which Kaempfer was employed, had established a trading outpost in Nagasaki, where the physician stayed from September 1690 to October 1692. During this period he compiled his *Amoenitatum exoticarum . . . Fasciculi*, a series of notes and drawings of the flora observed in his travels. Illustrations of *Arachnis flos-aeris*, *Dendrobium moniliforme*, and *Epidendrum domesticum* were included in the compilation which, however, was not published until 1712, only four years before his death.

Ambon, a small island off the east coast of New Guinea, was the center of the Spice Islands trade in the sixteenth, seventeenth, and eighteenth centuries. It was also the home of the famous naturalist-botanist G. E. Rumphius, who arrived in Ambon in 1653, a twenty-five-year-old clerk hired by the Dutch East India Company. Under a special retainer status he later spent his time in the self-appointed work of collecting, identifying, describing, and illustrating the indigenous flora of Ambon. He was the first to find and describe any member of the genus *Phalaenopsis*, the name then assigned being *Angraecum album majus*. The plants remained relatively unknown, though, until 1825, when the Dutch botanist, Karl Ludwig Blume, established the genus upon his rediscovery of the same species, known thereafter as *Phalaenopsis amabilis*. Rumphius' works were not published until many years after his death, appearing as the *Herbarium Amboinensis* in six parts between 1741 and 1750. This work became a valuable guide for future botanists.

One of the earliest efforts to further the botanical study of the Philippine Islands was the contribution of the Jesuit missionary, George Joseph Kamel, from 1688 to 1706. During his years in Manila he established a clinic for the medical care of the poor and underprivileged. Away from the clinic, he devoted himself to the describing and drawing of Philippine flora. His first published works appeared in the appendix to Ray's *Historia Plantarum* in 1704. Although many of the plants he described were orchids, his drawings of these plants did not appear until 1702–1709, when they were used in Jacob Petiver's *Garophylacium*.

The informative reports given by these and numerous other travelers stimulated an interest in Europe in these strange "parasites," as they were called, and a few attempts were made toward the end of the century to grow them in northern orangeries.

The first tropical orchid cultivated in Europe was figured in Paul

Hermann's *Paradisus Batavus* (1698) as the American *Epidendrum nodo-sum* (*Brassavola nodosa*). The plant, listed as *Epidendrum corassavicum folio crasso sulcato*, was grown in the garden of Casper Fagel, having been introduced into Holland from Curaçao.

The first tropical orchid introduced to England was a dried specimen of *Bletia verecunda* (syn. *B. purpurea*). A Quaker cloth merchant, Peter Collinson, obtained it from the Bahama Islands in 1731. According to John Martyn in his *Historia Plantarum Rariorum* (1732), the sender was unrecorded. A colored plate in this same volume lists the plant under the name of *Helleborine americana, radies tuberosa, foliis longis, angustis,* etc. Collinson received the specimen from Providence Island, and though the plant was desiccated, he took the tubers to the garden of Sir Charles Wager, who mulched them in a bed of bark for the winter. In the follow-ing spring, vegetative growth was noticed, and by summer flowers were produced. Linnaeus named the species *Limodorum tuberosum* in 1753, though it was later reclassified, the genus name honoring Mr. Louis Blet, a pharmacist and amateur botanist in Algeciras. A figure of this same species was shown in Miller's *Figures of the Most Beautiful Plants*, in 1760.

By 1737 two more of the hardy North American cypripediums were in cultivation in England. Miller's *Gardener's Dictionary* was published that year, and in it we find described the yellow Virginia Lady's Slipper (probably either *Cypripedium pubescens* or *Cypripedium parviflorum*, description is not sufficiently concise to ascertain the exact species), listed as *Helleborine virginianum flore rotundo luteo*. Also described was *Cypripedium spectabile*, the Canada Lady's Slipper, listed as *Helleborine canadensis sive Calceolus Mariae*.

The uses of *Vanilla planifolia* as a flavoring agent and perfume had been of interest in Europe since Cortés' conquest of Mexico in 1519. Plants, however, were not cultivated in England until 1739, when a packet of seed pods and cuttings were gathered near Campeche, Mexico, by Robert Miller. It is reported in the first edition of the *Gardeners' Dictionary* that the cuttings were planted in small pots and plunged into hotbeds of tanner's bark, whereupon they rapidly grew leaves and roots. Miller was intent upon successfully growing plants of this genus, for at that time spices and flavorings were valued commodities not readily ob-tainable. In his eighth edition (1768), another species, known as *Vanilla axillaribus*, is mentioned as being sent to him from Carthagena in New Granada. The plant is reported to have flowered, but it lived only one year. The exact date of this occurrence is not given, but a lucid descrip-tion of the flowers is. The blooms are described as similar to those of the "Bee Orchis," the somewhat longer flowers having helmets of a pale pink color and the labellums purple.

Meanwhile other authors and botanists continued to confuse the few then known species of *Vanilla*. In 1749 the Swedish botanist Carl von

Linné, known as Linnaeus, theorized that *Vanilla* was the source, as well as a species, of the *Orchis* genus, prescribing it as a powerful aphrodisiac elixir and publishing this theory in his *Materia Medica* that year. At that time, however, he must not have been absolutely certain of its generic category, because by 1753 he called it *Epidendrum Vanilla*.

Olof Swartz, another Swedish botanist, reestablished the genus *Vanilla* in 1799 describing a species whose fruits were scentless, evidently borrowing the name *Vanilla aromatica* from the fragrant vanilla of Mexico, though that species was still relatively unknown.

Salisbury claimed the specific epithet in 1807, when a plant of the Mexican species bloomed in cultivation in the garden of the Right Hon. Charles Greville at Paddington. *Myrobroma fragrans* was the name ascribed, but a year later Andrews published an illustration of the same specimen and named it *Vanilla planifolia*, claiming that it had been intro-

Vanilla planifolia, the "orchid of commerce," which was first used by the Aztecs as a flavoring agent.

duced by the Marquis of Bladford. Andrews' name was subsequently adopted, though by priority of publication it has been argued that Salisbury holds prior jurisdiction and the specific name *fragrans* should have been used. Though this plant actually *was* the vanilla of commerce, neither author apparently recognized it as such; Salisbury even stated that it was a different species than the then little-known *Vanilla planifolia* that was later to become of economic value.

Though the introduction of new species was sporadic, enthusiasm for orchids as decorative subjects increased among horticulturists. Linnaeus naively speculated, about the middle of the eighteenth century, that if the entire world could be searched, in all probability over one hundred *species* of orchids might be found! In all probability, at least that many were discovered within just a few decades.

The Royal Botanic Gardens, Kew, England, had been involved with the cultivation of tropical orchids since its beginning. Started as a nine-acre garden in 1759 in the grounds of the Dowager Princess of Wales (mother of George III), it remained a private garden for eighty-two years. At that time the West Indies were the most easily accessible tropical lands to Europe, and the first significant orchid importations into the Gardens were from those regions. *Epidendrum rigidum* was received there in 1760, followed by some *Vanilla* species in 1765. In 1768 the Gardens were known to contain twenty-four species of orchids, two of which were tropical. The others were indigenous British species. Dr. John Fothergill, returning from a journey to China in 1778, brought back the first Asiatic orchids—specimens of *Cymbidium ensifolium* and *Phaius tankervilliae.*

Aiton's *Hortus Kewensis*, an enumeration of the plants cultivated at the Gardens, first appeared in 1789, at which time fifteen "exotic" species were in cultivation. They were *Bletia verecunda, Epidendrum fragrans, Epidendrum cochleatum, Phaius grandifolius* (syn. *P. tankervilliae*), *Cypripedium spectabilis, Cypripedium acaule, Liparis liliifolia, Calopogon pulchellus, Habenaria fimbriata, Arethusa bulbosa, Satyrium carneum, Satyrium coriifolium, Bartholina pectinata, Serapias lingua,* and *Nigritella angustifolia.* From this group, *Epidendrum cochleatum* was the first epiphytic orchid known to have bloomed at Kew, this occurring in 1789. The following year *Epidendrum fragrans* also bloomed.

By 1813 the Gardens contained forty-six tropical species and about twelve more from Australia and South Africa. Nearly all these plants were tropical lowland or terrestrial species, for few epiphytic species—particularly the laelias, cattleyas, and odontoglossums from the tropical highlands—could survive the then prevalent conditions of culture.

In 1841 the Gardens passed into the hands of the government. William Jackson Hooker, professor of botany at the University of Glasgow, became its first official director. Hooker, a professional taxonomist, brought with him his own private herbarium and library, maintaining and increas-

Phaius tankervilliae, introduced in England by Dr. John Fothergill in 1778.

ing them until his death. His herbarium and a thousand of his personal volumes were purchased by the government after his death, becoming the basis of the Kew Herbarium, one of the largest collections of its type in the world.

Until the early 1800s the cultivation of orchids in Europe was not seriously undertaken; botanists and other men of letters looked upon them as "curiosities," and only a few scattered individuals attempted to grow them for esthetic purposes. The Horticultural Society of London, founded in 1809, became interested in orchids, however, and the subsequent interest in these plants as horticultural subjects assumed vast expansion within a relatively short period.

A history of the Orchid Family includes the names of many noted botanists and horticulturists, a number of whom have already been mentioned. A comprehensive survey of the introduction of orchidaceous plants to domestic culture, however, also involves persons renowned for

Cattleya labiata, the species which accelerated the "orchid craze" in England during the early 1800s. Illustration is a *Reichenbachia* print by H. G. Moon.

other endeavors. The names of two famous sea captains are remembered, among others, for their part in the progress of orchid introduction. During the collection of economic plants for Kew, Captain Bligh, of *H.M.S. Bounty*, brought some orchid plants back from Jamaica in the latter part of the eighteenth century, and, through his own botanists, Captain Cook introduced a number of orchids, as well as such economic plants as the breadfruit, collected on his trip around the world. Sir Joseph Banks and Dr. Daniel C. Solander, both Kew plantsmen, collected orchids in Australia while accompanying Captain Cook's expedition aboard *H.M.S. Endeavour* in 1780.

About 1812 plants of *Vanda, Aerides,* and *Dendrobium* were sent to England from India. During that same year Messrs. Conrad Loddiges and Sons began cultivating orchid plants in their Hackney nursery, signaling the beginnings of commercial orchid cultivation.

The Liverpool Botanic Garden was the recipient in 1810 of the first cattleya known in cultivation. The species was *Cattleya loddigesii*, which was sent from São Paulo, Brazil, by a Mr. Woodforde to a Mr. Shepherd of the Botanic Garden. The original plant and its subsequent divisions are reported to have bloomed every year following its arrival in England, but a published account of the species did not appear until 1819, when a plant belonging to Messrs. Loddiges was figured and described in their *Botanical Cabinet* as *Epidendrum violaceum.*

The most significant event influencing the orchid enthusiasm of English horticulturists was the first blooming of *Cattleya labiata* in cultivation. This occurrence heralded orchid growing as a highly fashionable pastime. The plants had been collected by Mr. William Swainson in 1818 in the Organ Mountains, in the vicinity of Rio de Janeiro, Brazil. Obviously the plants were not in bloom, and Swainson must not have considered them of botanical interest, much less of the Orchid Family, for he used them as packing material around other tropical plants which he was forwarding to England. Mr. William Cattley, of Barnet, a cultivator and introducer of tropical flora, was the recipient of at least some of these plants. Cattley, a patron of horticulture and one of the first to assemble a hobby collection of orchid plants, was apparently interested in the strange-looking plants used as packing, for he devised some method of growing them, and in November of that same year one of the plants bloomed. Cattley was extremely pleased, for the flowers were completely unlike anything seen before, the huge, trumpet-like labellum making this species the most attractive orchid thus far cultivated. Cattley wrote of it:

The most splendid, perhaps, of all Orchidaceous plants, which blossomed for the first time in Britain in the stove of my garden in Suffolk, during 1818, the plant having been sent to me by Mr. W. Swainson, during his visit to Brazil.

Upon viewing the first blooms of this heretofore unknown type, Dr.

John Lindley described and figured it, naming the genus in Cattley's honor. The large labellum was particularly impressive, so Lindley gave it the specific name of *labiata* (from Latin *labium*, meaning "lip"). The complementary specific name *autumnalis* was also applied, in allusion to its fall-blooming habit in the northern hemisphere.

The introduction of this unique and beautiful flower caused an immediate sensation among horticulturists, and in 1819 one of the plants was bloomed in the Glasgow Botanic Garden. A few more were later bloomed in other collections.

Until 1836 *Cattleya labiata* remained a treasured novelty. In that year Dr. Gardner located the habitat of the original plants and recorded in his *Travels in the Interior of Brazil*, 2nd edition:

Near the sea, and about 15 miles distant from the city [Rio de Janeiro], rises the Gavea, or Topsail Mountain, so called from its square shape, and well known to English sailors by the name of Lord Hood's Nose. It has a flat top, and rises about 2,000 feet above the level of the sea, to which it presents a nearly perpendicular precipitous face . . . . On the face of the mountain, at an elevation of several hundred feet, we observed some large patches of one of those beautiful large-flowered orchidaceous plants which are so common in Brazil. Its large rose-coloured flowers were very conspicuous, but we could not reach them. A few days afterwards, we found it on a neighboring mountain, and ascertained it to be *Cattleya labiata*. Those on the Gavea will long continue to vegetate, far from the reach of the greedy collector.

Dr. Gardner's explorations were carefully recorded, and a few days after his discovery of *Cattleya labiata* on the Gavea, in November 1836, he searched the opposite mountain. Of this excursion he wrote:

We made an excursion to a mountain called the Pedra Bonita, immediately opposite the Gavea . . . . Near the summit of the Pedra Bonita there is a small fazenda, or farm, the proprietor of which was then clearing away the forest that covers it, converting the trees into charcoal . . . . On the edge of a precipice on the eastern side, we found, covered with its large rose-coloured flowers, the splendid *Cattleya labiata*, which a few days before we had seen on the Gavea.

Gardner collected specimens at this location, some of which were used for drying:

It was with much difficulty and no little danger, that I could obtain about a dozen specimens of this, from the edge of a precipice on the Pedra Bonita Lynca. I collected, however, abundance of living plants.

The original location of *Cattleya labiata* remained unknown for eighteen years until Dr. Gardner's explorations, but soon afterward commercial horticulturists and wealthy private individuals began sending collectors to Brazil to search for this desirable plant. Much of the natural forest around Rio de Janeiro, however, had by then been destroyed to clear the ground for coffee plantations and the production of charcoal, as noted by Dr. Gardner. Thus, much of the natural habitat of *Cattleya labiata* was ruined, resulting in the almost total extinction of the species in that section. While unable to relocate *Cattleya labiata*, persistence on the part of the collectors resulted in the discovery of many other similar species of the genus *Cattleya*. Such forms as *Cattleya mossiae*, *Cattleya mendelii*, and *Cattleya trianaei* were promptly shipped to England, where they were classified as varieties of *Cattleya labiata vera* (*vera* being an addended name designating the "true" *Cattleya labiata*), the shape of the lip being the classifying determinant. Numerous collectors and growers thought themselves to be in possession of *Cattleya labiata*, but comparison with a dried specimen from one of the original plants preserved in the London Botanical Museum proved that though the plants and flowers were similar and sometimes as beautiful they were not *Cattleya labiata*.

The search continued, but so did the destruction of the forests around Rio de Janeiro. Dr. Gardner returned to Brazil in 1837 and wrote:

On my return from the Organ Mountains, I again visited this spot [Pedra Bonita], and found that a great change had taken place. The forest, which formerly covered a considerable portion of the summit, was now cut down and converted into charcoal; and the small shrubs and Vellozias which grew in the exposed portion had been destroyed by fire. The progress of cultivation is proceeding so rapidly for twenty miles around Rio, that many of the species which still exist will, in the course of a few years, be completely annihilated, and the botanists of future years who visit the country will look in vain for the plants collected by their predecessors.

Only in one other locality was Gardner able to find *Cattleya labiata*. On 29 March 1841 he discovered plants of the species, which also faced destruction, on the banks of the Rio Parahyba, the boundary between the provinces of Rio de Janeiro and Minas Gerais.

Thereafter, for nearly fifty years, the search for *Cattleya labiata* continued, but *Cattleya labiata vera*, the species on which the genus was founded, became only a memory. Two illustrations of *Cattleya labiata*, one a fine double-page illustration, are shown in Paxton's *Magazine of Botany*, the fourth volume, in 1837. These and a few earlier illustrations served for several decades as reminders to horticulturists and botanists that a prize had been lost. The rediscovery of *Cattleya labiata* in Pernambuco, fifty years later, was therefore a thrilling event in the annals of orchidology.

Prior to the introduction of *Cattleya labiata*, the culture of orchids was barely in its infancy, for the comparatively few species that were grown were usually chance finds by collectors in search of plants having more economic value, or by travelers and tradesmen who had brought orchid plants back with them as "curiosities." The striking beauty and showiness of the labiate cattleyas aroused much more general interest in the Orchidaceae, however. Importations received by Kew of plants from India, the West Indies, and Australia were the impetus for a special hothouse being built solely to house orchids. The Royal Horticultural Society also constructed an "orchid house" in the gardens at Chiswick.

Through its expanding collection of tropical plants, the Royal Horticultural Society gave rise to the popularization of the orchids among the wealthy classes. Messrs. Loddiges were also becoming fairly successful in cultivating the "Epidendrums" or "air plants," as nearly all the epiphytic species were termed, and increasing numbers of their plants began appearing at the newly established horticultural exhibitions. The fashionability of growing orchids on a hobby basis had its real beginning, perhaps, when William Spencer Cavendish, the sixth duke of Devonshire, noticed *Oncidium papilio* at one of the aforementioned exhibitions in 1833. Delighted with the remarkable character and singular charm of that species, the duke began forming a collection of orchids at Chatsworth. One of his acquisitions was a white Philippine phalaenopsis which he purchased from Hugh Cuming for 100 guineas. Several other species were later added to the Chatsworth collection via John Gibson and other

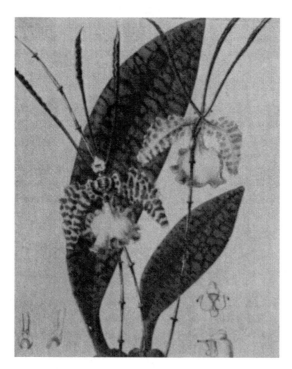

Oncidium papilio, the species which attracted the Sixth Duke of Devonshire to the hobby of orchid collecting.

The portage of live orchid plants from the mountainous regions of Asia and South America often was dependent upon the availability of mules and horses.

eastern explorers, employed by the duke as orchid collectors. Within ten years this was the largest private collection of orchids extant.

Among other amateur growers whose names are eulogized in early cultivation of orchids are Skinner and Bowring, Harrison and Moss of Liverpool, Cattley of Barnet, Rucker of Wandsworth, Day of Tottenham, and Bateman of Knypersly.

A number of commercial nurseries found it highly profitable to supply the demand for new species, and several hired collectors to travel into the tropical areas of the world where they might locate new sources of species which had already become horticulturally popular—and to collect new species which might stimulate further interest and profit. Bold, adventurous young men were sought, for the work of collecting was strenuous and fraught with danger. Thus the professional orchid hunter came into being: Warszewicz, Roezl, Bateman, Cuming, Linden, Wallis, Hartweg, Lobb, Low, Parish, and Welwitsch—names that were soon identified in connection with the discovery and introduction of hundreds of new previously unknown species. These hardy souls were counted among the most successful in their field. Unfortunately, many other new collectors set out, often ill-equipped both in knowledge of their destinations and in supplies. Many of them were never heard of again. Often the dangers involved were insurmountable—impenetrable forests, hostile savages, torrential rains, poisonous snakes, fierce animals, insects, tropical diseases, swirling rapids, and seasonal floods. The average European, of course, was often unprepared for such rigors and unexpected difficulties. Even seasoned collectors fell victim to the toll of lives lost in the orchid search—Falkenberg in Panama, Klaboch in Mexico, Wallis in Ecuador, Schroeder in Sierra Leone, Arnold on the Orinoco, Degance in Brazil, and Brown in Madagascar.

The mania for possessing orchid plants caused prices of all available new plants to climb rapidly. Great auctions were held in Liverpool and London in which 17 pounds for a single plant was not unusual. Some particularly rare specimens commanded a near-top price of 700 pounds, which was considered an "investment." Famous hobbyists, desiring their names perpetuated in botanical nomenclature, bid freely against one another in hopes of introducing, through their purchases, new species which might be endowed with the new owners' names.

Commercial orchid collectors were sent out in droves. As an example, in 1894 Messrs. Sanders sent twenty collectors into the jungles of the world, with two of them in Brazil, two in Colombia, two in Peru and Ecuador, one in Mexico, one in Madagascar, one in New Guinea, and

Typical mountain terrain in northern South America where the most intrepid of orchid seekers sought out rare and desirable species.

three in India, Burma, and the Straits Settlements. Whole areas were denuded of their trees in order to gather the epiphytic orchids gracing their upper branches. The areas where *Miltonia vexillaria* was found were said to have been cleared as if by forest fires, and on one particular search for *Odontoglossum crispum* in Colombia, 10,000 plants were collected with the result that 4000 trees were felled in order to reach the plants. As one area was stripped and the native vegetation ruined, the collector moved forward week by week, hacking down trees and depleting the natural wealth of orchids. An idea of this "slaughter" may be gauged from a letter in 1895 from Carl Johannsen, writing from Medellín:

I shall despatch tomorrow 30 boxes, 12 of which contain the finest of all the Aureas, the Monte coromes form, and 18 cases containing the great Sanderiana type all collected from the spot where they grow mixed, and I shall clear them out. They are now extinguished in this spot and this will surely be the last season. I have finished all along the Rio Dagua where there are no plants left; the last days I remained in that spot the people brought in two or three plants at a time and some came back without a single plant.

While orchid culture enjoyed its biggest "boom" in the British Empire, other countries were nonetheless engrossed in the novelty and beauty of the fascinating Orchid Family, the United States not the least among them.

The first known recipient of epiphytic orchids in the United States was Mr. John Wright Boott of Boston, Massachusetts. His brother James, then a resident in London, sent him a collection of plants about the year 1838, though Boott was known to have cultivated a few plants before 1829. A businessman, Mr. Boott enjoyed flowers as a leisure-time activity and maintained a small greenhouse in the yard of his residence at Bowdoin Square. Particularly enthusiastic about the plants received from his brother, during the next few years he imported more orchids, the more common species of *Cattleya*, *Dendrobium*, and *Epidendrum* becoming the basis of his collection.

At the same time, another eminent Boston horticulturist, Marshall P. Wilder, was cultivating tropical orchids. Records indicate that on 24 June 1837 he exhibited *Oncidium flexuosum* at a meeting of the Massachusetts Horticultural Society.

These collections effected a multiplication of interest in orchid growing in New England. Boott died about 1845, bequeathing his collection to John Amory Lowell, of Roxbury. Lowell built a greenhouse to accommodate the plants, and for ten years increased the collection by importations. One of the first orchids publicly displayed by Lowell was an immense specimen of *Dendrobium calceolus*. About 1853 he leased his country residence, selling the orchids to the tenant, who neglected them so badly that many died. Some of them, mainly oncidiums, were sold to the Misses Pratt at Watertown. Edward S. Rand bought the major portion of the remaining plants, removing them to his greenhouses in Dedham.

Mr. Rand was an enthusiastic cultivator, adding largely to his collection by importations from Messrs. Hugh Low & Son, of Clapton Nurseries, London. By 1856 this collection contained probably the finest specimen orchid plants in the country, among them a plant of *Dendrobium calceolus* four feet high and at least three feet in diameter, and a plant of "*Cattleya crispa*, as large as a small wash tub." About 1865 Mr. Rand sold his estate and presented his large collection of stove and greenhouse plants, including all the orchids, to Harvard College. The plants were placed in the greenhouses at the Cambridge Botanic Garden.

Other collections in the Boston area may be mentioned: Gardiner G. Hubbard, of Cambridge, grew fine specimens of stanhopeas and cyrtopodiums; William Gray, Jr., of Boston, maintained a choice collection of paphiopedilums; Frederick L. Ames, of Easton, grew fine rare species; and Messrs. Hovey had a small sales collection at Cambridge.

In the vicinity of New York, the veteran florist Mr. Isaac Buchanan brought the first *Cattleya mossiae* from London in September 1840 and soon afterward imported a collection of miscellaneous orchids from Brazil. Mr. Thomas Hogg had an extensive hobby collection in New York consisting mainly of stanhopeas, cattleyas, oncidiums, *Cycnoches ventricosum*, and *Aerides odoratum*. The breaking up of Hogg's collection in 1855–1856 gave still further impetus to orchid growing in the United States, particularly along the East Coast. Dr. James Knight bought some of the plants and imported others from Messrs. Low. Among many bloomed for the first time in the United States, *Dendrobium devonianum* was one of Dr. Knight's loveliest orchids.

Mr. Buchanan also bought numerous plants from the Hogg collection and began growing orchids on a large scale. Returning from Europe in 1856, he brought with him a large consignment of the best kinds then grown, which formed the starting nucleus of his collection.

Another portion of the Hogg collection passed into the possession of Cornelius Van Voorst, of Jersey City, and still another part went to Mr. Baker, of New York, an amateur collector. By 1857 Mr. Van Voorst had additionally obtained the collection of a Mr. Paulmerre, so that his greenhouses contained the finest collection in the country. About 250 species were represented, among which were nineteen of *Aerides*, forty cattleyas, fourteen odontoglossums, ten anoectochilus, thirty dendrobiums, sixteen laelias, and fine specimens of *Ansellia africana*, which two men could barely lift.

As time passed, orchid culture mushroomed along the Eastern Seaboard. The list of cultivators grew lengthy: M. Lienau, of Jersey City; John Cadness, of Flushing, Long Island; S. B. Dodd, of Hoboken; John Patterson, of Newark; Robert Buist and Caleb Cope, of Philadelphia; George Such, of South Amboy; a Mr. Mitchell of Tarrytown; General

Joseph Howland, of Tioronda, Matteawan; Louis Menand and Erastus Corning, of Albany; and General John F. Rathbone, of Albany, who expressed the same ardor for orchids that might have typified any one of the enthusiastic growers of that period:

I was so delighted with the plant and flowers that I caught the Orchid fever, which I am happy to say is now prevailing to considerable extent in this country, and which I trust will become epidemic. I purchased each year following a few plants. In 1867, that I might successfully grow this charming family of plants, I built a house exclusively for Orchids; and now I have a collection that will compare favorably with any in America.

And so the "fever" spread. Hobby orchid cultivation also flourished elsewhere. M. Pescatore, of St. Cloud, near Paris, was one of the first Europeans outside England to grow orchids as a leisure activity, having cultivated a large collection of plants for many years—as had Consul Schiller of Hamburg, Germany.

By the middle of the nineteenth century epiphytic orchids from both the eastern and western hemispheres had become widespread in popularity. They continued, however, as symbols of the wealthy classes. But upon the discovery of cool-growing species from the highlands of Mexico, Donald Beaton wrote in Paxton's *Magazine of Botany*:

You will thus see how desirable it is for the extension of the cultivation of this family that we should procure all the species that are to be found in the higher altitudes in Mexico and other places, to enable amateurs of limited means to cultivate a few beautiful plants of Orchideae; for hitherto this fine tribe of plants has only been enjoyed by the wealthier classes.

Adopting the same logic, in 1851 Benjamin S. Williams wrote a series of articles—"Orchids for the Millions"—for the *Gardeners' Chronicle*. This series was noted for its wide popularity and acceptance, soon becoming the *Orchid Grower's Manual*, published in seven editions from 1852 to 1894. The *Manual* was highly acclaimed, being accepted as the most authoritative work of the times dealing with the cultivation of orchids.

As previously mentioned, the Orientals had for centuries enjoyed orchids, and nobles and warriors had the distinction of being the few who were given the privilege of growing the endemic species of *Cymbidium*, *Angraecum*, and *Dendrobium*. The first orchids imported into Japan, however, came from England and France, sent for by the Viscount Itsujin Fukuba, who built the first greenhouse seen in the Orient. Upon completion of the nine- by thirty-six foot structure, in 1883 or 1884 the viscount received the species mentioned, most of them oncidiums, stanhopeas, and cymbidiums. Unfortunately, due to the rigors of the long voyage, many of the plants were dead upon arrival.

An Englishman living in Yokohama in 1891, a Mr. Dinisdel, sold some orchids to the Marquis Okuma, who built a greenhouse at his home and also purchased plants from a Chinese trader. The marquis attempted to hybridize plants in his collection, but the results of his attempts are unknown. In 1894 the Imperial "Shinjuki" Gardens erected greenhouses on its grounds and obtained plants also from Mr. Dinisdel. In that same year Viscount Fukuba's collection was transferred to the gardens.

The number of Oriental growers multiplied, but these consisted mainly of the moneyed classes—imperial aristocracy and their wealthy peers such as Prince Fushimi, Viscount Soma, Viscount Ijuin, Count Hayashi, Prince Shimazu, Prince Kuni, Baron Iwasaki, Baron Mitsui, Mr. Ro, Mr. Kaga, Korean Prince Rhee, and two Europeans residing in Tokyo.

Kew Botanic Gardens was perhaps the first of the major institutions to foster an interest in orchids both on the scientific and horticultural level, but, as the years passed and learning progressed, many other organizations and plant-minded groups made giant strides. The Royal Horticultural Society, formed in 1804, instituted its Floral Committee in 1859, empowering its members to award the First Class Certificate to plants of outstanding merit. The first plant to be so recognized was an orchid shown by Messrs. J. Veitch—*Cattleya* Dominiana, a cross of *C. maxima* × *C. intermedia*. The committee's work served beyond measure to popularize orchids and other outstanding garden plants, but, as the field of horticulture became more varied and specialized, the need for a special committee to deal only with orchids became evident, and so in 1889 the Orchid Committee was formed. Numbered among its fifteen members were such orchid notables as Mr. (later Sir) Harry J. Veitch, chairman of the committee, founder of the Royal Exotic Nurseries at Chelsea and the most prominent orchidist of the period; Baron Schroeder, owner of a famous orchid collection at the Dell; Professor (later Sir) Bayley Balfour, director of the Royal Botanic Garden, Edinburgh; William Boxall, the old Lowian collector; Joseph Charlesworth, a prominent nurseryman who was one of the first to raise orchids commercially by the laboratory method of seed germination; Sir Jeremiah Colman, who built up the fine Gatton collection of orchids; De Barri Crawshay, who grew fine odontoglossums and did much to develop improved hybrid strains; Sir F. W. Moore, superintendent at Glasnevin; J. T. Pitt, a blusterous gentleman who collected fine odontoglossums; and H. A. Tracy, an orchid specialist at Twickenham, particularly remembered for *Cymbidium tracyanum.*

On 12 May 1885 the first Orchid Conference was held in South Kensington, England, under the sponsorship of the Royal Horticultural Society. Both commercial and amateur cultivators of orchids met to exhibit specimens and to consider vital questions on the subjects of orchid culture and nomenclature. The planned program consisted of major talks by Harry Veitch on "Hybridization of Orchids," James O'Brien on

Early photograph of the Royal Horticultural Society's Orchid Committee engaged in judging blooming plants submitted for potential awards. At extreme left is Sir Harry Veitch, who served for many years as chairman of the committee.

"The Cultivation of Orchids," and a third topic on "The Nomenclature of Orchids" which was never presented because the participants became so involved in one aspect of the second talk—namely, the application of manure to orchids—that time ran out.

The society's library was founded in 1868, built around the fine collection of books and pamphlets which belonged to Dr. John Lindley, first editor of the *Gardeners' Chronicle* and proponent of what later became known as a system of "modern orchidology." The costs of fitting and furnishing the library were entirely defrayed by Sir J. Henry Schroeder in 1904, who spared no expense in making the room and its equipment worthy of its contents—more than 33,000 volumes and pamphlets devoted to horticulture, botany, and allied subjects. Further purchases, gifts, and bequests made it one of the leading horticultural libraries in the world.

From the standpoint of scientific orchidology, Harvard University produced one of the world's most renowned orchid scholars, Professor Oakes Ames, who, in the tradition of those great orchidologists who preceded him, Lindley and Reichenbach, became the leading orchid authority in the world. For forty years he received specimens, sent for identification and analysis, from correspondents all over the world. This resulted in the formation of an extensive herbarium and library. As an outgrowth of Professor Ames' work, Harvard became the "mecca" of U.S. orchidology, for he presented all his materials to the university in 1940, where they continue to grow to mammoth proportions. Through the development of this collection and library, numerous well-known orchidologists emerged and several important orchid floras were published—*The Orchids of North America* by Donovan Correll, the *Orchids of Guatemala* by Ames and Correll, the *Orchids of Kinabalu and the Philippines* by Ames, the *Orchids of Mexico* by Louis Williams, the *Orchids of Panama* by Williams and Paul Allen, the *Orchids of Trinidad* by Richard E. Schultes, the *Orchids of Peru* by Charles Schweinfurth, *Venezuelan Orchids Illustrated* by Leslie A. Garay and G. C. K. Dunsterville, and numerous other important works on the orchids of Colombia and Okinawa.

In the face of such development, culture, and study of orchids, it was almost inevitable that a group of orchid enthusiasts should get together for the purpose of mutual association and exchange of ideas on orchids and their cultivation. And thus it was that the idea of a national orchid society was born. The first meeting for the purpose of forming such an organization was held at Horticultural Hall in Boston on 25 March 1920. Numerous persons representative of both private and commercial orchid interests gathered there and voted to proceed with the organization of what would be called the American Orchid Society. Among the officers and trustees unanimously elected, Mr. Albert Cameron Burrage became president and Oakes Ames became a vice-president. Other well-known orchidists among the original hundred founders were George E. Baldwin, John T. Butterworth, Mr. and Mrs. Pierre S. DuPont, Clement Moore, Thomas Roland, Edwin S. Webster, Henry Hurrell, John Lager, Oliver Lines, Miss Eileen Low, Edward A. Manda, Fred K. Sander, and Charles Schweinfurth.

At a trustees' meeting held in the American Museum of Natural History in New York in November 1921 it was decided to publish a copy of the bylaws. Mr. Burrage very generously offered to bear the expenses involved and supervised the printing of the work. A thought of his, expressed therein, was prophetic:

It is hoped that this little pamphlet, giving the names of the one hundred founders of the American Orchid Society, the by-laws under which they are governed, and the officers who represent them, is the forerunner of a long line, each of which will portray in some way one of those lovely members of the great Orchid Family . . . , and which have so much interest not only for our ever increasing number of orchidologists, but also for flower lovers throughout the world.

For the next ten or twelve years American Orchid Society activities seemed centered primarily on orchid exhibitions to further promote the attraction of growing the "Queen of Flowers." Membership fluctuated between 150 and 200 all that time—almost on a selective and exclusive basis for orchids were even then considered the expensive playthings of landed and wealthy persons.

Then, at a meeting of the trustees in 1931, a far-reaching, progressive step was taken. It was suggested that the society publish a quarterly bulletin dedicated to timely subjects and news items of the orchid world and to become the official organ of the society. *The Orchid Review*, a monthly orchid periodical founded by Robert A. Rolfe in 1893, was until then the only major periodical available on the subject of orchids, and so an American counterpart was welcomed with avid response. David Lumsden, secretary of the American Orchid Society, was appointed as editor of the new publication, the first issue appearing in June 1932. That first quarterly bulletin consisted of thirty-two pages and dealt largely with articles on cypripediums. It also contained a portrait of Albert C. Burrage, then recently deceased, and a biographical sketch. The new *American Orchid Society Bulletin* was immediately successful, and publication was continued.

The society continued to thrive as well. The membership increased gradually, and many letters passed through the editor's hands from people who wanted to know more and more about growing orchids. Publicity for the society was further promoted through advertising and goodwill, so that by May 1939 membership had reached a then record high of 459. Then, in June of 1940, the *Bulletin* publication was stepped up to one issue per month under a new editor, Dr. Louis O. Williams, assisted by Gordon W. Dillon.

During World War II Dr. Williams went to Brazil to do research on the production of rubber. Dillon, who was working for the army on illustrations for survival manuals, was draft-free and was asked to take over editorship of the *Bulletin*, which he did in 1942.

Despite shortages of fuel and supplies during the war, orchid growing expanded. Reports of tropical orchids in their native habitats, as seen by U.S. servicemen, further stimulated plans for hobby orchid growing. And, for the first time after over twenty years of existence, American Orchid Society membership passed the one-thousand mark.

As the *Bulletin* became popularized, membership in the American Orchid Society continued to increase. All the while Gordon Dillon acted as a goodwill ambassador for the society and orchids in general. He went to orchid shows all over the nation, wrote reports on them, took photographs at shows and regional judgings, assembled slide programs from the photographs taken, gave lectures, and helped in a large way to stabilize the operation and organization of the society. The American Orchid Society soon became a "clearinghouse" of orchid data and knowledge, and Dillon's counsel and advice became increasingly sought as local orchid societies became affiliated with the American Orchid Society.

Dillon was appointed executive secretary to the society, and under his broadened direction of the society's activities and organization, orchid research and public interest in orchids blossomed in the United States at a pace comparable to the "orchid mania" of the early 1800s in England.

As executive secretary, Dillon was concerned with and involved in the management of the organization. Under his direction the society's membership had swollen to previously unreached records by the early 1950s, and he might well have been justified in resting on the laurels of his success in its growth. The society had become a symbol to orchid organizations the world over; national and state societies abundantly sprang into being; and interest in orchids reached an all-time high. Yet, despite all the progress, Dillon was increasingly disturbed by the lack of unity, the aimlessness, and the disparity of purpose he saw in the expanding "orchid fraternity."

New developments and cultural advances were appearing everywhere, but only those growers within close contact of one another benefited by them. Through their regional isolation it was evident that numerous of the world orchid societies were being deprived of the knowledge and guidance necessary for self growth. Seeing the need for closer ties, at a trustees' meeting of the American Orchid Society in the early 1950s he proposed to several of the board members the idea of a world orchid conference. The idea was enthusiastically received, and George Pring, then superintendent of the Missouri Botanical Gardens in St. Louis, Missouri, tentatively offered the gardens' facilities. Upon official approval by the Board of Trustees, planning for the First World Orchid Conference was launched, the entire operation resting in the hands of Dillon, Pring, and several others. In October 1954 the conference was held in St. Louis, sponsored by the American Orchid Society, and for the first time people from all the major orchid-growing areas of the world—whose orchid interests varied from those of the professional grower to the average hobbyist, from the scientific to the commercial—convened in common cause. This pioneering effort was eminently successful, one of its major achievements being the inauguration of a Standard American Orchid Judging System. The 601 registrants wholeheartedly endorsed the idea of further conferences, and so it was voted that the Second World Orchid Conference be held in Honolulu, Hawaii, in 1957.

The Second World Orchid Conference was just as successful as the first, as evidenced by nearly a thousand registrants. A major achievement was the establishment of an International Orchid Commission on Classification, Nomenclature, and Registration. This was followed in 1960 by the Third World Orchid Conference in London, jointly sponsored by the American Orchid Society and the Royal Horticultural Society. Here the dawn of orchid culture was united with the present, and a world approach to orchidology became a long-cherished reality. At this conference the burden of orchid hybrid registration was transferred from the shoulders of David F. Sander (who had carried the responsibility of this important work into the third generation of his family) to the Royal Horticultural Society. Here it was, also, that the Royal Horticultural Society voted to share in the work of future world orchid conferences by thereafter acting as co-sponsor with the American Orchid Society.

The Fourth World Orchid Conference of October 1963 attracted hundreds of orchid enthusiasts from all parts of the world to Singapore, where the Malayan Orchid Society hosted the conference. Here it was that East and West met and joined in common orchid unity and interest. A further major development was the presentation of the basic draft of the *Handbook on Orchid Nomenclature* and the establishment of a Handbook Committee to bring it to completion.

In April 1966 the Fifth World Orchid Conference brought over 1500 orchidists from thirty-one nations to Long Beach, California, where it was hosted by the Orchid Society of Southern California and again co-sponsored by the American Orchid Society and the Royal Horticultural Society. At its conclusion, the bonds of worldwide orchid friendship had been firmly tied. Its accomplishments were many—a World Orchid Conference Judging System was instituted and utilized for the first time; the World Orchid Conference was established as a self-sustaining organization; a fund for education and research was announced by the American Orchid Society; orchid editors of the world met on common ground, exchanging views and ideas toward more effective communication of orchid knowledge; and, perhaps most important, old and new friends met eagerly, casting off the restraints which for so many years prior to the conferences had kept them apart.

References

Adams, Helen H. 1943. *Cattleya labiata*, A History. *Amer. Orch. Soc. Bull.* 12, no. 5.

American Orchid Society Bulletin. 1966. Welcoming Address by Lewis C. Vaughn, General Chairman—Fifth World Orchid Conference 35, no. 7.

Arnold, Ralph E. 1958. *Bletia verecunda. The Orch. Rev.* 66, no. 780.

Arnold, Ralph E. 1932. Some Old Epidendrums. *The Orch. Rev.* 40, no. 473.

Arnold, Ralph E. 1959. Vanilla Flavour. *The Orch. Rev.* 67, no. 796.

Bateman, James. 1867. *A Second Century of Orchidaceous Plants.* Preface. L. Reeve & Co. London.

Boyle, Louis M. 1952. *Out West Growing Cymbidium Orchids and Other Flowers, The Story of El Rancho Rinconada.* Times-Mirror Press. Los Angeles.

Burbidge, Frederick W. 1953. Orchids. *The Orch. Rev.* 61, no. 725. (Reprinted from *Harper's New Monthly Magazine*, possibly 1886.)

Childers, Norman F., Héctor R. Cibes, and Ernesto Hernández-Medina. 1959. Vanilla—The Orchid of Commerce. Ch. 14 of *The Orchids—A Scientific Survey.* Carl Withner, ed. The Ronald Press Co. New York.

Cohen, Nellie. 1943. Florida Osmundine. *Amer. Orch. Soc. Bull.* 12, no. 1.

Curtis, Charles H. 1953. Men, Matters and Memories. *The Orch. Rev.* 61, no. 718.

Davis, Reginald S. and Mona Lisa Steiner. 1952. *Philippine Orchids.* William-Frederick Press. New York.

De Wolf, Gordon P., Jr. Kew and Orchidology. *Amer. Orch. Soc. Bull.* 28, no. 12.

Fort Lauderdale Orchid Society Newsletter. August 1966. Mrs. Rex Van Alstyne, ed.

Gauda, H. 1959. Orchid Growing in Japan. *The Orch. Rev.* 67, no. 790.

Hsia, Emile 1948. Orchids of the "Middle" or "Flowery Kingdom." *Orchid Digest* 12, no. 4.

Jones, Rodney Wilcox. 1941. *Cattleya labiata*—The Mystery Orchid. *Amer. Orch. Soc. Bull.* 10, no. 4.

Lorant, Michael. 1961. The Story of Vanilla. *The Orch. Rev.* 69, no. 821.

MacDonald, Norman. 1939. *The Orchid Hunters.* Farrar & Rinehart. New York.

Nagano, Y. 1953. History of Orchid Growing in Japan. *Amer. Orch. Soc. Bull.* 22, no. 5.

Nagano, Y. 1960. Orchids in Japan. *Proceedings of the Third World Orchid Conference.*—Historical Session. Staples Printers Ltd. London.

Nagano, Y. 1952. Three Main Species of Orchids in Japan. *Amer. Orch. Soc. Bull.* 21, no. 11.

Northen, Rebecca T. *Home Orchid Growing.* Rev. 3rd ed., 1970. Van Nostrand Reinhold Co., New York.

Orchid Review, The. 1893. Notes 1:225.

Orchid Review, The. 1931. Obituary: Albert C. Burrage. 39, no. 458.

Orchid Review, The. 1959. 100 Years of Awards to Orchids 67, no. 790.

Orchid Review, The. Potting Fibre for Orchids vol. 27, No. 313–314.

Orchid Review, The. 1893. The Hybridist 1:245.

Orchid Review, The. 1895. Vanillas of Commerce. 3, no. 34.

Parkinson, John. 1640. *Parkinson's Herbal.* London.

Rand, Edward S., Jr. 1888. *Orchid Culture.* Riverside Press. Cambridge, Massachusetts.

Richter, Walter. 1965. *The Orchid World.* English translation. E. P. Dutton & Co. New York.

Rolfe, Robert A. 1900. *Cattleya labiata* and Its Habitat. *The Orch. Rev.* 8, no. 96.

Sealy, J. R. 1959. Royal Botanic Gardens at Kew. *Science* 129, no. 3360.

Slousaronko, Aleksandi. 1966. Orchids in the U.S.S.R. *The Orch. Rev.* 74, no. 875.

van Steenis, C. G. G. J. 1950. Cyclopaedia of Collectors. *Flora Malesiana.* Series I, vol. 1.

Veitch, James, & Sons. 1887–94. *A Manual of Orchidaceous Plants. Epidendrea.* Vol. 1. H. M. Pollett & Co. London.

Watling, H. 1928. Researches into Chinese Orchid History. *The Orch. Rev.* 36, no. 424.

Withner, Carl L. 1959. Introduction and History of Orchid Culture. Ch. 1 of *The Orchids—A Scientific Survey.* Carl L. Withner, ed. The Ronald Press Co. New York.

Yamada, Rev. Masao. 1954. Modern Trends in Vandas. *Amer. Orch. Soc. Bull.* 23, no. 11.

Classification

IN 1885 THE EMINENT BOTANIST J. D. HOOKER ADVISED HIS PEERS: " . . . IT is only after much preliminary study, and with the aids of a complete library, . . . that descriptive botany can be effectively carried out; and it would be well for science if this were fully understood and acted upon."

This sage statement will hold as true in the whole future history of botanical classification as it was when originally spoken, for it contains the key phrase provisional to the fruition of any course of study—"if fully understood."

Taxonomy, the science of classification, though based on principles common to all classes of beings, has run a gamut of difficulties for years—particularly among the Orchidaceae. The often indistinct relations between genera and species, plus the varying interpretations of those relations, have made for several different systems of classification in the Orchid Family during its relatively brief taxonomic history.

Though enumerations and descriptions were made of the native European orchids during the time of the Doctrine of Signatures, the knowledge imparted dwelt principally with practical uses of plants, those particularly which contained substances that cured illness or alleviated pain.

Otho Brunfels (1489–1534), the first "German Father of Botany," provided a means of identifying medicinal herbs—the initial attempt at formal plant classification. His herbal, *Herbarium vivae Eicones* (1530–1536), was a compilation made directly from living plants, and illustrated therein were seven members of the Orchid Family: *Gymnadenia conopsea, Listera ovata, Ophrys fuciflora, Orchis militaris, Orchis morio,*

Orchis purpurea, and *Spiranthes spiralis.* This herbal was later regarded "either as the end of a long line of classical and medieval works on medicinal plants or as the beginning of modern taxonomy."

Not until the sixteenth and seventeenth centuries, however, concurrent with the rise of the experimental method in the physical sciences, did scholars begin the study of plants for their own sake. One of the first to enumerate plants from a purely botanical point of view was Kasper Bauhin, a Swiss contemporary of Galileo and Descartes who, in 1623, produced a nomenclator which gave the names and synonyms of the 6000-odd kinds of plants known to him. In this work, called the *Pinax,* the individual concepts of genera and species were recognized and used on a large scale for the first time.

The first fully systematic enumeration of the known flora of the world, comprising 7700 species, was prepared by the Swedish botanist Carl von Linné, known academically as Linnaeus. He apparently was the first to recognize the two major divisions of the Orchid Family, those later designated as Monandrae and Diandrae. His *Acta Societatis Regiae Scientiarum* established these divisions in 1740. His *Species Plantarum* (1753) emphasized the sexual system, which was based on the number and position of the stamens and pistils. Linnaeus did not separate plant families in this work, but the orchids were all listed in class XX under Gynandria (with stamens adnate to the pistil) and Diandria (with two stamens). This first edition described sixty-nine species of orchids in eight genera: *Orchis, Satyrium, Ophrys, Serapias, Limodorum, Arethusa, Cypripedium,* and *Epidendrum.* In his *Genera Plantarum* (1754) he adhered strictly to the binary system, each entity described with its generic and specific names.

By the late 1700s various other botanists such as Antoine Laurent de Jussieu* and Augustin Pyramus de Candolle had described and classified the then known orchids under various systems allied to that of Linnaeus.

In 1788 Olof Swartz published his *Prodromus Descriptionum Vegetabilium . . . in Indiam Occidentalem, etc.,* the first enumeration of West Indian plants, including orchids. Swartz, known later as the "first orchid specialist," followed the Linnean system, describing representatives of several different genera. Following his original work, in 1797–1806 he published an amplification, *Flora Indiae Occidentalis,* in which thirteen genera and twenty-seven species of West Indian orchids were recognized. In this work the various generic concepts consisted of brief descriptions limited to floral parts and discussion of the essential characteristics and relative position of each genus. The species, however, were fully described in as many aspects as Swartz knew, including roots, bulbs, stems, leaves, inflorescences, and fruit. Synonyms and native habi-

---

* The term Orchideae was ascribed to the Orchid Family by de Jussieu for the first time in August 1789.

Until a serious interest in the classification of orchids was developed in the early 1800s, the comparatively few epiphytic genera known were collectively known as "epidendra," alluding to their habit of growing on trees in the native habitat.

tats were likewise given, followed by notes on flowering season or a phrase distinguishing the plant from other related species. These two contributions formed the basis of many later treatises on the West Indies orchids.

Swartz's classification consisted of Orchids with one anther (twenty-four genera) and Orchids with two anthers (one genus: *Cypripedium*). This was noted in his article, "Groups of Orchids and the Species Described," in *Kongl. Vetenskaps Academiens Nya Handlingar*, volume 21. In this article he gave a detailed treatment of the twenty-five genera included.

A significant classification of the orchids of Australia, plus other complex plant families, was compiled by the Scotsman Robert Brown in the early nineteenth century. As a result of his visit to that southern continent (1801–1805), he wrote the *Prodromus Florae Novae Hollandiae et Insulae Van-Diemen* in 1810, a concise enumeration of the plant families present in Australia and New Zealand—the Orchideae among them. Brown was apparently the first botanist to use the term *Monandrae* in his descriptions of the native orchids, all of which were monandrous (having single anthers). Twenty-six genera and 113 species were treated in this work. Another important contribution by Brown was his re-classification of the orchids described in W. T. Aiton's *Hortus Kewensis, or a Catalogue of the Plants Cultivated in the Royal Botanic Garden at Kew* (1813). The system was Linnean, modified with Swartz's division into Monandria and Diandria. Brown included numerous new genera in his descriptions of forty-six genera and 115 species, supplementing information, where known, of synonyms, native habitat, date of introduction, and blooming season.

In 1818 the French botanist Louis Claude Richard listed and briefly discussed the important orchid works up to that time. The article, "De Orchideis Europaeis Annotationes," published in *Mémoires du Museum d' Histoire Naturelle*, also gave a valuable explanation of orchid plant anatomy in a new system of terminology which has been used ever since. Richard based his classification on the pollen being the characteristic determinant for separation, relegating Swartz's system to less importance. Though Richard's system was later considered regressive, his precise terminology and analyses of pollinia and reproductive systems proved to be a worthy addition to the expanding taxonomy of the Orchid Family. Richard's key to the genera of European orchids was based on pollen formation as follows: sectile, caudicle without a gland, granulose, and solid.

Carl Ludwig Blume, Director of the Rijksherbarium in Leyden, Holland, was the first to compile a key to the orchids of Java and the adjacent islands. In his *Tabellen en Platen voor de Javaansche Orchideën* (1825) he classified the orchids into three groups according to the nature of the pollen—granular, powdery, and waxy. Each genus was additionally given a tabular description of its basic floral anatomy and habit. As addenda to his initial work, the *Bijdragen tot de Flora von Nederlandsch Indië* was published the same year. These addenda introduced many new generic concepts, among them *Agrostophyllum*, *Spathoglottis*, and *Phalaenopsis* (the genus which Rumphius discovered and figured in his *Herbarium Amboinense* as *Angraecum*).

Blume's greatest work appeared in 1858. This was a small folio which elaborately described many previously described species as well as newer introductions. This work, *Florae Javae et Insularum adjacentium*, contained some of the most meticulous floral analyses and colored illustrations available in the literature of the Old World orchids.

Perhaps the most eminent of all the great systematic botanists was John Lindley, often referred to as the "Father of Modern Orchidology." Interested in horticulture at a time when the flourishing trade routes were enabling botanical exploration throughout the world, he became an orchidologist of extremely wide scope. Though he published numerous books on general plant classification, he is most noted for his contributions to orchidology. Among these was *The Genera and Species of Orchidaceous Plants*, an enumeration of all the then known species of the world—1980 in all. This work was considered the most comprehensive treatment in classifying the *Orchidaceae* (the term introduced and first used by Lindley, a modification of de Jussieu's *Orchideae*). Brief descriptions of the species were given, along with a detailed discussion of the family itself and previous literature published on orchids. Also included was *A Tabular View of the Tribes of Orchidaceae*.

Lindley is renowned also for his *Folia Orchidaceae*, which appeared between 1852 and 1859. This work was planned as a series of monographs of all the orchid genera, and, though unfinished, the major and most complex genera were treated. Each genus then known was described with all its component species, along with various keys.

Following Lindley, the German botanist Heinrich Gustav Reichenbach became the international authority on orchidology. Like Lindley, Reichenbach maintained an extensive orchid herbarium, dried specimens of which were the bases of hundreds of identifications and descriptions. During his twenty-four years of botanical fame, Reichenbach published his descriptions of new species chiefly in the *Gardeners' Chronicle* and the first four volumes of *Bonplandia*.

Reichenbach's most important works appeared in *Walper's Annales* and *Xenia Orchidacea; Beiträge zur Kenntniss der Orchideen* (Contributions to the Knowledge of the Orchids), a three-volume compilation of general orchid information that included monographs and keys of many genera. In addition, the text was profusely illustrated with hundreds of black and white sketches and watercolor drawings of the species described.

George Bentham in 1881 published the first of three great modern systems* of classification. His system, published that year in the *Journal of the Linnean Society*, was based on Lindley's five-tribe system—with modifications. In his detailed description of the tribes *Epidendreae*, *Vandeae*, *Neottieae*, *Ophrydeae*, and *Cypripedieae*, he included many subtribes and the genera inclusive of each. In 1883, under coauthorship with Sir Joseph Dalton Hooker, he published an expanded form of his system in the *Genera Plantarum*, following de Candolle's earlier outline.

Ernst Hugo Heinrich Pfitzer, another German botanist, devised a system of classification based on vegetative characteristics. Emphasis was placed particularly on leaves, stems, and inflorescences. His morphological observations and ideas were published in several journals. In 1889, upon request, he treated the Orchid Family in Engler and Prantl's *Die*

---

* The various systems developed by past orchidologists were based on principles which, while useful then, may not be applicable in present-day orchid classification. This is mentioned here only as a safeguard lest the reader err in applying those principles today.

natürlichen Pflanzen-familien. The system proposed varied widely from Bentham's: e.g., the *Apostasiaceae* were included in the subfamily *Cypripedilinae* under *Diandrae*; the *Diandrae* and *Monandrae* were initially separated on the basis of pollen characters; and the remaining majority of the system was devoted to an emphasis on vegetative characteristics.

In 1903 Pfitzer gave a detailed treatment of the *Cypripedilinae.* The work, entitled *Orchidaceae—Pleonandrae,* was published in Engler's *Das Pflanzenreich.* This work included *Apostasia, Neuwiedia,* and *Adactylus* (the three genera included under *Apostasioideae*), thus the addition of *Pleonandrae.* The components of the *Cypripedilinae* were divided into four genera—*Selenipedilum, Cypripedilum, Phragmopedilum,* and *Paphiopedilum,* and a key of each genus was given in sections, subsections, and species.

In 1906 a most comprehensive treatment of the Brazilian orchids was given in K. F. P. von Martius' *Flora Brasiliensis.* The section dealing with the Orchidaceae was done by a Belgian botanist, Celestin Alfred Cogniaux, who, using Pfitzer's system, spent eleven years on the study. Cogniaux incorporated the work of J. Barbosa Rodrigues, though he included numerous species found in the surrounding areas of northern South America, particularly the Guianas, Venezuela, Colombia, and Peru. Another of Cogniaux's contributions to the literature of orchid taxonomy was a monograph of the orchids of the West Indies. This work, published in 1910 in Ignatius Urban's *Symbolae Antillanae,* treated 500 species and ninety-six genera, becoming the leading reference source of all the orchids of the West Indies.

Robert A. Rolfe, like Lindley, became a recognized authority on the Orchid Family through his interest in gardening from an early age. For forty years after 1880, Rolfe occupied an eminent position at Kew as an assistant in the herbarium, and through his acquaintance with numerous horticulturists and gardeners, he identified many species and wrote prodigiously for various horticultural and scientific journals. Among his outstanding achievements were *Revision of the Genus Phalaenopsis* (1886), *A Revision of the Genus Vanilla* (1896), his monograph of orchids in the *Flora of Tropical Africa,* and a treatment of the Orchidaceae in the *Flora Capensis.* His "Evolution of the Orchidaceae" appeared in *The Orchid Review,* the periodical which he edited, in 1909–1912.

One of the most extensive and impressive series of works in orchidology was done by the German Fritz Kraenzlin. Lengthy and difficult monographs of complicated orchid groups were completed by Kraenzlin, among which were included keys, line drawings, and illustrations. A list of these important works is given herewith:

Orchidacearum Genera et Species volume 1 (1901). This monograph comprised the *Apostasieae, Cypripedieae,* and *Ophrydeae.*

Orchidacearum Genera et Species volume 2, Part 1 (1903-1904). The *Chloraeae* were treated in this monograph, including keys and plates of the lips and petals of the South American genera *Bipinnula*, *Asarca*, and *Chloreae*.

—monographs of the *Coelogyninae*, including *Coelogyne*, *Dendrochilum*, *Pleione*, *Pholidota*, etc., in A. Engler's *Das Pflanzenreich* (1907).

—monographs of the *Dendrobiinae*, Part I (1910).

—monographs of the *Dendrobiinae*, Part II (1911).

—a treatment of *Oncidium* (including *Cyrtochilum*), *Leochilus*, *Sigmatostalix*, and *Cryptarrhend* (1922).

—the *Pseudomonopodiales* (including *Lockhartia*, *Pachyphyllum*, *Centropetalum*, and *Dichaea*) (1919).

—a monograph of *Masdevallia* (with the genera *Lothiania*, *Scaphosepalum*, *Cryptophoranthus*, and *Pseudoctomeria*) in *Fedde Repertorium Specierum Novarum Regni Vegetabilis*, Beihefte 34 (1925).

—a monograph of *Polystachya* in Beihefte 39 (1926).

Writing for the *Journal of Botany*, Colonel M. J. Godfery added numerous articles on the orchids of Great Britain and Europe. A keen observer, Godfery chronicled his observations on the pollination of orchids by insects, very probably influenced by Charles Darwin's earlier work, *The Various Contrivances by Which Orchids are Fertilised by Insects* (1862). Godfery's *Monograph & Iconograph of Native British Orchidaceae* (1933) included essays on the evolution of the orchid flower, pollination and fertilization, evolution of species and genera, life cycle of the orchid plant, hybridism, and nomenclature. Also included was his "Key to the British Orchids." The entire work was richly profuse with line drawings, photographs, and watercolor drawings, with each of the forty-seven species described from living specimens. Also integrated into the work were discussions of his and others' observations of living specimens, with the published varieties and the common prevalent natural hybrids of Great Britain and other European areas.

The essays of Henry N. Ridley form valuable references in the groups he monographed. A traveler and collector of renown, Ridley became director of the Botanic Gardens at Singapore, from whence his most important contributions to orchidology emanated. Among his praiseworthy works are *A Monograph of the Genus Liparis*, *Flora of the Malayan Peninsula*, *A Revision of the Genera Microstylis and Malaxis*, and *The Genus Bromheadia*, all of which appeared in the *Journal of the Linnean Society* (1886–1891). Other important works included studies and keys of the orchids and flora of Borneo, Madagascar, and the Malay Peninsula.

Intensive study of the orchids of one large, specific geographical area characterize the contributions of J. J. Smith, a former director of the Government Botanic Gardens at Buitenzorg. His first important work (based on the herbaria of Europe's most famous botanical institutions, as well as on his own collecting and Blume's *Flora Javae* [1828]), was

Die Orchideen von Java (1905). Addenda followed (1908–1924) in which floral analyses of all the previously described species were illustrated by his own ink drawings. Much more of his work on the eastern orchids was published in the *Bulletin Botanique de Buitenzorg*, in which he added important data to the knowledge of species already described, as well as his own introduction of hundreds of new species. His *Artificial Key to the Orchid Genera of the Netherlands Indies, together with those of New Guinea, the Malay Peninsula and the Philippines* (1934) was considered especially valuable in the study of the orchids of the Eastern Hemisphere. Besides his treatments of the orchid flora of Amboina, Sumatra, and Dutch New Guinea, other notable works were his articles, "Sarcanthus Lndl. und die nächstverwandten Gattungen" and "Icones Orchidacearum Malayensium," a lengthy series of illustrations of Malayan orchids.

An early background of horticulture, plus the many compilations of former orchidologists, influenced the study of orchidology for Friedrich Richard Rudolf Schlechter, one of the most industrious and devoted orchidologists of recent times. Traveling continuously for nineteen years, he amassed about 20,000 collections from such regions as Africa, Sumatra, Java, Celebes, Borneo, New Guinea, and Australia. All this time he was writing and publishing his observations, adding new generic and specific concepts. In fact, in thirty-three years he published over 300 of his works. Most of his monographs appeared in the journal *Orchis* and the *Journal of Botany*, but many other publications, too numerous to mention in this résumé, also featured his knowledgeable works. His monographs are numerous:

Acrolophia (1894)
the *Disperideae* (1898)
Holothrix (1898–99)
the *Podochilinae, Acriopsis* (1900)
the *Diseae* (1901)
Xylobium, Townsonia, Bletilla (1911)
Altensteinia, Aa, Myrosmodes (1912)
Schomburgkia, Pleione, Gastrochilus (1913)
Pleione (1914)
Dichaea (1914–15)
Tainiopsis, Grammatophyllum, Grammangis, Houlletia (1915)
Cycnoches, Coryanthes, Anguloa (1916)
Laelia, Acineta (1917)
Aganisia, Sigmatostalix, Restrepia (1918)
Cochlioda (1918–19)
Brassavola (1919)
Eulophiella, Fernandezia, Rodriguezia (1920)
Basiphyllaea, Drakaea, Spiculaea, Schizochilus, Brachycorythis, Promenaea (1921)
Aspasia (1922)

Corysanthes (1923)
Cymbidium, Cyperorchis (1924)

Three major works have merited Schlechter's deserved recognition. *Die Orchideen*, a complete volume published in 1915, was a comprehensive coverage of orchid culture and a résumé of the whole field of orchid speciation. Through 1918–1924 a series of enumerations of species appeared. These encompassed the orchids of Middle America (*Kritische Aufzählung der bisher aus Zentral-Amerika bekanntgewordenen Orchidaceen*), those of China and Japan (*Orchideologiae Sino-Japonicae Prodromus*), and Venezuela, Colombia, Ecuador, Peru, and Bolivia (*Die Orchideenfloren der südamerikanischen Kordillerenstaaten*). Probably his most valuable work was his key to the orchids, *Das System der Orchidaceen*, published in 1926. This system, embracing a larger scope of material and generic concepts than any previous classification, emphasized the importance of similarities of the reproductive and vegetative structures in classifying the genera and species. Also, it excluded the *Apostasiaceae* from the Orchid Family.

Through a detailed study of the orchids of the Philippines, Oakes Ames became the world authority on those orchids, describing, in addition, a large number of new species. His orchid herbarium, rivaled only by the Lindley Herbarium at Kew and the Reichenbach Herbarium in Vienna, numbered nearly 96,000 sheets and included photographs, notes from other great collections, and the beautiful watercolor and pen drawings of his wife. Ames was an inveterate writer as well as an economic botanist and orchidologist, and contributed numerous masterful works to such publications as the *Philippine Journal of Science*, the *American Orchid Society Bulletin*, and *Botanical Leaflets of Harvard University*. His major works included *Orchidaceae: Illustrations and Studies of the Family Orchidaceae* in seven volumes (1905–1922); the *Schedulae Orchidianae* (assisted by Charles Schweinfurth) published in ten parts (1922–1930); *The Genus Epidendrum in the United States and Middle America* (1936); and *Drawings of Florida Orchids* (1947), illustrated by his wife, Blanche.

Hundreds of brilliant minds, in addition to those mentioned, have assisted in classifying the myriad representatives of this complex group of plants, and though perhaps not as well known as their professional counterparts, they have nevertheless contributed a collective and valuable storehouse of knowledge to the ever-expanding progression since the term *orchis* was originally coined by the philosopher Theophrastus.

References

Ames, Oakes. 1934. Ernst Hugo Heinrich Pfitzer—1846–1906. *Amer. Orch. Soc. Bull.* 2, no. 4.

Ames, Oakes. 1932. John Lindley (1799–1865). *Amer. Orch. Soc. Bull.* 1, no. 2.

De Wolf, Gordon P., Jr. 1956. Primary Classification in the Orchidaceae—A Critique. *Taxon* 3, no. 5.

Dillon, Gordon W. 1956. Some Principles and Family Background. *Amer. Orch. Soc. Bull.* 25, no. 10.

Dillon, Gordon W. 1957. Development of a System of Orchid Classification. *Amer. Orch. Soc. Bull.* 26, no. 4.

Dressler, Robert L., and Calaway H. Dodson. 1960. Classification and Phylogeny in the Orchidaceae. *Annals of the Missouri Botanical Garden.* 47.

Gardeners' Chronicle. 1858. Dr. Robert Brown, D.C.L., F.R.S., Foreign Member of the Academy of Sciences of the Institute of France. No. 24, p. 493.

Holttum, R. E. 1957. Henry Nicholas Ridley, C.M.G., F.R.S.—1855–1956. *Taxon* 6, no. 1.

Hurst, Rona. 1949. The R.H.S. and the Birth of Genetics. *Journ. of the Royal Hort. Soc.* 74, pt. 9.

Schultes, Richard Evans. 1951. Obituaries. *Proceedings of the Linnean Society of London.* Session 162, 1949–1950, pt. 2.

Schweinfurth, Charles. 1959. Classification of Orchids. Chapter 2 of *The Orchids—A Scientific Survey.* Carl L. Withner, ed. The Ronald Press Co. New York.

Vermeulen, P. 1953. *Orchis spectabilis* L. The American Species of Orchis—I. *Amer. Orch. Soc. Bull.* 22, no. 6.

Withner, Carl L. 1959. Introduction and History of Orchid Culture. Ch. 1 of *The Orchids—A Scientific Survey.* Carl L. Withner, ed. The Ronald Press Co. New York.

Cultivation and the
Methods Employed

ALTHOUGH ORCHIDS BECAME INCREASINGLY POPULAR AS ORNAMENTAL plants, and though great numbers of them began to be shipped to Europe in the beginning of the eighteenth century, the number of species successfully cultivated remained pitifully small. The then prevalent notion was that orchids were generally inhabitants of hot, steaming, tropical jungles, and due to the unusual habit of growth of most epiphytic species in their natural habitats, eighteenth-century botanists thoroughly misunderstood their cultural needs. As described by the naval officers who brought them back, their epiphytic habits of growth seemed to denote that they were parasitic.

As nearly as possible, jungle conditions were duplicated. Without realizing that in tropical countries there could be found climates as cool as that of England, gardeners devised a hot treatment for orchids. They placed the plants in "stoves"—structures of densely painted glass, coal fires, and brick flues, the hot, dry air circulating through hollow walls and passages. There were no movable windows; therefore there was no ventilation. The bricks were constantly drenched, creating a sickeningly humid and steamy atmosphere. A great deal of physical discomfort was always experienced by the plantsman who occasionally found it necessary to work within such an atmosphere.

Terrestrial orchids had become rather easily cultivated in mixtures of peat and loam, and since little attention was given to the physical differences between the terrestrial and epiphytic species, the same treatments were prescribed for all alike. Some growers used mixtures of rotted wood and leaves, plunging the pots in beds of tanner's bark or sawdust.

Under these conditions orchids succumbed by the thousands. The incidence of a plant blooming prior to its death was attributed to the grower's skill alone. The plants continued dying until, quite aptly, Sir Joseph Hooker dryly suggested that England had become the "grave of tropical orchids."

Despite the high mortality rate, plants were imported in larger and larger quantities. The exotic beauty of the flowers of the comparatively few plants that survived a blooming season or two so stimulated the desires of hobbyists that adventurers, seeking an easy means of making a lot of money, rushed off to the tropical regions where orchids grew, completely stripping many of these areas of their indigenous species. All orchids were taken, good or bad. Certain areas of Central and South America have had no naturalized orchids since.

Although a certain few collectors sent explicit cultural instructions with their shipments (going so far as to send the plants still attached to the very limbs of trees from which they were collected), the growers persisted in their stoves and tan-bark beds, and plants continued to

Early-day orchid growers failed to recognize the differences in cultural needs between the terrestrial and epiphytic orchids. As a result, epiphytic types, such as the oncidium above, were indiscriminately plunged into beds and pots of tanner's bark or sawdust—and perished by the thousands in the "stoves" of English gardens.

perish. Of the species in cultivation called Epidendrum,* Miller wrote in 1768:

There are nearly thirty species of this genus, which grow naturally upon trees in America and both Indies, but, as the plants cannot by any art yet known be cultivated in the ground, it would be to little purpose the enumerating of them here, though, could the plants be brought to thrive by culture, many of them produce very fine flowers of very uncommon form. I had three species of them sent me from America; these I planted with care in pots, which were placed in a stove, where they came so far as to show their flowers, but the plants soon afterwards perished.

The first East Indian orchids were brought to England in 1800, thanks to the efforts of Sir Joseph Banks. Three species of *Geodorum* and *Acampe longiflora*, along with *Aerides odoratum* from Cochin China, preceded the moderate additions of the following several years. An imperfect conception of the plants' needs was demonstrated, for they were grown experimentally in various composts—tanner's bark, decayed wood, etc.—under the hottest conditions obtainable.

Despairing of successfully maintaining live plants in the heavy composts being used, some growers tried other methods which, though more reasonable, were seldom successful because of the continued use of stoves. A few growers attempted to grow the epiphytic species suspended, without any compost at all. An item in the *Botanical Register* for 1817 relates of this method:

Air plants possess the faculty of growing when suspended so as to be cut off from all sustenance but that derived immediately from the atmosphere. Plants of other genera of this tribe, and even of a different tribe are endowed with a like faculty; in none, however, can such insulation be considered as the state of existence which suits them best, but merely as one they are enabled to endure, as a carp is known to do, that of being suspended out of water in a damp cellar.

This method met with limited success, for although the plants held onto life a little longer than in peat and loam, in time they died for lack of moisture and nutrients. The method did, however, help dispel the "parasite theory," for most of the plants survived long enough to demonstrate that they were not entirely dependent upon a host—and the then current notion was that a parasite, deprived of its host, would certainly soon die.

Further worthwhile steps were taken by Sir Joseph Banks in his use of wicker baskets and moss. In 1817 the *Botanical Register* spoke of the method:

* All the known epiphytic types, having been found growing "on trees," were at that time called epidendrums.

The method he pursues is to place the plants separately in light cylindrical wicker-baskets or cages, of suitable widths, of which the framework is of long slender twigs wreathed together at the bottom, and shallowly round the side; the upper portion being left open that the plant may extend its growth in any direction through the intervals, and yet be kept steady in its station, the ends of the twigs having been tied together by the twine that suspends the whole to the woodwork of the stove. A thin layer of mould is strewed on the floor of the basket, on which the root-stock is placed, and then covered lightly over with a sufficiency of moss to shade it and preserve a due degree of moisture, water being occasionally applied.

The advantage of having an aerated medium was of benefit to Banks' plants, and the success attributed to this method rapidly spread in the stoves of many other English growers. This was the precedent for the modern orchid basket, especially for such species possessed of pendent racemes. Such a container was deemed a necessity for growing stanhopeas, as Mr. Sigismund Rucker discovered accidentally. Rucker's grower was able to produce strong, healthy specimens of *Stanhopea* in ordinary pots, but he was mystified by the continued absence of blooms. One day his crock boy, passing through the doorway of the potting shed with an armload of plants, stumbled over the threshold and dropped his load. Pots were broken, of course, but the initial wrath of the grower turned to stunned surprise and joy, for one broken pot revealed two flower scapes encircling the interior of the pot in an effort to escape. Thus, the basic fundamentals of successful stanhopea culture were discovered, and another small facet of the slowly expanding knowledge of orchid cultivation was gained.

By attaching moss around the roots of his plants, the Rev. William Herbert, dean of Manchester, succeeded in establishing "Epidendra" on the stems of a tree. Notches were cut in the branches of the tree, the plant was inserted like a graft, and moss was stuffed around the roots, providing moisture and sustenance until the roots established themselves to the bark of the tree. Above the plants a pot of water was attached, in which a hole in the bottom of the pot allowed water to be conducted downward by means of a heavy string the approximate size of the hole, through which it passed. The idea had originated with Dr. Nathaniel Wallich, who had utilized a similar contrivance at the Botanic Garden of Calcutta.

The twenty-year period of 1832–1852 marked a decline of the intensity so characteristic of the orchid mania a few years previously—a circumstance that was chiefly attributable to a great falling off of the supply of new species, or at least of the species with which the amateur cultivator was able to succeed. New arrivals there were—the collections of Warszewicz, for example—but these consisted largely of species from the higher altitudes, cool-growing species that perished under hot treatment almost as rapidly as they were received. So difficult were these

Colonies of *Brassavola digbyana* growing in full sun on the branches of an "encino" tree in central Honduras.

species considered to be in cultivation that most growers declined purchasing even the most beautiful odontoglossums. The idea that all orchids necessarily needed hot treatment was induced by the fact that the first-discovered orchids were denizens of tropical coasts or riversides, or of the warm islands of the East and West Indies. Therefore, the ill success that followed the attempts to grow the species from the Mexican and Peruvian Andes was a discouraging element in orchid culture of the time.

John Lindley, apparently dissatisfied with the then current growing methods, set out to obtain information from the collectors—specific information which revealed exactly how and under what circumstances epiphytic orchids grew in their native tropic wilds. This information was, essentially, the beginning of the modern era of orchid culture. Disseminated among eminent amateur growers, the facts were applied literally, and in short order a "renaissance" occurred.

Sir Joseph Paxton, working in his experimental English cottage garden, was the first orchidist to abandon stoves and adopt Lindley's suggestions. He opened his greenhouses to the air and sunlight, giving his plants cool, buoyant atmospheric conditions—and they began to thrive. From his observations he formulated a set of rules which demonstrated that most orchids could be acclimatized if the proper conditions were provided. Through his practices and observations, Paxton standardized orchid culture, and Lindley exclaimed: "The success with which they (orchids) are cultivated by Mr. Paxton is wonderful. The climate in which this is effected, instead of being so hot and damp that the plants can only be seen with as much discomfort as if one had to visit them in an Indian jungle, is as mild and delightful as that of Madeira."

Paxton's success was epidemic. A turning point in orchid culture swiftly evolved and a new enthusiasm for the cool-growing species was generated. The *Gardeners' Chronicle* most adequately summed up this feeling in its issue of 10 October 1859:

The success of English gardeners which has attended the growth of orchidaceous plants inhabiting trees and rocks in tropical or subtropical countries has been one of the most signal marks of horticultural skill. Plants thought in 1820 to be uncultivable have been brought as much under command as Heaths or Ferns. In that year in the Royal Botanic Garden of Kew, into whose lap the British colonies had been pouring their treasures for a quarter of a century, nothing was to be found except *Cym. sinense* and *aloifolium*, *Epid. cochleatum*, *Rodriguezia secunda*, *Oncidium altissimum*, and a few more vulgar species which it was more difficult to kill than to keep alive. Now, go where we will, these plants so much abound that some have even come to be hawked about London streets.

Nevertheless it must be owned that if some succeed most admirably others fail deplorably, and we are beginning to discover that epiphytes after all demand to be treated with some attention to their peculiar nature. It is not enough to tie them to a block of wood or to pot them among peat or leaves or potsherds, or to keep the air about them always damp, as some imagine. There is always a principle behind, which principle must be looked at and studied, and so understood as to be rightly modified according to the nature of the plants. Some grow on trees, some on stones, many on the ground itself. Some bask in the hottest sun, others luxuriate in the open places of deep forests, or ride aloft on the branches of trees. There are also highland races that can only exist on the sides of mountains where clouds are always condensing, or that even struggle onwards towards the limits of alpine vegetation. . . . It is thus evident that he who would grow these plants successfully must have a good deal of intelligence, as well as the practical skill of a gardener. "Rule of Thumb" has nothing to say to orchid growing; it is only effective in orchid killing, as many a costly collection can testify. . . . Let those who are intrusted with the management of orchids think upon two things growing out of natural facts. Let them in the first place consider whether an atmosphere dry enough for succulents is likely to suit plants whose thin leaves can only retain their freshness while the air around them is as damp as that of a vinery forced in February. And in the next place let them try to reconcile their senseless system of "hard potting" with the peculiar habits of plants whose roots cannot bear to exist, either under pressure, or unless freely exposed to the action of a suitable atmosphere. We know that this hard potting has been used by first-rate growers in the case of Vandas and species of similar habit. But how is it used by them? Not for compelling roots to grow when and how Nature peremptorily forbids, but as a contrivance to steady long straggling stems which throw their arm-like roots into the air, and never attempt to produce them below the ground level. The application of this method of hard potting to cases having no sort of analogy is one of the most striking illustrations of the fatal effects of substituting ignorant practices for intelligent skill.

With the added knowledge of geographical and natural conditions of growth came improved culture and the use of potting media which more nearly approached the ideal. Blocks of wood from acacia, apple, pear, and plum trees were often used, on which plants were established and suspended from the sash bars of the greenhouses. Cork was another favorite material for this type of culture.

Once tanner's bark and loam were discarded, for many years fibrous peat was the accepted medium for epiphytic orchids. As the supply of this material gradually lessened though, sphagnum moss was mixed with it over a drainage of potsherds and charcoal. As fibrous peat became increasingly scarce, out of necessity of locating acceptable substitutes, many growers began using polypodium fiber. This medium, the fibrous roots of the fern *Polypodium vulgare*, grew in large quantities on rocks and trees in the Ardennes. The root masses were removed, cut fine with shears, mixed with chopped sphagnum moss, and then used in the usual manner of potting. While some genera flourished in this medium, *Odontoglossum* and allied genera, *Cattleya*, *Laelia*, *Dendrobium*, and *Paphiopedilum* often died, for a fungus that permeated the fiber caused the roots to sour and rot.

American growers followed the standards of orchid cultivation set by the Europeans for a long while, but the turfy peat and sphagnum moss so prevalent in the British Isles was not as readily available in the United States. Seeking a local substitute, growers found that the tough and fibrous roots of the osmunda fern proved suitable and was inexpensively available in the swampy areas of New Jersey, Pennsylvania, New York, and Florida. Because these roots were relatively long-lasting, afforded excellent aeration of the orchid roots, and provided good drainage, their use as a general-purpose potting medium was eagerly adopted in about 1900. A number of persons were thus enabled to establish a lucrative trade in collecting and supplying osmunda fiber to the hobby and commercial growers.

In Hawaii, Mexico, South America, the West Indies, and the several other tropical regions where orchid growing was becoming popularized, osmunda rapidly deteriorated in the torrential tropic rains. A natural material native to the tropic regions was therefore used: the stiff and fibrous trunks of the *Cyatheaceae* (tree ferns). This material was found to be far less water-absorptive, easily sawed into slabs and rafts (as well as shredded), and much longer-lasting. Osmunda fiber and clay pots were additionally difficult to obtain in Hawaii during the years of the Second World War. This was an additional factor in the switchover to the complete use of tree-fern fiber, an outgrowth of its first use in the Islands in the early 1930s as a material useful in making outdoor containers for flowering and ornamental plants.

The use of these materials grew in proportion to the increased numbers of persons who began growing orchids as a lasting hobby during those several decades. Commercial growers, seeing the great potential in retail plant sales, enthusiastically encouraged hobby orchid growing as a relaxing and interesting pastime, and the ranks of new orchid growers began to swell—particularly in the United States.

As the orchid industry expanded to record-breaking proportions, it was recognized that time-saving methods of production would have to be developed, particularly as it concerned potting media. While osmunda was satisfactory, dwindling supplies and expense prompted certain growers to experiment with other materials. Wood chips, leaf mold, buckwheat hulls, gravel, and many other natural products were tried. None proved entirely practical. Then, in 1951, an enterprising lumber mill owner, Mr. John Ivory of Dinuba, California, found a use for a waste product of his mill that very nearly revolutionized orchid culture. Mr. Ivory speculated that the waste bark left after the logs were stripped for processing might be useful as a soil conditioner and in other horticultural applications. With this in mind, he consulted with Mr. O. A. Matkin of the Soil and Plant Laboratory of Los Angeles. Matkin was a counselor for numerous orchid growers on the West Coast and thus considered orchid growing as a possible field in which the new product might be used. Both he and Dr. O. W. Davidson of Rutgers University guided several initial tests of the material as a potting medium for orchids. Results were highly favorable, and after a trial period of refinement of the product—screening out the wood and fine particles, distilling the barks to rid them of oils, esters and acids, and grading the bark chunks as to size—it was found that white fir (*Abies concolor*) of Oregon and Northern California and red fir (*Abies magnifica*) of the high Sierras were the most adaptable for orchid growing. The Douglas fir (*Pseudotsuga menziesii*) of Washington and Oregon was shortly thereafter also used in quantity.

In a short time, carload lots of fir bark were being shipped across country, to Europe and to Hawaii. Fir bark was an immediate success as an orchid-potting medium, for the costs were fractional as compared to osmunda and other media, and the savings in potting time were very substantial, particularly in large commercial orchid ranges. A number of bark "mixes" were gradually introduced, in which varying proportions of poultry-grade peat moss, oak leaves, redwood bark fiber, sand, and perlite were incorporated. These mixes were modified to meet the climatic requirements of the various regions in which they were used, and the orchid world advanced another cultural degree.

Good management and advanced cultural techniques led to unqualified success in greenhouse orchid growing over the years. The aspiring orchid grower without a greenhouse, however, usually found himself handicapped, for though he might place his plants in advantageous outdoor locations during the spring and summer (in the northern temperate zones, at least), during the inclement seasons of the year the plants had to be brought back into the house, where they invariably received too little light for optimum growth and normal flowering. Indoor gardening of other families and groups of plants was practiced widely in the period following World War II, and those hobbyists who were growing and blooming saintpaulias and gloxinias under artificial lights—in apartments, basements, and bay windows—set an example for indoor orchid growing. Meanwhile, the experimental work by Robert Casamajor and Dr. Fritz Went, at the Amelia Earhart Laboratories in California, proved that certain orchids, too, could be grown and flowered entirely under artificial light sources. A new concept of indoor orchid growing was born and supplemental artificial lighting solved the problem for many hobbyists of successfully growing orchids in the home. One of the most outstanding and successful persons to grow orchids under lights was Dr. Aphrodite J. Hofsommer of Webster Groves, Missouri. Attending the First World Orchid Conference in St. Louis in 1954, Dr. Hofsommer was inspired by a discussion on the use of fluorescent lights in orchid culture. This seemed to be just the answer for her expanding collection of windowsill orchids, so she and her husband converted an extra coal bin in their basement into a fluorescent-lighted orchid-growing area which she called the "Green Thumb Room." Orchid plants were placed on gravel-filled trays and the light fixtures were suspended eight to ten inches over the leaf tops. Within a year her "light culture" proved tremendously successful, and for several years thereafter her observations and results were published in the *American Orchid Society Bulletin.* The response by other indoor gardeners and orchid hobbyists was infectious, for Dr. Hofsommer's pioneering on the hobby level was instrumental in proving that orchids could be grown under nearly any set of conditions—and cultural limitations were cast off by hundreds of new orchid growers.

The wartime development of plastic materials was another significant contribution to orchid cultivation. These materials were found to be highly useful in greenhouse construction, the advantages being that they were lightweight, inexpensive, and easily handled. Commercial growers, in particular, found that they could quickly erect large enclosed plastic

Orchids grown entirely under artificial lights in the basement "Green Thumb Room" of Dr. Aphrodite Hofsommer's home in Webster Groves, Missouri.

structures to handle the inevitable overflow of rapidly growing seedlings common to every commercial orchid range, and thus easily accommodate and grow on thousands more plants for seasonal and wholesale demand. Both flexible and rigid plastics were used at much less expense than glass houses, a great advantage being that they could easily be dismantled at the end of a season and the growing area used at various times of the year in the production of other profitable crops.

The use of plastic as a structural material in greenhouses opened new vistas of growing for hobbyists as well. Larger hobby orchid houses were built at much less cost than the average small glasshouse and orchid collections could thereby be enlarged, as was inevitably the result.

The evolution of the orchid hobby has been an ascending one. Each step of the way has provided a more substantial foundation for further development and experimentation. Cultural perfection has become a standard ideal among growers everywhere—and the sharing of ideas, developments, and cultural methods have provided the orchid fraternity, no matter how far-flung its members, a unity and spirit of cooperation never before attained in its history.

References

Arnold, Ralph E. 1932. The Evolution of the Orchid Pot. *The Orch. Rev.* 40, no. 464.

Arnold, Ralph E. 1932. Orchid Composts, A Retrospect. *The Orch. Rev.* 40, no. 474.

Ashton, E. R. 1925. Tropical Orchids: Their History and Cultivation. *The Orch. Rev.* 33, no. 382.

Orchid Review, The. 1894. The History of Orchid Cultivation—Part I, Vol. 2, no. 14.

Orchid Review, The. 1894. The History of Orchid Cultivation—Part II. Vol. 2, no. 15.

Orchid Review, The. 1894. The History of Orchid Cultivation—Part III. Vol. 2, no. 17.

Orchid Review, The. 1956. Men, Matters and Memories. Vol. 64, no. 756.

Orchid Review, The. 1894. Polypodium Fibre as a Substitute for Peat. Vol. 2, no. 20.

Veitch, James, & Sons. 1887–94. *A Manual of Orchidaceous Plants.* Vol. 1. *Epidendreae.* H. M. Pollett & Co. London.

White, R. Brooman. 1894. Polypodium Fibre versus Peat. *The Orch. Rev.* 2, no. 21.

The Development of an Industry

COMMERCIAL ORCHID CULTURE HAD ITS BEGINNINGS ALMOST AS SOON AS orchids became popular as ornamental plants. Various horticultural firms, in hopes of supplying the demand for new and unusual plants, hired collectors to travel worldwide, scouring the tropical haunts where orchids and other novelties were known to occur.

It is not surprising that commercial orchid growing began in England because, concurrent with the Elizabethan era and the eighteenth century, greenhouses and conservatories were erected with an eloquence unparalleled since that time. The culture of horticultural curiosities was taken up by men of wealth, position, and prestige to the extent that greenhouse growing became the most refined branch of the art of horticulture. The Victorian era followed with a flourish of interest in gardening, particularly the exotic varieties then being found in subtropic and tropic regions. The travels of Captain Cook, Sir Joseph Banks, Alexander von Humboldt, and others, further introduced England's gardeners to a wealth of new plant materials, stimulating an insatiable demand for ever more strange and attractive plants. Professional gardeners and growers were, of course, quick to meet the opportunity of supplying the desired flowers and plants.

One of the earliest nurseries to cultivate orchids for sale was that of Messrs. Conrad Loddiges and Sons of Hackney, England. Beginning in 1812 to cultivate orchids, they continued as the principal commercial orchid cultivators in Europe until the breaking up of their establishment in 1852. During those forty years the Loddiges were recognized as the most influential and authoritative in the field of orchid culture, and the number of species introduced into cultivation by the firm was considerable.

Gardeners on private estates, as well as hobby enthusiasts, contributed to the growth of commercial orchid culture through their purchases. Among the many firms established—some now nearly forgotten—the following were eminent: Messrs. B. S. Williams and Sons of the Victoria and Paradise Nurseries, Upper Holloway; Messrs. Rollison of Tooting; William Bull and Sons of King's Road, Chelsea; Messrs. Shuttleworth and Carder; Messrs. James Brooke & Co. of Fairfield Nurseries, Manchester; Messrs. Cowan of Southgate; Messrs. Whately and Newton, Kenilworth; Messrs. Backhouse of York; and Messrs. Heath of Cheltenham.

Another early and famous English nursery firm venturing into the culture of tropical orchids was the Chelsea nursery of James Veitch and Sons, established about 1808. Messrs. Veitch's famous line of plant collectors—the Lobb brothers, A. R. Endres, F. W. Burbidge, Charles Curtis, Walter Davis, Gustav Wallis, David Burke, and others—sent home prodigious numbers of new species, rare plants that were carefully cultivated under the most studied conditions, approximating the natural atmospheres of the original habitats as closely as possible. Concerning the excellence of culture practiced at Veitch's, a visitor to the firm wrote in the *Gardeners' Chronicle* in October 1859:

I may here remark that a son of the proprietor, who kindly showed me over the nursery, informed me that a great deal of success that attended their orchid growing arose from a careful consideration of the climate and habits of the plants in their native countries, and assimilating as much as possible that state here, instead of jumbling them up together as is often done, to the utter ruin and destruction of many valuable plants.

The firm's most distinctive accomplishment was its work of pioneering in the field of orchid hybridization. In the hands of their competent foreman, Mr. John Dominy, Veitch's produced the first man-made orchid hybrid, *Calanthe Dominii*, in 1856. And for nearly twenty years the Veitch establishment was the only place in the horticultural world where orchid hybrids were available—twenty-five hybrids produced in all. John Seden succeeded Mr. Dominy upon the latter's retirement, carrying on the tradition established in the newly flourishing field of orchid hybridization.

After over a century of management by the Veitch family, the firm was divided and sold upon the retirement of Sir Harry J. Veitch in 1913, the Langley nursery going to Mr. J. M. Black and Mr. Sidney Flory. The newly organized firm, known as Black & Flory, Ltd., retained its distinction as the first commercial nursery devoted solely to the culture of orchids.

Under the original family name, Stuart Low & Co. is known as the oldest orchid firm in England. Established by Mr. Hugh Low in 1820 as a general nursery for choice greenhouse plants, the firm remained for several generations in the same family. Originally established eight miles from London as Messrs. Hugh Low & Co. of Clapton, the firm was one of the first to receive orchids from abroad, soon becoming actively engaged in the exciting and profitable business of growing orchids. On the death of the founder, the firm passed into the management of the second son, Mr. Stuart Henry Low, a first officer aboard one of the East India Service tea clippers; he reluctantly left the sea to manage the family business. The establishment then became Stuart Low Co., and the eldest son, Sir Hugh Low, in the consular service in Malaya, sent orchid plants back to his brother, introducing a number of species new to horticulture and botany.

Though established in 1860, several decades after the initial interest in commercial orchid culture began, the name Sander became as familiar and famous as most of the great firms that preceded it. Having served an apprenticeship with the noted seed firm of Messrs. James Carter & Co., Mr. Henry F. C. Sander founded the House of Sander in George Street, St. Albans. Mr. Sander's intention was to build his business into a seed establishment—which he did most successfully. At Carter's he had become well acquainted with Benedict Roezl, an orchid collector who urged him to go into commercial orchid cultivation. Roezl's suggestions were appealing, and in 1872 Sander gave up the seed business and built a new nursery at the Camps, St. Albans. Four acres were covered by sixty greenhouses and thousands of orchids were stocked therein by the numerous plant collectors hired by the firm. At one time Sander had twenty-three full-time collectors in his employ. Much of his success at bringing home new and rare orchids was due to the information passed on by Roezl and his nephews about the regions of the tropics with which they had become familiar.

The business flourished, and in 1894 a tract of land was purchased in Bruges, Belgium, upon which a larger nursery was built. In the 1880s and 1890s the firm became recognized as the horticultural showplace of Europe and was visited by numerous members of nobility. In this period some two million orchid plants were handled in the St. Albans nursery, where some of the finest orchid species changed hands for thousands of guineas. Over 100 men were employed to unpack and pot the new importations.

A tract of land was purchased at Mamaroneck, New York, where osmunda fiber was processed and, later, a large nursery was built in Summit, New Jersey. But because of the distance and managerial difficulties, the nursery was sold to John Lager and Henry Hurrell, Americans who were both originally English gardeners.

In 1902 Mr. Sander's three sons were taken into the business: C. Fearnley Sander, Frederick K. Sander, and Louis Sander. World War I seriously hampered the importation of orchids, but, undaunted, the Sander family supplemented the shortage of new plants by beginning a program of hybridizing with their own stock—the third firm to utilize Dr. Burgeff's symbiotic method of seed germination.

Upon the death of their father in 1920, the sons became partners. To counteract newly imposed tariffs, another nursery was purchased from the Cowan brothers at Southgate, this to be known as Sanders of Watford. During this period, and at his own expense, Frederick K. Sander initiated a register of orchid hybrids dating from 1856. This work, in the trust of the Sander family until 1961, became the famous and internationally used *Sander's List of Orchid Hybrids*.

Louis died in 1936, leaving his brothers in control. The deaths of Frederick in 1951 and Fearnley in 1957 necessitated a reorganization of the business, and it was left to Roger and David, sons of Fearnley, to take over management. Roger supervised the Watford nursery and David managed the St. Albans establishment, additionally continuing the work begun by his uncle as registrar for the Acting International Registration Authority. In 1957, upon family agreement, the firm was liquidated, the Bruges establishment passing into the sole proprietorship of Roger Sander—the Watford branch under his son John's management—and the St. Albans establishment transferred to David Sander, who continued his family's orchid-growing tradition under the title of David Sander's Orchids, Ltd., at Selsfield, East Grinstead.

McBean's Orchids, Ltd. was founded in 1879 as a general nursery by Mr. James Ure McBean, a florist and nurseryman of Cooksbridge. Mr. McBean first purchased a few orchid plants for his cut-flower trade in 1894, but his youngest son, Albert Alexander McBean, became so enticed by the lure of orchids that within ten years all fifteen of the greenhouses were filled with these plants.

Upon being taken into partnership with his father in 1903, Albert McBean assumed the management of the business, which became known as J. & A. McBean. Hybridizing was begun in 1906, seedlings being raised for years under the symbiotic culture method. Later, Professor Lewis Knudson traveled to England to demonstrate the new nonsymbiotic method of orchid seed germination, and Mr. Sidney B. Rothwell, the firm's grower, began the application of the method at the Cooksbridge nursery.

Following his father's death in 1910, Albert McBean managed the firm for thirty-eight years, and with his passing in 1942 the business was incorporated as a private company known as McBean's Orchids, Ltd., under the management of Mr. Rothwell.

The firm of Charlesworth & Co. was founded by Joseph Charlesworth in the 1880s. Mr. Charlesworth established his first nursery at Heaton, Bradford, Yorkshire, leaving the wool business to go into commercial orchid growing. He traveled to the South American Andes during his first year of business, collecting and shipping back to England great numbers of the cool-growing odontoglossums. As a result of this trip, McBean's was the first to introduce the highly coveted "Premier" type of *Odontoglossum crispum*. A few years later Mr. Shuttleworth joined in partnership with Charlesworth and the firm became Charlesworth, Shuttleworth & Co.

In 1894 Mr. Charlesworth began a program of hybridization. Becoming interested in the experiments of Noel Bernard and Hans Burgeff, he began raising orchid seedlings by the fungal method. Together with Dr. J. Ramsbottom he achieved marvelous results with odontiodas and odontoglossums. As far as records indicate, this was the first attempt to use scientific methodology in the commercial production of orchid seedlings. Writing in 1922, Ramsbottom stated:

... It is probable that the work of the fungus is to introduce carbohydrates into the seed, but so far as I am aware, no one has yet succeeded in chemically stimulating the seeds of Odontoglossum and similar plants.* It is with these that the late Mr. Joseph Charlesworth, of Haywards Heath, had as uniform a success as is possible. Usually in one of the culture flasks as many seeds germinate as can find room, germination even taking place on the sides of the flasks. No one who has seen such a culture flask, the transplanted seedlings, the growing and then flowering plants, can doubt for a moment that the natural type of germination is occurring; ... When the appropriate fungus is obtained and the ordinary methods of Orchid culture are grafted on to the laboratory methods, the numerically insignificant results obtained in the epoch-making test tubes of Noel Bernard become the millions of seedlings appearing like a green sward in the houses of Messrs. Charlesworth and Co.

The Charlesworth-Shuttleworth partnership was dissolved a few years later, the firm once again becoming Charlesworth & Co. Prospering, Mr. Charlesworth noted the need for expansion and, in 1906, a branch nursery was established at Haywards Heath. Climatic conditions at the new nursery proved so superior to those at Bradford that in 1908 all the firm's plants were moved to Lyoth Common, Haywards Heath, and the Bradford nursery was disposed of. Mr. Charlesworth died in 1920, and in 1923 the firm became a private company.

These, then, were the "giants" of the industry which brought England to the forefront as the orchid-growing center of the world by the end of the nineteenth century. Other prominent firms by that time were Mansell & Hatcher, Ltd., of the Cragg Wood Nurseries, Rawdon, Leeds; Harry Dixon and Sons, Spencer Park Nurseries; and Armstrong & Brown, Ltd., at Tunbridge Wells.

At the turn of the century the enthusiasm for orchid growing re-

* In reference to Lewis Knudson's then-newly-perfected method of germinating orchid seed without the presence of mycorrhizal fungus.

mained unabated. The great English and Belgian firms were at the height of their fame, and large numbers of showy tropical orchids were grown in France to supply the flourishing cut-market trade. Otto Beyrodt had long since established a large nursery for orchids in Berlin which competed favorably with the established firms on the Continent.

Gradually, however, the interest in imported species waned as commercial success in orchid hybridization increased. Furthermore, the most rewarding regions of the New World had been fairly searched, and the chances of discovering new and unusual species lessened. In the United States at that time commercial orchid cultivation was coming into its own. Previously, because that nation was preoccupied with an early struggle for existence—a major war and revolution and, later, a great civil strife—little time or effort could be given to the comparative luxury of orchids. After the Civil War, however, great impetus was given to material comforts and esthetic pursuits, and by the 1890s there were seven commercial firms growing orchids for sale and cut-flower production in the United States. Others followed, and of these, the following were probably the most prominent and long-lasting:

Butterworth's, Framingham, Massachusetts: The continuation of a business founded by Charles J. Power in 1848, Butterworth's was one of the early commercial orchid establishments in the United States. Employed by Power in 1891 to take charge of the establishment, John Thomas Butterworth was so successful that, with Mr. Power's inducement, he took over the business in 1896, continuing an interest in orchids that began in his boyhood in England. Beginning with the commercial sale of paphiopedilums, Butterworth soon built up a stock of about a dozen different genera of orchids, including *Cattleya* and *Oncidium*, through the purchase of two or three private collections each year. Gradually one line of crops after another was discontinued and orchids substituted until, in the 1920s, Butterworths were known primarily as orchid specialists. Fine miltonias became a hallmark of the firm.

Armacost & Royston, Inc., Los Angeles, California: Armacost & Royston, Inc., a famous West Coast orchid firm established by Walter L. Armacost and F. E. Royston in 1911, began importing cattleyas and phalaenopsis a year later. Realizing that success depended on securing the finest parent stock available for hybridizing, the firm imported some of the best known hybrids from England in 1921 and sowed their first seed a year later. By adopting Knudson's nonsymbiotic method of seed germination, the orchid division of the company was built up to magnificent size—approximately 100,000 square feet of glass devoted exclusively to orchids, made possible largely by a practical application of laboratory methods to commercial cultivation. Their first hybrid seedling bloomed in 1926. Soon thereafter they were producing sufficient quantities of *Cattleya* hybrids to supply and sell freight carload quantities—in all probability, the first orchid firm to handle such large numbers of marketable plants. Their first carload was shipped east in 1929, seven years after they began hybridizing, and as many as three to four carload lots were shipped out each year for some time thereafter.

George E. Baldwin & Co., Mamaroneck, New York: Early training with Charlesworth & Son at Haywards Heath, England, was the basis of Mr. George Baldwin's founding of an orchid business in 1906. Baldwin imported great quantities of plants, devoting much time to hybridizing and the growing of seedlings. The result was a large commercial collection of superior-quality hybrids that amateur and commercial grower alike bought in quantity.

Lager & Hurrell, Summit, New Jersey: Famed for its large collection of genera and species, this firm was begun by John E. Lager and Henry Hurrell, both of whom had grown up with wide horticultural experience in England. Founded in 1880 by H. F. C. Sander, the firm was purchased by Lager and Hurrell in 1895. Mr. Lager soon thereafter spent two years in South America collecting plants to stock the business. The going was difficult during the early years because plants had to be collected, greenhouses had to be built, and the plants had to be grown on before they could be turned to profit. At that point they began seriously to grow orchids for the cut-flower market. White flowers, particularly those varieties of *Laelia anceps*, became especially valuable because of the demand for their use in weddings, and as a result of having these types available, Lager & Hurrell came into prominence. As their collected stocks of rare species increased, private estates and public park conservatories found the firm a ready source of desirable plants. Consequently, the firm markedly influenced orchid culture in the United States and came to have the most varied commercial collection in the nation.

Edward A. Manda, Inc., West Orange, New Jersey: This firm, founded in 1906 by another pioneer in American orchid growing, Joseph A. Manda, was highly instrumental in creating enthusiasm among amateur orchid growers. Mr. Manda became interested in orchid hybridizing while working with the old florist firm of Pitcher & Manda in Flushing, Long Island, New York, from as early as 1885. His special interest was paphiopedilums, and while serving his apprenticeship he hybridized and introduced several hybrids of the genus. His *Paphiopedilum* Arnoldianum (*Paph. concolor* × *Paph. superbiens*) is said to be the first American-made orchid hybrid, its first flowering occurring in 1890. The production of cut flowers was secondary, for Manda was interested primarily in the production of plants, largely from backbulb propagations. He grew several thousand plants of *Paphiopedilum insigne* var. *sanderae* and made numerous purchases of large established collections, from which he also propagated. Major emphasis was on the sale of plants and the stock of species and hybrid cattleyas received major attention at a later date, when his son Edward entered the business. Both felt it was important to maintain high quality and to sell at a lower price than in former years. Thereby the delights of orchid growing were to become economically feasible for a great number of amateur growers.

Thomas Young Nurseries, Inc., Bound Brook, New Jersey: The profit to be gained by combining business with pleasure was ably demonstrated by an enterprising hobbyist named Thomas Young. Cut orchid flowers alone were the basis of his success. This firm's development reads like the typical "rags to riches" story, as published in the Plainfield, New Jersey, *Courier-News*, dated 16 May 1938:

... Thomas Young, an orchid lover, began the business of raising orchids in 1905 with more of a desire to putter around with the plants than to make any kind of sizable profit. The Young Nurseries, at that time, meant two small greenhouses, where orchids were grown as a specialty, and gardenias were grown on the side.

The name "nurseries" was rightfully applied, for like a chemist trying to learn more and more about a formula, Young watched and studied and coddled his orchid plants until they became the most important flower cultured in this area.

So large did the business become that along about 1929, Mr. Young was faced with two problems, either he would have to expand the business and get into production in a large way, or he had to sell out. Since he had begun the business more for the pleasure of raising the plants than for the income, he chose the latter course.

It was not long after this orchid genius advertised his wish to retire from the business that he had received every type of offer imaginable from small retail florists to huge Wall Street investment concerns and chain department stores. Through Carl Beckert, now president of the company, this fast expanding business was corralled for the unbelievably high figure of $2,500,000, by Reybarn, Inc. and Selected Industries, Inc. of Wall Street. Young left Bound Brook after the sale for a trip to England and thence into retirement ...

Fennell Orchid Company, Homestead, Florida: Mr. Lee A. Fennell went into the orchid business in Cynthiana, Kentucky, in 1888, moving the business to Lexington, Kentucky, about 1910, and then again to Homestead, Florida, in 1922. He opened the "Orchid Jungle" in 1923 in a native hammock, clearing paths through the verdant subtropical growth and establishing orchid plants on the native trees and in slat houses. Here it was that the first commercially raised orchid seedlings in Florida were germinated in quantity—1000 plants of *Brassolaelio-cattleya* Dorothy Fennell. Mr. Fennell was a strong advocate of orchids being grown by hobbyists and was perhaps the forerunner in making South Florida one of the nation's leading orchid centers. A number of commercial growers in Florida were by 1925 selling orchid plants and flowers. Among others, John B. Seeds began his nursery in 1919, and W. A. Manda established a range in Palm Beach.

The world's gardeners had become greatly aware of the widespread interest being shown in orchid growing by the early 1900s. The introduction of new orchid hybrids went on apace; greater knowledge of general cultural requirements was rapidly absorbed; and the laboratory work of Noel Bernard and Hans Burgeff, in the symbiotic methods of raising orchid plants from seed, opened the way to amateur and commercial orchid growing on an increasingly larger scale. Great private collections and large orchid nurseries in England, France, Belgium, and Germany particularly prospered, and the North American production of orchid plants and cut flowers rose rapidly. Then, 1914—and World War I.

In Europe, particularly, horticulture suffered drastically. Fear and destruction were widespread, and numerous good orchid collections were destroyed by the havoc and ruin of war. Other collections were necessarily abandoned and left to the mercy of fire, bombs, and freezing. On the other side of the world, however, with less fear of invasion, hybridization and the new techniques of culture and flower production continued to develop and improve. At this point it might be said that Europe began to fall behind as the world's leading center of orchid cultivation.

The Armistice of 1918 was a great relief to the world, but insofar as orchid development was concerned, England had lost six to eight years, Belgium even more—and there still remained long-range economic problems to overcome.

In the United States, meanwhile, it was found that cymbidiums flourished in outdoor plantings in California. Mr. William Hertrich, then employed by Mr. Henry E. Huntington of San Marino, was particularly interested in seeing what orchids could be grown outdoors. At his suggestion, Mr. Huntington purchased a number of plants while on a trip to England, and of his outdoor planting experiments, Hertrich stated years later:

I planted the first Cymbidiums in the rockery near the entrance to the Huntington home about 1910. This planting was to be an experiment to test the hardiness of various genera of orchids, including also Odontoglossums, Calanthes, Coelogynes, Miltonias, Laelias, Cypripediums and Stanhopeas. The Cymbidiums proved to be the one genus best adapted to our local climate.

The plants grew without special attention among other shade-loving plants such as begonias, cyclamens, primulas, ferns, etc. The flowers produced were of good quality and fairly regular, particularly *Cymbidium lowianum* . . .

Thus a new regional industry was born, and California ultimately became well known among the leading U.S. producers of commercial cymbidiums. Prominent among the early commercial growers was Mr. John Carbone, an Italian immigrant who first began growing orchids in California in the early 1900s, and though he remained an amateur at heart, he built up a large establishment with more than four acres under glass, sixteen large greenhouses containing some 90,000 blooming-sized plants of *Cattleya*, *Phalaenopsis*, *Dendrobium*, *Vanda*, and *Odontoglossum*. His cymbidium houses were looked upon as a horticultural wonder—row upon row of handsome hybrids in sixteen- to twenty-inch pots, each producing hundreds of blooms. Many of his plants carried flowers as large as some cattleyas. Through his excellent culture, experience, and advice, many others were inspired, particularly to grow cymbidiums.

As far as can be determined, the first commercial outdoor planting of California cymbidiums was in 1926, and the first large showing of cymbidium orchid plants in bloom that were grown outdoors in Southern California was made at the Pasadena Flower Show in 1937.

World affairs gradually returned to order after World War I and orchid growers everywhere looked toward a bright future. Amateur growers showed an even greater interest in orchids, and the commercial aspects of plant and cut-flower sales increased. Professor Lewis Knudson, of Cornell University, perfected his laboratory method of germinating orchid seed asymbiotically—a major breakthrough in the production of large numbers of plants and just the sort of boost the orchid world seemed to need. H. G. Alexander, managing the famous Westonbirt collection of orchids for Sir George Holford, in England, introduced the magnificent white *Cymbidium* Alexanderi 'Westonbirt,' forerunner of a long line of polyploid cymbidiums that revolutionized hybridizing in that genus. And new commercial firms began to rise to eminence all round the world.

But once again a disastrous world war intervened. World War II caused an incalculable loss, even more drastic than its predecessor, for the horrors of armed conflict were greatly magnified and more far-reaching, the result of advanced, powerful, and destructive weapons and machines. Again the losses to orchid cultivation were staggering. Restrictions on the use of coal and other fuels forced several European firms to let their plants freeze, while some English and Belgian collections were shipped to the United States for safekeeping and sale. A major loss to the orchid world was the bombing in 1943 of the Botanical Museum at Dahlem-Berlin, Germany, in which the vast collection of

Professor Rudolph Schlechter's herbarium and voluminous notes were completely destroyed. A similar great loss occurred in the Philippines when, at the end of the Japanese occupation in 1945, the Philippine National Herbarium, containing the major work of Dr. Elmer Merrill on Philippine orchids, was looted and burned by the retreating enemy. The herbarium, containing about half a million mounted specimens, was reduced to ashes.

The war ended, once again leaving Europe hard-hit—and once again leaving the United States preeminent as the world's leading orchid capital. Commercial collections in Australia and South America also began to appear. Servicemen returning from the South Pacific particularly aroused a widespread interest in the strange and unusual species they reported seeing in such far-flung regions as New Guinea, Borneo, Malaya, the Solomon Islands, and other shores. Commercial growers once again turned to peacetime interests. The Hawaiian Islands, particularly, began to have a marked influence on the tide of commercial orchid cultivation, this influence precipitated by the increasing stream of tourists, both prewar and postwar, who flocked to these verdant isles.

Along with its year-round pleasant climate, by the late 1920s Hawaii had become famed for its pineapple, sugar, and bananas. Naturally,

Experimental outdoor cultivation of cymbidiums under protective cover led to the development of a regional industry in California in the 1930s and 1940s.

tropical flowers abounded. High average temperatures, humidity, and abundant sunshine made it a veritable paradise of orchid growing. Chinese emigrants first brought orchids to Hawaii in the 1860s, primarily *Cymbidium ensifolium* and *Phaius tankervilliae*. Mr. Herbert Shipman had imported a few cattleyas to Hilo as far back as 1905, but not until the early 1930s did orchid growing begin to "catch on" in the islands. Among the earliest professional orchid growers in Hawaii, Mr. Y. Hirose of Hilo was one of the most prominent. In 1930 he began a broad program of buying species; in 1933 he flasked his first cross; and by 1942 he was shipping flowers and plants by air. An orchid society had been formed in 1938 and culture classes were taught by Professor Edward A. White of Cornell University. Later, the Department of Adult Education held classes in hybridizing. In short, Hawaii emerged as another "star on the horizon" in the commercial production of orchids.

Vanda Miss Joaquim, a primary cross of *Vanda hookeriana* × *Vanda teres* obtained by a grower of Singapore in 1893 and named for his daughter, was the forerunner of the million-dollar orchid industry in Hawaii. Mr. Lester W. Bryan of Hilo, on assignment in the Far East in 1930 for the Hawaiian Sugar Planters' Association, saw *Vanda* Miss Joaquim at the Singapore Botanical Gardens and realized almost immediately that this orchid could successfully be grown outdoors in Hawaii. Obtaining twenty-eight cuttings of the plant from the gardens, he took them back to Hilo where he propagated them by stem cuttings. In time his original cuttings amounted to a field of 10,000 blooming plants. Very shortly other growers saw the potential of this orchid as a paying crop

A commercial planting of vandas in Singapore

and within a few years there were thousands of islanders growing it. Cane stock sold at $1.00 per foot, and thousands of feet of stock exchanged hands. On the cut-flower end of the operation, individual flowers averaged 35¢ apiece. Because of their excellent keeping qualities, the flowers of this Vanda were found perfect for a number of purposes—in leis, particularly, where thousands of them were used for local and tourist consumption. Even more profitable, however, was the market on the mainland, where planeloads of the blooms, sold by the pound, were used on holidays, as "free orchids for every lady" in store openings, and in decorating floats in such events as the Annual Pasadena Tournament of Roses and the Rose Festival in Portland, Oregon. Thus the orchid-growing industry was launched.

During this period *Vanda* species and hybrids were imported in quantity by Robert and Milton Warne from the Philippines, India, and East Asia. Commercial hybridization of this genus began on a grand scale, and vandas became established as the "people's orchid" in Hawaii. The wartime "boom" provided the average person with the means of owning a few plants and vanda cultivation became an ordinary practice for most gardeners. Even the housewife planted vanda hedges in her yard, and the cities and towns of Hawaii became more beautiful—attracting even more tourists and flower lovers. Other orchid genera were found to grow just as easily—dendrobiums, phalaenopsis, cattleyas. Hundreds of large and small commercial orchid nurseries were organized and formed, and by the mid-1950s Hawaii became recognized as one of the leading commercial orchid-growing centers of the world.

Orchid hybridization continued unabated, and as the number of new hybrid introductions increased, it was also increasingly noticed that every so often there appeared individual plants which showed more vigorous growth as well as larger, better-shaped, and more heavily textured flowers. Such plants were easily recognized as desirable types, and orchid growers everywhere vied for their possession. Some investigation in the study of orchid chromosomes had been made by plant physiologists—K. L. Hoffman in 1930; O. Hagerup and G. A. L. Mehlquist in 1947; and R. E. Duncan and R. A. MacLeod in 1948–1949. Their researches were published in various horticultural and botanical journals. Mehlquist determined that polyploidy existed in cymbidiums in 1949 and reported that three natural tetraploids were then known: *Cymbidium* Alexanderi 'Westonbirt,' *Cymbidium* Pauwelsii 'Comte d'Hemptinne,' and *Cymbidium* Swallow (a hybrid of the first two). The most comprehensive work in this area, however, was conducted by Dr. Harry Kamemoto while studying at the Department of Floriculture and Ornamental Horticulture, Cornell University. In the course of his investigations he discovered that one of the laeliocattleyas he used showed irregular pairing in the microsporocytes of the young buds (the average for members of the *Cattleya* subtribes is twenty pairs in the microsporocytes of young buds, with forty chromosomes in root tips), thus leading to the discovery of polyploidy in cattleyas in 1950. The significance of this discovery was a giant step forward in commercial orchid cultivation, profoundly influencing the progress of orchid breeding.

Armed with the knowledge of natural polyploidy occurring in the important commercial genera, growers systematically began searching their collections for plants with possible polyploid characteristics. Laboratory determinations were made by the hundreds, by microscopic chromosome counts of the root tips, and when particular plants were affirmed as polyploids, they were immediately reserved as stud plants. A new race of commercial orchids was thus produced, and growers everywhere began the process of upgrading their stock by the hybridization and development of new plant varieties possessing improved substance of the blooms, broader and somewhat shorter sepals and petals, and general superiority over their diploid progenitors.

The process of developing polyploid orchid hybrids in quantity was lengthy and time-consuming—and not always attended by complete success and satisfaction. Chance segregation of genes invariably produced progeny with not all the hoped-for characteristics, and much valuable growing space and time were involved in each new cross, large numbers of which had to be discarded. Then, in 1960, Dr. George M. Morel of the Institut National de la Recherche Agronomique at Versailles, France, published a technique of clonal propagation of orchids by multiplication of the apical meristem, mainly as a method aimed at freeing cymbidiums of virus. For a few years the significance of this technique was little appreciated. Then in 1964 Morel wrote about the quantity production of plants by the meristem method, and a sudden awakening occurred in the orchid world. Messrs. Vacherot & Lecoufle of Paris, who had worked in cooperation with Morel in his experiments, were the first to capitalize on the new technique, mass-producing huge quantities of a few of their select cattleyas and cymbidiums. Like wildfire, the technique was thereafter adopted by commercial growers throughout the world. Thus it became possible to obtain large numbers of plantlets, seedling size, all propagated from a single award-quality or seasonably profitable plant; and the entire scope of commercial orchid culture, from cut-flower production down to retail plant sales to the hobbyist, was advanced another degree.

These periods in the history of commercial orchid culture, with their trials, tribulations, hazards, trends, and milestones, have contributed immeasurably to the achievements of present-day orchid growing. Constantly striving toward the goal of perfection in cultural techniques, the commercial orchid grower—from the earliest to the present—has prevailed as the backbone of an industry which supports and fosters orchid growing for profit and pleasure. To him the average "John Doe" orchidist may justifiably doff his cap.

References

American Orchid Society Bulletin. 1941. Visiting Your Neighbors—The Butterworths, Framingham, Massachusetts. Vol. 10, no. 7.

Arnold, Ralph E. 1954. Other Days. *The Orch. Rev.* 62, no. 738.

Curtis, Charles H. 1948. The House of Veitch—Part I. *Journ. of the Royal Hort. Soc.* 73, pt. 9.

Dillon, Gordon W. 1958. Orchid Growers of England—I. Orchid Survey of Europe. *Amer. Orch. Soc. Bull.* 27, no. 11.

Gardeners' Chronicle. 1921. Henry F. C. Sander—Obituary. Vol. 69, no. 1775.

I'Anson, George. 1934. A Lifetime of Orchid Madness. *Asia* 34, no. 8.

Lott, Mrs. Young C. 1948. A History of Orchid Growing in Florida. *Amer. Orch. Soc. Bull.* 17, no. 12.

Moir, W. W. Goodale. 1966. Early Orchid Introductions into Hawaii. *Bull. of the Pac. Orch. Soc. of Hawaii* 24, no. 2.

Orchid Review, The. 1921. In Memoriam: Henry F. C. Sander. Vol. 29, no. 338.

Orchid Review, The. 1960. A Guide to British Orchid Growers. Vol. 68, no. 802.

Orchid Review, The. 1962. Sander's Century of Orchid Growing. Vol. 70, no. 833.

Richter, Edna M. 1947. The Meeting Place Host—Butterworths—Master Propagators. *Amer. Orch. Soc. Bull.* 16, no. 4.

Richter, Walter. 1965. *The Orchid World* (English translation). New York: E. P. Dutton & Co.

Veitch, James H. 1906. *Hortus Veitchii.* London: James Veitch & Sons Ltd., Chelsea.

White, Edward A. 1945. *American Orchid Culture* (second printing, third edition). New York: A. T. De La Mare Co., Inc.

Hybridization

THE SPONTANEOUS HYBRIDIZATION OF PLANTS FAR OUTDATES THE BIRTH OF
agriculture, yet, remarkably, the intentional crossing of plants cannot be
traced back further than the early eighteenth century. Evolutionary
studies indicate that natural-occurring orchid hybrids are probably very
ancient—though orchid hybridization is only of comparatively recent
advent. This perhaps is the reason for the Orchid Family having the
most comprehensive and detailed list of hybrids of any known botanical
group.

The first substantial information concerning orchid hybridization is
recorded by Rev. William Herbert, dean of Manchester, who reported
in a paper entitled "On Hybridization Among Vegetables" in 1847, in
the second volume of the *Journal of the Horticultural Society of London*, that he was able to obtain well-formed capsules on plants fertilized
with pollen from another species. In the paper he remarked:

Cross breeding among Orchidaceous plants would perhaps lead to very
startling results; but, unfortunately, they are not easily raised from seed. I
have, however, raised Bletia, Cattleya, Orchis (Herminium), Monorchis and
Ophrys aranifera from seed; and if I were not during the greater part of the
year absent from the place where my plants are deposited, I think I could
succeed in obtaining crosses in that order. I had well-formed pods last spring
of Orchis by pollen of Ophrys as well as of other species of Orchis which had
been forced; and if I had remained on the spot I think I should have obtained
some cross-bred Orchidaceous seed. An intelligent gardener may do much
for science by attempts of this kind, if he keeps accurate notes of what he
attempts, and does not jump at immature conclusions.

Following Dean Herbert's report, two years later Dr. F. W. Moore, curator of the Royal Botanic Garden at Glasnevin, contributed an article to the *Gardeners' Chronicle* entitled "On Growing Orchids from Seeds." The article stated that Moore had raised orchid seedlings at least five years previously. Among the plants cultivated from seed were *Epidendrum elongatum, Epidendrum crassifolium, Cattleya forbesii,* and *Phaius (Thunia) albus.* Dr. Moore gave no information as to how the parent plants were pollinated, whether by their own pollen or by that of other flowers of the same species. The resultant seeds, however, are reported to have vegetated freely. In his article Dr. Moore particularly stressed the difficulty of keeping the seedling plants alive during their first year of existence.

Robert Gallier, a gardener to Mr. Tildesley of Staffordshire, reported in the *Gardeners' Chronicle* in 1849 that he had successfully obtained seed from a pod produced on *Dendrobium nobile* by the pollen of *Dendrobium chrysanthum.* Seedlings were produced, Gallier stated, but all soon perished.

Verification of fact is usually based on proven results, and the first successful result of man's ingenuity at artificially creating orchid hybrids was *Calanthe* Dominii, a hybrid produced by Mr. John Dominy, of the Veitch Royal Exotic Nursery. A friend of Dominy's—a surgeon, Dr. John Harris—who had studied botany during medical school, understood the nature of the orchid column, and it was he who suggested to Dominy the possibility of orchid hybridizing, demonstrating that the orchid column was actually a more complex modification of the anthers and pistils of other flowering plants, and that the application of the pollen masses to the viscous stigmatic surface was analagous to the powdery pollen dusting of the pistils in the more common flowering plants. With Dr. Harris' encouragement, Dominy began cross-pollinating cattleyas in 1853. At about the same time he made a cross of *Calanthe furcata* and *Calanthe masuca.* The seed was collected and sown in 1854; two years later the first flowers opened, on 28 October 1856. That was an immediate sensation in horticultural circles. Orchid hybridization was finally considered more than just a possibility. Taxonomic botanists, faced with the classification of man-made creations in the already complicated Orchidaceae, were greatly disturbed by the inception of orchid "mules," and perhaps one of the best-remembered statements in the history of orchidology was prompted by this first hybrid. John Lindley, upon viewing the plant, exclaimed, "You will drive the botanists mad!" It is doubtful, however, that the great orchidologist was terribly troubled by the introduction of artificial breeding in orchids, for in 1859, in the 2 January edition of the *Gardeners' Chronicle,* he wrote about the new hybrid:

On the 28th October, 1856, Mr. James Veitch, jun., of the Exotic Nursery,

Chelsea, brought to the writer of this memorandum a flower of a Calanthe which combined the peculiar hairy forked spur and deeply lobed lip of the white *Calanthe furcata*, with the violet colour and broad middle lobe of the lip of *C. masuca*. One might have said that the flowers were just intermediate between the two in all respects. A botanist could not have referred the plant either to the one or the other of those two species; nor on the other hand could he have regarded it as a new species. He would perhaps have considered it either as a purple flowered *C. furcata*, or a fork-spurred small flowered *C. masuca*. Had hybrids been suspected to occur among Orchids the plant would have been pronounced a cross. And such it was.

It appears that it had been raised in the Exeter Nursery by Mr. Dominy, Messrs. Veitch's indefatigable and very intelligent foreman, between *C. masuca* and *C. furcata*. The seed was obtained in 1854 by crossing those two species, was immediately sown, and in two years the seedlings were in flower. Nor is it the least remarkable circumstance connected with this production that it grows and flowers freely, while *C. masuca* is a "shy" plant. We therefore propose, with much pleasure, that the name of the hybrid be *Calanthe Dominii*, in order to put upon permanent record the name of the first man who succeeded in this operation. He is indeed especially entitled to this distinction not only in consequence of having produced other Orchidaceous mules, among which we understand are Cattleyas, but because of his eminent success in raising such plants from seed, as a matter of horticultural business.

Because variation had already been shown in many of the species then in cultivation, Dr. Lindley began to wonder about the possibility of many of them being natural hybrids, and in the same memorandum he wrote:

But although mule Orchids have never before been obtained artificially, are we quite sure that they have not been produced spontaneously? This is a grave botanical question which science cannot elude. It must be looked in the face; and if it should appear that species have been unduly multiplied in ignorance of so important a fact, why in that case botanists must retrace their steps as best they may. It is greatly to be feared that they will be compelled to do so. For instance, is it not probable that *Aerides maculosum* is a natural cross between *A. affine* and *A. crispum*? In the gardens there is a Saccolabium, on which we have long had an eye and which we now suspect to be a natural mule between *S. guttatum* and *Blumei*. In the genus Orchis are most suspicious forms placed round *O. militaris*, which demand careful study; there also we have *Morio-papilionacea* and *purpureo-militaris* of Timbal, *Simio-purpurea* of Weddell, and some other, all probably natural mules. The genus Ophrys will doubtless be found in the same state; and if so what may not be feared for tropical genera such as Oncidium, Odontoglossum, Epidendrum, Dendrobium, and Cattleya? Whatever else these facts and speculations may produce, among them this at least is certain, that in the future too much care cannot be taken to avoid founding species upon marks of doubtful value, especially in dealing with garden plants. What with heteranthism, dimorphism, pelorism, and hybridism our favourite Orchids may be found to assume as many disguises as an actor.

Lindley's speculations echoed the thoughts of all conscientious botanists, for the introduction of Dominy's hybrid calanthe made plain the need of a reevaluation of previous orchid taxonomy.

Meanwhile, Dominy's cattleya seedlings continued to grow and in August 1859 five blooming plants were displayed in London at a meeting of the Horticultural Society (later to become the Royal Horticultural Society). The new hybrid was called *Cattleya* hybrida.

Even as early in the annals of orchid hybridization as this second hybrid, the need for detailed records was demonstrated—Dominy had failed to accurately record the cross! Besides the fact that many of the *Cattleya* species were somewhat confused during that period, Dominy's oversight emphasized the ensuant confusion possible when parentages are not recorded. First listed as *granulosa* × *harrisoniae*, then as *granulosa* × *loddigesii* and *guttata* × *intermedia*, it was finally accorded, by the characteristics of the flower, to be *guttata* × *loddigesii*.

Dominy continued his experiments in orchid hybridization, becoming renowned as the authority in the field. And for fifteen years Veitch's was the only nursery where orchid hybrids were produced. Many intergeneric crosses were attempted, as many fraught with disappointment as with success. Among those which resulted only in dry chaff or empty pods were *Acanthophippium curtisii* × *Chysis bractescens*, *Bletia hyacinthina* × *Calanthe masuca*, *Chysis aurea* × *Zygopetalum sedenii*, *Odontoglossum bictoniense* × *Zygopetalum maxillare*, and *Zygopetalum mackayi* × *Lycaste skinneri*. Still, the failure encountered proved a valuable basis of learning the natural affinities between orchid genera. Even the culture of the seedlings successfully reaching maturity was no simple task, particularly in the early stages of growth. In his *Manual of Orchidaceous Plants*, Harry J. Veitch told of the difficulties involved:

Capsules were produced in abundance which in due course proved their maturity by dehiscing and thus the desired seed was at hand. Then arose a great difficulty, a difficulty which still exists, namely, to discover the most suitable method of raising seedlings. The seeds of orchids are minute chaffy bodies of extreme lightness; so minute are they that an ordinary pocket lens is powerless to enable one to know whether the seeds are likely to contain a germ or are merely lifeless dust. When growing wild it is evident that the contents of the mature capsules after dehiscence are more or less scattered by the wind, perhaps wafted to great distances until they settle on the branches of trees, on shelving rocks or other suitable substrata where the seeds can germinate and the seedlings firmly affix themselves. Following or at least believing that we were following Nature, so far as the altered circumstances of artificial cultivation allowed, every method or available means that could be thought of was brought into request to secure the germination of the seed. It was sown upon blocks of wood, pieces of tree-fern stems, strips of cork, upon the moss that surfaced the pots of the growing plant, in fact, in any situation which seemed to promise favourable results. . . .

Further statements related that the latter method was the most successful.

Acknowledging his appreciation for the early suggestions of his friend, Dr. Harris, Dominy named the first hybrid *Paphiopedilum* in honor of that gentleman. The cross, named *Paphiopedilum* Harrisianum, was bloomed from a mating of *Paphiopedilum villosum* and *Paphiopedilum barbatum* in 1869.

In reference to naming the new paphiopedilum in Dr. Harris' honor, H. G. Reichenbach had this to say in the *Gardeners' Chronicle* for 30 January 1869:

These splendid acquisitions are due to the unrivalled skill and sagacity of Mr. Dominy. Now, we are told that it was Dr. Harris of Exeter who gave Mr. Dominy the idea of hybridising orchids, at a time when we knew nothing about the European Orchid mules, and when there was not the least indication of the present great excitement of mind as to the limits and origins of species.* The showy plant now described could not as Mr. Dominy well observes, bear a better name than that of *Cypripedium* (*Paphiopedilum*) Harrisianum, in honour of the gentleman to whom we are indebted for so much.

In the same issue Reichenbach also discussed the merits of orchid hybrids, in close agreement with those views given earlier by Lindley:

There are various opinions as to the value of hybrids. We hear there are some gentlemen who shrink from the apparition of such plants even among Orchids. No doubt, hybrids of doubtful origin, which make their appearance without certificates of birth and parentage are most troublesome both to men of science and amateurs. Thus the study of garden specimens of Pelargonium, Cacti, Ericas, is very irksome and often impossible. But if the origin of all of these doubtful plants were known, would it not be a grand thing for science? And so it is with Orchids.

Dominy produced the following twenty-five hybrids prior to his retirement in 1880, a twenty-two-year period of orchid hybridization with Messrs. Veitch:

HYBRID	PARENTAGE	DATE BLOOMED
Calanthe Dominii	*C. furcata* × *C. masuca*	October 1856
Cattleya hybrida	*C. guttata* × *C. loddigesii*	
Cattleya Dominiana	*C. maxima* × *C. intermedia*	

* By this time Charles Darwin's *Origin of Species* had been published.

Hybrid	Parentage	Date bloomed
Calanthe Veitchii	*C. rosea* × *C. vestita*	1859
Dossinimaria Dominii	*Haemaria discolor* ×	
	Dossinia marmorata	June 1861
Goodyera Veitchii	*Haemaria discolor* ×	
	Macodes petola	July 1862
Cattleya Aclandi-Loddigesii		
(syn. *C.* Brabantiae)	*C. loddigesii* × *C. aclandiae*	July 1863
Cattleya Exoniensis	*C. mossiae* or *C. labiata* ×	
	L. crispa	September 1863
Cattleya Devoniensis	*L. crispa* × *C. guttata*	September 1863
Laelia Pilcheri	*L. crispa* × *L. perrinii*	May 1864
Anoectochilus Dominii	*Goodyera discolor* ×	
	Anoectochilus xanthophyllus	May 1865
Cattleya Quincolor	*C. forbesii* × *C. aclandiae*	June 1865
Cattleya Manglesii	*C. lueddemanniana* ×	
	C. loddigesii	August 1866
Phaius Irroratus	*Phaius grandifolius* ×	
	Calanthe vestita	1867
Phaius Inquilinus	? × ?	May 1867
Cypripedium Harrisianum	*C. villosum* × *C. barbatum*	1869
Selenipedium Dominianum	*S. caricinum* × *S. caudatum*	1870
Cypripedium Vexillarium	*C. barbatum* × *C. fairieanum*	1870
Aerides Hybridum	*A. affine* × *A. fieldingii*	1870
Laelia Veitchiana	*C. labiata* × *L. crispa*	1874
Cattleya Felix	*L. crispa* × *C. schilleriana*	1876
Laelia Caloglossa	*C. labiata* × *L. boothiana*,	
	possibly *L. crispa*	1877
Cattleya Picturata	*C. guttata* × *C. intermedia*	1877
Dendrobium Dominianum	*D. nobile* × *D. linawianum*	1878
Laelia Dominiana	*C. dowiana* × *L. boothiana*,	
	possibly *L. crispa*	August 1878

Dominy's success with man-made hybrids greatly stimulated the interest of amateur and commercial orchid growers alike, accentuated, perhaps, by the publication of Charles Darwin's *On the Fertilisation of Orchids by Insects* in 1862.

The first to follow Dominy successfully was a Mr. Cross, gardener to Lady Ashburton at Melchet Court in Hampshire. Cross' first efforts were *Paphiopedilum insigne* hybrids. *Paphiopedilum* Ashburtoniae (*P. barbatum* × *P. insigne*) appeared in 1871; *Paphiopedilum* Crossii (*P. insigne* × *P. venustum*) flowered two years later. Additional paphiopedilum hybrids were introduced by Mr. Cross from time to time.

Numerous other gardeners and operators joined the expanding rank and file of hybridizers, the most notable of these probably being Mr. John Seden, successor to Dominy at the Exeter nursery of Messrs. Veitch. In a thirty-nine-year career with the Veitches, Seden became as famed for his hybridization as had Dominy, with over 500 hybrids created before his retirement in 1905. Among his accomplishments, Seden was the first to demonstrate, by hybridization, that natural hybrids do occur in the wild, supporting Dr. Lindley's ideas of the intermediate character of some of the "species" located. It had been known, or at least postulated, as early as 1787, that some of the European terrestrial orchids such as *Gymnadenia, Nigritella,* and *Orchis* were interbreeding and producing progeny of intermediate character. Natural hybridization in the tropical species was not considered, however until a unique plant in a consignment of *Phalaenopsis amabilis* flowered in 1852, distinctly different than *Phalaenopsis amabilis.* Dr. Lindley wrote of the plant:

It is not improbable that this beautiful plant is a natural mule between *P. amabilis* and *P. rosea.* It agrees with the former in foliage and in the tendrils of the lip; with the latter in colour, in the acuteness of its petals and in the peculiar form of the middle lobe of the lip. . . . Flowers halfway in size between *P. amabilis* and *P. rosea.*

At the suggestion of this parentage, Seden later made the cross. Upon blooming, the single surviving plant proved to be identical with the suspected natural hybrid which Lindley had named *Phalaenopsis intermedia.*

Within a short time it became apparent that a hybrid record was needed. In 1871 F. W. Burbidge published a list of eighteen orchid hybrids in the *Gardeners' Chronicle,* giving the parentage where known, and establishing a precedent in consistent publication of new hybrids, for the *Gardeners' Chronicle* made the hybrid listing a regular feature of its publication.

Ernst Bohnhof published a *Dictionnaire des Orchidees Hybrides* in Paris in 1895, and A. E. Hopkinson's *Orchid Hybridist's Handbook,* which listed known orchid hybrids to the end of 1894, was published in 1896. The most inclusive listing of that period, however, seems to have been one by Mr. George Hansen, foreman of the Sierra Agricultural Experiment Station, a department of the University of California at Jackson. Hansen was a native Englishman formerly associated with orchid growing in England ten years before going to the United States. His list, published in London as *The Orchid Hybrids,* included all those known up to 15 October 1895. All available data were given on each hybrid listed—seed and pollen parentage, date of first showing, synonyms, names of hybridizer and exhibit, and references to publications and illustrations. First and second supplements were later added. In 1909 Hurst and Rolfe published the *Orchid Stud Book,* the most comprehensive of all hybrid listings until then. This book was to become a classic in orchid literature because it was a great forward step in the organization of orchid hybrid listings.

Numerous hybrid lists were published, but that which ultimately became considered most comprehensive was begun by Frederick K. Sander. In 1901 he published the *Orchid Guide*, a thirty-two-page alphabetical listing of known hybrids. A second edition was published in 1915, including all the registered hybrids between 1901 and 18 July1915. Another edition appeared in 1921. The Sander family became justifiably well-known for its work in the registration and publication of new orchid hybrids, and in 1946 all the registered hybrids were listed in a single volume called *Sanders' Complete List of Orchid Hybrids.* Three further addenda appeared between 1946 and 1960, at which time the Royal Horticultural Society assumed the burdensome responsibility of International Registrar of Orchid Hybrids, relieving the Sanders of over a half century of devoted service to orchidology. By that time hundreds of new orchid crosses were being registered each month by amateur and professional growers alike.

References

De Wolf, Gordon P. 1950. Beginning to Hybridize Orchids—A Preliminary Survey of Orchid Breeding. *Amer. Orch. Soc. Bull.* 19, no. 1.

Gardeners' Chronicle. 1899. Hybrids and Their Raisers. Vol. 26, no. 665.

Lenz, Lee W. 1956. John Dominy—Pioneer Orchid Hybridizer. *Amer. Orch. Soc. Bull.* 25, no. 10.

Lenz, Lee W. and Wimber, Donald E. 1959. Hybridization and Inheritance in Orchids. Ch. 7 of *The Orchids—A Scientific Survey.* Carl L. Withner, ed. The Ronald Press Co. New York.

Menninger, Emma D. 1956. One Hundred Years of Orchid Hybridization. *Amer. Orch. Soc. Bull.* 25, no. 10.

Orchid Review, The. The History of Orchid Hybridization, Part I. Vol. 1, no. 1.

Sanders' Complete List of Orchid Hybrids. 1946. Gibbs & Bamforth Ltd. St. Albans, England.

Veitch, James, & Sons. 1887–94. *A Manual of Orchidaceous Plants.* Vol. 1—*Epidendreae.* London: H. M. Pollett & Co.

Veitch, James H. 1906. *Hortus Veitchii.* Chelsea, London: James Veitch & Sons Ltd.

Scientific Application

NEW THEORIES AND IDEAS OFTEN SUFFER THE MISFORTUNE OF BEING RE-jected or completely ignored, especially in the face of long-established and comfortable beliefs and methods of doing things. Science in all its fields has been subject to such treatment since its beginnings. Science and technology, of course, are relative newcomers in mankind's history. Prior to the nineteenth century, philosophy and science were considered one and the same—a carry-over of Aristotelian philosophy plus an over-lay of emotion. Aristotle's blending of the two was so effective that his philosophical science was not easily laid aside even though increasingly technical discoveries and thoughts seemed to contradict the established principles. Derision, blindness, and indecision often resulted, and for science the proof was in the doing.

Sex in plants had been shown experimentally by Rudolf Jacob Cam-erarius in 1694, so that by his teachings, late fifteenth-century gardeners arrived at a basic understanding of the reproductive structures of the more common flowers. The functions of stamens and pistils were easily evident and most gardeners were able to produce seed from the plants entrusted to their management. By 1717 the plant hybridizer's skill be-came evident by the recorded descriptions of horticultural hybrids which began to appear. The orchid flower, however, remained a mys-tery. Because plantsmen could not understand the nature of the orchid column, artificial pollination seemed highly improbable, if not com-pletely impossible. Pollination, therefore, was considered a rare and purely spontaneous occurrence in the Orchidaceae.

While serving an appointment as head master of the school at Span-dau, Germany (1774–1780), Christopher Konrad Sprengel observed the fertilization of endemic orchid flowers by insects. This phenomenon among Sprengel's nature studies was published as *Das entdeckte Geheimniss der Natur* (The Discovered Secret of Nature) in 1793. Little attention was given to Sprengel's report, however. Because he was relatively unknown, minor credence was attributed to his work and, embittered by this response, Sprengel abandoned his botanical interests completely. Long after his death, however, it had to be recognized that he was the first to have published his observations on the natural pollination of orchids.

Despite the ignorance surrounding the reproductive processes of the Orchidaceae and the brash theories that orchids could not be pollinated outside of their native habitats, John Lindley reported that "about the year 1832, *Prescottia plantaginea* was raised abundantly in the garden of the Horticultural Society; and it has been rumored for some time that seedling epiphytes are coming forward in certain Continental nurseries." Thus, at last, some of the aura of mysticism had been cleared away. Satisfactory explanation of the physiology of orchid fertilization was yet forthcoming, however.

Though it was popularly believed that the orchid column was a sterile anther, Lindley's illustrator, Francis Bauer, would not accept this hypothesis and attempted, on the basis of his theories of fructification, to explain the functions of the columnar organs as he believed they operated. Though he was actually in error, Bauer *was* approaching the true aspects of orchid pollination.

Robert Brown became interested in the mystery of fecundation in the Orchid Family and meticulously reviewed all the theories which had been expressed on the subject from 1760 to 1831, including those of Swartz, the two Richards (father and son), Dupetit-Thouars, Blume, and others. His own observations on the tissue structure of orchids led him to the apt conclusion that the only way in which the impregnation of the ovules is effected is through the direct contact of the pollen and the stigma. Brown's critical investigations were thorough, and during his research he noticed (the first in the scientific field to do so) that all cells contain nuclei. This achievement itself was a great technical discovery. The results of his investigations appeared in 1833 as his famous paper, "On the Organs and Mode of Fecundation in Orchideae and Asclepiadeae," in *Transactions of the Linnean Society*, volume 16.

John Lindley was also concerned with the features of pollination and hybridization of orchids but was cautious not to be swayed by conjecture. Of the then-current explanations given by botanists concerning the pollination of orchids, he wrote some prefatory remarks in Francis Bauer's *Illustrations of Orchidaceous Plants* (1830–1838):

Opinions are divided as to the manner in which impregnation occurs in this order. Mr. Bauer adduces a great many facts to show that it does not take place, as in other plants, by actual contact between the pollen and the stigmatic secreting surface, but that it is effected by absorption of the fecundating matter by the stigmatic gland from the pollen through the caudicula.

On the other hand Dr. Brown, M. Adolphe Brongniart, and others, suppose that impregnation is effected here as elsewhere by contact between the pollen and stigma. It is alleged that pollen tubes are emitted by the pollen after it has adhered to the stigma, that these tubes descend the stigmatic canal, and mix themselves among the ovules over the surface of the placentae, and that in some cases the pollen tubes have been traced into the foramina of the ovules. The latter is a remark of Dr. Brown's whose skill and faithfulness as an observer are above all question.

For a long time I adopted the views of Mr. Bauer, but additional experience, a careful observation of Orchidaceae in a state of cultivation, and a verification of some of the facts last described, have caused me to alter my opinion, to acquiesce in the conclusions of Dr. Brown, and to regard the phenomena represented by Mr. Bauer as connected with circumstances not belonging to impregnation. It is now well known that cultivated Orchidaceae, which rarely fruit if unassisted, may be made to bear fruit with certainty, if they are artificially impregnated. The effect of such impregnation is firstly to hasten by many days the decay of the flower, and secondly, to fill the stigmatic canal with pollen tubes, which may be traced without difficulty even up to the very maturation of the fruit.

The determination of this point does not however diminish the value of Mr. Bauer's observations; it only leaves the facts he describes still to be accounted for; and it is a most curious subject of enquiry to investigate the exact uses of so singular and peculiar a sexual apparatus as that with which Orchidaceae are furnished.

The seeds are generally enveloped by a loose cellular testa, which is frequently open at the lower end, at the period of maturity. They contain a nucleus, whose apex is directed towards the base of the seed, and which is either covered by two extremely thin membranes, frequently prolonged at the point into a tube, or is coated by a brittle crustaceous integument. At that end of the nucleus which is next the apex of the seed, is uniformly found a very distinct chalaza of a deep brown, or a bright brown colour. The interior of the nucleus is a cellular fleshy homogeneous body, and must be regarded as an embryo destitute of albumen.

Lindley's observations, as chronicled, were apparently quite concise. The exactness of his description could hardly be questioned concerning the appearance, both external and internal, of the impregnated orchid ovary and ripe seeds. His confidence in Dr. Brown's observations was also well founded, for they proved factual. Strange, then, that Lindley should close his remarks by stating, "Nothing certain is known of the germination of Orchidaceae." He must have indeed been a very cautious man.

The first emergence from the philosophical maze concerning the nature of things was effected by a naturalist named Charles Darwin, whose *Origin of Species* shook the foundations of natural history in 1859. This work was received with suspicion and open hostility by many naturalists, for it was looked upon as an attack on their cherished prejudices and prepossessions. Nevertheless, certain facts supported Darwin's views, and a large body of naturalists began seriously to contemplate the logic of his theories on natural selection and evolution. One of his major interests was the Orchid Family, to which study he applied himself assiduously. In 1862 he presented to the Linnean Society of London his paper on the sexual forms of *Catasetum*, a genus which had previously confused all of botany because of its extraordinary dimorphism. That same year his treatise *On the Fertilisation of Orchids by Insects* was published. This classic work not only removed all doubt concerning the function of the pollinia but additionally focused the attention of natu-

Angraecum sesquipedale, the Madagascan species which Charles Darwin speculated on, noting that it would very likely be necessary for some form of long-tongued moth to pollinate such a flower. Years after his prediction, the moth (below) was discovered and suitably named *Xanthopan morgani praedicta*.

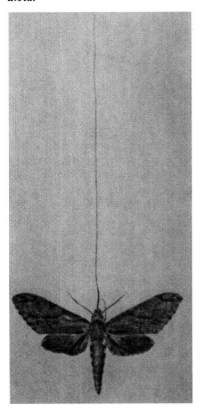

ralists on the complex symbiotic relationship between orchids and insects. This contribution earned him the well-deserved respect of the scientific community—and paved the way toward a much expanded basis for artificial orchid hybridization.

For many years following Darwin's reports, and the successful production of numerous hybrids by John Dominy, the records of hybrid parentages were diligently recorded. The crosses made were experimental in nature, however, for the promiscuous selection of parent plants was conducted without benefit of genetic knowledge. The first to delve into the complexity of orchid genetics was Charles C. Hurst, biologist-botanist-geneticist who initially became interested in orchids after reading Darwin's *Fertilisation of Orchids* in 1894. Armed with inspiration, he formed a collection of plants and began to make experimental crosses between species of different tribes and genera. His observations were published in *The Orchid Review* in 1897 and 1898, titled "Curious Crosses." In 1897 he read the outline of a paper before the Royal Horticultural Society in which he emphasized the importance of chromosomes. In this outline, the full details of which were published in the society's *Journal* the following year as "On Some Curiosities of Orchid Breeding," he enumerated the behavioral characteristics of orchid hybrids, based on his own experiments and those of numerous correspondents. His description of fertilization in orchids was followed by a description of the chromosomes: "The essence of fertilization consists in the removal of one-half of the nuclear elements from the egg cell of the mother and the replacing of them by an equal number from the pollen cell of the father, and in this way Professor Weismann accounts for the different phenomena of heredity, reversion, and variation . . . which have puzzled philosophers and naturalists from Aristotle to Darwin." Orchid chromosomes had not yet been counted, but Hurst strongly indicated that the foregoing theory could explain the results found in orchid hybrids. This was three years before the rediscovery of Gregor Mendel's works, and it was not until 1902 that Sutton located the Mendelian factors in chromosomes. Hurst's paper gained for him a fellowship in the Linnean Society, for the value of his clarification of genetic principles was viewed invaluable Thus the variation evident in hybrid progeny could be explained in part. In 1899 he read a paper to the Royal Horticultural Society which enunciated a law of partial prepotency in orchid hybrids—for all practical purposes the yet undiscovered Mendelian law of dominance and segregation.

Further studies by Hurst concerning the occurrence of natural hybrids among orchids led to the presentation of an article to *Nature* in 1898 on the "Origin of Orchid Species." Other of Hurst's works, based on his application of Mendelian theories to *Paphiopedilum* (he was the first to apply them to orchids) aided in determining many measurable

Eulophiella rolfei, a hybrid cross of *E. Elizabethae* × *E. Peetersiana*. This first registered hybrid in the genus was made by the Charlesworth firm and named in honor of Robert Allen Rolfe in 1917.

characters in the breeding of plants. In 1902–1903 he discovered the existence of complementary color genes in albino orchids and worked out a formula in 1912 for breeding albino orchid hybrids. That same year he discussed the application of genetics to orchids at an orchid conference in London, indicating that red forms of *Odontoglossum crispum* and yellow *Cattleya* hybrids could be developed by following Mendel's law. In 1909 he and Robert A. Rolfe published the *Orchid Stud Book*, enumerating all the known artificial orchid hybrids to 1907. The *Stud Book* listed twenty-three bigeneric hybrids, two trigeneric hybrids, and over 2000 primary hybrids. This work was perhaps the major stimulus leading to the systematization of orchid hybridization, the reduction of synonymy, and the foundation on which was built Sander's great work, the ever-valuable *List of Orchid Hybrids*.

Orchids had long been known to grow in close association with fungal hyphae at their roots. Without realizing what the function of the fungi was, Link first observed this interesting yet puzzling phenomenon in 1840 in young goodyera seedlings. Schleiden von Reissek, in 1847, became aware of their relationship and attempted to extract the fungi, which we now know as *mycorrhiza* (the term first coined by the German botanist A. B. Frank, in 1885). He found that in *Orchis morio* the mycorrhiza was present in almost all the cortical cells, though in the tropical epiphytic orchids the mycorrhizal masses were arranged only singly at the periphery of the root. Studies by Wahrlich, published in 1886, established that the roots of orchids invariably contain mycorrhiza, a deduction made after taking 500 representative samples at random in the Orchid Family. Others suspected a symbiotic dependence of one upon another, though published observations were singularly few. The limited number of commercial nurserymen who were successful in germinating orchid seed carefully concealed their operations. Numerous methods were attempted—sowing the seed on sphagnum moss, on wet bricks, on cork slabs, and many other materials. The most successful method seemed to be by sowing the seed on the rooting medium at the base of the seed-bearing parent. Nevertheless, even then successful germination was a rare chance occurrence. In character with the ideas of the time, growers presumed that a secret force emitted from the mother plant or its roots determined the chances and percentage of successful germination. Yet they persisted in their experimentation. Sometimes pieces of root from mature plants were added to the substratum, bringing about a greater degree of germination.

By the turn of the century some botanists had tried to isolate the mycorrhiza and cultivate them in pure cultures, but all attempts failed and they were thus unable to prove the existence of an interdependence between orchids and mycorrhizal companions.

It was the work of a young French biologist, Noel Bernard, that demonstrated once and for all that the presence of the mycorrhiza was essential, in a symbiotic relationship, to the germination of orchid seeds. Bernard began his studies on orchid mycorrhiza in 1899, following them up with great determination. Through diligent observation, both in the laboratory and in the field, he was able to extract the mycorrhiza and inoculate seeds in sterile cultures. His experiments included placing orchid seed on a nutritive agar solution contained in test tubes, some of which were inoculated with the mycorrhiza and some left untreated. Those on the mycorrhiza-treated agar germinated quickly, while those on the untreated agar remained almost dormant. Through these experiments he concluded that the germination of orchid seed in nature *was* dependent on the presence of the mycorrhiza. His results were published in various journals from 1904 to 1909, though the far-reaching consequences of his work were but little realized at the time. While Bernard's experiments proved a point, he was not so short-sighted as to deny that orchid seed might someday be germinated without the presence of mycorrhizal fungi. At the Ghent Floralies in 1908 he speculated that it should be possible, by experimentation, to find some artificial medium which would play the same part as the fungus had hitherto played in the germination of orchid seed.

During the same period, Professor Hans Burgeff of Wurzberg, Germany, was making similar observations and experimenting with orchid mycorrhiza, though unaware of Bernard's research. Had each known of the other's work, they could undoubtedly have accelerated development in the studies by a comparison of notes and results. Bernard died unexpectedly in 1911, however, so there was little chance for collaboration. Meanwhile, Burgeff's works, *Die Wurzelpilze der Orchideen, ihre Kultur und ihr Leben in der Pflanze* (1909), and *Die Anzucht tropischer Orchideen aus Samen auf Grundlage der symbiotischen Verhältnisse von Pflanze und Wurzelpilz* (1911) became the foundation of expanded development of the methods which made it possible to raise seed in quantity. Commercial orchid cultivation, particularly, benefited from Burgeff's techniques, for he eliminated the necessity of much tedious laboratory procedure for the commercial growers by providing them pre-infected cultures in which seed of their own crosses could be sown.

Following the work of Burgeff and a number of contemporary workers, opinions remained in conflict concerning the absolute essentiality of mycorrhizal fungi in connection with the germination of orchid seed. Lewis Knudson, a plant physiologist at Cornell University, had been investigating albino corn and had devised techniques of culturing the seedlings under sterile conditions on a medium containing sugar. He became interested in the fungi relationships of orchids in 1917 and, reviewing the work of Bernard and Burgeff, became convinced that while their experiments were good, the interpretation of their results was faulty. His earlier work in the organic nutrition of corn seedlings and leguminous plants served as background experience and, learning that Bernard and Burgeff's control cultures had always contained starch as an energy source, he reasoned that the fungus itself did not cause germination because it invaded the orchid seed but that it converted the starch of the culture medium to sugar. Therefore, if the orchid seed were provided with sugar and nutrients, they would germinate just as easily without the fungus. Experiments were devised in which culture tubes were prepared with a purely synthetic medium consisting of calcium nitrate, ammonium sulfate, potassium phosphate, magnesium sulfate, iron phosphate, cane sugar or glucose, agar, and water. When the sugar was omitted, germination commenced but growth soon ceased. When sugar was provided, practically every seed produced a seedling. Continued investigation during a period of about eight years clearly refuted the idea of the necessity of a fungus.

In the early phases of his work Knudson found it nearly impossible to obtain live orchid seed, for the few growers who were producing seed were either unwilling to part with it or the costs of such seed was prohibitive. Through Professor Liberty Hyde Bailey, he learned of a Cornell graduate in Florida, Theodore L. Mead, who was greatly interested in orchids and who had raised some orchids from seed. With Bailey's encouragement, he wrote to Mr. Mead, and as a result Mead supplied him with viable seed of several hundred crosses over a period of five years. Out of this developed the asymbiotic method of seed germination in 1922 which made possible the raising of orchid seedlings by the millions, revolutionizing the entire orchid industry. Knudson's techniques were adopted everywhere and unlimited numbers of species and hybrid crosses were raised, to the point where plants and cut flowers by the hundreds of thousands well represented the scientific breakthrough that put commercial orchid production on its feet. Hobby orchid growers, too, learned Knudson's asymbiotic method and began to make and register their own hybrid crosses. By the middle 1940s, each monthly issue of *The Orchid Review* saw the introduction of increasingly larger numbers of new hybrids.

Robert Brown had, of course, discovered in 1831 that all living cells contain nuclei. He was followed by a large company of botanists who became interested in plant cytology. Ironically, cell structure and genetics in the Orchid Family received thereafter comparatively little attention, until Charles Hurst began his studies of orchid inheritance. But even though his investigations pointed the way to sounder breeding programs, orchid breeders paid little heed to his conclusions and results. For nearly forty years thereafter, orchid genetics received little attention. Then, in 1945, R. E. Duncan discovered a phenomenon in the tissues of *Paphiopedilum wardii* which he called aneusomaty, or the presence of varying numbers of chromosomes in different cells. This was followed by extensive studies in that genus (Mehlquist, 1947; Duncan and MacLeod, 1948–1949). *Paphiopedilum* was especially useful for cytological work, it was found, because of the large chromosome size and strong affinity for chromosomal stains. Further meiotic irregularities of chromosome behavior which sometimes resulted in aneuploid chromosome numbers were observed by Hagerup in 1947, and this gave additional support to the explanation of the occurrence of plants which had different chromosome numbers, even though their siblings had the same genetic constituents.

At about the same time, Dr. Gustav A. L. Mehlquist was investigating the cytology of cymbidiums. Among his findings, in 1949 he reported that three well-known *Cymbidium* hybrids had been found to be tetraploids—*Cymbidium* Alexanderi 'Westonbirt,' *Cymbidium* Pauwelsii 'Comte de Hemptine,' and *Cymbidium* Swallow, a progeny of the first two.

Though commercially the most important, members of the *Cattleya* tribe were studied little. The small size of their chromosomes, coupled with the relatively high numbers in each cell, made them especially difficult to count. Furthermore, ordinary staining techniques did not yield satisfactory results. The earliest published reports of chromosome studies in that tribe were by Hoffman (1930), who verified that a diploid chromosome number of 40 was found in *Cattleya trianaei, Epidendrum nocturnum, Epidendrum raniferum*, and a hybrid of *Laeliocattleya* Canhamiana × *Laelia tenebrosa*.

In 1949 Harry Kamemoto, research assistant in the Department of

Floriculture and Ornamental Horticulture at Cornell University, was prompted by the lack of cytological research in this group to work out the development of a suitable technique for determining chromosome numbers in the sporocytes and root tip cells of the cattleyas and their allies with very small chromosomes. This technique opened the way for a much expanded study, particularly in the creation of new horticultural varieties.

Continued investigation included species and hybrids, and by 1950 Kamemoto discovered that a number of improved commercial varieties were actually triploids and tetraploids, thus expanding the vigorous growth, large flowers, good form, and heavy substance which characterized such plants as *Cattleya* Balmar, Joyce Hannington, Bow Bells, and many others. Kamemoto additionally studied the behavior of chromosomes in various hybrids during the meiotic divisions of the pollen mother cells. He observed that the chromosomes paired regularly in various species and hybrids within the genus *Cattleya* and also in certain *Laeliocattleya* hybrids. These studies served as a useful guide in selecting future plants for breeding. Such plants, hybridized with others of equal and comparable chromosome numbers, were the basis of a new "breed" of orchids which readily found their places in national award lists and in cut-flower production.

Equipped with the knowledge imparted by such a vast amount of scientific research, it seemed that orchid growers the world over were no longer shackled by ignorance and lack of available cultural methods. Nevertheless, limitations did exist. Large-scale orchid production is a costly and time-consuming business, and commercial growers in particular found that it was not always profitable to make numerous crosses, for they very often did not have the available time and greenhouse space necessary for growing large blocks of seedlings on to maturity. Because hybrid orchids are highly heterozygous, their progeny are highly variable, and despite the advances made in hybridizing over the previous years, even by the use of excellent stud plants, the resulting percentages of high-quality progeny are always low. It is—and always has been—a costly proposition, therefore, to raise large numbers of a cross to maturity in order to select only a few of the very best clones.

Most commercial orchid growers maintained a few small lots of select plants in their collections which were ideal for their purposes—dependable blooming at the desired time of year, fine form and texture, good keeping qualities, etc. Their major problem was the slow rate at which these plants could be propagated vegetatively. It was a painstaking and lengthy process to assemble a commercial collection that could provide sufficient high-quality cut flowers to meet seasonal demands. Then, almost by chance, a solution was provided in 1960 by Dr. Georges M. Morel, director of the National Institute of Agricultural Research at Versailles, France.

In the course of a study Dr. Morel was conducting on virus diseases of cymbidiums, he discovered in 1956 that it was possible to obtain virus-free orchid plants by tissue-culturing the apical meristem of new vegetative growths. In such tissue it was found that virus organisms were not usually present. The method was not new, for it had been employed previously with horticultural subjects such as dahlias, carnations, and potatoes. But Morel was the first to apply the technique to orchids. By aseptically dissecting the young buds and excising the apex of the meristem, he demonstrated that it was possible to promote virus-free plantlets in culture media just as if growing plants from seed. The protocorm-like growths which preceded actual differentiation of roots and leaves often divided into clumps of four or five identical structures, each of them producing a new plant identical in every respect to the plant from which the original meristem apex was excised. A report of these results was published in the *American Orchid Society Bulletin* in July 1960, but while orchid growers heralded Morel's achievement, the commercial possibilities implied in the report seemed to escape notice.

The spontaneous proliferation of these plant tissues was of more than passing interest to some plant physiologists. At the same time that Morel saw the possibilities of a rapid means of clonal multiplication, Dr. Donald Wimber of the Brookhaven National Laboratories in Bethesda, Maryland, was also conducting experimental procedures along the same lines. He published his results, the "Clonal Multiplication of Cymbidiums through Tissue Culture of the Shoot Meristem," in 1963— but still the orchid-growing populace did not elicit much response. Then, in 1964, Morel explicitly spelled out that the proliferation process could be induced artificially in several genera and that by sectioning the protocorm-like bodies and transferring them to new media, new plantlets from a single bud could be produced *ad infinitum*! He stated that "if each protocorm gives only four new ones per month, it is possible to obtain more than 4,000,000 plants in a year from a single bud." By that time his first meristem-propagated plants of *Cymbidium*, *Miltonia*, and *Phaius* (propagated five and six years previously) had bloomed— identical in every characteristic to the "donor" plant. This was the proof that commercial orchidists needed; almost overnight they were having their choicest plants propagated in quantity.

A host of unanswered questions and unsolved problems in orchidology yet remain to challenge scientific inquiry. The magnitude of the Orchid Family is itself a phenomenon that invites the question "Why?" Much of our present knowledge about orchids is based on past research, and there is every reason to expect that future generations of orchidists will be enticed into scientifically investigating the nearly limitless aspects of orchidology. The results of their researches will, indeed, be orchid history in the making.

References

Ames, Oakes. 1937. Pollination of Orchids through Pseudocopulation. *Amer. Orch. Soc. Bull.* 6, no. 2.

Ames, Oakes. 1944. The Pollinia of Orchids. *Amer. Orch. Soc. Bull.* 13, no. 6.

Bernard, Noel. 1906. Fungus Co-operation in Orchid Roots. *The Orch. Rev.* 14, no. 163.

Brown, Robert. 1833. On the Organs and Modes of Fecundation in Orchideae and Asclepiadeae. *Trans. of the Linn. Soc.* 16. London.

Burgeff, Hans. 1959. Mycorrhiza of Orchids. Ch. 9 of *The Orchids—A Scientific Survey*. Carl L. Withner, ed. New York: The Ronald Press Co.

Costantin, J. 1913. The Development of Orchid Cultivation and Its Bearing upon Evolutionary Theories. *Annual Report Smithsonian Institution*, pp. 345–358.

Curtis, J. T. 1955. Pure Research in Relation to Orchid Culture. *Amer. Orch. Soc. Bull.* 24, no. 1.

Darwin, Charles. 1903. *Various Contrivances by which Orchids are fertilised by Insects*. 2nd rev. ed. New York.

Forbes, Henry O. 1885. On the Contrivances for ensuring Self Fertilization in some Tropical Orchids. *Journ. of the Linnean Society* 21.

Gardeners' Chronicle. 1890. Heredity. Vol. 7, no. 181.

Gardeners' Chronicle. 1903. Mendel's Methods of Plant Breeding. Vol. 33, no. 838.

Gardener's Chronicle. 1841. Miscellaneous—The Late Francis Bauer, Esq. No. 2. January 9.

Gardeners' Chronicle. 1858. The Late Robert Brown, L.L.D., F.R.S., etc. No. 38.

Gibson, William Hamilton, and Helena Leeming Jelliffe. 1905. *Our Native Orchids*. New York: Doubleday, Page & Co.

Hurst, Rona. 1949. The R.H.S. and the Birth of Genetics. *Journ. of the Royal Hort. Soc.* 74, part 9.

Kamemoto, H. 1951. Polyploidy and Orchid Breeding. *Na Pua Okika O Hawaii Nei* 1, no. 1.

Kamemoto, H. 1950. Polyploidy in Cattleyas. *Amer. Orch. Soc. Bull.* 19, no. 7.

Kamemoto, H. and Randolph, L. F. 1949. Chromosomes of the Cattleya Tribe. *Amer. Orch. Soc. Bull.* 18, No. 6.

Knudson, Lewis. 1924. Further Observations on Nonsymbiotic Germination of Orchid Seeds. *Botanical Gazette* 77, no. 2.

Knudson, Lewis. 1922. Nonsymbiotic Germination of Orchid Seeds. *Botanical Gazette* 73.

Knudson, Lewis. 1951. Nutrient Solutions for Orchids. *Botanical Gazette* 112, no. 4.

Knudson, Lewis. 1927. Symbiosis and Asymbiosis Relative to Orchids. *The New Phytologist* 26, no. 5.

Lambeau, F. 1933. Germination of Orchid Seeds. *The Orch. Rev.* 41, no. 482.

Mehlquist, Gustav A. L., and Clovis, Jesse F. 1957. Counting Chromosomes in Orchids. *Amer. Orch. Soc. Bull.* 26, no. 6.

Menninger, Emma D. 1954. Tetraploid Cymbidiums. *Amer. Orch. Soc. Bull.* 23, no. 3.

Orchid Review, The. 1900. Germination of Orchid Seedlings. Vol. 8, no. 91.

Orchid Review, The. 1933. Men, Matters, and Memories. Vol 41, no. 480.

Orchid Review, The. 1900. Mycorrhizas of Orchids. Vol. 8, no. 94.

Orchid Review, The. 1915. Orchid Culture and Evolution. Vol. 23, no. 267.

Orchid Review, The. 1922. Orchid Mycorrhiza. Vol. 30, no. 345.

Randolph, L. F. 1951. Chromosomes and Orchid Breeding. *Amer. Orch. Soc. Bull.* 20, no. 7, 8.

Rayner, Chevely. 1916. Recent Developments in the Study of Endophytic Mycorrhiza. *New Phytol.* 15, no. 8.

Rolfe, R. A. 1918. Root-Fungi of Orchids. *The Orch. Rev.* 26, nos. 301, 302.

Scully, Robert M., Jr. 1966. Aspects of Meristem Culture in the Epidendrum Alliance. *Tech. Paper* 823. Univ. of Hawaii Agric. Experiment Sta.

Stearn, William T. 1960. Two Thousand Years of Orchidology. Historical Session—*Proceedings of the Third World Orchid Conference.* Rochester, Kent, England: Staples Printer Ltd.

Wilson, Gurney. 1906. Fungus Co-operation in Orchid Roots. *The Orch. Rev.* 14, no. 161.

A Chronological Guide to Descriptive and Taxonomic Orchid Literature

PUBLISHED WORKS ON THE ORCHIDACEAE ARE DISPERSED THROUGHOUT BOtanical and horticultural literature. Many such treatises form part of the floras of different countries, while others are less technical, being devoted to the popularization of orchids on the aesthetic level. Larger works, given exclusively to orchids, have been compiled by eminent botanists and number among the most valuable contributions to orchidology. The chronological listing given here contains many of each, and includes works published in a host of languages—Latin, English, French, German, and other European and Oriental languages. Cultural publications are largely omitted in this listing, beyond those of early historic significance. This list is far from complete insofar as the descriptive literature of orchids is concerned, also, though as nearly as possible, it contains the most important of the published works on orchids.

1228	Chao Shih-ken. *Orchid Guide for Kuei-men and Chang-chou.*
1247	Wang Kuei-hsüeh. *Wang's Orchid Guide.*
1552	*Badianus Manuscript.*
1590	Chou Lu-ching. *Secrets in Orchid Culture.*
1600	(Author unknown.) *A Monthly Cultivation Book for Orchids.*
	(Author unknown.) *An Orchid Guide for Fukien.*
1605	Carolus Clusius. *Exoticum Libri Decem.*
1611–93	Mao Hsiang. *Orchid Talks.*
1633	John Gerard. *Herball or Generall Historie of Plantes.*
1640	John Parkinson. *Theatricum Botanicum.*
1698	Paul Hermann. *Paradisus Batavus.*
1702–09	Jacob Petiver. *Garophylacium.*

1703   H. A. Rheede tot Draakenstein. *Hortus Indicus Malabaricus.*
1704   George Joseph Kamel. *Ray's Historia Plantarum* (Appendix).
1712   Engelbert Kaempfer. *Amoenitatum exoticarum . . . Fasculi.*
1728   Jo-an Matsuoka. *Igansai-ranpin.*
1732   John Martyn. *Historia Plantarum Rariorum.*
1737   Philip Miller. *Gardener's Dictionary.*
1741–50 G. E. Rumphius. *Herbarium Amboinensis.*
1760   Philip Miller. *Figures of the Most Beautiful Plants.*
1753   Linnaeus. *Species Plantarum,* ed. 1.
1762   Linnaeus. *Species Plantarum,* ed. 2.
1789   A. L. Jussieu. *Genera Plantarum.*
1794   Hipólito Ruiz and José Antonio Pavón. *Florae Peruvianae et Chilensis Prodromus.*
1797   Hipólito Ruiz and José Antonio Pavón. *Florae Peruvianae et Chilensis Prodromus.* Ed. 2 (Orchidaceae, Clas. 20, Gynandria diandria).
1799   Olof Swartz. *Dianome Epidendri generis Linn.* in Schrader's *Journal fur die Botanik.* Vol. 2, pt. 4.
1800   Olof Swartz. In Kongl. *Vetenskaps Academiens nya Handlingar,* Stockholm. Vol. XXI.
1805   Olof Swartz. *Genera et Species Orchidearum systematice Coordinatarum.* Schrader's neues Journal.
         C. L. Wildenow. *Species Plantarum,* Vol. 4.
1810   Robert Brown. *Prodromus Florae Novae Hollandiae.*
1813   Robert Brown. In Aiton's *Hortus Kewensis,* ed. 2, Vol. 5.
1815–23 S. Edwards and others. *Botanical Register.*
1815–25 Humboldt, Bonpland and Kunth. *Nova Genera et Species Plantarum,* Vols. 1, 7.
1817   L. C. Richard. *De Orchideis europaeis.*
1817–33 Conrad Loddiges. *Botanical Cabinet.*
1818–20 John Bellenden Ker. *Select Orchideae from the Cape of Good Hope.* In *Journal of Sciences and Arts.* Vols. 5, 6, 8, 9.
1821–25 John Lindley. *Collectanea Botanica.*
1822   Aubert du Petit-Thouars. *Histoire particulière des plantes orchidées recueilliés sur les trois îles australes d'Afrique, de France, de Bourbon et de Madagascar.*
1824–25 P. de La Llave and Johannis Lexarza. *Novarum Vegetabilium Descriptiones.* Vol. 2.
1824–47 John Lindley. *Botanical Register.*
1825   C. L. Blume. *Bijdragen tot de Flora van Nederlandsche Indie* Stuk 6, 7, 8.
1826   John Lindley. *Orchidearum Sceletos.*
         C. Gaudischaud. *Voyage autour du monde.*
1827   Br da. *Genera et Species Orchidearum quas in Java collegerunt Kuhl et Van Hasselt.*
1827–64 W. J. Hooker. *Botanical Magazine.*
1828   Achille Richard. *Monographie des orchidées des îles de France et de Bourbon.*
1830–32 Nathaniel Wallich. *Plantae Asiaticae Rariores.*
1830–38 John Lindley and Francis Bauer. *Illustrations of Orchidaceous Plants.*
1830–40 John Lindley. *The Genera and Species of Orchidaceous Plants.*

1831   Robert Brown. *Observations on the Organs and Mode of Fecundation in Orchideae and Asclepiadeae.*

1832   William Roxburgh. *Flora Indica*, Vol. 3.

1834–49   Joseph Paxton. *Magazine of Botany.*

1835   John Lindley. *Upon the Cultivation of Epiphytes of the Orchid Tribe.* Trans. Hort. Soc. of London. Vol. 1, ser. 2.

1835–45   E. Poppig and S. Endlicher. *Nova Genera et Species quas in regno chilense, peruviano, et in terra amazonica collegerunt.*

1836   S. Endlicher. *Genera Plantarum.*
         John Lindley. *Notes on the Cape Orchidaceae of Drege,* in Companion to Bot. Mag., Vol. 2.
         John Lindley. *Notes on some Genera and Species of American Orchidaceae* Bot. Mag., Vol. 2.

1836–38   E. Poppig and S. Endlicher. *Nova Genera ac Species Plantarum.* 1 (Orchidaceae), 1836; 2 (Orchidaceae), 1837–38.

1837–40   Knowles and Westcott. *Floral Cabinet.*

1837–43   James Bateman. *The Orchidaceae of Mexico and Guatemala.*

1838–41   John Lindley. *Sertum Orchidaceum.*

1840–56   Robert Wight. *Icones Plantarum Indiae occidentalis.* Vols. 3, 5.

1841   A. Richard. *Monographie des orchidées recueilliés dans la chaine des Nilgherries, Annales des Sciences Naturelles.* Vol. 15, ser. 2.

1842–45   John Lindley. *A Century of New Genera and Species of Orchidaceae.* Annals of Natural History. Vols. 10, 12, 15.

1845–82   L. Van Houtte. *Flore des Serres et des Jardins de l'Europe.*

1846   John Lindley. *Orchidaceae Lindenianae.*

1847   A. Richard. *Tentamen Florae Abyssinicae.*

1847–52   Heinrich G. Reichenbach. *Orchidographische Beiträge.* Linnaea. Vols. 19–25.

1848   C. L. Blume. *Rumphia*, Vol. 4.

1848–60   Heinrich G. Reichenbach. *Orchideae per annos 1846–55 descriptae.* Walper's Annales. Vols. 1, 3, 6.

1849   G. Gordon. *Notes on the Proper Treatment of Epiphytal Orchids.* Journ. Hort. Soc. London. Vol. 4.
         C. L. Blume. *Collection des orchidées les plus remarquables de l'archipel indien et du Japon.*

1850   In de la Sagra, D. Ramon. *Historia Física, Política y Natural de la Isla de Cuba.* Pt. 2, 11, Botanica (Orchidaceae).

1851   W. Griffiths. *Notulae ad Plantas asiaticas.* Vol. 3.

1851–53   John Lindley. In *Paxton's Flower Garden.*

1852   F. Josst. *Beschreibung und Cultur der tropischen Orchideen.*
         Heinrich G. Reichenbach. *De pollinis Orchidearum genesi ac structura et de Orchideis in artem ac systema redigendis.*

1852–57   Heinrich G. Reichenbach. *Garten-Orchideen,* in Botanische Zeitung, Vols. 10–15.

1852–59   John Lindley. *Folia Orchidacea.*

1852–94   Benjamin S. Williams. *The Orchid Grower's Manual* (7 editions).

1853   Theodor Irmisch. *Beiträge zur Biologie und Morphologie der Orchideen.*
         J. G. Beer. *Practisches Studium an der Familie der Orchideen.*
         W. H. De Vriese. *Illustrations d'orchidées des Indes orientales.*

1854–93   C. Lemaire, E. André and others. *L'Illustration horticole.*

1854–94　E. Regel and L. Witttmack. *Gartenflora.*
1854–1900　Heinrich G. Reichenbach. *Xenia Orchidacea.* Vol. 1, 1854–1858; vol. 2, 1862–1874; vol. 3 (with Fritz Kraenzlin), 1878–1900.
1856　　　Prillieux et Riviere. *Observations sur la germination d'une orchidée.* Annales des Science naturelles. Vol. 4, ser. 1.
　　　　　J. M. Fabre. *Sur la germination des ophrydées, etc.* Ann. Sci. Nat. Vol. 5, ser. 4.
1857　　　T. Moore. *Illustrations of Orchidaceous Plants.*
1857–58　John Lindley. *Contributions to the Orchidology of India.* Journ. Linn. Soc. Vols. 1, 3.
1858　　　C. L. Blume. *Flora javanica nova series.* Vol. 1.
1859　　　Prillieux. *Sur la dehiscence du fruit des orchidées.*
1860　　　Joseph D. Hooker. *Orchideae of Tasmania.* Flora Tasmanica. Vol. 2.
　　　　　Jean Linden. *Pescatorea, Iconographie des orchidées.*
1861　　　C. Oudemans. *Ueber die Luftwurzeln der Orchideen.*
1862　　　Charles Darwin. *Fertilisation of Orchids by Insects.*
　　　　　M. P. Duchartre. *Note sur le Phalaenopsis Schilleriana.* Journal de la Société impériale d'Horticulture. Vol. 8.
1862–84　Robert Warner. *Select Orchidaceous Plants.* Vols 1, 2, 3.
1863　　　J. G. Beer. *Beiträge zur Morphologie und Biologie der Orchideen.* Grisebach. *Flora of the British West Indian Islands.*
1863–78　George Bentham. *Orchideae of Australia.* Flora australiensis, Vol. 6.
1864　　　H. Leitgeb. *Ueber die Luftwurzeln der Orchideen.* Denkschrift Wiener Academie.
　　　　　J. Meyen. *Luxemburg Orchideen.*
1864–74　James Bateman. *Monograph of Odontoglossum.*
1864–94　J. D. Hooker. *Botanical Magazine.*
1865　　　Crüger. *Fertilisation of the Flowers of Coryanthes macrantha.* Journ. Linn. Soc. Vol. 8.
1866　　　Th. Wolfe. *Beiträge zur Entwickelungsgeschichte der Orchideenblüthe.* Pringheim's Jahrbuch. Vol. 4.
1867　　　J. Bateman. *A Second Century of Orchidaceous Plants.*
　　　　　J. D. Hooker. *Orchideae of New Zealand.* New Zealand Flora.
1869　　　H. G. Reichenbach. *Beiträge zur Orchideenkunde Central-Amerikas.*
1869–78　and 1882. W. Wilson Saunders and H. G. Reichenbach. *Refugium Botanicum.* Vol. 2.
1869–88　H. G. Reichenbach. *New Garden Orchids. Gardeners' Chronicle.*
1871　　　P. Van Tieghem. *Recherches sur la structure du pistil.* Les Memoires de l'Institut de France. Vol. 21.
　　　　　H. G. Reichenbach. *Beiträge zur systematischen Pflanzenkunde.*
1873　　　H. G. Reichenbach. *Enumeration of the Orchids collected by Rev. C. Parish in the neighbourhood of Moulmein.* Trans. Linn. Soc. Vol. 30.
1874　　　F. W. Burbidge. *Cool Orchids and How to Grow Them.*
1875　　　S. Jennings. *Orchids and How to Grow Them in India and other tropical climates.*
1875–88　R. D. Fitzgerald. *Australian Orchids.*
1876　　　Edward S. Rand. *Orchids grown at Glen Ridge, near Boston, Massachusetts.*

1877   H. G. Reichenbach. *Orchidiographische Beiträge.* Linneae. Vol. 7.
1877–82 Barbosa Rodriguez. *Genera et Species Orchidearum novarum.* Part 1, 1877; Part 2, 1881–82.
1877–87 E. Pfitzer. *Beobachtungen über Bau und Entwickelung der Orchideen.* Natürlicher Verein Heidelberg. Flora der deutschen botanischen Gesellschaft.
1878   Du Buysson. *L'Orchidophile.* Traité théorique et pratique sur la culture des orchidées.
         M. R. Gérard. *Sur l'homologie et le diagramme des orchidées.*
1879   A. Grisebach. *Symbolae ad floram argentinam.* In Abhandl. Königl. Gesell. Wissen. Göttingen 24.
         M. Treub. *Embryogénie de quelques Orchidées.*
1880   E. De Puydt. *Les orchidées, histoire iconographique.*
1881   G. Bentham. *Notes on Orchideae.* Journ. Linn. Soc. Vol. 18.
         E. Pfitzer. *Grundzüge einer vergleichenden Morphologie der Orchideen.*
1881–85 W. B. Hemsley. *List of Garden Orchids. Gardeners' Chronicle.*
1881–93 Godefroy-Lebeuf. *L'Orchidophile. Journal des Amateurs d'Orchidées.*
1882   Harry Bolus. *Notes on Some Cape Orchids.* Journ. Linn. Soc. Vol. 19.
1882–94 R. Warner and B. S. Williams. *The Orchid Album.* Vols. 1–11.
1883   G. Bentham and J. D. Hooker. *Genera Plantarum.* Vol. 3, Orchideae.
1884   E. Boissier. Flora Orientalis. *Orchideae.* Vol. 5.
         H. Bolus. *Orchids of South Africa.* Journ. Linn. Soc. Vol. 20.
         H. O. Forbes. *On the Contrivances for ensuring Self-fertilisation in some tropical Orchids.* Journ. Linn. Soc. Vol. 21.
         H. Baldwin. *The Orchids of New England.*
1884–87 H. Bolus. *Contributions to South-African Botany.* Pt. 1, 1884; Pt. 2, 1885; Pt. 3, 1887. Journ. Linn. Soc. Bot.
1884–94 L. Linden and others. *Lindenia, une iconographie des orchidées.*
1885   Henry N. Ridley. *The Orchids of Madagascar.* Journ. Linn. Soc. Vol. 21.
         H. Bolus. *Orchids of South Africa.* Journ. Linn. Soc. Vol. 22.
         H. G. Reichenbach. *Ueber das System der Orchideen.* Bulletin du Congrès internationale de St. Petersburgh.
1886   H. N. Ridley. *The Genus Liparis.* Journ. Linn. Soc. Vol. 22.
         E. Pfitzer. *Morphologisches Studium über die Orchideenblume.*
         M. T. Masters. *On the Floral Conformation of the genus Cypripedium.* Journ. Linn. Soc. Vol. 22.
         A. D. Webster. *British Orchids.*
1886–92 Robert A. Rolfe. *Garden Orchids. Gardeners' Chronicle.*
1887   Robert A. Rolfe. *Bigeneric Orchid Hybrids.* Journ. Linn. Soc. Vol. 24.
         E. Pfitzer. *Entwurf eines natürlichen Systems der Orchideen.*
         H. N. Ridley. *A Review of the Genera Microstylis and Malaxis.* Journ. Linn. Soc. Vol. 24.
         M. Mobius. *Anatomie der Orchideen.* Pringsheim's Jahrbuch. Vol. 18.

1888   H. N. Ridley. *Notes on Self-fertilisation and Cleistogamy in Orchids.* Journ. Linn. Soc. Vol. 24.

H. Bolus. *South African Orchids.* Journ. Linn. Soc. Vol. 25.

H. Bolus. *The Orchids of the Cape Peninsula.* In Trans. S. Afr. Phil. Soc. Vol. 5, pt. 1.

R. A. Rolfe. *A Morphological and Systematic Review of the Apostasieae.* Journ. Linn. Soc. Vol. 25.

E. Pfitzer. *Untersuchungen über Bau und Entwickelung der Orchideenblüthe.* Pringsheim's Jahrbuch. Vol. 19.

1888–94   F. Sander. *Reichenbachia, Orchids Illustrated and Described.*

1889–90   J. D. Hooker. *Orchideae of British India.* Flora of British India. Vols. 5, 7.

1889–93   R. A. Rolfe. *List of Garden Orchids.* Gardeners' Chronicle.

1889–96   F. H. Woolward. *The Genus Masdevallia.*

1890   R. A. Rolfe. *On the Sexual Forms of Catasetum.* Journ. Linn. Soc. Vol. 27.

W. Watson and W. Bean. *Orchids, their Culture and Management.*

1891   H. N. Ridley. *The Genus Bromheadia and Two new genera of Orchids from the East Indies.* Journ. Linn. Soc. Vol. 28.

1891–93   Marquess of Lothian and Miss F. H. Woolward. *The Genus Masdevallia.* Pts. 1–5.

1891–94   R. A. Rolfe. *New Garden Orchids, Decades I–VII.* Kew Bulletin.

1892   Stein. *Orchideenbuch: Beschreibung, Abbildung und Kulturanweisung.*

1893   D. Bois. *Les Orchidées.*

The Orchid Review, an illustrated monthly journal. R. A. Rolfe, ed.

C. Moore. *The Orchideae of New South Wales.* Flora of New South Wales.

Max Schulze. *Die Orchideen Deutschlands, Deutsch-Oesterreichs und der Schweiz.*

Fritz Kraenzlin. *Beiträge zu einer Monographie der Gattung Habenaria.* Engler's Botanisches Jahrbuch. Vol. 16.

Fritz Kraenzlin. *Orchidaceae Africanae.* Engler's Botanisches Jahrbuch. Vol. 17.

1893–1913   H. Bolus. *Icones Orchidearum Austro-africanarum extra-tropicarum.* Vol. 1, 1893–96; vol. 2, 1911; vol. 3, 1913.

A. Cogniaux. Martius' *Flora Brasiliensis Orchidaceae.*

1894   Frederick Boyle. *About Orchids, A Chat.*

H. A. Burberry. *The Amateur Orchid Grower's Guide Book.*

O. de Kerchove. *Le livre des orchidées.*

M. Schulze. *Die Orchidaceen Deutschlands, Deutsch-Oesterreichs und der Schweiz.*

1895   B. Grant. *The Orchids of Burma.*

J. D. Hooker. *A Century of Indian Orchids.* In Ann. Roy. Bot. Gard., Calcutta. Vol. 5.

R. Schlechter. *Beiträge zur Kenntnis neuer und kritischer Orchideen aus Südafrica.* In Engler, Bot. Jahrb. 20, Beibl. 50.

1895–1914   F. Kraenzlin. *Orchidaceae Africanae.* In Engler, Bot. Jahrb., pp. 22–51.

1896   H. N. Ridley. *An enumeration of all Orchideae hitherto recorded from Borneo.* Journ. Linn. Soc. Bot. Vol. 31.
        H. N. Ridley. *The Orchideae and Apostasiaceae of the Malay Peninsula.* Journ. Linn. Soc. Bot. Vol. 31.

1897   R. Schlechter. *Orchidaceae africanae novae vel minus cognitae.* In Engler, Bot. Jahrb., 24.

1897–98 R. A. Rolfe. In Thiselton-Dyer, Flora of Tropical Africa (*Orchideae*, vol. 7).

1897–1914 F. Kraenzlin. *Orchidaceae africanae.* In Engler, Bot. Jahrb., 24, 48, 51.

1898   G. King and R. Pantling. *The Orchids of the Sikkim-Himalaya.* In Ann. Roy. Bot. Gard. Calcutta. Vol. 8.

1899   H. Correvon. *Album des orchidées de l'Europe centrale et septentrionale.*

1901   *Sander's Orchid Guide.*

1904   W. Mueller and F. Kraenzlin. *Abbildungen der in Deutschland und den angrenzenden Gebieten . . . Orchideen-Arten.*
        G. G. Niles. *Bog-trotting for Orchids.*

1905   W. H. Gibson and H. L. Jelliffe. *Our Native Orchids.*
        J. J. Smith. *Die Orchideen von Ambon.*

1905–22 Oakes Ames. Fasc. 1, 1905; Fasc. 7, 1922. *Orchidaceae: Illustrations and Studies of the Family Orchidaceae.*

1905–39 J. J. Smith. *Die Orchideen von Java.*

1906   A. Cogniaux. *Notes sur les orchidées du Brésil et des régions voisines.* Bull. Soc. Roy. Belg., p. 43.
        J. F. Duthie. *The orchids of the North-western Himalaya.* Ann. Roy. Bot. Gard., Calcutta. Vol. 9.

1907   H. N. Ridley. Materials for a Flora of the Malayan Peninsula. *Orchideae.* Pt. 1.

1908   E. G. Camus, P. Bergon and A. Camus. *Monographie des orchidées de l'Europe, de l'Afrique septentrionale, de l'Asie Mineure, etc.*

1908   *Orchidaceae*, in Gray's New Manual of Botany. 7th ed.

1909   M. R. Goyena. Flora Nicaraguense (*Orchidaceae*).

1909–10 A. Cogniaux. In Urban, I. Symbolae Antillanae (*Orchidaceae*) 6.

1909–34 J. J. Smith. *Die Orchideen von Niederländisch Neu-Guinea.*

1910   O. Ames. *The genus Habenaria in North America.* Orchidaceae 4.
        W. Fawcett and A. B. Rendle. Flora of Jamaica. 1 (*Orchidaceae*).
        C. Reiche. *Orchidaceae Chilenses.* Anal. Mus. Nac. Chile. 2nd sec. Bot., no. 18.

1910–11 R. Schlechter. *Revision der Orchidaceen von Deutsch-Samoa.* Fedde Repert. 9.

1911   Richard S. Rogers. *An Introduction to the Study of South Australian Orchids.*
        R. Schlechter. *Beiträge zur Kenntnis der Orchidaceen-Flora von Sumatra.* Engler, Bot. Jahrb. 45, Beibl. 104.
        R. Schlechter. *Zur Kenntnis der Orchidaceen von Celebes.* Fedde Repert. 10.

1911–23 R. Schlechter. *Die Orchidaceen von Deutsch Neu-Guinea.* Fedde Repert. Beih. 1, 1911–14; *Figuren-Atlas zu den Orchidaceen von*

Deutsch Neu-Guinea, Fedde Repert. Beih. 21, 1923.

1912   R. Schlechter. *Plantae Chinenses Forrestianae.* Notes Roy. Bot. Gard., Edinburgh 24.

1912–13   R. A. Rolfe. In Thiselton-Dyer, Flora Capensis (*Orchideae*, vol. 5). J. J. Smith. *Vorläufige Beschreibungen neuer papuanischer Orchideen.* Pts. 6 (1912), 11 (1913), in Fedde Repert. 11–12.

1913   R. Schlechter. *Orchidacees de Madagascar* (Orchidaceae Perrierianae madagascarienses) in Anal. Mus. Col. Mars. Ser. 3, 1.

1914   O. Ames. *The Orchids of Guam.* In Phil. Journ. Sci. C. Bot. Vol. 9. F. Kraenzlin. In F. Sarasin and J. Roux. *Orchidaceae von Neu-Caledonien und den Loyalty-Inseln.* Nova Caledonia, Bot. 1.

1914–21   R. Schlechter. *Die Orchidaceen von Mikronesien.* In Engler, Bot. Jahrb. 52 (1914); 56 (1921).

1914–27   F. Kraenzlin. *Die Orchideen.* Ed. 1, 1914–1915; ed. 2, 1927.

1915   O. Ames. *The genera and species of Philippine Orchids.* Orchidaceae V.

        R. Schlechter. *Kritische Aufzählung der bisher von Madagaskar, den Maskarenen, Komoren und Seychellen bekanntgewordenen Orchidaceen.* Beih. Bot. Centralbl. Vol. 33.

        R. Schlechter. *Orchidaceae Stolzianne, ein Beitrag zur Orchideen-Kunde des Nyassa-Landes.* Engler, Bot. Jahrb. Vol. 53.

1916   R. Schlechter. *Orchidaceae Perrierianae* (Collectio secunda). Beih. Bot. Centralbl. Vol. 34, abt. 2.

        R. Schlechter. *Herzog's bolivianische Pflanzen III.* In Meded. van's Rijksherbar., Leiden. No. 29.

1917   L Hauman. *Quelques orchidées de l'Argentine.* Anal. Mus. Nac. Hist. Nat., Buenos Aires. Vol. 29.

1917–45   J. J. Smith. *Orchidaceae novae malayenses.* Pts. 8–18, in Bull. Jard. Bot. Buitenz., Fedde Repert. and Blumea.

1918   F. C. Hoehne. *Orchidaceas novas e menos connecidas dos Arredores de São Paulo.*

        R. Schlechter. *Kritische Aufzählung der bisher aus Zentral-Amerika bekanntgewordenen Orchidaceen.* Beih. Bot. Centralbl. Vol. 36, abt. 2.

        R. Schlechter. *Versuch einer natürlichen Neuordnung der afrikanischen angraekoiden Orchidaceen.* Beih. Bot. Centralbl. 36 (2).

1919   R. Schlechter. *Orchideologiae Sino-Japonicae Prodromus.* Fedde Repert. Beih. 4.

1919–22   R. Schlechter. *Die Orchideenfloren der südamerikanischen Kordillerenstaaten.* 1, Venezuela, Fedde Repert. Beih. 6, 1919; 2, Colombia, Fedde Repert. Beih. 7, 1920; 3, Ecuador, Fedde Repert. Beih. 8, 1921; 4, Peru, Fedde Repert. Beih. 9, 1921; 5, Bolivia, Fedde Repert. Beih. 10, 1922.

1919–26   R. Schlechter. *Beiträge zur Kenntnis der Orchidaceenflora von Parana.* Fedde Repert. 16, 23.

1920   O. Ames and C. Schweinfurth. *The Orchids of Mount Kinabalu, British North Borneo.* In Orchidaceae 6.

1921   O. Ames. *A Bibliographic Enumeration of Bornean Plants.* Journ. Straits Branch Roy. Asiat. Soc. Special No. (Orchidaceae).

L. Hauman. *Notes sur le genre "Chloraea" Lindley.* Mém. Acad. Roy. Belg.

L. Hauman. *Orchidées Argentines.* Anal. Soc. Cient. Argent. Vol. 90.

1921–29   E. G. Camus and A. Camus. *Iconographie des orchidées d'Europe et du bassin méditerranéen.*

1922   O. Ames. *A discussion of Pogonia and its allies in the northeastern United States.* Orchidaceae 7.

R. S. Rogers. *South Australian Orchids.* In J. M. Black, Flora of South Australia.

R. Schlechter. *Beiträge zur Orchideenkunde von Zentral-Amerika,* 1, *Orchidaceae Powellianae Panamensis.* Fedde Repert. Beih. 17.

R. Schlechter. *Neue Orchidaceen Papuasiens.* Engler, Bot. Jahrb. Vol. 58.

1922–1930   O. Ames and C. Schweinfurth. *Schedulae Orchidianae,* Nos. 1–10.

1923   R. Schlechter. *Beiträge zur Orchideenkunde von Zentral-Amerika,* 2. *Additamenta ad Orchideologiam Costaricensem.* Fedde Repert. Beih. 19.

1924   O. Ames. *An Enumeration of the Orchids of the United States and Canada.*

H. N. Ridley. *The Flora of the Malay Peninsula. Orchideae* 4.

R. Schlechter. *Beiträge zur Orchideenkunde von Colombia.* Fedde Repert. Beih. 27.

R. Schlechter. *Contributions to South African orchideology.* Ann. Transvaal Mus. Vol. 10.

R. Schlechter. Plantae Sinenses. *Orchidaceae,* in Meddel. fran Göteborgs Botaniska Trädgard. Vol. 1.

1924–25   O. Ames. *Enumeration of Philippine Apostasiaceae and Orchidaceae.* Enum. Phil. Flow. Pl. (Bur. Sci. Pub. 18, Orchidaceae.)

R. Schlechter. *Orchidaceae Perrierianae, Ein Beitrag zur Orchideenkunde der Insel Madagaskar.* Fedde Repert. Beih. 33.

1925   R. Schlechter. *Die Orchideenflora von Rio Grande do Sul.* Fedde Repert. Beih. 35.

J. J. Smith. *Die Orchideen der zweiten Frankfurter Sunda-Expedition,* 1909–10. Meded. van's Rijksherbar., Leiden, 53.

C. B. Tahourdin. *Native Orchids of Britain.*

1925–27   O. Ames. In P. C. Standley and S. Calderón. *Lista preliminar de las Plantas de El Salvador (Orchidaceae).*

1925–39   G. Keller and R. Schlechter. *Monographie und Iconographie der Orchideen Europas und des Mittelmeergebietes,* 1 (Schlechter, 1925–28); 2 (Keller and von Soó, 1930–36); 3 (Keller, 1931–35); 4 (Keller and von Soó, 1935–38); 5 (Keller, 1939). Fedde Repert. Sonderbeih. A.

1926   P. Brühl. *A Guide to the Orchids of Sikkim.*

F. Kraenzlin. *Monographie der Gattung Polystachya,* Hook. Offprint from Fedde Repert. 39.

J. J. Smith. *The Orchidaceae of Dr. W. Kaudern's expedition to Selebes,* 1917–1920. Svensk Bot. Tidskrift 20.

1927   E. Coleman. *Pollination of the orchid Cryptostylis leptochila F.v.M.*

Vict. Nat. Vol. 44.

J. J. Smith. *Beiträge zur Kenntnis der Flora von Borneo.* Mitteil. aus dem Instit. fur allgem. Bot. Hamburg 7 (*Orchidaceae*)

1928   O. Ames. In Standley. *Flora of the Panama Canal Zone.* (*Orchidaceae*).

E. E. Pescott. *The Orchids of Victoria.*

Jany Renz. *Zur Kenntnis der griechischen Orchideen.* Fedde Repert. 25.

J. J. Smith. *Additions to the orchid-flora of Selebes.* Bull. Jard. Bot. Buitenzorg. Ser. 3, 10.

J. J. Smith. *Orchidaceae Buruenses.* Bull. Jard. Bot. Buitenz. Ser. 3, 9.

1928–40   R. Schlechter and G. Keller. *Monographie und Iconographie der Orchideen Europas und des Mittelmeergebietes.*

1929   E. Coleman. *Pollination of an Australian Orchid by the male ichneumonid Lissopimpla semipunctata Kirby.* Trans. Entomol. Soc. Lond. 76 (2).

F. C. Hoehne. *Contribuições para o conhecimento da flora orchidologica brasílica.* Pt. 1, 1929; pt. 2, 1930. Archiv. Instit. Biolog., 2 and 3.

F. Kraenzlin. *Neu-Caledonische Orchidaceen.* Viertel. Naturf. Gesell., Zurich, 74.

Jany Renz. *Über neue Orchideen von Rhodos, Cypern und Syrien.* Fedde Repert. 27.

R. Schlechter. *Figuren-Atlas zu den Orchideenfloren der südamerikanischen Kordillerenstaaten.* Fedde Repert. Beih. 57.

R. Schlechter. *Orchidaceae Buchtienianae.* Fedde Repert. 27.

1929–38   J. J. Smith. *Icones Orchidacearum Malayensium,* in Bull. Jard. Bot. Buitenz. Suppl. Vol. 2, 1929–34; vol. 3, 1938.

1930   E. H. Pelloe. *West Australian Orchids.*

Jany Renz. *Beiträge zur Orchideenflora der Insel Kreta.* Fedde Repert. 28.

H. M. R. Rupp. *Guide to the Orchids of New South Wales.*

R. Schlechter. *Blütenanalysen neuer Orchideen, 1. Südamerikanische Orchideen.* Fedde Repert. Beih. 57.

J. J. Smith. *On a collection of Orchidaceae from the northern Moluccas.* Bull. Jard. Bot. Buitenz. Vol. 11, ser. 3.

1931   F. Kraenzlin. *Orchidacearum Sibiriae Enumeratio.* Fedde Repert. Beih. 65.

E. Nelson and H. Fischer. *Die Orchideen Deutschlands und der angrenzenden Gebiete.*

R. Schlechter. *Blütenanalysen neuer Orchideen, 2, Mittelamerikanische Orchideen.* Fedde Repert. Beih. 59, 2.

1931–36   K. Schuster. *Orchidacearum iconum index.* Fedde Repert. Beih. 60.

J. J. Smith. *Additions to our knowledge of the orchid flora of Borneo.* Brittonia 1.

J. J. Smith. *On a collection of Orchidaceae from Central Borneo.* Bull. Jard. Bot. Buitenz. Ser. 3, 11.

1932   Jany Renz. *Die Orchideenflora von Ostkreta* (Sitia). Fedde Repert. 30.

R. Schlechter. *Blütenanalysen neuer Orchideen, III. Afrikanische und madagassische Orchideen.* Fedde Repert. Beih. 68.

J. J. Smith. *Orchidaceae selebenses Kjellbergianae.* Bot. Jahrb. 65.

1933   E. Coleman. *Pollination of orchids: genus Prasophyllus.* Vict. Nat. 49.

M. J. Godfery and H. M. Godfery. *Monograph and Iconograph of Native British Orchidaceae.*

J. J. Smith. *Enumeration of the Orchidaceae of Sumatra and neighboring islands.* Fedde Repert. 32.

1933–34   R. Schlechter. *Blütenanalysen neuer Orchideen, IV. Indische und malesische Orchideen.* Fedde Repert. Beih. 74.

1933–56   Victor S. Summerhayes. *African Orchids.* Kew Bull. Vols. 5–9; Vol. 18–23.

1934   J. J. Smith. *Beiträge zur Flora von Papuasien XX.* Bot. Jahrb. 66.

1936   O. Ames. *The Genus Epidendrum in the United States and Middle America* (with F. Tracy Hubbard and C. Schweinfurth).

F. C. Hoehne. *Orchidaceas dos Herbarios de Alexandre Curt Brade e do Museo Nacional.* Bol. Mus. Nac. 12.

1937   O. Ames. In P. C. Standley, *Flora of Costa Rica* (*Orchidaceae*, pt. 1). Field Mus. Nat. His. 18, Publ. 391.

F. C. Hoehne. *Orchidaceae novae brasilienses.* Engler, Bot. Jahrb. 68.

1938   J. Acuña. *Catálogo Descriptivo de las Orquídeas Cubanas.* Bol. Técn. 60. Estación Experimental Agronómica.

1939   H. Stehlé. *Flore Descriptive des Antilles Françaises.* Vol. 1. *Les Orchidales.*

1940–53   F. C. Hoehne. *Flora Brasilica* (*Orchidaceae*) 12. Pt. 1 (genera 1–12), 1940; pt. 2 (genera 13–43), 1945; pt. 6 (genera 97–114), 1942; pt. 7 (genera 115–147), 1953.

1941–51   Charles Schweinfurth. *Orchidaceae peruvianae I–VIII.* Bot. Mus. Leafl. Harvard Univ. 9–15.

1942   W. H. Nicholls. *Additions to the Orchidaceae of Victoria.* Vict. Nat. 59.

H. M. R. Rupp. *Corybas or Corysanthes?* Vict. Nat. 59.

1943   H. M. R. Rupp. *The Orchids of New South Wales.*

1944   D. Deinum. *De Orchideen van Nederland.*

1946   Hermano Léon. *Flora de Cuba,* 1 (*Orquídeas*).

1946–49   L. O. Williams and P. H. Allen. In Woodson and Schery's *Flora of Panama. Orchidaceae,* Ann. Mo. Bot. Gard.

1947–49   W. H. Nicholls. *Additions to the Orchidaceae of Western Australia.* Vict. Nat. 64 and 65.

1948   O. Ames. *Orchids in Retrospect.*

Jany Renz. *Beiträge zur Kenntnis der süd- und zentralamerikanischen Orchideen.* Pt. 1. *Orchidaceae-Cranichidinae.* Candollea 11.

1949   F. C. Hoehne. *Iconografia de Orchidaceas do Brasil.*

1950   R. S. Adamson and T. M. Salter. *Flora of the Cape Peninsula. Orchidaceae.*

D. S. Correll. *Native Orchids of North America North of Mexico.* Chronica Botanica. Vol. 26.

1951   L. O. Williams. *The Orchidaceae of Mexico.* In parts in Ceiba.

W. H. Nicholls. *Orchids of Australia.*
V. S. Summerhayes. *Wild Orchids of Britain.*

1952   Reginald S. Davis and Mona Lisa Steiner. *Philippine Orchids.*

1952–53 O. Ames and D. S. Correll. *Orchids of Guatemala.* Nos. 1, 2, Fieldiana: Botany.

1953   R. E. Holttum. A Revised Flora of Malaya. Vol. 1, *Orchids of Malaya.*

1955   A. Duperrex. *Orchidées d'Europe.*

1958   Mariano Ospina H. *Orquídeas Colombianas.*

1958–61 Charles Schweinfurth. *Orchids of Peru.* Nos. 1, 2, 3, 4, Fieldiana: Botany.

1959–72 G. C. K. Dunsterville and L. A. Garay. *Venezuelan Orchids Illustrated.* Vols. I, II, III, IV, V.

1960   Richard Evans Schultes. *Native Orchids of Tobago and Trinidad.*

1964   Frederick W. Case, Jr. *Orchids of the Western Great Lakes Region.*

1965   Alex D. Hawkes. *Encyclopedia of Cultivated Orchids.*

1966   E. A. C. L. E. Schelpe. *An Introduction to the South African Orchids.*

1966   H. Santapau and Z. Kapadia. *The Orchids of Bombay.*
L. van der Pijl and Calaway H. Dodson. *Orchid Flowers: Their Pollination and Evolution.*

1967   Calaway H. Dodson and Robert J. Gillespie. *The Biology of the Orchids.*

1968   Frank Piers. *Orchids of East Africa.*
V. S. Summerhayes. *Florida of Tropical East Africa—Orchidaceae (Part 1).*

1972   Carlyle A. Luer. *The Native Orchids of Florida.*

Please see page 317 for additional literature references.

Part II:

Makers of Orchid History

Introduction

FROM ITS COMMENCEMENT OVER A CENTURY AND A HALF AGO, THE HISTORY of orchid cultivation is replete with details of wonder and interest. The facts concerning the introduction of orchids to European glasshouses and gardens, the difficulties necessarily overcome before their cultivation was properly understood, and the long list of illustrious names who have each played an important part in orchidology, all combine to make the history of the Orchid Family an absorbing and unique study.

Interesting stories of accomplishment and adventure dramatize the lives and careers of those noteworthy men involved in the history of orchids. Some will be seen as pioneers forging through unexplored regions and, as a result, adding to an expanding knowledge of geography, ecology, taxonomy, and natural science. Others, flourishing with the crest of orchid interest prevalent in the middle 1800s, established markets of demand and supply in the fields of hobby and commercial orchid culture. And still others are honored for their technical contributions toward the development of scientific orchid study. The legacy which they have collectively bequeathed to present-day orchidists has added immensely to our knowledge of the orchid flora of the far reaches of the earth.

In most instances the major figures involved in the progression of achievement in orchidology have been humble, self-effacing, dedicated persons. Their accomplishments weren't always widely recognized or known—nor attended by plaudits and praise. Their lot in life was not always comfortable, particularly those who worked and collected in the wilds. Most of them left this life having never gained fame or fortune, and a few even died in near poverty. Yet, despite the infirmities and misfortune that befell many, it is almost certain that not one of them could have been as well satisfied in any other chosen field. Considering them as a body, the leading figures of orchid history have assuredly been a diverse and heterogeneous combination of courage, stamina, talent, determination, and knowledge. These individuals were intensely and devotedly involved in orchid interests, and each—through his studies, plant introductions, travels, and discoveries—has added invaluable data to the benefit of ensuing generations of orchidists.

Carl von Linné (1707-1778)

AMONG THE FIRST OUTSTANDING SYSTEMATIC BOTANISTS, CARL VON LINNÉ (known academically as Linnaeus) was certainly the most famous. Orchidology as a study was yet nonexistent in the eighteenth century; only as recently as 1731 had the first tropical orchid (*Bletia verecunda*) been carried back to England from one of the colonial outposts in the Bahamas. All plants interested Linnaeus, however, and by his remarkable accuracy of observation and philosophical mind, he became the most eminent naturalist-botanist of his time. His arrangement of plants based on a system of sexual relationships prepared the way for many later systems of classification.

Carl von Linné was born near Stenbrohult, in the province of Sma-land, Sweden, on 24 May 1707. He developed an early interest in botany and physiology, but his father, a Lutheran minister of small monetary means, was unable to further his son's interests. Nevertheless, in 1727 Linnaeus began the study of medicine at Lund, entering Upsala University the following year. Poverty continued to hinder him but through the assistance of Olaf Rudbeck he was able to continue his studies. In the meantime he was curator of the botanical gardens at the university.

In 1732 Linnaeus was given government aid to make a study of the flora of Sweden and Lapland, and soon thereafter he published his *Lapland Flora*. Later he studied mineralogy at Fahlun and in 1735 received a degree from the Harderwyk University in Holland. During his stay in Holland Linnaeus became associated with many eminent naturalists and, as a result of his botanical researches, especially as relating to plant classification, he occasionally announced original discoveries. His greatest and most important contribution was the development of the binomial system of nomenclature for scientific names of plants and animals—a "tool" which was widely adopted, revolutionizing all branches of biology.

His first treatise on orchids appeared as "Species Orchidum" in *Acta Societatis Regiae Scientiarum, Upsala*, 1740. In this work he established, for the first time on record, technical names for orchid genera and species. Those genera listed were *Cypripedium, Epidendrum, Limodorum, Liparis, Ophrys, Orchis*, and *Serapias*. The species given were *Cypripedium calceolus, Habenaria viridis* (as *Satyrium viride*), *Orchis coriophora, Orchis maculata*, and *Serapias rubra*.

After visits to Germany, France, and England, Linnaeus became president of the Stockholm Academy and in 1741 was made professor of medicine in Upsala. The following year saw him accept the professorship of botany.

In 1753 his important work *Species Plantarum* was published, in which he introduced his sexual system founded on the number and position of the stamens and pistils in plants. There was no designation of plant families as such, but all the orchids were placed in class XX under two categories: Gynandria (stamens adnate to the pistil) and Diandria (two stamens present). In this first edition he listed eight genera of orchids, including fifty-nine species within those genera.

In his *Genera Plantarum* (1754) the eight orchid genera then known were described at length. His diagnoses were commonly based on the descriptions by older botanists and herbalists, on the dried specimens of Clayton from Virginia, on the common species of Europe, and on his own earlier works. Throughout this work he adhered strictly to the binary system of nomenclature, i.e., the generic name (such as *Orchis*) followed by the specific name (as *spectabilis*). Of the eight genera described, all but *Epidendrum* were based on native European orchids that were entirely terrestrial. The genus *Epidendrum* was designed specifically to encompass epiphytic orchids and included *Vanilla, Arachnis, Luisia, Vanda, Brassavola, Broughtonia, Dendrobium, Cymbidium, Oncidium, Phalaenopsis,* and *Rhynchostylis.*

Other of his works include *The Natural System, Fundamental Botany,* and *Philosophy of Botany.*

He died on 10 January 1778.

References

Dillon, Gordon W. 1956. Some principles and family background. Understanding the Orchid Family—I. *Amer. Orch. Soc. Bull.* 25, no. 10.

Garay, Leslie A. and Sweet, Herman R. 1966. *Orchid Stamp News.* 2, no. 2.

Vermeulen, P. 1953. *Orchis spectabilis* L. The American Species of Orchis—I. *Amer. Orch. Soc. Bull.* 22, no. 6.

Worldscope Encyclopedia. 1953. Unabridged. Vol. 7. New York: The Universal Guild, Inc.

Joseph Banks (1743–1820)

THE HISTORY OF EACH SCIENCE WILL ALWAYS INCLUDE A PLACE OF RECOGnition for the patron as well as the practitioner. Heralding the era of worthwhile, full-scale plant collecting came Sir Joseph Banks, wealthy landowner and for forty-two years (1778–1820) president of the Royal Society. During that period he was the "dictator" of British botany, and may well be called the father of modern plant hunters as well as the promulgator of modern techniques of plant hunting.

Joseph Banks, son of a wealthy British landsman, was born in London in 1743. At the age of nine he was sent to Harrow School and from there to Eton at the age of thirteen. He was not considered a particularly good student; he especially detested the classical studies. Conversely, he was inordinately fond of sports and outdoor recreation, and was so enamored of play that he seemed incapable of concentrating on study. After a year at Eton he was still making no headway in scholastic work, but this was shortly to change. The turning point in his life stemmed seemingly from a sudden recognition of the wonders of nature with which his everyday activities brought him in contact. Becoming intensely interested in insects and plants, he resolved to study botany. He began his private herbarium at that youthful age, paying women who collected "simples" for the druggists' shops to bring him specimens also. When, during a school holiday he found *Gerard's Herball* on his mother's dressing table, he began to study seriously. He frequently visited the herb garden of the Apothecaries' Company, and with the aid of the book was able to identify many of the plants he observed there.

At the age of seventeen Banks entered Oxford. While he was attending the university, his father died, leaving the boy a large fortune and estate. Botany was not taught as a subject at Oxford, but with his inheritance Banks was able to hire a private tutor, Israel Lyons, astronomer and botanist. From Oxford the young scientist entered Cambridge, where he excelled so admirably in his studies of natural history that he gained an honorary degree at the age of twenty-one and was elected a Fellow of the Royal Society two years later. Discontinuing his work at Cambridge, he later left college in order to devote himself more fully to the study of natural science.

In 1766 an Admiralty vessel was sent to Newfoundland to investigate the fisheries there. Banks took the opportunity offered him to travel aboard the ship and thus had his first glimpse of adventure—a glimpse that merely served to whet his appetite for more. On this first journey the ship barely escaped sinking, and much of Banks' collection of Newfoundland plants was thrown overboard. A few hardy shrubs were the only tangible evidence remaining of the specimens collected.

He did not have to wait long for another voyage; the Royal Society had been planning an expedition to the South Seas, with Lieutenant James Cook chosen as commander and Banks as director. Banks, then only twenty-five, was overjoyed and immediately set about making preparations. Selecting the best personnel available, he engaged Dr. Daniel Solander to accompany him. He employed four artists and a complement of servants, as well as the best equipment available for the collections he hoped to make. Dipping unstintingly into his personal funds, he used up 10,000 pounds sterling. In a letter to Linnaeus, John Ellis wrote of Banks' preparations: "No people ever went to sea better fitted out for the purpose of natural history, or more elegantly."

On 25 August 1768 sail was set on H.M.S. *Endeavour* on this projected great voyage of exploration to the Pacific. The first collection of plants was made at Tierra del Fuego, on the southernmost tip of South America. At Tahiti the ship's astronomers took observations of the transit of Venus, and under Banks' direction the ship set southward toward the unknown. It was then 25 August 1769, the first anniversary of their departure from England. Six weeks more at sea and they reached New

Zealand and Australia, then known as New Holland. Here was another rich field for collecting, and the first landing place was so abundant that they named it Botany Bay. A jotting from Banks' journal reads:

3rd May (1770). Our collection of plants was now grown so immensely large that it was necessary that some extraordinary care should be taken of them, lest they should spoil in the books. I therefore devoted this day to that business and carried ashore all the drying paper, nearly 200 quires, of which the larger part was full, and spreading them upon a sail in the sun, kept them in this manner exposed the whole day, often turning them. 4th May. Myself in the woods, botanising as usual; now quite devoid of fear, as our neighbours have turned out such rank cowards.

Banks and Solander both contracted malaria in the Malay Archipelago and both nearly died. Two of their companions had previously died from exposure in January 1770 on Tierra del Fuego. And once again shipwreck was narrowly avoided off the Queensland coast. There were, indeed, difficulties to be met.

Finally, after nearly three years' absence, they turned homeward. This voyage, recorded in the journals of both Banks and Solander, opened new vistas of study for European botany. It was also the knowledge acquired through his experiences of plant discovery, the hazards of collecting, and plant preserving that entitled Banks to a preeminent position at Kew.

Princess Augusta, widow of Frederick Prince of Wales and mother of George III, had been developing a botanical garden in the grounds of Kew House since 1759. This was a great opportunity for Banks, because upon the Princess' death in 1772, George III immediately moved to Kew House from adjoining Richmond Lodge, joining the two properties to form Kew Gardens and inviting Banks to assist him as director. Banks made the most of this position, inaugurating the policy of close cooperation with the crown and sending out many collectors to bring back new plants for the gardens and herbarium.

Dr. Solander had meanwhile remained in Banks' employ as librarian and secretary, additionally sorting and classifying specimens. The two friends made a further expedition together—to Iceland, where they spent a month exploring Mt. Hecla and collecting plants. They returned via the Hebrides Islands, where they also did some collecting. In addition, they collected orchids when visiting Australia with Captain Cook's expedition of 1780 in H.M.S. *Endeavour*, the first to bring orchid specimens back from that region. In honor of his voyages and explorations, Banks was created a baronet in 1781.

Dr. Solander died in 1782, before the work of classifying the collected plants could be completed. Banks did not complete the work after Solander's death, nor did he publish his diary of that historic voyage. He had previously gone to great expense in getting plates prepared for the 800 plants collected, however. Engraved on copper, 700 were finished, and of the 360 New Zealand species collected, 200 plates were prepared. Botanists were puzzled, therefore, when these plates were not published, although the British Museum sent Thomas Kirk a set of impressions from the plates, some of them signed by Sydney Parkinson, the chief artist of the expedition who had died on the return voyage.

Banks, of course, was involved with many outside affairs. Hawkesworth had used much of Sir Joseph's diary notes in the compilation of *Cook's First Voyage*, which may have been at least partial reason why he did not publish them himself. Another reason was that after the death of Solander, Banks acted as chief counselor to all the king's scientific matters, which occupied much of his time. In this position he had control of the Royal Gardens at Kew.

Upon discussion of the colonization of New South Wales, Banks suggested that the site of the first settlement should be Botany Bay, and from the beginning he acted as patron of the infant colony. By his arrangements, several shipments of useful trees and plants were sent to the colony, and gardeners were appointed as caretakers. Again, here was opportunity to obtain new exotic plants for Kew Gardens. Collectors were dispatched and many rare plants were sent back. Collectors were also sent to the West Indies and the Cape, and Kew became the foremost place in the world as a botanical garden. Later, Sir Joseph established botanical gardens in Jamaica and Ceylon.

Banks consulted the king with the idea that breadfruit of the Pacific tropical islands might be grown with advantage in the West Indies. A commission was granted to undertake this venture, and Banks organized the preparations. He was personally acquainted with Lieutenant William Bligh, who at twenty-two was appointed master of H.M.S. *Resolution* under Captain Cook on his third voyage. Bligh was selected to transport the trees and to command H.M.S. *Bounty* on the voyage. The undertaking was abortive, however, and the well-known mutiny organized by Fletcher Christian was the result. Some years later Bligh was again sent for the same purpose and was successful.

Banks was elected president of the Royal Society in 1778, an office he kept for the next forty-one years. Certain reforms were his first official actions in his new capacity. For years there had been no bars to membership in the society; men aspiring to prestige and distinction—but with no scientific merit—had been freely admitted. Banks maintained that the society's work would be far more effective if only interested scientists and wealthy men who wished to patronize science were chosen as members. There was much opposition to this proposal, but Banks won. He proved to be constantly active as president, yet continued to be a munificent patron of science. His house, his library, and the whole of his valuable collections were at all times available to men of science.

By Sir Joseph's efforts the first East Indian orchids were brought to England in 1800. His suggested cultural techniques were of major significance in breaking through the widespread misunderstanding and ignorance which had been previously associated with their culture.

As an internationalist Joseph Banks was a great humanitarian. During time of war enemy ships were often captured by the British Navy, and sometimes foreign naturalists found themselves prisoners. Immediately upon hearing of such incidents, Banks would intervene and all natural science collections involved would be returned to their rightful owners. During the war with France ten collections were returned by Sir Joseph's efforts to Paris, and numerous men of science were liberated from foreign prisons. On one occasion some Danish supply ships were captured by England, and the Icelanders awaiting the supplies found themselves in a state of famine. Through Banks' intercession, however, permission was gained to send provision ships to the island.

While president of the Royal Society Banks also aided many young botanists. To Robert Brown he offered the post of naturalist to survey the coasts of Australia with the expedition under Captain Flinders in 1801. Brown was most successful during the four-year voyage, returning with a rich harvest of plants from that continent.

When Linnaeus' family found it necessary, for financial reasons, to sell his extensive collection of insects, shells, minerals and plants, Banks offered to take it on condition that a buyer could not be found in Sweden; he felt the collection should not leave the collector's homeland. A second offer was made, though, so Banks referred James Smith, a wealthy young naturalist, to Linnaeus' family, and Smith bought the collection. This led to the foundation of the Linnean Society in London, a significant contribution to the cause of natural history. Upon Smith's death the society bought the entire collection. Sir Joseph became the first honorary member.

The first medal of the Royal Horticultural Society was struck in 1811 and was awarded to Banks for his services to the society from its inception. He had been among those present on 7 March 1804 in a room in a house in Piccadilly, when the society was first organized.

This great patron of science died at the age of seventy-seven at Spring Grove on 19 June 1820. In his will he left provision that the artist Francis Bauer be enabled for the rest of his life to continue his drawings of the new plants at Kew. To Robert Brown he bequeathed his house in Soho Square, plus his library and herbarium, which Brown in turn donated to the British Museum.

After Banks' death, Dawson Turner, one of his friends, recovered part of the diary of the voyage with Captain Cook, and Turner's grandson, Joseph D. Hooker, used it in compiling the interesting *Journal of Sir Joseph Banks.*

Botanist, explorer, patron of science, trustee of the British Museum, director of Kew Gardens—Joseph Banks' name is indeed prominent among the many distinguished men of that long reign of George III. Largely through his accomplishments, the fields of botany and horticulture—and orchidology—entered the initial stages of scientific development.

References

Gardeners' Chronicle. 1867. No. 35.

Gilmour, John. 1946. *British Botanists.* London.

Glenn, Rewa. 1950. *The Botanical Explorers of New Zealand.* Wellington.

Lemmon, Kenneth. 1962. *The Covered Garden.* London: Museum Press Ltd.

Rolfe, R. A. 1956. Notes. *The Orch. Rev.* Vol. 64, no. 758.

van Steenis, C. G. G. J. 1950. Cyclopaedia of collectors. *Flora Malesiana.* Vol. 1, ser. 1.

Walkabout. 1962. Sydney. December.

Franz Bauer (1758–1840)

Dᴜʀɪɴɢ ᴛʜᴇ ᴄʟᴏsɪɴɢ ᴅᴇᴄᴀᴅᴇs ᴏꜰ ᴛʜᴇ ᴇɪɢʜᴛᴇᴇɴᴛʜ ᴄᴇɴᴛᴜʀʏ ᴀɴᴅ ᴛʜᴇ opening years of the nineteenth, Sir Joseph Banks was the guiding light of English naturalists. With unbounded enthusiasm and ample wealth to further any cause he considered worthy, he rendered incomparable service to the study of natural science. Among those who benefited by his patronage were botanists, explorers, and plant illustrators.

A keen eye, an unusual perception of floral and vegetative organization, and artistic skill were the necessary attributes of a successful botanical illustrator. Such a combination has always been rare. Still, Sir Joseph was able to find such a talent in Franz Bauer, whose perfect drawings have found lasting value in the annals of orchidology.

Franz Bauer was born at Feldsberg, Austria, on 4 October 1758. His father, who was painter to Prince Liechtenstein, near Vienna, died while Franz and his two brothers were infants, but not without leaving them a heritage of artistry. All three showed an early predilection for art. Franz in particular gave early evidence of his talent; a botanical drawing of his—of *Anemone pratensis*—was engraved and published when he was only thirteen years old.

Bauer went to England in 1788 with the intention of proceeding to Paris to seek his fortune, but Sir Joseph Banks, aware of his rare artistic talent, persuaded him to stay in England, hiring him at 300 pounds per year for life on condition that he reside at Kew as botanical painter for the Royal Gardens. His agreement to these terms enabled him to pursue his own interests in botanical illustrating, independent of the demands of the public and booksellers, and hundreds of illustrations of the plants received by travelers and navigators were the result. Accuracy of delineation and coloring, elegance of execution, and physiological and anatomical truth were unexcelled in Bauer's work, and he was readily honored by botanists, horticulturists, and orchidists.

Bauer's talents were so appreciated that he was appointed drawing master to Princess Elizabeth. His courtly bearing did not equal his artistic elegance, however, and his services, which were given free of charge, were dispensed with. At that time he was working on the tribe of heaths, then being introduced chiefly from the Cape. Engravings of his drawings, colored by Queen Charlotte and the princess under his supervision, were later sold at public auction, along with other of the queen's effects.

Toward the end of the century Bauer commenced his *Illustrations of Orchidaceous Plants*, subsequently published by Dr. John Lindley.

Bauer's abilities were not limited only to illustrating; he later became interested in the diseases of corn, and his skill in the use of the microscope aided in many discoveries important to agriculture. In this field he also did a few short papers on wheat smut, for which he received fifteen guineas—the only money received in his professional career beyond that paid to him in his position at Kew.

In 1816 Sir Everard Home, engaged in research concerning the anatomical structures of the foot of the common house fly, communicated with Sir Joseph Banks on the problems encountered in the work, and Sir Joseph immediately introduced him to Bauer. This led to a profitable and enduring friendship, for Bauer solved the problems successfully. Continuing the work with Sir Everard, he produced many concise drawings and dissections of creatures such as the earthworm, lamprey, conger eel, the metamorphosis of the frog, and the process of incubation from the egg to the complete chicken. More important, his work on the human eye and the structure of brain, nerves, blood, lungs, urethra, and muscular fiber led to great improvement in the treatment of disease and human suffering. Much of this work was published in *Philosophical Transactions of the Royal Society.*

All the while Bauer continued his drawings of Kew plants, including ferns and new orchids as they were introduced. He also studied the structure of cotton, flax, wood, and the hair of human races, establishing an unassailable position in scientific research. It was said of him that "nothing prevented his acquiring an extraordinary degree of fame, except his remarkably unobtrusive modesty—he worked rather for the credit of others, than for his own."

Thirty of Bauer's paintings appeared in Alton's *Delineations of Exotic Plants* (1796), and the five engravings therein attest to his masterful style. His own *Strelitzia Depicta* (1818) contained lithographs so elaborately painted as to be virtual original watercolors. Another set of his lithographs appeared in *Illustrations of Orchidaceous Plants* (1830–1838). These, which show botanical details only, were unfortunately transferred to stone by an inexperienced amateur and are thus of inferior quality.

In his frequent connection with orchids, Bauer formed theories on the process of their fertilization. In this then relatively misunderstood function he was a pioneer, and though his ideas were somewhat erroneous, the value of his observations led to further inquiry and investigation concerning the "unusual" sexual apparatus peculiar to orchids.

Oncidium baueri

The following observations are quoted, following Bauer's death, from a commentary given in the *Gardeners' Chronicle* of January 1841:

Few men, perhaps devoted their existence so entirely to an uninterrupted observation of natural objects, and enriched science with so many discoveries; and still fewer have been so indifferent to all ordinary considerations; for Bauer regarded his talents merely as a stepping-stone to that tranquility and happiness which ought to be the ulterior object of all science and all acquirements. For many of his latter years, Mr. Bauer was unable to quit his house; but though his body was thus as it were chained down, his mind remained active and unconfined, ranging over every field of inquiry connected with his pursuits. With his microscope and unrivalled pencil, he raised a creation of his own—a treasury of facts—to which he might have pointed the more proudly (had such a feeling moved him) as this accumulation caused no sigh, and justified no envy. He exhibited the life of a scientific artist and philosopher in its most exalted form. The common objects of ambition had no charms for him; power, wealth, or fame, with him were empty sounds; and what many have called obscurity, makes him in reality more truly bright and great. Mr. Bauer's name will always be associated with microscopical inquiries; for although he was unassisted by the improvements introduced into modern optical instruments, his sagacity generally enabled him to supply the deficiencies of his apparatus. Of the many performances of Mr. Bauer, his illustrations of the structures of Orchidaceous plants deserves especial mention, because they show that his mind was fully impressed with the laws of vegetable organization long before they were recognised to the world. He was the first to elucidate the real structure of these curious plants, although the result of his labours was not made known till long after others had received the credit of the discovery. The published records of Mr. Bauer's fame are few. It is among the portfolios of the British Museum, that those must seek who wish to become acquainted with his labours.

Bauer died at Kew on 11 December 1840, time having treated him kindly; free from suffering, natural causes claimed him at the age of eighty-two. He was buried at the side of Gainsborough and Zoffany.

By order of his executors, his effects were sold at auction on 24 November 1841. About forty lots of his material were sold, including not only his small library and several copies of his illustrations of the plants at Kew but numerous original sketches from nature studies and 100 drawings illustrating the germination and vegetation of wheat and diseases of corn, with manuscript notes. Also included were the drawings of his late brother, Ferdinand Bauer, and his microscopes and microscopical preparations. His collection of drawings connected with Sir Everard Home's researches in comparative anatomy was offered to the College of Surgeons, but upon that institution's refusal to purchase them, they were sold to the king of Hanover.

Bauer is commemorated in the Orchid Family by *Coelia baueriana*, *Galeandra baueri*, and *Oncidium baueri*.

References

Bauer, Francis. 1830–38. *Illustrations of Orchidaceous Plants* (with notes and prefatory remarks by John Lindley.) London: J. Ridgeway & Sons.
Blunt, Wilfrid. 1950. *The Art of Botanical Illustration.* London: Collins.
Gardeners' Chronicle. 1841. Miscellaneous—The late Francis Bauer, Esq. No. 2.
Gardeners' Chronicle. 1841. Mr. Francis Bauer's sale. No. 2.
Orchid Review, The. 1933. Francis Bauer, 1758–1840. Vol. 41, no. 486.

Olof Swartz (1760–1818)

Since the time of Linnaeus few Swedish botanists have enjoyed a greater degree of fame than Olof Swartz. This cannot be attributed to the length of time during which he worked in the cause of science, for he died at a relatively early age, or to the number and comprehensive nature of his publications. Rather, it was mainly due to those publications being devoted to extensive tribes of plants which had but little attracted the attention of botanists, such as the Orchidaceae, the ferns, and the mosses. Imparting knowledge and distributing materials freely, Swartz delighted in seeing science promoted by others as well as himself, and all authors on the subject of botany had him screen their works before committing them to print. The orchids were of prime interest to him. Upon certain fixed principles, he formed new genera, published many illustrations, and added numerous unusual and novel species. By these efforts and interests Swartz became known as "the first orchid specialist."

Olof Swartz was born on 21 September 1760, at Nordkoping, Sweden. Situated on the Motola River, Nordkoping was a famous shipping port. One of its local manufacturing establishments belonged to Olof's father.

In 1778 he was sent to the University of Upsala. Under the instruction of Linnaeus' son (the famed "father of modern botany" had died the year Swartz entered his formal studies), Swartz gained great proficiency in the various branches of natural history, as he did also in the study of medicine. During the summer months of 1779–1782, away from studies, he made excursions in the provinces of Sweden. Familiarizing himself with the natural entities of his native land, he traversed the districts bounded on the west by the Gulf of Bothnia, Lapland, as far as Lulea, Finland, and the islands of Oeland and Gothland.

At the age of twenty-three Swartz felt the desire to visit distant and tropical regions. After spending the winter studying and arranging the collection he had already formed (having already written his *Dissertatio da Methodo Muscorum*, his history of Gentiana-pulchella, and his inaugural treatise to the Faculty of Medicine), he left Sweden in 1783. He went to North America, where he spent a year, and then to Jamaica, Santo Domingo, other islands of the West Indies, and to the shores of South America. At each place he diligently collected the native flora. In 1786 he went to England, where he studied and examined the vast collection of material in the Banksian Herbarium, comparing the plants that he had himself brought home with this and other collections.

In 1789 he returned to Sweden, where he was immediately made a member of the Academy of Stockholm. Again he made exploratory journeys through various parts of the Swedish dominions, particularly the northern provinces, the Norwegian alps, and part of Lapland. In 1790 he was named president of the Academy at Stockholm, and in 1791 professor at the Belgian Agricultural Institution. At about that time he was married to the daughter of Dr. Bergius, of Upsala. Unfortunately, she lived only until 1797, leaving Swartz a son and a daughter.

Dr. Swartz's time became increasingly devoted to botany, the rich collections he had amassed leading him to enter into correspondence and exchange with the naturalists of other countries. His botanical fame was well founded by then; his published works spoke well for him. His *Prodromus Descriptionum Vegetabilium . . . in Indiam Occidentalem, etc.*, published in 1778, was the first enumeration of West Indian plants, including seven genera of orchids, following the Linnean system of binomial classification. His *Florae Indiae Occidentales* (1797–1806) was an amplification of the earlier work, but recognizing thirteen genera and twenty-seven species of orchids. Descriptions of the genera were limited to floral parts, followed by a discussion of the essential characteristics and the relative position of the genus. The species were the object of rather lengthy descriptions, including the roots, bulbs or stems, leaves, inflorescences, flowers, and fruiting bodies. Synonyms and habitat were also given, often accompanied by notes on the flowering season or a short phrase distinguishing the plant from a related species. These two works were destined to become the foundation for all the later contemporary treatises on the orchids of the West Indies.

In 1800 Dr. Swartz published a series of articles which were probably the first devoted exclusively to orchids—*Orchidernes Slägter ach Arter Upstallde* (Groups of Orchids and the Species Described). These appeared in *Kongl. Vetenskaps Academiens Nya Handlinger*, volume 21. Detailed diagnoses of the floral parts were given, and each of the twenty-five genera included were divided into orchids with one anther (twenty-four genera) and those with two anthers (one genus, *Cypripedium*). This division was apparently the first formal recognition of the two great divisions of the Orchid Family which were later designated as Monandrae and Diandrae. Many new species were added, especially West Indian ones, in the *Genera et Species Orchidearum, systematice coordinatarum*, 1806.

Swartz was presented with the orders of Wasa and the Polar Star in recognition of his work, and in 1811 he was made secretary of the Academy of Science. In 1813 he was offered a professorship in the Carolinian Institution.

Dr. Swartz had always pursued his numerous studies and avocations with great zeal, often to the detriment of his health. His constitution had never been vigorous in the first place, and the attacks of illness which he sustained might have been avoided had he given more attention to his person. He labored in his various tasks and employments until September of 1818, when, after an illness of eleven days, he died of a "nervous fever."

References

Dillon, Gordon W. 1956. Some Principles and Family Background—Understanding the Orchid Family—I. *Amer. Orch. Soc. Bull.* 25, no. 11.

Journal of Botany. Brief Memoirs of the Life of Olof Swartz, with Extracts from his letters. Vol. 2.

Robert Brown (1773–1858)

Following upon a rational system of nomenclature proposed by Linnaeus, Sir Joseph Banks' travels and plant introductions further served to stimulate a feverish intensification in the field of classification. The whole study of natural history was seething with new ideas and concepts which scientists and naturalists seized upon and applied determinedly, methodically, and often blindly. Classification became almost an end in itself through a half century of describing, assessing, and cataloguing, through which an eventual seeking of relationships and natural order emerged.

Australian orchid taxonomy was closely linked to the philosophical interest in natural history in the nineteenth century, but not until Linnaeus' system of binomial classification was applied were the broad and sound principles of the system worked into a model sufficiently influential to affect the interest of all the natural scientists of the time. This "tool" of classification, which supported a fledgling theory of natural patterns of adaptation and biological selection, was carried to Botany Bay by a Scottish physician named Robert Brown. The surge of ideas resulting from that journey affected every level of science thereafter.

Robert Brown was born on 21 December 1773, at Montrose, Scotland, the son of a clergyman of the Episcopalian church. Little is known of his early life except that he was educated at Montrose Grammar School, a fellow student of Joseph Hume. He later studied at Marischal College, Aberdeen, and at the age of sixteen began the study of medicine at Edinburgh University, where his interest in botany developed. Plants had been his first love since early boyhood, and his six-year study of botany at Edinburgh was a special joy for him. His capacity for biological science—especially the branches of classification—attracted the attention of his professors, who predicted his future eminence.

Brown left the university without receiving a degree, so in order to support himself and still devote time to botany, he joined a regiment of Scotch home guards, the Fifeshire Regiment of Defencibles stationed in the north of Ireland. His appointment was as assistant surgeon and ensign. While there he assiduously studied plants and the works of established botanists. An early interest in collecting and keeping was furthered in the regimental service, and Brown acquainted himself with all possible information relating to the plants he acquired and from which he made dried specimens. During this period he became acquainted with Sir Joseph Banks through the discovery of a rare moss, a specimen of which he had previously sent to Banks, then virtually "Emperor" of the world of science.

At the close of the century the Admiralty fitted out an expedition for the survey and exploration of the Australian coasts and Sir Joseph Banks selected Brown, then twenty-eight years of age, to accompany its commander, Matthew Flinders, as naturalist on the sloop H.M.S. *Investigator*. The expedition included Ferdinand Bauer (brother of Franz Bauer) as botanical illustrator, Mr. Peter Good as gardener, and William Westall as landscape painter. The *Investigator* sailed on 19 July 1801. The following year, after stops at Madeira and the Cape of Good Hope, it arrived at King George's Sound, on the southeast coast of Australia. During the three-week survey of the harbor, Brown collected more than 500 species of plants, the majority of them new to science. Botanizing was conducted also at Port Jackson, Sandy Bay, the northern shores, the Gulf of Carpenteria, the Pelew and Wellesley Islands, and then at Wessel Islands, where the ill health of Captain Flinders, the appearance of scurvy among the crew, and the rotting of the ship's timbers made it necessary for them to change course to Timor to replenish their provisions. Thereafter they cruised the south and west coasts, arriving at Port Jackson in June 1803, having lost many of the crew from dysentery.

Though ill fortune seemed to follow them, Brown was nonetheless gratified with the results of their explorations. Nearly 3800 botanical specimens had been collected during the four-year venture, about 120 of them orchids. Twenty-two of Australia's seventy-eight indigenous orchid genera were introduced and named by Brown on the basis of this trip. Sir Joseph Banks was also pleased, and in a reply to Brown's report on the first part of the voyage he commented:

Your commander deserves . . . great credit for the pains he must have taken to give you a variety of opportunities of landing and botanising. Had Cook paid the same attention to the Naturalists, we should have done more at that time. However, the bias of the public mind had not so decidedly marked Natural History for a favourite pursuit as it now has.

At Port Jackson the *Investigator* was condemned as unfit for further service; inspection showed that the ship's timbers were rotting and flaking dangerously. Captain Flinders hired another vessel, the *Porpoise*, and sailed for England. Brown and Bauer remained behind with the intention of exploring the island continent for eighteen months, after which it was agreed that Flinders would rejoin them in another ship for the completion of the survey. The *Porpoise*, however, was shipwrecked in Torres Strait. Flinders and a few of the crew managed to escape and later hired a small schooner. But the little ship leaked so badly that they were forced to dock at Mauritius, where the vessel was seized by the French governor, and Captain Flinders was held prisoner from December 1803 to June 1810.

Meanwhile, Brown and his companions explored the Blue Mountains and other distant reaches of the New South Wales settlement, the islands of Bass Strait, and Tasmania—all the while making collections. Among the orchids, his most important discoveries included *Cymbidium canaliculatum, Dendrobium canaliculatum, Dendrobium rigidum,* and *Dendrobium discolor* (originally classified as *Dendrobium undulatum*). In the Hawkesbury foothills he found *Sarcochilus falcatus, Cymbidium suave, Dendrobium speciosum, Dendrobium aemulum,* and *Dendrobium linguiforme.* Combing the sandstone areas around Sydney, he discovered and established numerous of the terrestrial orchid genera—*Pterostylis, Dipodium, Prasophyllum, Calochilus, Lyperanthus, Cryptostylis, Microtis, Caladenia, Corysanthes, Caleana, Glossodia, Orthoceros, Eriochilus, Acianthus,* and most of their species. The genera *Diuris* and *Thelymitra* had already been established, but Brown added twenty or more species.

Duplication of epithets was a common occurrence in those days when so much classifying was being done and new lists were slowly circulated. For this reason several of Brown's introductions were later given new names. *Neottia australis*, for instance, became *Spiranthes sinensis*, and *Calanthe veratrifolia* was later changed to *Calanthe triplicata*. In all, Brown discovered nearly a quarter of all the Australian orchid species in his search. Such monumental results were due largely to his keen perception and extremely sharp eyesight. His classifications often depended upon his observation of the minutiae upon the minute—the almost imperceptible division of pollen masses, rudimentary petals, scarcely noticeable calli, etc.

As a result of Captain Flinders' continued absence at the appointed time for departure, the naturalists took advantage of an alternate opportunity for the return to England, again aboard the rotten old *Investigator*, for no other ship could be diverted from carrying trade cargoes. They arrived home in October 1805. Most of the collections and drawings from the expedition arrived safely with them, though an extensive duplicate set of the south-coast plants and all the living material had gone down in the wreck of the *Porpoise*.

Upon Brown's return, the Board of Admiralty directed him to publish the botanical results of the expedition. One portion of the report was published in the *Prodromus Florae Novae Hollandiae* and another in the appendix to the narrative of Captain Flinders' voyage, published in 1814.

Soon thereafter Brown succeeded Dr. Dryander as Sir Joseph Banks' librarian, also receiving the appointment of librarian to the Linnean Society of London, for which he prepared and presented a series of botanical papers. The sexual structure of orchids was the topic of his material. Pointing out the significance of the glands found in the stigma of some orchids, he separated the genus *Orchis*, where the glands are contained in a pouch, from the genera *Gymnadenia* and *Habenaria*, in which bare glands are found. In November 1813 he announced the discovery of the nucleus—that part of the cell which later formed the basis of knowledge in genetics.

On the death of Sir Joseph Banks in 1823, and by the terms of his will, Brown became the possessor of the Banksian Herbarium for the remainder of his life, after which it was to pass to the British Museum. In addition, Brown received the remainder of the lease of Sir Joseph's house in Soho Square, in London. Brown at once offered the herbarium to the British Museum on condition that he be appointed keeper of the botanical department with a suitable salary, which offer was accepted. Brown continued to reside in the Soho Square house, which had become the center of scientific society in London, renting an unused portion of the building to the Linnean Society until the expiration of the lease, after which its removal to Burlington House by the government coincided with that of the Royal and Chemical Societies.

At a later period Brown took an active interest in perfecting scientific instruments, and when qualitative improvements in microscopes were commenced, he bought fine instruments from both British and foreign makers. Though generally unacquainted with optics and mechanics, his knowledge of minute vegetable structures enabled him to suggest so many improvements to opticians and manufacturers that his name was thereafter identified with the development of microscopical science.

Brown was known to retain his knowledge almost selfishly and was notoriously reserved concerning his collections. These he neither dispensed freely nor allowed others to profit by, scarcely even to inspect. One incomplete set of Australian plants was given to the Banksian Herbarium, but it was not available for consultation. This and another imperfect set were later deposited in the British Museum under Brown's custody, where knowledge of their existence was long held from the public, and until his death, neither collection was available for general use.

Brown held the office of president of the Linnean Society for several years. He retired in 1853, after which he ceased active participation in scientific societies and pursuits. His interest and enthusiasm continued, however, especially in the Linnean and Royal Societies. In the spring of 1858 he suffered an attack of bronchitis which weakened him considerably and from which his recovery was slow. Dropsy and lack of appetite supervened, and he gradually sank, succumbing a few months later, his mental awareness and memory keen to the last.

Robert Brown had a natural reserve that rendered him slow and reluctant to publish the results of his work. He was extremely cautious in his methods of investigation, and a fear of error or inaccuracy in communicating information may have been the basis of his unobtrusive nature. As a consequence of his reluctant nature, even the valuable geographical and nautical results of the *Investigator* brought him little recognition.

According to a biographical sketch about Brown in the *Gardeners' Chronicle* of 18 September 1858:

So deep was the veneration in which Brown was held by his contemporaries during his lifetime, and he was allowed to enjoy the prerogative he assumed of reserving to himself the sole use for upwards of half a century of collections made at the nationel expense. He was permitted to do so, even by those whose scientific progress suffered most, and whose sphere of usefulness was seriously contracted, through being deprived of access not only to the unpublished materials and collections which he possessed, but to those of which nothing could be authentically known, save through his own published writings.

References

Ames, Oakes. 1941. Pollination in Coryanthes. *Amer. Orch. Soc. Bull.* 10, no. 6.

Gardeners' *Chronicle.* 1858. Dr. Robert Brown, D.C.L., F.R.S., Foreign Member of the Academy of Sciences of the Institute of France. No. 25.

Gardeners' *Chronicle.* 1858. The late Robert Brown, L.L.D., F.R.S., etc. No. 38.

Kerr, Ronald. 1964. The sharp eyes of Robert Brown. *Aust. Orch. Rev.* 29, nos. 1, 3.

Kerr, Ronald. 1966. The tool that moved the world. *Amer. Orch. Soc. Bull.* 35, no. 4.

van Steenis, C. G. G. J. 1950. Cyclopaedia of collectors. *Flora malesiana.* Vol. 1, ser. 1.

Vermeulen, P. 1953. *Orchis spectabilis* L.–The American species of Orchis–I. *Amer. Orch. Soc. Bull.* 22, no. 6.

William George Spencer Cavendish (1790–1858)

VOGUES ARE USUALLY SET BY PERSONS OF INFLUENCE AND RENOWN; THUS it was that orchids became fashionable in the glasshouses and conservatories of the British upper classes.

Through its expanding collection of tropical plants in the early 1800s, the Royal Horticultural Society was influential in introducing new species of orchids, and the Messrs. Loddiges were moderately successful in cultivating the epiphytic "air plants." But the fashion of growing orchids as a hobby really began when the sixth duke of Devonshire became interested in them. The duke's interest was the prelude of a craze which spread throughout the world.

William George Spencer Cavendish, son of the fifth duke of Devonshire and the beautiful Duchess Georgiana, was born in Paris on 21 May 1790. The parents were overjoyed at the birth of a son, for after sixteen years of wedded life and two daughters, the long-desired male heir had been born. The child was even taken before the queen, and Louis XVI and Marie Antoinette, still unsuspecting of their impending doom, showed an interest in the baby.

The young duke-apparent was educated at Trinity College, Cambridge, England, graduating B.A. in 1811 and proceeding to LL.B. in 1812. In the same year that he gained his initial degree, his father died, and he succeeded to the title and a great fortune at the age of twenty-one. His mother had died five years previously, in 1806.

The duke had a bountiful natural inheritance besides his material gains—handsome bearing, high rank, and a tendency for extravagance. He had a fine literary taste also, and was especially interested in old English dramatic literature. In 1812 he purchased the library of Thomas Dampier, bishop of Ely, for 10,000 pounds, and in 1821 the dramatic collections of John Kemble. Many of the paintings from Devonshire House and Chiswick were removed to enrich his gallery at Chatsworth.

Public duties were also important to him. As the head of a famous Whig house he remained strong to the liberal tradition of his family. He supported and voted for measures such as Catholic emancipation and the abolition of slavery, and was particularly concerned for the children working in factories for fifteen hours daily. In 1832 he presented a petition in the House of Lords in favor of reducing the number of daily working hours in the factories. Twice he held the office of chamberlain, but resigned finally in 1828. His wealth and standing naturally made him a popular figure in aristocratic society, and his high spirits and gaiety added to this attraction. In those days he was a personal friend of the Prince Regent.

Though seemingly blessed with good fortune, the duke was afflicted with chronic deafness at an early age, and as this disability increased, it cut him off more and more from the public duties normal to a man of his rank. This caused a difficult gap in his life, and though he had the makings of a statesman, his deafness closed the door to any such career or endeavor. As time passed he became increasingly lonely. He and his sisters corresponded copiously, for he was greatly attached to his family, but he remained very much at a loss for real occupation and interests. Though he did not go through life without female ties and attachments, he never married. He became known as the "Bachelor Duke" and spent large amounts of money on books and works of art—though not very happily—and added a huge wing to Chatsworth. He gave lavish entertainments and balls which were the talk of society, and at times his expenditures exceeded even his large income.

Previous to all this the duke had held no special interest in horticulture, but his home bordered the grounds of the Horticultural Society, and he was frequently wont to stroll from one property to the other on a pleasant day, observing the society's plants and flowers and becoming curious about the activities therein. During his walks he often noticed a short, pleasant-looking young man who, he was told, was the gardener in charge of creepers and new plants. This young man was Joseph Paxton. Paxton's general bearing and alertness were appealing to the duke, and in their talks the duke found Paxton to possess a higher-than-average intelligence. When the post of head gardener at Chatsworth became vacant in the spring of 1826, it was not surprising, therefore, that Paxton came to mind in regard to filling the position. Paxton was on the point of seeking a career in America, but when the duke's offer came, he accepted quickly. Thus began the formation of a lengthy and enduring friendship.

The duke thereafter interested himself in horticulture, and under Paxton's supervision his gardens became world renowned. So engrossed became the duke in horticultural activities that he was later elected president of the Royal Horticultural Society, and it was in a society's exhibit in 1833 that he became enamored of orchids. By this time he had worked up to considerable enthusiasm about gardening, building hothouses and steadily accumulating tropical plants and orchids at Chatsworth. But rare and desirable plants remained extremely scarce, so it was decided to send a collector to India to bring back new plants. Paxton had an intelligent young man, John Gibson, under his charge at Chatsworth, who, in his opinion, was suited for the task. It was known that the mountains of Assam contained an abundance of tropical plants, especially orchids, and since a new governor-general, Lord Auckland, was about to take up his appointment in India, the duke was able to arrange for Gibson to travel on H.M.S. *Jupiter* with Auckland to Calcutta. That trip and others involving various collectors proved most successful, and within ten years the Chatsworth collection of orchids was the most famous in England.

The duke spared no expenses in maintaining and adding to his properties. A magnificent conservatory designed by Paxton—300 feet long, 145 feet wide, 60 feet high—was erected, covering almost an acre of ground. This structure later served partly as a model for the building erected in Hyde Park for the Great Exhibition of 1851. Cavendish also spent huge amounts in the upkeep of his country residences at Chiswick, in Middlesex; Hardwick Hall, in Derbyshire; Bolton Abbey, in Yorkshire; and Lismore Castle, in County Waterford.

The duke became a privy councillor and was made a Knight of the Order of the Garter in 1827, and from that time until 1834 he was lord chamberlain of the households of George IV and William IV. Among other titles, he was lord-lieutenant of Derbyshire and was elected presi-

Cymbidium devonianum

dent of the Royal Horticultural Society on the death of the first holder of that office, T. A. Knight, in 1838.

The orchid as a status symbol was a well-established concept by that time, and the desire to own increasingly more of these remarkable plants, both in number of acquisitions and rarity of species, became a mark of the wealthy and landed gentry. And the Chatsworth orchid collection for many years remained the model by which amateur orchidists in England patterned their growing collections.

The duke's deafness had always hampered him, and as he grew older his general health also deteriorated steadily. A nervous semi-hypochondriac disposition frequently paralyzed his activities as well. The decline progressed, and his death occurred at Hardwick Hall on 17 January 1858, at the age of sixty-seven.

The memory of this pioneer orchid hobbyist is still brought to mind in the many species honoring him. Among orchids there are *Cymbidium devonianum, Dendrobium devonianum, Oncidium cavendishianum,* and *Galeandra devoniana.*

References

Curtis' Botanical Magazine. 1931. *Dedications & Portraits 1827–1927.* Compiled by Ernest Nelmes and Wm. Cuthbertson. London: Bernard Quaritch Ltd.

Markham, Violet R. 1935. *Paxton and the Bachelor Duke.* London: Hodder & Stoughton Ltd.

Hugh Cuming (1791–1865)

FOLLOWING UPON THE INTRODUCTION OF "NATURAL PLANT CURIOSITIES" brought back from an increasing number of expeditions, plus the fashionability of orchids as "stove" plants, it was natural that enterprising men should endeavor to supply a growing demand for these rare tropical epiphytes. Thus emerged the professional orchid collector. One of the most sagacious of these was Hugh Cuming, an Englishman who roamed the western oceans seeking and discovering great quantities of natural wonders—not the least of which were new and unusual orchids.

Hugh Cuming was born to parents of modest means at West Alvington, Kingsbridge, in the county of Devon, England, on 14 February 1791. As a child he displayed an avid interest in plants and shells, and through his acquaintance with Colonel Montagu, the then celebrated author of *Testacea Britannica*, his love of natural history was encouraged and developed.

At the age of thirteen he was apprenticed to a sailmaker. Here he was brought into contact with seafaring men who fired his imagination with their stories of remote ports and life at sea. Seeking adventure, in 1819 he shipped out on a voyage to South America, settling in Valparaiso, Chile, which had just received its independence from Spain. From there he actively commenced collecting shells in an ample field. Here he met Mr. Nugent, the British consul, and Lieutenant Frambly, a noted conchologist, who both stimulated and assisted him in shipping plants and shells back to England. The specimens were eagerly received, and returning ships brought increasing orders for exotic materials.

In 1862 Cuming gave up his business and completely devoted his time to collecting. For this purpose he commissioned a yacht to be built according to his own specifications. Christened the *Discoverer*, the yacht was designed expressly for the collection and stowage of objects of natural history. For nearly twelve months Cuming cruised among the islands of the South Pacific, dredging and collecting on sea and shore. Easter Island, the Tuomotos, and the Society Group were included in his travel repertoire, and during a visit to Pitcairn Island, he was the house guest of John Adams, one of the survivors of the *Bounty* mutiny, forty years before. Returning to Valparaiso with his boat stocked full of plants and shells, Cuming was commended by the authorities, who were highly impressed with his work of the past year. Consumed with the ambition to increase the collection of shells in the British Museum, he consigned numerous cases to that institution. He also sent many more cases of pressed plants—and as much living material as possible—to the botanical gardens of England. Shortly afterward plans were made for an extended trip along the coast of Chile and Mexico. The Chilean government, further honoring Cuming, granted him duty-free anchorage in its ports and the privilege of purchasing stores free of duty. He was also furnished with letters to the authorities of all the states he visited, who received him with hospitality and extended every facility available. For two years he explored the Chilean coast, adding plants and shells from as far north as Acapulco, Mexico.

Concluding the trip, Cuming returned to England. The Zoological Society had just previously been organized, and Cuming's arrival in 1831 was considered a great event, his accumulated stores of plants, animals and shells becoming the subject of discourse at numerous memorable meetings. He soon became acquainted with men at the top of their professions—directors of museums and botanic gardens—and supplied fresh material to them and the Zoological Society for thirty-four years thereafter.

In 1835 he made ready for another exploration, this time in an area rich in natural phenomena and relatively untouched by naturalists—the

Philippine Islands. Recommendations from the Chilean government and letters from the authorities at Madrid assured him of a welcome by the Philippine missionaries and officials and acceptance by the people. With freedom to travel where he wished, he continued to collect shells but, more particularly, he became interested in the rich and varied flora of the islands. In his four years of combing the Philippines, Singapore, St. Helena, and the Malacca areas, he filled his storage chests with a magnificent series of land shells, the likes of which had not previously been seen. He was aided greatly in these collections, hiring the services of local school children who gladly scoured the woods and forests for plants and snails. This enabled him to assemble the richest collection gathered by a single individual up to that time.

His orchid discoveries were numerous as well, and he became the first to ship living orchids successfully from Manila to England. Letters to Dr. William Hooker of the Botanic Gardens at Glasgow reveal that "Orchidea also is worthy of notice; of plants 3,500 species." Messrs. Loddiges were the recipients of at least one shipment sent from Manila. *Aerides quinquevulnerum, Dendrobium anosmum, Dendrobium superbum, Grammatophyllum scriptum, Phalaenopsis amabilis* var. *aphrodite*, and *Vanda lamellata* are only a few of the species which were introduced through his collecting. A number of others bear his name: *Coelogyne cumingii, Podochilus cumingii, Bulbophyllum (Cirrhopetalum) cumingii*, and *Liparis cumingii*, to mention a few.

His vast assemblage of materials, immediately distributed to museums at home and abroad, included 130,000 specimens of dried plant material, 30,000 conchological species and varieties, large numbers of birds, reptiles, quadrupeds and insects, and numerous living orchid plants—thirty-three of them hitherto unpublished species.

Before his sojourn to the Philippines, Cuming had brought together by purchase, exchange, and discovery the finest and most valuable collection of shells then in existence. His Philippine additions increased this to an enormous extent, and from then until the end of his life he continued in the arrangement and addition of the collection. He was determined to build the greatest shell collection in the world. In the *Philippine Journal of Science* he is quoted as stating: "The greatest object of my ambition is to place my collection in the British Museum that it may be accessible to all the scientific world and where it would afford to the public eye a striking example of what has been done by the personal industry and means of one man." Toward this end, in later years he financed several collectors to carry on the work.

A glimpse of Mr. Cuming is given in a commentary of E. L. Layard, a close friend with similar conchological interests:

I can see the old gentleman now! His heavy florid face beaming over his white "choker" and his extensive, prominent white frilled shirt and black vest; he always dressed in black—I only knew him when he was like the larger of his two portraits—he gave it to me himself, and wrote his name on it in my presence. And this reminds me, I do not think he could do more than write his name. All his letters to me were written by his secretary, though signed by himself.

The rigors of his years at sea began to exact their toll on him before his return to England. In correspondence with Dr. Hooker he remarked, "The ill health and fatigue that I have experienced has been very great, my eyes are much injured by the sun; in short I am ten years older than I ought to be." He had long been subject to chronic bronchitis and asthmatic attacks, each successive paroxysm causing his friends increased reason for alarm. Following a visit to the Crystal Palace on 26 July 1865, he suffered a major recurrence of his ailments. Symptoms of dropsy, to which he had previously been subject, reappeared, and on the tenth of August he died in his house at 80 Gower Street, London. His shell collection, which had been the object and comfort of his life, surrounded him in his last days and he continued to occupy himself in its contemplation until within just a few hours of his death.

References

Davis, Reginald S., and Steiner, Mona Lisa. 1952. *Philippine Orchids*. New York: The William-Frederick Press.

Gardeners' Chronicle. 1865. Miscellaneous—The late Mr. Hugh Cuming. No. 35.

Kline, Mary C. 1961. Hugh Cuming—collector extraordinary. *Amer. Orch. Soc. Bull.* 30, no. 5.

Standley, Paul. 1928. Flora of Panama Canal Zone. *Contrib. U.S. Nat. Herb.* 27.

van Steenis, C. G. G. J. 1950. Cyclopaedia of collectors. *Flora malesiana*. Vol. 1, ser. 1.

Karl Ludwig Blume
(1796–1862)

By what means are we to judge the bearing and conduct of an individual pioneering in a new field? Can we afford to assess the merit of his contributions to be jaded by considerations of his personality? These are questions which we must ask ourselves seriously in light of today's sophisticated scientific researches. Years ago, when all branches of scientific investigation were in their infancy, the matter was far different. Pride and vanity often preceded the disrepute of investigators whose achievements were nonetheless worthy. Orchidology, too, has seen its share of dissension and discord on this account. Among the earliest of orchidologists to become as well known for his obstinacy and determination to adhere to his own principles as for his contributions, was Karl Ludwig Blume. Frustration and conflict of opinion were his companions during a major portion of his life.

Karl Ludwig Blume was born in Brunswick, Germany, in 1796, and though numerous biographical references exist about him, little is known of his childhood years and early interests. It is known, however, that he was educated for the medical profession. His inquiries into native medicines led him to Java in 1817, where he began to study botany. There he was appointed inspector of the vaccine and assistant director of the Buitenzorg Botanic Garden. It seemed that he had an astonishing capacity for work and an ambition no less great, for he collected largely and began to publish while yet little acquainted with the work already done in the scientific institutions of Europe.

In 1822 he succeeded Reinwardt as director of the Botanic Garden. It was during this administration, in 1825, that his *Tabellen en Platen voor de Javaansche Orchideen* appeared, providing the first exact orchid knowledge of the mainland of Java and adjacent islands. In this work he prepared a key to the Javanese orchids in which the various genera were divided into three groups according to the granular, powdery, or waxy nature of the pollen grains. Each genus was next listed in tabular form with descriptions of the sepals, lip, column, anther, pollinia, and habit. Next he diagrammed a series of careful floral analyses of one or more species within most of the genera. As additions to the flora of Java, in that same year he published *Bijdragen tot de Flora von Nederlandsch Indië* (Contributions to the Flora of the Dutch Indies), in which numerous new concepts were presented—detailed descriptions of the genera and brief summaries of the component species. A number of the generic concepts (such as *Agrostophyllum*, *Spathoglottis*, and *Phalaenopsis*) are still recognized as good genera, though others (*Dendrolirium* and *Trichotosia*, for instance) have been reduced to synonymy or sections of larger genera.

In 1826 Blume left the Indies for reasons of health and economy and went to Holland, where he was appointed director of the State Herbarium at Leyden in 1829. On this occasion the government gave him the honorary title of professor and decorated him with the Order of the Dutch Lion. Both of these distinctions were motivated by the services Blume had already given the state. At Buitenzorg he had done useful work in making a catalog of the Botanic Garden, and by his *Bijdragen* he had established his reputation as a great botanist. His rich collections constituted the departure for the beginning of the new herbarium, which already ranked with the great collections of the period, and his appointment as director justified great hope.

But the way proved stormy. To begin with, Blume was extremely possessive of his collections and herbarium and was widely recognized as being overly vain and ambitious. Attaching great importance to the privilege of monopolizing his institution, it did not take long for him to enter into conflict with his colleagues. More than one collision of opinions resulted. Then in 1844 the government decided to start an herbarium at the Botanical Garden at Buitenzorg. This occurrence seemed to be so dangerous, in Blume's mind, to the interests of the Leyden herbarium, that he believed he had to protest the action. He judged that it was a question of protecting a condition necessary to the life of his own establishment. A second state herbarium of the Indies could only lessen the value of the herbarium at Leyden as a center of information for the study of the flora of the Dutch Indies. Moreover, it was inevitable that an institution situated in the colonies and identical to that at Leyden would gather the same specimens and distribute duplicates, thus detracting from the principal resources of the Leyden collections. This collision of interests resulted in a lively battle which was decided in favor of Buitenzorg, without according compensation to the establishment at Leyden. Perhaps fear of bestowing too great a responsibility on an ambitious man was a factor. It was not incontestable that the decision in favor of Buitenzorg would do much to hurt the state herbarium by taking away its principal privilege: monopoly.

Blume was especially reproached by his colleagues for having been so little disposed to permit others to profit from his precious collections. This rather questionable opinion grew little by little into real opposition, which ended by involving even members of the government.

Neither the official complaint, taken to the government by Miquel and de Vriese, nor even new regulations (1850) much less favorable to the Leyden institution, could modify the line of conduct Blume followed. With unflinching tenacity he clung to his particular principles, even though he lacked the means to go on with what constituted a dictatorial system. The determination of those vast collections demanded too much, even from the energy of a hard-working intellectual like Blume, and so the government appointed an assistant curator in 1854 to aid with the work, no other means apparently being at its disposal. Thus Blume ended by finding himself isolated among his colleagues and deprived of government favor. The last years of his directorship were bitter, with continual conflict.

Nevertheless, Blume carried on his studies independently during those years of crisis. Among his principal orchid works of that period was *Rumphia*, vol. IV (1835–1848), his reorganization of Rumphius' work transposed into the Linnean system of classification. His *Flora Javae et Insularum adjacentium* appeared in 1858 as a small folio containing elaborate descriptions of many species previously described by himself and others. This work was elaborately illustrated by some of the most beautiful colored plates and most meticulous floral analyses to be found among the literature of the Old World orchids.

Blume died on 3 February 1862, leaving to posterity a rich heritage upon which subsequent modern floras of the island of Java were based, the beautiful plates of his *Flora Javae* remaining as indispensable aids to investigators of the orchids of the entire East Indies.

References

Goddijn, W. A. 1863. Mededeelingen Van's Rijks Herbarium, Leiden (in no. 62A). *Journal of Botany*. 1, ser. 2.

Schweinfurth, Charles. 1959. Classification of orchids. *The Orchids—A scientific survey*. Chapter 2. New York: The Ronald Press Co.

van Steenis, C. G. G. J. 1950. Cyclopaedia of collectors. *Flora malesiana*. Vol. 1, ser. 1.

Withner, Carl L. 1959. Introduction and history of orchid culture. *The Orchids—A scientific survey*. Chapter 1. New York: The Ronald Press Co.

Robert Wight (1796-1872)

Twelve years after William Roxburgh's introduction of the first living specimens of East Indian vandas, aerides, and dendrobiums into England, a young Scottish physician named Robert Wight was sent to Madras as surgeon to a native regiment. The floral riches of India attracted him soon thereafter—to the extent that he was eventually to provide an extensive description of that country's flora, orchids being prominent in his work.

Robert Wight was born at Milton, Duncra Hill, East Lothian, Scotland, on 6 July 1796, son of a writer to the Signet in Edinburgh. The twelfth of a family of fourteen, young Wight was educated at the Edinburgh High School and professionally at Edinburgh University, where he took a medical degree in 1816.

After one or two voyages as a ship's surgeon in 1819 he went to India, where he was first assistant surgeon and later full surgeon of the 33rd Regiment of Native Infantry in the East India Company's service. His botanical propensities must have been eminent even then, for within three years he was transferred to Madras, where he was given charge of the Botanic Gardens and afterward appointed naturalist to the East India Company. While at the Botanic Gardens, from 1826 to 1828, he made extensive collections during a tour of the southern provinces of India, sending Sir William Hooker (then at Glasgow) a large number of plants collected in Madras. Because his primary duties were as a medical officer, he was never liberally supported by the government of Madras, so it was mostly by his own resources that he made botanical collections and later published his work.

In 1828 the government discontinued his post at the Botanic Gardens and reassigned him to regimental duties as garrison surgeon at Negapatam. Here he accumulated another great assortment of plants which he distributed in 1832–1833 to various scientific organizations in Europe. Meanwhile, in 1831 he went on sick leave to England where, in collaboration with Dr. G. Walker-Arnott, he prepared the *Prodromus Florae Peninsulae Indiae Orientalis*, which described nearly 1400 species. This was the first attempt at a flora of any part of India in which Linnaeus' natural system was used. Unfortunately, Dr. Walker-Arnott died before the work was completed, and thus only one volume came into being.

Wight returned in 1834 to India, where he served an additional two years in the Indian army—not, however, without continuing a diligent study of Indian plants. As a matter of fact, his collections grew so large that it often took several carts to carry them on a march. All the while his sights were on the compilation and publication of an extensive and illustrated work on the plants of India.

Leaving the army in 1836, Wight took a position with the Revenue Department, where he supervised the growing of cotton, tobacco, and other products.

In 1838 his *Illustrations of Indian Botany* was commenced, followed soon thereafter by the *Icones Plantarum Indiae Orientalis*, a work of fifteen years' duration. Six volumes were published, comprising 2101 uncolored figures. Volume 3 contained thirty-six descriptions and illustrations of Indian orchids, and part 1 of volume 5 carried 134 more delineations of orchids. Some of the drawings are copies of those made in Calcutta by Roxburgh; some are by native artists laboriously trained by Wight to draw and lithograph; and some are by himself. In volume 5 he remarked that ". . . to master these, however, is a work demanding both time and patience on the part of the inquirer. Being well aware of this, as well as of the interest which attaches to this order, I have been induced, at the risk of falling into many blunders, to devote an unusually large space of this work to its elucidation even at this late stage of my progress." In it, species of the following genera were illustrated: *Arundina, Oberonia, Dienia, Microstylis, Liparis, Eria, Coelogyne, Dendrobium, Bulbophyllum, Cirrhopetalum, Phaius, Ipsea, Eulophia, Aerides, Vanda, Saccolabium, Polystachya, Diplocentrum, Sarcanthus, Aeceolades, Cym-*

bidium, Cyrtopera, Aceras, Platanthera, Peristylis, Habenaria, Satyrium, Diseris, Cephalanthera, Epipactis, Spiranthes, Zeuxine, Cheirostylis, Monochilus, Goodyera, Anoectochilus, Euphrobosces, Mycaranthes, Phreatea, Oxysepala, Aggeianthus, Lichinora, Bromheadia, Chiloschista, Josephia, Acriopsis, Podochilus, Pattonia, Cytheris, Cottonia, Taeniophyllum, Cryptochilus, Apetalon, Pogonia, Podanthera, Cypripedium, and *Cullenia.*

Early in his studies Wight saw that the Linnean system was insufficient for the classification of Indian plants and, by a clear perception of affinities and a most significant interpretation of structures, he gave worthy evidence of being far above the level of a mere descriptive botanist. Owing to his background of experience in horticultural work, he advanced the idea that extratropical plants within the tropics could be acclimatized by self-hybridization, thus modifying their needs so as to adapt them to successful culture in higher temperatures than found in their native habitats—a view supported by proof at later dates in a number of plant families.

Though somewhat isolated from the great botanical institutions, Dr. Wight was in constant communication with the leading European botanists and on terms of warmest friendship with the Hookers, John Lindley, Walker-Arnott, and others. To these and his friends, he endeared himself by his great congeniality, fortitude, and generosity. The herbarium at Kew was particularly enriched by the contribution of Wight's plants and notes through the years.

Wight retired from public service in 1853 and returned to England, where he managed a sixty-acre farm and, together with a Dr. Waring, assisted as well in the editing of a *Pharmacopoedia for India.*

As Wight advanced in years, failing health prevented him from working, but he continued to foster the interests of those engaged in botanical studies. In 1871 he generously presented his Indian herbarium to Kew. It contained all his type specimens and consisted of more than 4000 species.

At the age of seventy-six, on 26 May 1872, he died at his country residence near Reading, England, leaving a widow, four sons, and a daughter.

A perusal of Wight's separately published works to various scientific journals would include *Hooker's Botanical Miscellany* and *Journal of Botany, Companion to the Botanical Magazine, Madras Journal of Science, Annals of Natural History, Edinburgh Philosophical Journal, Journal of the Indian Agricultural Society, Calcutta Journal of Natural History,* and *Gardeners' Chronicle.* A list of his communications may be found in the Royal Society's *Catalogue of Scientific Memoirs.*

Orchid species bearing Dr. Wight's name are *Aerides wightianum, Doritis wightii,* and *Saccolabium wightianum.*

References

Curtis' Botanical Magazine. 1931. *Dedications and Portraits 1827–1927.* Compiled by Ernest Nelmes and Wm. Cuthbertson. London: Bernard Quaritch Ltd.

Gardeners' Chronicle. 1872. The Late Dr. Robert Wight, F.R.S. Vol. 50, no. 22.

Gray, Asa. 1873. Scientific Papers. *Amer. Journ. of Science and Arts* 5, ser. 3.

King, Sir George. 1899. The Early History of Indian botany. *Journ. of Bot.* 37, no. 443.

John Lindley (1799-1865)

As increased numbers of new orchid genera and species were introduced to the sales rooms, glasshouses, and herbaria of Europe in the 1800s, the terminology or "language" of the Orchid Family became increasingly confusing. Seeing the need for a systematic classification of the orchids, John Lindley developed a system of enumerating all the known orchids of the world, thus becoming known as "the father of modern orchidology."

Descendant of a Yorkshire family, John Lindley was born at Catton, near Norwich, England, on 5 February 1799. His father was a well-known nurseryman, renowned as the author of *A Guide to the Orchard and Kitchen Garden*.

Young Lindley was educated at the Grammar School at Norwich. Though he had difficulty in learning lessons by rote, he distinguished himself by his quick and industrious nature. At that time his interests led him to the study of plants and antiquities, and he is known to have spent much of his pocket money in renting books on those subjects. He read with such avidity that his schoolmates called him "Old Antiquity." He left school when he was about sixteen and went to Belgium on business transactions for his father. On his return he remained a few years with his father, devoting himself untiringly to botanical, horticultural, and entomological pursuits.

At Norwich, Lindley became well acquainted with William Hooker, to whom he supplied plants and insects from time to time. In 1818 or 1819 he went to London and there was employed as assistant librarian by Hooker's son, Sir Joseph. The younger Hooker also thought highly of Lindley and recommended him to Mr. William Cattley, who was looking for an editor for the *Collecteana Botanico*, an enumeration of many of Cattley's fine plants. This work was published in 1821.

With proceeds from his *Rosarum Monographia*, published in 1820, Lindley bought a dissecting microscope and a small herbarium, an important addition to his own expanding collection. The herbarium received the whole of what he called his leisure hours. In this work his wife assisted in its arrangement and conservation; though it was inferior to some others in extent, it was surpassed by none in condition.

In 1822 he became garden assistant secretary to the Horticultural Society. At that time the garden at Chiswick was being formed by William Spencer Cavendish, the sixth Duke of Devonshire, partly under Lindley's supervision. Both jobs were performed ably and well, and in 1826 he was appointed sole assistant secretary to the Horticultural Society, in which capacity he attended to duties in both London and Chiswick. From this point on Lindley became the mainspring of the society, advancing its financial position and maintaining its working efficiency. The position required his daily attendance during office hours in Regent Street, or once a week at the garden, in addition to frequent extra work in the early morning. Mr. Sabine, Honorary Secretary of the society, resigned his post in 1830 owing to untoward circumstances that taxed his energy and well-being. The customary, expensive fetes held at the garden had failed to promote the objectives of the society, and though Mr. Sabine's hopes and expectations had been high, difficulties resulted. Working with George Bentham, who had succeeded Mr. Sabine as Honorary Secretary, Lindley worked out a plan for holding general exhibitions of flowers and fruits at the garden instead of the larger, costly exhibitions previously held. These exhibitions proved to be the means of restoring the society to its former prosperity, and similar exhibitions, based on Bentham and Lindley's, were held in all parts of the country.

Seeing the need for a first-rate horticultural journal, Lindley and other gentlemen, including Sir Joseph Paxton, founded the *Gardeners' Chronicle* in 1841. Lindley became its editor, doing his utmost to raise the prestige of horticulture and, through his great knowledge of plants and their requirements, clearly laying before the public the physiological laws involved in the various operations of gardening. Through his columns he staunchly advocated the improved education of gardeners and worked to detect fraud and expose the practices of the unprincipled.

As wealthy amateurs began collecting orchids, Lindley seized the opportunity for an intensive study of the genera and species. By his investigations, he was the first to make a substantial classification of the Orchid Family. Though the system was later modified to meet expanding needs, its basic simplicity made it valuable to horticulture. Here is Lindley's classification:

I. Anther one only
  A. Pollen masses waxy.
    1. No caudicula or separable stigmatic gland.
      Tribe I. *Malaxeae* (or *Malaxideae*)
    2. A distinct caudicula, but no separable stigmatic gland.
      Tribe II. *Epidendreae*
    3. A distinct caudicula, united to a deciduous stigmatic gland.
      Tribe III. *Vandeae*
  B. Pollen powdery, granular, or sectile.
    1. Anther terminal, erect.
      Tribe IV. *Ophreae* (or *Ophrydeae*)
    2. Anther terminal, opercular, lying over the rostellum.
      Tribe V. *Arethuseae*
    3. Anther dorsal, behind the rostellum.
      Tribe VI. *Neotteae*
II. Anthers two
      Tribe VII. *Cypripedeae*

In his position as orchid authority for British horticulture, Lindley began receiving a steady stream of material for study and identification, and his herbarium became the repository of the types and duplicates of numerous new genera and species from all parts of the world. To this he added his own skillfully done analytical pencil sketches and ink and watercolor drawings.

Prior to Bentham's resignation in 1841, nearly all the activities of the Honorary Secretary, plus his own duties, fell on Lindley's shoulders. He subsequently took the designation of vice-secretary, the succeeding honorary secretaries taking very little active part in the management. He continued in this office until 1858, resigning to become secretary to the society and member of council, a position which he held until failing strength and the overwhelming responsibilities of the Exhibition of 1862 obliged him to give up all active participation in management of the society's affairs.

Lindley had been in poor health for some years previously. In 1851

Epidendrum lindleyanum

he had acted as a juror to investigate and report on the foods displayed in the Great Exhibition of that year. The burden of this office, compiled upon his other duties, was so trying that as a consequence he became seriously ill. He recuperated after a period of rest and resumed his work with his usual vitality, but when the 1862 Exhibition commenced, he was induced against the advice of his family to take charge of the whole colonial department. Constant headaches began to plague him, but he refused to give up his post. By the time the exhibition was closed his mental and physical health had been so severely impaired that he was never to recover fully. Soon thereafter he was compelled to resign the secretaryship of the society. His good friend, H. G. Reichenbach, later recalled:

Traces of the mental exhaustion which saddened Lindley's last years are to be found in some of his last works. It was exceedingly painful to me when I went to him, the excellent man whom I had known ever since 1849, and found that he did not remember one of his favourites—he who shortly before was one of the most active workers; and he felt the full weight of the affliction, upon which he expressed himself with such touching eloquence to Bateman and myself. I still see him in the verandah at Turnham Green, as he appeared one October evening, when he called after me, bidding me not to forget to pay him a visit as often as I come to England. Except his household and physician, I was the last who saw him.

Dr. Lindley's family and friends were aware of his fragile health, but his death took them somewhat by surprise. He retired for the night on Tuesday, 31 October; the following morning he was taken by a seizure and died very shortly afterward. Present at his burial on 5 November were Bentham, J. D. Hooker, T. Thompson, Reichenbach, and many other friends.

Though John Lindley's life seemed centered in the Horticultural Society, many other activities and pursuits, in which he actively engaged, were important to him. He lectured both at University College and at the Botanic Garden of the Society of Apothecaries at Chelsea; in this latter establishment he held the office of Praefectus Horti. His connection with University College had begun in 1829, and he continued to lecture there until 1862. Upon his resignation he was made Emeritus Professor and was subsequently appointed to the office of Examiner of Botany at the University of London from 1861 to 1863. He never read his lectures to the students; instead, he outlined and planned carefully, profusely illustrating his discussions with large, rough drawings.

His journalistic contributions were prodigious. A partial listing of his major works follows:

1829	*Synopsis of the British Flora*
1830	*Outlines of Botany*
1832	*Introduction to Botany*
1833	*Nixus Plantarum*
1835	*Key to Structural and Systematic Botany*
1836	*Natural System of Botany*
1837	*Monograph on the Victoria regia*
1837–38	*Ladies Botany*
1838	*Flora Medica*
1839	*School Botany*
1841	*Elements of Botany*
1846	*The Vegetable Kingdom*
1849	*Medical and Economic Botany*

Several of these works were published mainly for the use of his classes. These by no means were his only journalistic efforts, however. In addition to drawing up the greater part of Loudon's *Encyclopedia of Plants*, he conducted all except the first few volumes of the *Botanical Register*. With but little assistance he edited Lindley and Paxton's *Flower Garden*, besides contributing to several of Paxton's works in horticultural botany. He wrote all the botanical articles in the *Penny Cyclo-*

paedia down to the letter *R*, and a *Treatise on Botany*, published by the society. From his pen issued the greater part of the eighth, and the whole of the ninth volume of Sibthorp's *Flora Graeca*, published from 1835 to 1837, and from 1831 to 1837 he worked with William Hutton on the *Fossil Flora of Great Britain*, three volumes containing figures and descriptions of fossil vegetables found in the country.

As in elementary botany, he commenced in horticulture with a small work entitled *Outlines of Horticulture*. *Theory of Horticulture* followed, published in 1840, reproduced in America, and translated into nearly every European language. A second edition was issued in England in 1855.

His particular attentions had been more exclusively devoted to orchidaceous plants for years. Between 1830 and 1840 his *Genera and Species of Orchidaceous Plants* was issued in parts; a second edition, under the title of *Folia Orchidaceae*, was begun in 1852, but was never completed, the last part having been issued in May 1859. The *Sertum Orchidaceum*, a folio of beautifully colored plates, appeared in numbers and was completed in 1838.

Lindley was a frequent contributor to the *Transactions of the Horticultural Society* from 1822 to 1848, drawing up reports on the new plants in the society's garden and on ornamental plants—adding notes of morphological and physiological interest. In the volumes of the *Transactions of the Linnean Society* several other important papers by Lindley are to be found, mainly in reference to orchids.

Lindley was a member of about sixty scientific societies, including every notable botanical and horticultural society in Europe and America. He became a Fellow of the Linnean Society in 1820 and of the Royal Horticultural Society in 1828. In 1832 he received his Ph.D. from the University of Munich. In 1834 he was elected an honorary member of the Royal Academy of Science of Berlin and became a corresponding member of the French Institute in 1853. In 1857 he received the Royal Medal from the Horticultural Society, awarded "in recognition of the value of his labours in various branches of scientific botany, and more especially for his learned and comprehensive works on the natural orders of plants, on the Orchidaceae, and on theoretical and practical horticulture."

Lindley was of average height, with dark brown hair and ruddy complexion. He had only one useful eye, the other having been blind since infancy. He was short of temper and unlikely to be patient with those who opposed him; at the same time, however, he was warm-hearted and had a generous disposition. He was married to the daughter of Anthony Freestone of St. Margaret's, Southelmham, Suffolk, in 1823, by whom he had three children.

An impressive list of orchids honors Lindley's name. Besides the genera *Lindleyella* and *Neolindleya*, there are *Barkeria lindleyana*, *Cattleyopsis lindleyana, Eulophia lindleyana, Maxillaria lindleyana, Odontoglossum lindleyanum, Physosiphon lindleyi, Sobralia lindleyana, Spiranthes lindleyana,* and *Bulbophyllum lindleyana.*

The total of this great horticulturist-botanist's accomplishments would be more than staggering to those of even above-average abilities, and the following quotation, published in 1865 in the *Journal of Botany*, may indicate the regard he was afforded by his contemporaries:

The orchids were his particular favorites, and the various works he wrote on them will probably be regarded as the most favorable specimens of what he has done and what he could do; and let us own that there are few botanists who would not be glad to have written them, as there are few whose botanical career has been more useful than that of John Lindley.

References

Ames, Oakes. 1932. John Lindley (1799–1865). *Amer. Orch. Soc. Bull.* 1, no. 2.

Dillon, Gordon W. 1957. Development of a system of orchid classification. Understanding the Orchid Family—II. *Amer. Orch. Soc. Bull.* 26, no. 4.

Gardeners' Chronicle. 1865. The late Dr. Lindley. Nos. 45, 46.

Reichenbach, H. G. 1917. Dr. Lindley. *The Orch. Rev.* 25, no. 292.

White, C. T. 1940. A history of Australian orchids. *Australian Orch. Rev.* 5, no. 4.

George Bentham (1800–1884)

THERE WERE MANY IMPORTANT WORKERS IN ORCHIDOLOGY AFTER LIND-
ley's death: Reichenbach, Cogniaux, and others. Their works contributed much to the expanding knowledge concerning the Orchidaceae,
but George Bentham was the first to publish, in 1881, the first of the
modern systems of orchid classification. Bentham maintained what became known as the "idealistic" approach to plant classification—the first
tribe arbitrarily representing that which is closest to the perfect orchid,
with the less perfect forms in other tribes and subtribes in descending
order. Bentham remained firm in traditional methodology, even when
Charles Darwin's influence was strong in taxonomy and the evolutionary
concept.

George Bentham was born on 22 September 1800, at Stoke, near

Portsmouth, England. His father was General Sir Samuel Bentham, then inspector of all the royal dockyards. While a boy, young Bentham lived for a period in St. Petersburg, Russia, where he became fluent in the Russian language. From 1814 to about 1826 he lived with his family near Montpellier, France. His interest in botany began there, where he examined the wild plants of Angoulême and Montauban and, afterward, he did further research into the flora of the Pyrenees.

As a result of his excursions alone and with Dr. Walker-Arnott, Requien, and Audibert, his first work, *A Catalogue of Plants Indigenous to the Pyrenees and Bas Languedoc*, was published in French in 1826. In the preface to this volume, stress was laid on the verification of the original type specimens, a point which at that time was not judged particularly important. This was a source of aggravation to Bentham, who vigorously disapproved of the "extreme multiplication of badly defined species"—which led him to redescribe the French species of *Cerastium*, *Orobanche*, and *Helianthemum*. This led to protests and adverse criticism, but Bentham was adamant, stating that "if I have ventured to differ from that learned botanist (Dunal), as to the number of species (of *Helianthemum*), it is because I have observed on living specimens that the characters upon which they have been established are very variable and too intricate not to introduce yet greater confusion into this difficult genus." In reference to such variation, Bentham insisted on the impropriety of affixing separate names to accidental or minor variations, and advocated that no name should be given to a variety unless a permanent change occurred in numerous individual plants, of which a regular series of intermediate forms would demonstrate the connection with the primitive species.

On his return to England in 1826 Bentham at first concentrated on studying law but shortly gave up legal interests and devoted himself exclusively to botany. He became associated with the Royal Horticultural Society at a time when that organization was receiving a great many new species and genera from the collectors it had despatched to numerous foreign areas. Thus it was that he met John Lindley, with whom a most congenial friendship developed. Together they undertook the introduction and determination of the many new plants received from David Douglas, Karl Hartweg, and others.

Bentham was secretary to the society from 1829 to 1840, and it was during his secretariat that the famous Chiswick fetes were begun. The first exhibition was held in the society's garden in 1833. For the occasion a tent 150 by 100 feet in diameter was purchased, and it is recorded that 1700 people attended.

From that time on Bentham devoted his time to elaborating monographs of genera and orders, or preparing floras of various countries. In this work he gradually accumulated a large herbarium and library which was of inestimable aid in his research. In 1854 he donated this important assemblage to the nation with the condition that it be made available to the public and that he be provided the facilities at Kew to continue his compilations. There, day after day, he labored determinedly over his monographs, allowing himself little relaxation beyond his annual trips, usually spent on the Continent. Even then much of his time was taken by visits to and study in botanical establishments.

Bentham frequently contributed to Sir William Hooker's botanical publications. Two major works entrusted to him were the preparation of the *Flora of Hong Kong* and *Flora Australiensis*, the latter being a seven-volume work in which he was assisted by Ferdinand Mueller, government botanist of Victoria, Australia. This first complete account of the Australian orchids totaled 129 pages.

Investigations into the flora of the greater part of the world and numerous monographs of genera and orders, together with his constant association with the leading botanists of Europe—plus his powers as a linguist—all combined to make him especially qualified to undertake a *Genera Plantarum*. He was undismayed by the magnitude of the task before him; in conjunction with Sir Joseph Hooker, the publication of the work was begun in 1862. Though each author was apportioned equal shares of the work, Bentham undertook some of the most laborious portions so as to lighten Hooker's labors and relieve him of anxiety as to their mutual progress. They were not content with condensations of preceding descriptions; instead, they examined and compared every genus of which there were specimens in the herbarium, adjusting synonymy, collating descriptions published by others, and furnishing references to the literature—thus forming a meaningful and magnificent work, completed in April 1883. Included was an amplification of Bentham's system of the Orchidaceae, published earlier. Only five tribes were included in it, with the addition of subtribes and genera:

Tribe I.	*Epidendreae* (nine subtribes)
Tribe II.	*Vandeae* (eight subtribes)
Tribe III.	*Neottieae* (six subtribes)
Tribe IV.	*Ophrydeae* (four subtribes)
Tribe V.	*Cypripedieae* (no subtribes)

During the course of its publication Bentham wrote and published various lengthy notes and commentaries in the *Journal of the Linnean Society* in which he discussed the structure, affinities, and geographical distribution of many of the orders at greater length than the plan of the *Genera* allowed.

For more than twenty years Bentham labored incessantly at his work. An example of the diligence so characteristic of the man is quoted from the *Gardeners' Chronicle* of September 1884:

Late one afternoon, at the end of a week, when most of the officials were thinking of concluding their labours for the day, Bentham came to the end of his revisions of the Orchids—a task that had occupied him for many consecutive months. Without taking pause, as most people would have done after the accomplishment of such a task, Bentham simply summoned an attendant, and requested that the Gramineae—the grasses—might be brought to him, and then and there he entered upon another task before whose magnitude and intricacy most men would recoil.

Of a quiet and retiring nature, Bentham shunned rather than sought acclaim. He was little known except by his closest friends. Strangers and slight acquaintances might even have judged him reserved to the point of being brusque and cold. Actually, he was warm-hearted and generous; not only his time, but his own private funds were placed at the society's disposal, and all his efforts seemed directed in securing its prosperity and usefulness. He accepted the presidency of the society in 1861, devoting himself to the advancement of its causes for thirteen years. No detail was too trivial to merit his consideration. As well as the duties of president, he shared largely in the work of the secretary, treasurer, librarian, and editor. In this position, his philosophic mind and business tact established him as more than merely a systematic botanist. His theories relating to the life history of organized beings, hybridism, dimorphism, and geographic and geological distribution, elicited much scientific controversy in the face of the Darwinian theories, but his persistence and quiet temperament added persuasive argument to his ideas.

The honors conferred upon Bentham came late in his life and had to be pressed upon him. Only after several years was he persuaded to become a Fellow of the Royal Society, who awarded him their greatest honor, the Royal Medal. He was also a member of the Institute of France and was associated with most of the scientific organizations of the world. His name is perpetuated in a number of plants, among them the orchid genera *Benthamia* and *Neobenthamia*.

It was no great surprise, though it caused utmost sorrow, that he died in his eighty-fourth year on 10 September 1884. His old friend, Sir Joseph Hooker, was present at his side during his last hours.

References

Dillon, Gordon W. 1957. Development of a system of orchid classification. Understanding the Orchid Family—II. *Amer. Orch. Soc. Bull.* 26, no. 4.

Gardeners' Chronicle. 1884. Mr. George Bentham. Vol. 22, nos. 559, 560.

White, C. T. 1940. A history of Australian orchids. *Aus. Orch. Rev.* 5, no. 4.

Joseph Paxton (1801–1865)

HORTICULTURAL SKILL WAS A MARK OF DISTINCTION IN NINETEENTH-century England. Money could buy impressive country estates and pretentious furnishings, but it could not provide a fundamental knowledge of the arts and crafts necessary for creating the type of beauty the owners desired in their gardens and conservatories. These aesthetic attributes were usually gained by the employment of experienced plantsmen and gardeners. In the ranks of such men, Joseph Paxton exemplified the top; his unofficial title as England's "Prince of Gardeners" well bespoke the esteem in which he was held in horticultural circles.

Joseph Paxton was born on 3 August 1801 at Milton Bryant, Bedfordshire, England, where his father was a farmer. Of humble means, Paxton was unable to attend the fine schools. At the age of fifteen he selected gardening as his profession and for two years was employed in the garden of Sir Gregory Osborne Page Turner, Bart., at Battlesden Park, near Milton Bryant. The following three years were spent at Woodhall Park, near Watton, Herts., in the gardens of Samuel Smith, Esq., where he acquired a thorough practical knowledge of the most important branches of horticulture. For two more years he was a gardener at Battlesden.

In the fall of 1823 he went to London, finding employment in the garden of the duke of Somerset at Wimbledon. About this time the duke of Devonshire leased some ground to the Horticultural Society, which commenced the formation of an experimental garden at Chiswick. This endeavor presented an excellent opportunity for young gardeners, and Paxton eagerly took advantage of the chance to further obtain all the requirements of his profession. On the recommendation of Joseph Sabine, Honorary Secretary of the Horticultural Society, he was admitted to the new garden on 13 November 1823. Advancement came rapidly, for in 1824 he was promoted to foreman of the arboretum. Here it was that he became acquainted with the duke of Devonshire, who frequently came to Paxton for advice and consultation on new trees and shrubs. Paxton's bearing and intelligence impressed the duke, and, needing a gardener for his extensive grounds, he inquired of Mr. Sabine as to Paxton's capabilities for the position. "Young and untried," stated Sabine, yet he was enthusiastic in Paxton's behalf—and young Paxton went to Chatsworth. In his own words:

I left London by the Comet coach for Chesterfield, and arrived at Chatsworth at half-past four o'clock in the morning of the 9th of May, 1826. As no person was to be seen at that early hour I got over the greenhouse gates by the old covered way, explored the pleasure ground and looked round the outside of the house. I then went down to the kitchen garden, scaled the outside wall, and saw the whole of the place, set the men to work there at six o'clock, then returned to Chatsworth, and got Thomas Weldon to play me the waterworks, and afterwards went to breakfast with poor Mrs. Gregory and her niece; the latter fell in love with me, and I with her, and thus completed my first morning's work at Chatsworth at nine o'clock.

He married that same niece, Miss Sarah Brown, in 1827. Meanwhile, he had begun a marvelous transformation at Chatsworth. Said the duke:

In a very short time a great change appeared in pleasure-ground and garden; vegetables, of which there had been none, fruit in perfection, and flowers. Twelve men with brooms in their hands on the lawn began to sweep the labourers to work with activity. The kitchen garden was so low, and exposed to floods from the river, that I supposed the first work of the new gardener would be to remove it to some other place, but he made it answer. In 1829 the management of the woods was entrusted to him, and gradually they were rescued from a prospect of destruction. Not till 1832 did I take to caring for my plants in earnest. The old greenhouse was converted into a stove, the greenhouse at the gardens was built, the arboretum was invented and formed. Then started up Orchidaceae, and three successive houses were built to receive the increasing numbers. In 1835 the intelligent gardener, John Gibson, was despatched to India to obtain the *Amherstia nobilis* and other treasures of the East. The colossal new conservatory was invented and begun in 1836; the following year Baron Ludwig was so charmed with its conception that he stripped his garden at the Cape of the rarest produce of Africa. Paxton had now been employed in the superintendence and formation of my roads; he made one tour with me to the West of England, and in 1838 contrived to accompany me for an entire year abroad, in which time, having gone through Switzerland and Italy, he trod in Greece, Turkey, Asia Minor, Malta, Spain, and Portugal. In his absence he managed that no progress should be checked at home. A great calamity ruined the expedition he had set on foot to California; the unfortunate Wallace and Banks, young gardeners from Chatsworth having been drowned in Columbia River. He went with me in 1840 to Lismore, and in that year the conservatory was finished. The village of Edensor was new-modelled and rebuilt between 1839 and 1841, and the crowning works have been the fountains and rock-garden.

Paxton's overall abilities transcended the realm of gardening alone. Financial arrangements which he suggested to the duke were so well taken as to foster such success that the duke entrusted him with the superintendence of his large estates at Derbyshire. Paxton's reputation grew as great among the aristocracy as among his own class, and his worth was nobly appreciated. He and the duke formed such a compatible friendship that they often had occasion to dine together at the duke's table.

In the midst of a period when new orchids were being introduced and their cultivation was in an experimental stage, Paxton developed an abiding interest in them. The duke's orchid collection was also constantly enlarging, so that within ten years of its formation it had become the largest private orchid collection in the country. Paxton collaborated closely with John Lindley, then secretary of the Horticultural Society and the most prominent orchidologist of the times. Lindley had been disturbed by the lack of success most gardeners encountered in attempting to cultivate tropical orchids in "stoves," and suggested to Paxton that a more rational system of cultivation should be adopted. Forthwith Paxton opened up the greenhouses, providing cool air and ventilation to the orchids. This treatment had a marked influence on the plants, for they began to flourish. Lindley widely expounded the advantages of Paxton's methods, and the latter became well known for having standardized orchid culture. In later years Paxton's cultural techniques were recognized as the beginnings of "modern" orchid cultivation.

The salient aspects of Paxton's methods were that he provided separate houses or compartmented houses for orchids from different climates; maintained a lower average temperature than was usually given by other orchid growers of the day; introduced more efficient ventilation by which a larger volume of fresh air was admitted into the houses, especially during the growing season; occasionally watered the walkways and stagings in the greenhouses in order to provide a moist atmosphere; and developed an improved method of potting, with special regard to efficient drainage and greater attention to root development.

Journalism was also one of Paxton's specialties. Already producing his beautifully illustrated *Paxton's Magazine of Botany*, in 1841 he became one of the founders of the *Gardeners' Chronicle*. The first volume of his *Magazine* was published in 1834. Even as early as that date the changing of plant names by botanists bothered gardeners and horticultural journalists, and in the introduction of his first volume Paxton wrote:

As great confusion often exists amongst cultivators, in consequence of our very eminent Botanists so frequently changing the names of plants after their introduction, great care will be taken to constantly adhere to the names first given, if at all consistent. In some cases the change is indispensable.

Pleased at the avidity with which his volumes were accepted by British horticulturists, Paxton wrote in the advertisement to volume 2:

The increasing interest exhibited during the past year, in the introduction and cultivation of Flowering Plants, may in a great measure account for the very extensive sale of the Magazine of Botany, which, without doubt, now surpasses that of any other work of the kind in the country. From this unexpected success the author is led to hope that his endeavours, however humble, have in some degree met the wants and wishes of his countrymen.

The first orchid Paxton illustrated in his *Magazine* was *Cattleya intermedia*, a double-page illustration showing a spike of five flowers grown in Earl Fitzwilliam's gardens at Wentworth House. He was extremely pleased with the response shown to this picture, and in succeeding volumes he included orchids increasingly. Enthusiasm continued on a grand level, and in the third volume Paxton wrote: "The plants most in esteem now by the scientific Botanists are unquestionably Orchideae, . . . " Thus Joseph Paxton, by his excellence of culture and the dissemination of published pictures and information, was responsible in large part for the accelerated popularity in orchid growing.

Great opportunity for achievement was afforded Paxton in 1850. At that time he was erecting a peculiarly built greenhouse which he had designed for the cultivation of the newly introduced aquatic plant, the *Victoria regia*. At the same time, plans were being formed for the first Great Exhibition. Two hundred and forty designs had been submitted to the building committee for the purpose of housing the exhibition.

None of the plans submitted, however, complied with the requirements for the purpose of the event. Paxton, hearing of the situation, submitted a design which was accepted with great approbation. A great domed glass structure was erected—a marvel of beauty and ingenuity for all who viewed it. For his services to the exhibition, Queen Victoria was pleased to confer the honor of knighthood upon Paxton.

Sir Joseph took a great interest in education and spent much of his time in later years overseeing the papers prepared by horticultural students for discussion at their evening meetings. He was a vice-president of the Royal Horticultural Society, a Fellow of the Linnean Society, and a benevolent friend and subscriber to the Gardeners' Royal Benevolent Institution. He became director of a railway as well as a liberal in politics, voting in favor of every measure which he thought likely to benefit his fellow man. In 1854 he was returned as member of Parliament for Coventry and represented that body continually until his death.

The one improvement for which he became perhaps most well known in the gardening world was the invention and introduction of inexpensive greenhouses for the greater populace.

Sir Joseph was finally felled by death on 8 June 1865.

The orchid genus *Paxtonia* is named in his honor.

References

Curtis, Charles H. 1956. Men, matters and memories. *The Orch. Rev.* 64, no. 756.

Gardeners' Chronicle. 1865. The late Sir Joseph Paxton. No. 24.

Gardeners' Chronicle. 1865. Miscellaneous—The late Duke of Devonshire and Sir Joseph Paxton. No. 27.

Markham, Violet R. 1935. *Paxton and the Bachelor Duke.* London: Hodder & Stoughton Ltd.

George Ure Skinner
(1804-1867)

BY 1834 THE "ORCHIDOMANIA" IN ENGLAND WAS WIDESPREAD. THE COUN-
tries of the New World were being combed for their orchid treasures
and thousands of plants were being shipped to the Continent. The little-
known Republic of Guatemala was at that time an unwrought mine of
natural history; therefore, whatever was sent to Europe from there was
almost sure to be new. George Ure Skinner, an English merchant residing there, became famous for his collections.

George Ure Skinner was born on 18 March 1804, the second son of
the Very Rev. John Skinner, dean of Dunkeld and Dunblane. His grandfather was the primus of the Scottish Episcopal Church and bishop of
Aberdeen, and his great-grandfather was a well-known ecclesiastical
historian of Scotland and one of the best Hebrew and Latin scholars of

his era. With such a heritage of scholarly forebears, it is rather curious that young Skinner did not follow the academic trail. His inclinations were entirely different.

As a child he was an ardent nature lover and in early youth was bent on joining the navy. His father had other plans for him, however, and in deference to his father's wishes he became a clerk in the banking house of Barclay, Bevan & Co., of London. He subsequently removed himself to Leeds, where he entered business as a general merchant. Leeds did not hold him long, though.

In 1831 there occurred an opportunity for trade relations with the Republic of Guatemala, and Skinner at once accepted and set sail for that country. There it was that he entered into partnership with Mr. McKlee, and thus the well-known mercantile house of Klee, Skinner, & Co., of Guatemala came into being.

Skinner had not been in Guatemala long when he became deeply impressed with its vast resources, nearly all of which were allowed to go to waste in the unsettled condition of the country. With great resourcefulness he undertook the extensive cultivation of indigo and cochineal, which later numbered among the staple exports of the republic. Other projects followed, but incursions by savage Indian hordes hampered their development, and Skinner often found it necessary to bear arms against the invaders.

In 1834 he still had not even heard of orchids. He was, however, much interested in the birds and insects of Guatemala and spent considerable time in collecting them. One of his shipments of specimens to the Museum of Natural History at Manchester, England, attracted the attention of James Bateman, then a horticultural student at Oxford. Bateman was, of course, eager to seize the first chance of obtaining botanical material from a relatively untouched area, and so he wrote to Skinner, explaining by means of descriptions and sketches the sort of plants orchids were, hoping to interest the man in searching for them. The day Mr. Bateman's letter arrived, Skinner later repeated many times over, was as it were a birthday, for it gave a fresh interest to his life which lasted to the end of his days. Though untrained in botany, he soon recognized the orchids which were described in Bateman's letter and began collecting at once. At the earliest opportunity he sent a box of carefully packed plants to Bateman, all of which were new to England. Among the shipment were plants of *Barkeria skinneri* (which Bateman asked Dr. Lindley to name after its discoverer), *Epidendrum aromaticum, Cattleya aurantiaca, Oncidium cavendishianum, Oncidium leucochilum,* and *Odontoglossum bictoniense*—the latter being the first of the genus to reach England alive.

When Skinner heard of the success of his shipment, he was extremely pleased, and thereafter it rarely occurred that a mail shipment left Guatemala without a letter from Skinner announcing some new discovery or seeking the orchid news of England, particularly as pertained to the plants introduced by himself.

The list of Skinner's orchid introductions is lengthy, nearly 100 species. Besides those mentioned, he was the first to find *Odontoglossum grande* (his favorite orchid), *Odontoglossum uro-skinneri, Odontoglossum rubescens, Odontoglossum pulchellum, Schomburgkia tibicinis, Epidendrum stamfordianum, Epidendrum alatum, Cattleya skinneri, Stanhopea saccata, Cycnoches ventricosum* and *egertonianum, Laelia superbiens, Epidendrum cnemidophorum, Lycaste skinneri* (later changed to *Lycaste virginalis*), and many more. Though the orchids were his favorite plants, he did not neglect other botanical tribes, as is shown by names such as *Aquilegia skinneri* and *Uro-skinnera speciosa*, names given by Lindley to other of Skinner's introductions. In the Orchid Family his name is further commemorated by *Mormodes skinneri*, and *Epidendrum skinneri*.

His contributions to ornithology were also considerable, with not less than twenty species of birds sent to British museums for the first time.

Skinner was ever ready to give his services to science and natural history and was happy to lend a helping hand to any traveler or naturalist

Lycaste virginalis (*L. skinneri* Ldl.), the national flower of Guatemala and showy discovery of George Ure Skinner.

who came his way. He heartily rejoiced at the successes of others as much as if they had been his own, and thus assisted Mr. O. Salvin, one of England's most eminent ornithologists, in his earliest Guatemalan wanderings. Through him, Captain Dow, of the American Packet service, and many others, were first led to study and love nature. In kindness to his friend James Bateman, in 1860 he took that gentleman's eldest son under his care and the boy returned with him to Guatemala following one of Skinner's visits to England.

During the period when orchids were at a peak of popularity and interest in England, the orchid sales at Stevens' Auction Rooms were originated by Skinner. When in England, he might always be found there sorting, arranging, and cataloguing cargoes of imported orchids. To him the work was a labor of love, and he was as willing to do it in behalf of a stranger as much as for himself—always, however, claiming a few specimens as prerequisites, which he presented as gifts to his friends. At his disposal were extensive collections made by Warszewicz in Peru and Veragua in New Grenada, but as these were all "cool" orchids and looked upon as unmanageable, most of them were given away.

At the Veitch Exotic Nursery in Chelsea, a glass house for the accommodation of his own importations was generously placed at his disposal, and he could often be found there on visits to England. The whole Veitch establishment fascinated him, and the Veitch family was especially close to his heart.

Having worked hard all his life, he at length resolved to retire from business, putting his thirty-five years of collecting behind and settling for the remainder of his life in his native land. A widower for many years and then past sixty years of age, he looked forward to joining his two daughters and aged mother who had for some time resided with the Rev. James Skinner at Newland, near Malvern, England. With this in mind he sailed from England to Guatemala on 2 December 1866 with the intention of winding up his affairs and then returning to England in the fall of the next year. Had he been able to carry out these plans, he would have crossed the Atlantic Ocean forty times. Fate decreed otherwise, however. He reached Colon the first week of January 1867 and crossed by rail to Panama. Finding that the first ship leaving that port for the Pacific was overcrowded, he decided to wait for a week until the arrival of the next vessel. In the meantime he set about collecting plants and birds with his usual enthusiasm. On Sunday of that week he returned to Colon for church services, dining in the evening on board the *Danube*. There, it is presumed, he contracted yellow fever, for on Monday he felt uncomfortable; on Tuesday he was gravely ill; and on Wednesday, 9 January, he died.

His last letter—written in high spirits and full of plant gossip—was to his old friend Mr. Veitch. It was written on the fourth, with a postscript added on the sixth. The mail that bore it home also carried the sad and unexpected tidings of his death.

References

Ames, Oakes, and Correll, Donovan S. 1952. Orchids of Guatemala. *Fieldiana: Botany* 26, no. 1. Chicago Natural History Museum.
Gardeners' Chronicle. 1867. The late Mr. G. Ure Skinner. No. 8.

Friedrich Martin Josef Welwitsch (1806–1872)

IN READING OF THE LIVES OF INFLUENTIAL MEN IN THE FIELD OF BOTANY, one becomes aware of an odd coincidence; a large number of them gave up promising careers in other fields in order to devote themselves to plants. Many chose to wander and explore the far reaches of the world, sending their new discoveries to botanical gardens and educational institutions. Their personal preferences were for life in the wilds, unhindered and at liberty to blaze their own paths. Others preferred the herbarium approach to plant study—cataloguing, systematizing, and publishing their results. Few such individuals had the opportunity and backing to do both—nor the combination of scientific aptitude and self-discipline along with great physical stamina and courage. One such individual who did possess those qualities, and who distinguished himself magnificently in the annals of orchid discovery, was an Austrian physician named Friedrich Welwitsch, one of the earliest botanists to systematically explore the virgin territory of West Africa. His orchid discoveries, as well as a large number of botanical "curiosities" found in Angola and Benguela, were probably the most rewarding and enlightening finds since that period when Australia was first opened to botanizing.

Friedrich Martin Josef Welwitsch was born at Marisaal, Carinthia, Austria, on 5 February 1806, one of a large family. His father was the owner of an extensive farm and surveyor of a district in Carinthia. It was due to his father's influence that the boy acquired his first taste for botany because, while accompanying the elder Welwitsch in his walks over the countryside, he was encouraged to seek out the various native plants and identify them by means of an old herbal. A town apothecary also assisted him in his early botanical studies.

When the time came for his higher education, he was sent to the University of Vienna and enrolled in law school; he fared poorly in legal studies, however, as his irresistible tendency toward natural science was too distracting. His father was displeased and withdrew the young student's allowance, leaving him to fend for himself. For a short time thereafter he supported himself as a theatre critic, but with a view to more congenial living he entered the medical faculty of the university, at the same time pursuing the study of botany with increased fervor. He spent much time in the Botanical Museum at Vienna and soon became well known to Professor Eduard Fenzl and other botanists for his love of collecting, his scientific knowledge of native flora, and his merit as a contributor to the accurate knowledge of the flora of the Vienna Basin and lower Austria. His first publication, *Observations on the Cryptogamic Flora of Lower Austria*, appeared in the *Beiträge zur Landeskunde von Wien* in 1834, winning for him a prize given by the mayor of the city.

He graduated in medicine in 1836, his thesis being *A Synopsis of the Nostochineae of Lower Austria*. Shortly thereafter his life's course began to define itself. Having attended a meeting of the German Naturalists' Association, his thoughts became fixed on foreign travel, and in a short while his dreams became real.

In 1839 Welwitsch was commissioned by the Wurtemberg Unio Itineraria to collect the plants of the Azores and Cape Verde Islands. He accordingly left Vienna in the summer of that year and arrived in Lisbon in July. He unfortunately found himself unavoidably detained there (no reason or explanation given in available references) and so made use of his time by making an extensive collection of the plants of the district. So attracted did he become by the country that he ultimately made arrangements to remain in Portugal through the winter instead of proceeding to the Atlantic islands. He never returned to Austria.

He remained in Lisbon as a botany teacher, having charge at different times of the Botanic Gardens at Lisbon and Coimbra. In addition, he supervised the gardens of the duke of Palmella throughout Portugal. All the while he explored the country and made large botanical collections. Over 56,000 specimens were distributed to the Unio Itineraria, and complete series were deposited in the herbaria of the Academy of Sciences at Lisbon and Paris. His own private herbarium contained over 9000 species, each represented by a large series of well-preserved specimens selected to show all stages and conditions of growth.

In 1850 the Portuguese government, under Queen Dona Maria, resolved to send a scientific expedition to its West African possessions, a double purpose being to obtain information on the natural products of the region and to develop its economic interests. Welwitsch was selected for this important mission, and in August 1853 he set out for Loanda, the capital of Angola, fully equipped, accredited with full powers by the government, and with complete liberty to act at his own disposal. He reached Angola at the end of September, at once beginning a series of collecting excursions. He devoted nearly a year to the investigation (his travels forming a huge triangle with 120 miles of coastline as base), ultimately returning to Loanda. Thereupon he set out for the interior, following the Bengo and reaching the district of Golungo-Alto, where he established his new base for further explorations.

He spent two years in arduous and exhaustive search, forging through almost impenetrable forests. During this time he suffered repeatedly and severely from fevers, scurvy, and ulcerated legs. His enthusiasm never waned, however, and he assiduously continued his work. During this period he made the acquaintance of Dr. David Livingstone, then (October 1854) on his way to Loanda, having traveled the whole distance from Cape Town. The two explorers spent quite some time together, and their meeting convinced Welwitsch to abandon a plan he had previously entertained of trying to make his way across the continent to the Portuguese possession on the east coast—a task which Livingstone accomplished during the next two years.

Welwitsch's further explorations took him to southwest Africa, in an arid plateau region inland from Cape Negro, where he amassed an awesome collection of materials, orchids not the least among them. One interesting discovery, a terrestrial orchid allied to *Lissochilus*, possessed broad leaves nearly five feet long, a flower stem ten to twelve feet high, and a spike of blossoms about 1½ feet long bearing twenty to twenty-five rose-colored flowers. This was probably the largest and most magnificent of all terrestrial orchids hitherto discovered. He additionally discovered over sixty other species, a number of which were later named in his honor: *Liparis welwitschii, Eulophia welwitschii, Lissochilus welwitschii, Listrostachys welwitschii, Corymbis welwitschii, Brachycorythis welwitschii, Habenaria welwitschii,* and *Disa welwitschii.*

After seven years of wandering the wildest regions of West Africa, Welwitsch returned to Lisbon in 1861. His collections were undoubtedly the earliest of any importance made in southern tropical Africa, the orchids including many first collected by him, a number of which have not been recollected since. In addition to the specimens being well collected and preserved, his locality and other biological notes were exceptionally comprehensive for the period in which he worked and often still provide the only information available on the specific points mentioned.

In Lisbon he commenced a critical examination of his African material. He discovered, however, that there was a great lack of comparative collections, literature, and qualified botanists in Portugal, and the task of naming and arranging his specimens became increasingly difficult. It was obvious that he would need references at one of the great scientific centers, and so, with a grant from the Portuguese government, Welwitsch took his collections to London in 1863. There he worked steadily from early morning till late at night, frequently suffering from recurrent fevers and other ailments resulting from his years in Africa. All his work, though, was characterized by precision and completeness. Despite this excellence, however, he never became well known in London's scientific circles, and in some cases he was probably underrated because of his difficulty in expressing himself clearly in English. For this reason he was somewhat withdrawn. He, nevertheless, kept himself up to date on all that was published in botanical science, industriously naming and arranging his collections in accordance.

After two years in London, word reached him that malicious rumors were being circulated in botanical circles in Portugal to the effect that he was selling his Angolan collections and living in sumptuous luxury. Without a formal hearing of any kind, the Portuguese government discontinued his subsistence allowance six months after the attack. Welwitsch became embittered and, as a result, developed a suspicious and averse reaction to society in general. But he continued to labor at his collections, alone and absorbed in his work.

In the summer of 1872 a fire in the house where he lodged scorched and blackened some of his collections. This incident caused him a severe nervous disorder. A painful illness followed, lasting about six weeks, and on the evening of 20 October he died, working to the last on his valuable African collections.

His herbarium was bequeathed to the British Museum, but this led to prolonged litigation on the part of the Portuguese government, ending in a compromise whereby the British Museum received one set of Welwitsch's plants. Some went to Portugal, and others were distributed to various European herbaria.

In the early days the importance of his collections was fully recognized, but because of the division of the collections it was not easy thereafter to examine the material as a whole. This led to the collections being neglected for some time afterward. Later, as the wide geographical ranges of African orchids were more and more recognized, the identity of the Welwitsch gatherings often became a crucial matter, and the assurance of accuracy in the taxonomy of African orchids made it almost absolutely necessary to consult the Welwitsch material. Many of his orchid findings, thought formerly to be restricted to Angola, became known to occur over wide areas of tropical and South Africa as well.

Welwitsch was well recognized for his achievements by the bestowal of four or five orders. He was a member of the Leopoldo-Corolinian Academy, a fellow of the Zoologico-Botanical Society of Vienna, a fellow of the Linnean Society, and a member of other scientific organizations.

Among his important published works on the flora of Africa are *Sertum Angolense* in the *Transactions of the Linnean Society*, 1869; a catalogue of the African plants collected by Welwitsch, prepared by W. P. Hiern and others and published by the British Museum, 1896–1901; and his contributions to Professor Daniel Oliver's *Flora of Tropical Africa*. Welwitsch's orchids were never published collectively in any single work, but a careful perusal of the literature mentioned conveys the magnitude and importance of his pioneer discoveries in tropical Africa.

References

Curtis' Botanical Magazine. 1931. *Dedications and Portraits 1827–1927*. Compiled by Ernest Nelmes and Wm. Cuthbertson. London: Bernard Quaritch Ltd.

Gardeners' Chronicle. 1872. Obituary. No. 43.

Gardeners' Chronicle. 1865. Notices of books—No. 1.

Gray, Asa. Scientific papers—1889. *American Jour. of Sciences and Arts* 396, 3rd ser.

Journal of Botany. 1873. 11: 1–11.

Leopoldina. 1872. 8: 10, 11.

Thiselton-Dyer, W. T. 1898. *Flora of Tropical Africa*. Preface of Vol. 7: *Hydrocharideae to Liliaceae*.

Charles Robert Darwin
(1809-1882)

NOT UNTIL THE LATTER HALF OF THE EIGHTEENTH CENTURY DID THE STRUC-
tural peculiarities of orchid flowers attract the serious attention of naturalists. Lee (1765) became interested in these curious structures, followed by Kurt Sprengel (1793), who observed the role of insects in the
pollination of orchids. Wechter (1801) observed that native terrestrial
orchids failed to set seed unless visited by insects, and Robert Brown's
paper on the reproductive structures of orchids, read before the Linnean Society in 1831, established the presence of the nucleus, the "heart"
of the living cell. A few weeks later a young naturalist set sail on
H.M.S. *Beagle*, an epoch-making voyage that resulted in biological discoveries that were to shake the foundations of scientific and religious
opinion and change the philosophical attitudes of mankind. This young
man was Charles Darwin, the learned and versatile "evolutionist" whose

observations of the orchid's reproductive parts led to the confirmation of his theory of evolution through natural selection and competition. Much of what orchidology now knows of the relationships of orchids and insects is based on Darwin's discoveries over 100 years ago.

Charles Robert Darwin was born at The Mount, Shrewsbury, England, on 12 February 1809. He was the son of Dr. Charles Waring Darwin and the grandson of Dr. Erasmus Darwin, a naturalist whose speculations were to have a profound influence on the younger family scion.

Young Charles was educated at the grammar school at Shrewsbury, thence he went to Edinburgh (1825) and afterward to Cambridge. He did not excel in school, however. He was, in fact, considered rather below the common standard in intellect. He became a pupil of Professors Henslow and Sedgewicke at Cambridge, and under their guidance his consuming interest in botany began to bear fruit. He received his degree at Cambridge in 1831 and shortly thereafter, at the age of twenty-two, joined a hydrographical survey as an unpaid naturalist on H.M.S. *Beagle*. For five years he served aboard the *Beagle*, studying the flora, fauna, and geology of numerous temperate, subtropical, and tropical districts surrounding South America. This historic round-the-world voyage which Darwin later referred to as "by far the most important event in my life," laid the foundations for the remainder of his life's work, placing him among the foremost of rising naturalists. The results of his services were given in his *Journal of Researches* into the geology and natural history of the countries visited.

Darwin was not a robust man even in his young manhood but he was a zealous naturalist who refused to be shackled by illness; on his return to England he began to write and experiment extensively, despite poor health, exploring all the sciences of earth, life, and man. Thus he rose to renown. Few were privileged to know him on a close personal level, however, for owing to his always feeble health and retiring nature, he seldom entered into social functions or close personal relationships. Instead he labored diligently and introspectively in the pursuit of scientific study. By his work at the Geological Society, and by his numerous papers on coral reefs, the natural history of the cirrhipeds, and many other biological researches he gained fame as an authority.

In 1838 he accepted the appointment as secretary of the Geological Society and was elected to the Royal Society the following year. Meanwhile, he had married his cousin, Emma Wedgwood, and settled in Down, Kent, shortly thereafter. Years of study and writing followed.

Darwin held that no higher plant could fertilize itself for a perpetuity of generations without the intercession of being cross-fertilized with some other individual. This theory he published in 1859 in his work entitled *On the Origin of Species by Means of Natural Selection*. This work brought him controversial fame as it called down upon him a shower of blame and abuse for propounding such a theory without providing absolute proof.

Native terrestrial orchids grew in abundance near Darwin's home and, because they were the "most singular and modified forms in the vegetable kingdom," he began an extensive study of their reproduction in order to prove his theory of cross-fertilization against that of self-fertilization. With his sons and his friends often assisting him in his observations, he spent unnumbered hours in the garden and fields making notes on the number of flowers that set seed; setting up controls by the use of nets and bell jars; catching bees and moths and examining the pollen masses that adhered to their heads and bodies; artificially pollinating flowers by the insertion of a pencil or a fine bristle; and examining the showy markings and structures of species which were consistent in attracting natural pollinators. Early in his researches he noted the pollination of *Orchis pyramidalis* by a particular moth, and studied such unusual adaptations as the "flinging" of pollen onto the pollinator in the genus *Catasetum* and the pollination of *Ophrys* by pseudo-copulation.

The studies were of such interest to Darwin that he shortly initiated a copious correspondence with Sir Joseph Hooker (then assistant director at Kew), and in a letter to Hooker in October 1861 he stated, "I never was more interested in any subject in my life than this of Orchids."

As his interest in the order became intensified, he began to study the pollinating devices of tropical orchids: the shooting mechanism of *Catasetum* species, the "bucket" lip of *Coryanthes*, and many others. Observing the remarkably lengthy nectary of *Angraecum sesquipedale*, he predicted that it must be necessary for some certain moth with a foot-long tongue to be the pollinating agent for this remarkable species.*

Finally gathering sufficient evidence to uphold his theories, in 1862 Darwin published his classic work, *On the Fertilisation of Orchids by Insects*. This work put forth the results of his observations and not only removed all doubt regarding the function of the pollinia, but drew the attention of naturalists to the complex symbiosis existing between flowering plants and food-seeking insects. The introduction of this book states his purpose:

... In my volume "On the Origin of Species" I gave only general reasons for the belief that it is an almost universal law of nature that the higher organic being require an occasional cross with another individual; or, which is the same thing, that no hermaphrodite fertilises itself for a perpetuity of generations. Having been blamed for propounding this doctrine without giving ample facts, for which I had not sufficient space in that work, I wish here to show that I have not spoken without having gone into details.

* Darwin did not live to see his prediction proved, though it was observed some years later that such a moth (*Xanthopan morgani praedicta*) with a proboscis over a foot long does, indeed, exist in Madagascar.

I have been led to publish this little treatise separately, as it is too large to be incorporated with any other subject. As Orchids are universally acknowledged to rank amongst the most singular and most modified forms in the vegetable kingdom, I have thought that the facts to be given might lead some observers to look more curiously into the habits of our several native species.... This treatise affords me also an opportunity of attempting to show that the study of organic beings may be as interesting to an observer who is fully convinced that the structure of each is due to secondary laws, as to one who views every trifling detail of structure as the result of the direct interposition of the Creator.

As the facts were brought together to bear on Darwin's theory, the tide of feeling among naturalists turned in his favor. Known for his honesty, his persistent study habits, and his unprejudiced devotion to truth, he gained immediate support from such men as Sir Joseph Hooker, Professor Huxley, Mr. George Bentham, and others. Their "conversions" to a belief in evolution were remarkably rapid, and even the educated minority of the population at large soon grasped evolutionary concepts.

For the remainder of his life Darwin studied, researched, and made many important contributions to geology, zoological geography, taxonomy, ecology, and animal breeding. He died on 19 April 1882, at the age of seventy-three.

Other of his important works in the various fields of science include *The Structure and Distribution of Coral Reefs, The Descent of Man, Geological Observations in South America, Insectivorous Plants, Cross and Self-Fertilisation in the Vegetable Kingdom, Formation of Vegetable Mold, Emotions in Man and Animals, Principles of Variation Under Domestication,* and *The Power of Movement in Plants.*

Darwin's orchid studies became the basis of a number of later works by succeeding naturalists and botanists, but while his contributions to orchidology were theretofore unprecedented in pollination studies, their importance is equally shared in science as a breakthrough which resulted in theories that changed the whole foundation of scientific knowledge.

References

American Orchid Society Bulletin. 1940. Vol. 9, no. 6, p. 151.

Ames, Oakes. 1937. Pollination of orchids through pseudocopulation. *Botanical Museum Leaflets* 5, no. 1. Cambridge, Massachusetts: Harvard University Press.

Ames, Oakes. 1941. Pollination in Coryanthes. *Amer. Orch. Soc. Bull.* 10, no. 6.

Ames, Oakes. 1944. The pollinia of orchids. *Amer. Orch. Soc. Bull.* 13, no. 6.

Darwin, Charles. 1903. *Various Contrivances by which Orchids are Fertilised by Insects.* 2 ed., rev. New York.

Gardners' Chronicle. 1882. Death of Charles Darwin. Vol. 17, no. 434.

Gibson, William Hamilton, and Jelliffe, Helena Leeming. 1905. *Our Native Orchids.* New York: Doubleday, Page & Co.

Orchidata. 1966. 5, no. 6.

Worldscope Encyclopedia. 1953. Vol. 4. The Universal Guild, Inc.

James Bateman (1811–1897)

ORCHIDS CONTINUED TO INCREASE IN POPULARITY AS ORNAMENTAL PLANTS, and larger numbers of them appeared in the glasshouses and conservatories throughout England. Ironically, great numbers of them perished because of the widespread misunderstanding, prior to the introduction of Sir Joseph Paxton's cultural methods, of their requirements. Systems of classification were being developed, monographs of genera were being published, and many other technical aspects were being explored, but there remained a desperate need for published cultural information on the horticultural level. Toward this end James Bateman, an early and enthusiastic orchid hobbyist, was instrumental in the spread of growing techniques, by the many semitechnical and popular books and articles he authored.

James Bateman was born at Redivals, Bury, England, on 18 July 1811. At Oxford he received his B.A. in 1834 and his M.A. in 1845. Like many other famed orchidologists, Bateman took an early and abiding interest in botany. While attending Magdalene College, Oxford, on one occasion he was required to write out half the Book of Psalms as punishment for absenting himself from class beyond a prescribed period. He had stopped at a local nursery to buy a plant of *Renanthera coccinea*, which had caught his eye. This plant was to become the beginning of his fine orchid collection at Knypersley Hall.

Bateman's father encouraged his son in horticulture, and in 1833 young Bateman hired a botanical collector named Colley to go to Demerara, chiefly to search for orchids. By this venture about sixty species of orchids were sent back alive, a third of them new to cultivation. One of these was named *Batemannia colleyi* by John Lindley, thus commemorating both employer and collector.

Bateman was an industrious hobbyist anxious to establish acquaintance with anyone who lived in areas where orchids grew naturally. Learning that the Natural History Museum at Manchester had received shipments of birds and animals from one George Ure Skinner, Bateman wrote to the collector. Thus began a most productive relationship between collector and horticulturist. As each shipment of plants was received from Guatemala, Bateman established them in his greenhouse at Knypersley Hall, flowered them, and had them identified by contemporaries in London but particularly by John Lindley. Within ten years he possessed the finest examples of Guatemalan orchids then available in England.

Several fine orchid books emanated from his pen. From the standpoint of size alone, his *Orchidaceae of Mexico and Guatemala* is monumental. Issued in parts from 1837 to 1843, it consists of forty huge folio plates, twenty-seven inches in height by fifteen inches in width, and includes descriptions and cultural advice. Only 125 copies of this gigantic volume were issued. The drawings were specially prepared for Bateman by Mrs. Withers, flower painter for Queen Adelaide. The plate depicting *Odontoglossum bictoniense* is of particular historic interest because it pictures the first member of the genus introduced to cultivation.

Bateman moved to Kensington in 1860, where he compiled the texts for many of the new orchids figured in *Paxton's Botanical Magazine*. Reissued in 1867 in one volume, these texts and figures became known as *A Second Century of Orchidaceous Plants*.

During the ten-year period of 1864–1874 Bateman issued his *Monograph of Odontoglossums*, the introduction of which recalls the mistaken manner in which "cool" orchids were cultivated in stoves. "But," stated Bateman, "no sooner had a few houses, constructed and managed on the cool-culture system, made it clear that the orchids of temperate regions were prepared to submit to the skill of the cultivator, that a general raid was made upon the more accessible countries in which they were known to abound, more especially certain districts in Mexico and New Granada. To the latter country collectors were simultaneously sent off by the Horticultural Society, by Mr. Linden, and by Messrs.

Low and Co., and all these rival envoys, much to their own mortification, and chagrin, found themselves sailing for the same destination in the same steamer on the same errand."

The *Monograph* was originally intended to be concluded with an analysis of the genus and a conspectus of all its known species, but this section never appeared, the thirty plates issued being the entirety of the work.

Bateman also contributed to the *Gardeners' Chronicle*, doing a series of papers entitled "Dies Orchidianae," under the pen name of Serapias, and he published a *Guide to Cool Orchid Growing* in 1864.

His horticultural associations were many. He served as a fellow of the Linnean Society from 1833 and as a fellow of the Royal Society from 1838. He lectured to the Royal Horticultural Society for many years, and that organization awarded him the Veitch Memorial Medal in 1885.

On 27 November 1897, at the age of eighty-six, James Bateman passed away at Worthing, Sussex.

References

Curtis' Botanical Magazine. 1931. *Dedications and Portraits 1827–1927*. Compiled by Ernest Nelmes and Wm. Cuthbertson. London: Bernard Quaritch Ltd.

Garden, The. Obituary. Vol. 52, no. 1359.

Orchid Review, The. 1931. Records of the past. Vol. 39, no. 461.

Wilson, Gurney. 1950. Bateman's "Odontoglossum." *The Orch. Rev.* 58, no. 682.

Karl Theodore Hartweg (1812-1871)

CENTRAL AND SOUTH AMERICA WERE EASILY THE "TREASURE TROVES" OF the orchid world in the 1800s and the areas most frequented by orchid seekers attempting to supply the voracious "orchid mania" then current in England. Many intrepid collectors entered the field either in the service of commercial nurseries or on their own, both with a view toward ready profit. The competition was fierce indeed, for having once located and collected the plants, it was often a race to get them shipped back to the salesrooms of England by the most expedient means. As a scientific organization, however, the London Horticultural Society was interested in new plants for the sake of study, not profit; thus they had no great urgency to acquire large quantities of single species. And so, by sending out a young German collector named Karl Hartweg to Mexico and tropical America, there resulted the most variable and comprehensive collection of New World orchids made by a single individual in the first half of the century.

Karl Theodore Hartweg, a descendant of a long line of gardeners, was born 18 June 1812, at Karlsruhe, Germany. He received an excellent education in botany and at an early age was employed by the Paris Jardin des Plantes and afterward by the London Horticultural Society, where his aptitude and intelligence soon attracted attention and led to his being sent to Mexico in 1836 to collect seeds and plants for introduction into English gardens. William Jackson Hooker, director of the Royal Botanical Gardens at Kew, confidently anticipated that Hartweg would do great justice to British plant study and wrote in *The Companion to the Botanical Magazine* in January 1837:

... Mr. Theodore Hartweg embarked for Mexico in the service of the Horticultural Society, to whom therefore all living plants, roots, and seeds will be sent: but that useful Institution has generously allowed him to dispose of dried specimens of plants on his own account, which he will do at the rate of £2 the hundred species. All applications, however, for shares must be made through the Horticultural Society, by letters addressed either to Mr. Bentham, or to Mr. Lindley. From the capital of Mexico, Mr. Hartweg will go to Guanaxato and proceed northward ... keeping as much as he can to the Tierra fria. He will remain in the country two or three years, that is, if the state of it will admit of botanizing; but it is so disturbed, that he may probably have to take another direction and visit Bolivia, which presents a yet more interesting field. Whichever way he goes, we are authorized in anticipating great things from him.

For seven years Hartweg roamed Mexico, Central America, northern South America, and Jamaica, making important discoveries, including numerous coniferous trees of the Mexican highlands and large numbers of new orchids which he successfully introduced into cultivation. In his own journals he described in detail the botany of the regions explored. George Bentham described the Hartweg collections under the title of *Plantae Hartwegianae*, the publication of which commenced in 1839 and extended over several years.

Hartweg returned to England in 1843 and the society was so pleased with his work that they sent him on a second mission to Mexico and California, with the same objectives and under the same auspices, in 1845. This mission was completed in 1848. Arriving at Vera Cruz in November 1845, he crossed Mexico to Mazatlán, on the Pacific Coast. There it was, on his first journey to Zaquapan, on the eastern side of the snowclad Orizabas, that he found the orchid *Hartwegia purpurea*, so named in acknowledgment of his success as a collector by Dr. John Lindley.

Because of political difficulties between the United States and England over possession of Alta California, Hartweg was unable to obtain passage to California until May 1846, arriving in Monterey on 7 June. From there he journeyed to San Francisco, the Sacramento Valley as far north as Chico, and into the Sierra foothills. Other trips took him southward to Soledad and San Antonio and the Santa Lucia Mountains. The many plants introduced in the course of these journeys, especially hardy plants, trees, and orchids, were of great satisfaction to the Horticultural Society.

Following the California expedition, Hartweg was appointed director of the Grand Ducal Gardens of Swetzingen, in Baden, Germany, where he died on 3 February 1871, leaving several sons and a legacy of worthy and important achievement in plant discovery and introduction.

References

Alden, Roland H., and Ifft, John D. 1943. *Early Naturalists in the Far West.* San Francisco: California Academy of Sciences.
Gardeners' Chronicle. 1871. Obituary. No. 10.
Journal of Botany. 1871. Botanical News. Vol. 9.
McKelvey, Susan Delano. 1955. *Botanical Explorations of the Trans-Mississippi West 1790–1850.* Jamaica Plain, Massachusetts: Arnold Arboretum of Harvard University.

Josef Ritter von Rawicz Warszewicz (1812–1866)

THE NAME WARSZEWICZ HAS LONG BEEN ASSOCIATED WITH NUMEROUS showy orchids of Central America, many of which became well known to hybridizers. The collector for whom these plants were often named had many unique experiences, and though funds were often insufficient, he made lengthy expeditions into tropical forests, collecting, exploring, and despatching his finds to the botanical gardens and herbaria of Germany and England.

Josef Ritter von Rawicz Warszewicz was born in Wilno, Lithuania (of Polish extraction), in 1812. Little is revealed of his childhood, but he is known to have joined the staff of Jundzill's Botanical Garden as a young man. He became embroiled in the first Polish revolution, however, and had to foresake his homeland.

In the years 1840–1844 he was employed as an assistant in the Botanical Garden at Berlin, where his industrious nature made him a highly capable gardener; here his large herbarium was later deposited.

In 1845, the year Warszewicz finished his studies at the Botanical Garden, Messr. Van Houtte, a horticulturist of Ghent, Belgium, advertised for a suitable man to accompany a Belgian colony to Guatemala in order to collect tropical plants and seeds for commercial sales purposes. Upon recommendation by a friend, Warszewicz was hired for the assignment and left Ostend for Guatemala in December 1844. Almost immediately after his arrival in Central America the Van Houtte greenhouses began receiving consignments of tropical plants, mainly orchids.

In 1846 Warszewicz established himself in Guatemala as an independent collector, gathering seeds, living plants, and dried specimens which he sent to Europe. In the gardens of his friends and patrons Warszewicz cultivated the great quantities of plants which he had collected from the mountains of Guatemala and dispatched them wholesale to Europe. His success was such that brought a new era to German horticulture, being the first time that a man who was as industrious and intelligent as others who sent their collections only to England, should make shipments directly to the various gardens in Germany. The gardens at Hamburg, Berlin, Erfurt, and the Botanical Garden in Zurich all received annual shipments of seeds, tubers, and bulbs. During all this time until the end of his travels, Warszewicz imported enormous quantities of orchids, and the descriptions of a number of new species of this family which he introduced were published by H. G. Reichenbach in *Bonplandia*.

Warszewicz passed several years exploring and collecting in various parts of Central America. Almost without means and accompanied only by a single Indian, in 1848 he set out from Guatemala to undertake a great journey through Central America. There for long months he lived in Indian huts, subsisting on maize and fruits from the forest. Especially rich were his collections in Panama, where he climbed the 16,000-foot Chiriqui Volcano. He discovered *Cattleya dowiana* in Costa Rica. Unfortunately, the plants he was able to send to Van Houtte arrived in poor condition and perished in spite of the painstaking cultural efforts taken with them. Specimens later sent by a Mr. Acre arrived successfully and bloomed to perfection. In Colombia the following year, Warszewicz discovered and collected *Cattleya warscewiczii*.

In 1850 he returned to Europe after an attack of yellow fever. On his return to Cracow Dr. Czerwiakowski, of the botanical garden of that city, offered him a position, but Warszewicz would not accept. Instead, he went to Berlin, where he met H. G. Reichenbach and assisted him for awhile in his work, describing more than 300 orchid species. Unaccustomed to such sedentary work, however, in the beginning of 1851 he embarked for South America. By the end of that year he was in Guayaquil, Ecuador, where he was robbed of money and equipment, whereby

Cattleya warscewiczii

he lost all that he had gained from his earlier journeys. From there he continued to Bolivia and Peru, spending some time in Lima in 1852. Each of his trips brought shipments of orchids, as well as many other plants of horticultural value, to botanical gardens in Cracow and Berlin. He discovered several new species of *Gesneriaceae*, and his *Canna warscewicza* became one of the most outstanding parents in the hybrid progeny of the genus.

The Horticultural Society of London offered to have him travel at their expense, but Warszewicz declined, for he wished to wander and continue his collecting without following a prescribed route or turning his collections over to a single organization, preferring to distribute his material without restriction. At this time his importations were highly prized, especially in England, and it was there that orchids he had collected brought prices as high as twenty-five pounds sterling per plant.

In Peru he followed the Marañón River, again discovering a great number of new orchids which Professor Reichenbach described. A recurrence of yellow fever in 1853, however, once again compelled Warszewicz to leave his orchid-hunting grounds, and he returned to Cracow where Dr. Czerwiakowski offered him the post of supervisor of the Botanical Gardens. He accepted the position and retained it until, after a short illness, he died on 29 December 1866. His collections of dried specimens were bequeathed to the Berlin Botanic Garden.

Many orchids remain to honor the name and memory of this great collector. Besides *Cattleya warscewiczii*, previously mentioned, he is commemorated in *Cycnoches warscewiczii*, *Catasetum warscewiczii*, *Miltonia warscewiczii*, *Paphiopedilum caudatum* var. *warszewiczianum*, *Sobralia warscewiczii*, *Brassia warscewiczii*, *Epidendrum warscewiczii*, *Mesospinidium warscewiczii*, *Oncidium warscewiczii*, *Stanhopea warscewiczii*, and the genus *Warszewiczella*.

There would seem to be a discrepancy between the spelling of his name—Warszewicz—and the specific names of plants honoring him. His own name is the correct spelling, but the mistaken specific spellings remain by virtue of early nomenclature and publication.

References

Bonplandia. 1854. II Jahrgang. No. 8.
Gardeners' Chronicle. 1867. No. 9.
Ogrodnictwo. 1927. Numero consacré a la mémoire de J. Warszewicz. Vol. 23, no. 1.
Sampolinski, Jerzy. 1963. Josef Warszewicz—A famous orchid collector. *The Orch. Rev.* 71, no. 840.
Standley, Paul. 1928. Flora of Panama Canal Zone. *Contrib. U.S. Nat. Herb.* Vol. 27.

John Gibson (1815-1875)

STURDY YOUNG MEN WERE REQUIRED IN THE TASK OF TRAVELING TO THE tropics in search of orchids and other plants. Among the earliest—and youngest—of the plant collectors was John Gibson, a gardener working for the duke of Devonshire in the 1830s. The prior orchid collections of William Roxburgh and Dr. Robert Wight in India were very likely the stimuli by which Sir Joseph Paxton suggested to the duke that orchids should be sought there, and young Gibson was sent.

John Gibson was born at Cheshire, England, in 1815 and began his gardening career under the supervision of his father, who for many years was in the service of Sir Edmund Antrobus, at Eaton Hall, near Congleton, Cheshire. At seventeen years of age young Gibson was apprenticed to Joseph Paxton, then gardener to the duke of Devonshire, at Chatsworth. Here it was that Gibson found his beginnings in the world of orchidology.

Orchids were then beginning to become popular among cultivators, and the Chatsworth plants, placed in a two-light frame in a bed of tan bark, evoked much interest and curiosity. Paxton, aware of John

Gibson's enthusiasm for these novel and beautiful plants, sent him to study their cultivation under Mr. Cooper, a successful orchid grower of the day.

By 1835 the duke had begun the formation of a fine private orchid collection, and at Paxton's suggestion he decided on expediting a trip to India for the purpose of obtaining plants. In preparation for this expedition, Gibson was sent to London to inspect the major nurseries, especially to take notice of the orchids and rare plants at the Loddiges firm, and the herbaria of Mr. Lambert and others. Thereafter, in mid-1835 it was arranged that Gibson should accompany Lord Auckland, the newly appointed governor general, in charge of a large collection of medicinal plants for introduction into India. He left England in September, stopping and staying over in Madeira, Rio de Janeiro, and the Cape of Good Hope over a period of several weeks. Arriving at Calcutta in March 1836, he presented Lord Auckland's consignment of plants to Dr. Nathaniel Wallich, then director of the Calcutta Botanic Garden. Having fulfilled this duty, he was free to begin his quest for orchids, and at Dr. Wallich's suggestion he proceeded to Chirra Poongee, in the Khasia Hills. This was prior to the establishment of an overland route to India, so it was necessary to wait until the seasonal rains had filled the tributaries of the Brahmapootin River, which then afforded the only direct means of reaching the planned collecting site high in the Himalayas.

Gibson discovered many species, which were regularly dispatched to Dr. Wallich through direct postal communication, who then forwarded the collections to England. At the end of the collecting period, late in 1836, Gibson returned to Calcutta. He left this city again with his collections in March 1837, arriving back in London early in July. Besides the other plants he brought back, he introduced many orchids, among which could be mentioned *Dendrobium devonianum, Dendrobium cambridgeanum, Dendrobium formosum, Dendrobium paxtonii, Dendrobium densiflorum, Dendrobium gibsonii, Anoectochilus setaceus, Phaius albus, Phaius wallichii, Vanda teres, Coelogyne gardneriana, Coelogyne wallichiana, Saccolabium denticulatum, Saccolabium calceolare,* and *Camarotis purpurea.*

On his return to Chatsworth Gibson was appointed foreman of the exotic plant department under Joseph Paxton. In 1849 he left Chatsworth, accepting an appointment as superintendent of Victoria Park, then under construction. Greenwich Park was added under his supervision in 1850, and Battersea Park was entrusted to him in 1858. Soon afterward, Kennington Park, the grounds of Chelsea Hospital, and those of the Royal Military Asylum were placed under his charge.

Gibson was one of the first public gardeners to break away from the formal symmetry of flower gardening, bringing to focus instead, the beauty and form of individual plants and naturalistic groupings. His influence proved lasting.

In the London International Horticultural Exhibition and Congress of 1866, Gibson took a very active part. Working with a determination and skill that contributed largely to the success of that occasion, he laid out plans for the interior of the huge tent used to house the exhibition and carried out its superintendence with such success that the phrase "Gibson's three acres of Eden" long afterward recalled vivid memories of the grand event.

On the death of Mr. J. Mann in 1871, Gibson was elected to fill the vacant position of superintendent of St. James, the Green, Hyde Park, and Kensington Gardens. Gibson, however, had for some time been afflicted with paralysis—a malady that necessitated his removing himself from all public duties. His office as superintendent of Hyde Park was given to his son. His condition steadily worsened, and on 11 June 1875 he died at his home, Argyle Lodge, South Kensington.

References

Gardeners' Chronicle. 1872. John Gibson. No. 26.

Gardeners' Chronicle. 1875. Obituary. Vol. 3, no. 55.

Lemmon, Kenneth. 1962. *The Covered Garden.* London: Museum Press Ltd.

van Steenis, C. G. G. J. 1950. Cyclopaedia of Collectors. *Flora malesiana.* Vol. 1, ser. 1.

John Dominy (1816-1891)

THE PROGRESS OF ORCHID HYBRIDIZATION IS WELL TABULATED, AS EVIDENCED by comprehensive listings of Burbidge, Bohnhof, Hurst, Sander, and the Royal Horticultural Society. This is so probably because of the relatively few decades since the technique of artificial orchid hybridization was commenced. Plant breeding was practiced for centuries before hybrid orchids were introduced, but owing to an incomplete understanding of the sexual apparatus of the orchid flower, botanists and gardeners were unable to cross-pollinate orchids until late in the nineteenth century. But the wisdom and skill of a practiced nurseryman, John Dominy, combined to introduce a new strata in orchid growing.

John Dominy was born at Gittisham, Devonshire, England, in 1816. While very young he decided on gardening as his profession and by the time he was eighteen he had completed his term of apprenticeship in a private garden. Thereafter he entered the nursery of Messrs. Lucombe, Pince & Co. of Exeter. He remained there only two or three months,

taking a position with Messrs. Veitch & Co. at their Exeter establishment. There he remained until 1841, when he accepted an appointment
as head gardener to J. P. Magor of Redruth, with whom he stayed for
nearly five years. He then returned to the Veitch nursery, working both
at Exeter and at their new Chelsea establishment. He spent the rest of his
working years with the Veitch organization.

Though Dominy was an excellent cultivator of greenhouse plants, his
fame grew from his accomplishments in hybridizing. Orchids were his
specialty in this line, so much so that few people are aware that he was
also a most successful breeder of nepenthes and, to a lesser extent,
fuchsias.

Dominy's breakthrough in orchid hybridization is well known. His
fame is based on his development of the first man-made orchid hybrid
and his eminence in orchid hybridization for twenty-five years thereafter (see pages 77-81). He rapidly rose to high esteem in horticultural
circles, and for his achievement in raising *Laeliocattleya* Exoniensis, in
1864 the Devon and Exeter Horticultural Society presented him with
"a piece of plate" in recognition of the value of his experiments in hybridizing carried on while a member of their association.

Upon the announcement of his impending retirement there appeared
an article in the *Gardeners' Chronicle* of 12 June 1880, which read:

We hear that Mr. Dominy, whose name has now for forty years been associated with Messrs. Veitch's establishments, is about to retire. Few men connected with horticulture have deservedly gained so much esteem and respect
from the wide range of people with which his position has brought him in
contact, and still fewer have so indelibly fixed their mark upon any family of
cultivated plants as has Mr. Dominy upon Orchids, Nepenthes, etc., by the
number of hybrids with which, by his skill and assiduous perseverance, the
gardens of this country have become enriched; for it may truly be said, that
of the hundreds of collections of these plants which now exist there are none
of note that do not contain some or other of the fine things he has raised. . . .
Others have since followed, and are still following the track in which Mr.
Dominy has been the pioneer, and without detracting in the least from their
praiseworthy work still the name of Dominy will ever be intimately associated
with this, the slowest and most patience-taxing of all operations connected
with the gardener's art. Mr. Dominy retires whilst yet hale, and with his love
for horticulture undiminished.

Upon his actual retirement the Council of the Royal Horticultural
Society presented him with the Gold Flora Medal for "his successful
labours as a raiser of hybrid orchids, nepenthes, and other garden
plants." A few years later the society again honored him by presenting
to him a gold watch and a purse of 200 guineas through their president,
Sir Trevor Lawrence, who stated:

For nearly forty-three years Mr. Dominy had been in the service of Messrs. Veitch—a fact in itself which spoke volumes in his favour; and, indeed, his high personal character was well known to them all. But it was not altogether on this score that his friends had combined to do him honour, but rather on account of his achievements as the first raiser in this country of hybrid orchids.

Dominy maintained his interest in horticultural pursuits for many years after his retirement and regularly attended the meetings of the Royal Horticultural Society's Floral and Orchid Committees, of which he was a member.

After a short illness he died on 12 February 1891 and was buried at Exeter.

References

Gardeners' Chronicle. 1880. Retirement of Mr. Dominy. Vol. 13, no. 337.

Gardeners' Chronicle. 1880. Vol. 14, no. 343.

Gardeners' Chronicle. 1881. Mr. Dominy. Vol. 15.

Gardeners' Chronicle. 1881. The Dominy Testimonial. Vol. 16, no. 404.

Gardeners' Chronicle. 1881. Reports of Societies. Vol. 16, No. 407.

Gardeners' Chronicle. 1891. Obituary. Vol. 9, No. 216.

Gardeners' Chronicle. 1891. Obituary. Vol. 9, no. 218.

Gardening World, The. 1890–1891. 7: 393.

Hortus Veitchii. 1906. Chelsea, London: James Veitch & Sons Limited.

Lenz, Lee W. 1956. John Dominy—Pioneer Orchid Hybridizer. *Amer. Orch. Soc. Bull.* 25, no. 10.

Orchid World, The. 1916. The Centenary of John Dominy. Vol. 6, no. 7.

Joseph Dalton Hooker (1817–1911)

MENTION OF THE NAME HOOKER IN CONNECTION WITH BOTANY AND HORTIculture is practically synonymous with the history of the Royal Botanic Gardens at Kew—a story of progressive expansion and development.

Joseph Dalton Hooker was born into a family of scientists on 20 June 1817, at Halesworth, Suffolk, England. His grandfather had long taken pride in the cultivation of rare plants; his maternal grandfather, Dawson Turner, had been interested primarily in cryptogams and had published various works on mosses and ferns of Ireland and England; and his father, William Jackson Hooker, was a professor of botany at Glasgow University before becoming director at Kew.

Joseph first became interested in mosses, taking particular notice of them as a young child. Later he collected insects and terrestrial orchids, often in company with his father on expeditions into the highlands. He was educated at Glasgow High School and University, his father being his instructor as well as holiday companion.

In 1839 he took his M.D. at the University. He had finished his medical studies successfully, also being well versed in botany and natural science, and it was then that a great opportunity occurred that influenced his whole life's course. This opportunity came in young Hooker's appointment as assistant surgeon and naturalist aboard H.M.S. *Erebus* on an Antarctic expedition commanded by Sir James Ross. *Cook's Voyages* and the *Voyage of the Beagle* had been the delights of Hooker's boyhood, and the expedition thus enabled him to see those lands about which he had read and dreamed. New Zealand, Australia, Tasmania, Kerguelen, Tierra del Fuego, and the Falkland Islands became realities for him, and from each location large collections of plants were made from which a great amount of botanical information resulted. Six volumes were later devoted to the botanical accounts of the four-year trip, two under each of the three titles, *Flora Antarctica* (1844–1847), *Florae Novae Zelandiae* (1852–1855), and *Flora Tasmaniae* (1855–1860). These and other publications consequent on the voyage were well received and appreciated. Less well known were Hooker's elaborate meteorological observations, made all during the voyage.

In 1841, while Joseph was yet traveling, his father was appointed director of Kew. This was a glad event for the Hookers, for they had always hoped that Kew could be a public garden. Father and son soon laid plans for a wider scope of these famous gardens. On his return to England Joseph visited the Continent, meeting botanists and exchanging plants for Kew. After lecturing on botany at Edinburgh for a few years he was appointed botanist of a geological survey in Wales to investigate fossil flora.

In 1847 Joseph Hooker visited the Himalayas, spending three years studying the geography and flora of the regions visited, and making extensive collections. From a horticultural point of view this was the most productive of Hooker's travels. The account of the expedition, including details on the endemic orchids, was told in his *Himalayan Journals*, the two volumes of which were published in 1854. An interesting feature given in his *Journals* was the manner in which the expedition was outfitted. "My party," Hooker wrote, "mustered 56 persons. These consisted of myself and one personal servant, a Portuguese half-caste, who undertook all offices and spared me the usual train of Hindu and Mahomedan servants. My tent and equipment, instruments, bed, box of clothes, books and papers required a man for each. Seven more carried my papers for drying plants and other scientific stores. The Nepalese guard had two coolies of their own. My interpreter, the coolie *sirdar* (a headsman) and my chief collector (a Lepcha) had a man each. Mr. Hodgson's bird and animal shooter, collector and stuffer with their ammunition and indespensables had four more. There were, besides, three Lepcha lads to climb trees and change the plant papers, and the party was completed by fourteen Bhutan coolies laden with food consisting chiefly of rice with ghee, oil, capsicums, salt and flour. I carried myself a small barometer, a large knife and digger for plants, note book, telescope, compass and other instruments, whilst two or three Lepcha lads who accompany me as satellites carry a botanizing box, thermometers, sextant and artificial horizon, measuring tape, azimuth compass and stand, geological hammer, bottles and boxes for insects, sketch books etc. arranged in compartments of strong canvas bags."

Explorations in Sikkim and other westward journeys with Dr. Thomas Thomson occupied over a year. A second Himalayan trip in 1849 led to trouble at the court of the regent of Sikkim, and Hooker was forcibly detained for twelve months, at the end of which he was nearly assassinated. He returned to England in 1851.

Soon after his return from India Hooker was appointed examiner in botany for the Medical Service. At the same time he busied himself with the examination and distribution of his collections. And in conjunction with Dr. Thomson he began a *Flora Indica*, but only one volume was published because Thomson returned to India and Hooker took on new duties by his appointment to the post of assistant director at Kew under his father.

In 1860 he traveled to Syria and Palestine, the principal result of which was the discovery of the famous cedars of Lebanon. Much of the botanical information gained on that trip was published in *Smith's Dictionary of the Bible*.

As assistant director, Joseph Hooker did much systematic work, the most important of which was the preparation with George Bentham of the *Genera Plantarum*, the first of which was issued in 1862. He also contributed his *Handbook of the New Zealand Flora* (1864–1867) to the Kew colonial floras.

When Sir William Hooker died in 1865 Joseph succeeded him as director of Kew. Administrative duties occupied much of his time thereafter, but this did not prevent him from the continuation of his scientific work and the unceasing introduction and culture of plants, especially those of economic value. Great activity was also shown at Kew during Hooker's directorate, and not only did he give his labors but often his own earnings as well.

Hooker had felt for some time that the study of botany was in need of revision. His idea was that students should increasingly study the plants as well as dried specimens, and his aim was to set forth questions that required thought rather than rote memory. He considered botany "a science of observation" and effected the arrangement of the palm and temperate houses at Kew to duplicate as nearly as possible natural geographical distribution and similarities of habitat.

Another great botanist, John Lindley, had died the year that Joseph Hooker assumed the directorate. Lindley's herbarium was acquired from his executors and presented to Kew by the government, and thus the Kew Herbarium took on added importance. The general collections were later presented to Cambridge University, but the 3000 specimens in the orchid herbarium were retained at Kew.

In 1871 Hooker undertook a botanical expedition to Morocco and the Atlas Range in company with John Ball and George Maw, and in 1877 he accompanied the American botanist, Asa Gray, on a journey to Colorado, Utah, the Rocky Mountains, the Sierra Nevadas, and California. All the while he recorded his observations, classified specimens, and worked out new methods of reforming botanical studies.

Hooker was president of the Royal Society for five years, and even in that capacity he was able to make reforms. He effected a reduction of the ordinary subscription rate by asking for donations from wealthy members, thus making it possible for the scientist of meager resources to become a fellow. Actually, he had reluctantly accepted the presidency for, as he expressed it, he had an aversion to high places.

Hooker was a lifelong friend of Charles Darwin. The two collaborated mutually in their scientific work, and Hooker was especially influenced by Darwin's theories on evolution. With the whole outlook of botany in a state of change, Hooker was significantly impressed with Darwin's *Origin of Species*. The geographical distribution of plants was to him an essential part of the study of botany, for he no longer believed that a species was fixed but that plants adapted themselves to their environments and so changed.

Mormodes hookeri

Hooker's abilities as a writer were fantastic. Only a small percentage of his published works could be given here. The complete list, published in the *Kew Bulletin* for 1912, covered more than sixteen pages. As a biographer he wrote the life of Darwin, a sketch of his father's life, and a journal on Sir Joseph Banks. Besides sharing in the production of the *Genera Plantarum*, he was also editor of the *Icones Plantarum* and the *Botanical Magazine*, for forty years editing the 91st to 130th volumes of the latter.

Though it is necessary to pass over most of his books and papers, his monumental *Flora of the British Isles* cannot be overlooked. In it he described many orders, among them the Orchidaceae, including 116 genera and nearly 1300 species. The number of orchids figured in the *Botanical Magazine* during his editorship was also very great, as were his other contributions to orchidology. He studied the orchids of Ceylon and New Zealand, and as far back as 1854 published an important paper on the structure and fertilization of *Listera*. There are several references to his work in Darwin's *Fertilisation of Orchids*.

Hooker's position as a scientist was duly recognized by the learned bodies of his own and foreign countries. Academic distinctions gained during the seventy active years of his life included the honorary degree of D.C.L. of Oxford and that of LL.D. of Cambridge, Edinburgh, Dublin, and Glasgow. In 1869 he was made C.B., in 1877 K.C.S.I., and in 1897 G.C.S.I. He was also the recipient of many honors and medals from the Royal, Linnean and Geographical Societies and from the Society of Arts. In 1907, on his ninetieth birthday, he received the Order of Merit.

Sir Joseph passed away in his sleep on 10 December 1911, at the Camp, Sunningdale, Berkshire. It had been hoped that his ashes would be placed in Westminster Abbey next to Darwin's, but Hooker's wish had been to be buried beside his father in the family grave in the churchyard of Kew Green, and this desire was honored.

His name is perpetuated in the orchid genera *Josephia* and *Sirhookera*, as well as in *Mormodes hookeri*, *Oncidium hookeri*, *Paphiopedilum hookerae*, *Pleione hookeriana*, and *Vanda hookeriana*.

References

Curtis' Botanical Magazine. 1931. *Dedications and Portraits 1827–1927*. Nelmes, Ernest, and Cuthbertson, Wm., comps. London: Bernard Quaritch Ltd.
Gardeners' Chronicle. 1871. Dr. J. D. Hooker, C.B., F.R.S. No. 1.
Gardeners' Chronicle. 1885. Vol. 24, no. 622.
Gardeners' Chronicle. 1905. Sir Joseph Hooker. Vol. 37, no. 941.
Gilmour, John. 1946. *British Botanists*. London.
Glenn, Rewa. 1950. *Botanical Explorers of New Zealand*. Wellington.
Lemmon, Kenneth. 1962. *The Covered Garden*. London: Museum Press Ltd.
Orchid Review, The. 1912. Vol. 20, no. 229.

Jean Linden (1817–1898)

THOUGH THE GREATEST SHARE OF ORCHID COLLECTING HONORS WAS CLAIMED by British horticulturists and botanists, many personalities from other countries were instrumental also in the discovery and introduction of new species. As orchid cultivation gained in fashionability in England, horticulturists in Belgium were quick to recognize that trade in tropical and subtropical orchids could be profitable. One of these enterprising men was Jean Linden, a native of Luxembourg who imported more than 1100 different species into Belgium.

While still a youth he moved to Belgium, where he became one of the first students at the Faculty of Sciences in the newly founded University of Brussels. At the age of nineteen he was entrusted in 1835 by the Belgian government with a scientific mission to South America. Accompanied by Funck and Ghiesbrecht, he landed at Rio de Janeiro on 24 December of that year after an unpleasant three-month voyage. His explorations included trips to the provinces of Rio, Espirito Santo, Minas Geraes, and São Paulo. His collections from these regions were publicly exhibited in Brussels in 1837, at a period when interest in tropical plants was most intense. That same year he traversed both the north and west of Cuba and the following year the interior of Mexico, visiting all the eastern slopes of the Mexican cordilleras, the Peak of Orizaba, the Ana-huac Plateau, and the volcano Popocatepetl.

A complete account of all his wanderings would read like a journal, because further explorations led him to a host of regions. Vera Cruz, Yucatan, Campeche, Chiapas, and the Laguna de Términos were included in his Mexican explorations. At the latter place he contracted a severe attack of yellow fever from which he barely recovered and which entailed a painful three-month convalescence. Scarcely had he regained his health when he journeyed by sea into Tabasco State, traveling thence to northern Guatemala (at that time in a state of revolution) and returning along the Gulf of Mexico. Further trips took him to Havana, the United States, many parts of Venezuela, and Colombia. In all these areas he sought the mountainous regions, solely occupied with ascertaining the possibility of growing orchids at cool temperatures.

In about 1841 a few English growers, including Mr. Backer of Birmingham, Mr. Rucker of Wandsworth, and the Rev. J. Clowes of Manchester, hired Linden to collect orchids for them in Colombia and Venezuela. Linden was highly successful in this task, discovering (among many other worthy plants) *Anguloa clowesii* and *Anguloa ruckeri*. The former was flowered in Rev. Clowes' collection in 1844 and was thus seen for the first time in Europe.

On this expedition to the highest summits of the Venezuelan and Colombian Andes, Linden found orchids blooming in a region where the temperature fell to the freezing point every morning. Concerning this discovery, he remarked many years later:

. . . It was, however, only in the Cordilleras of the Venezuelan and Colombian Andes that my Orchid discoveries attained their greatest importance. From the time of Alexander von Humboldt, who only indicated a few species of Orchids, up to my arrival in the Andes, the most brilliant representatives of the Cattleyas and Odontoglossums, as well as many other species of great merit, were still undiscovered. I had the good fortune to arrive first, but I was closely followed by Hartweg, travelling for the Royal Horticultural Society of London. We met at Bogota, and it was during an excursion that we took together that we discovered, near Pacho, *Odontoglossum crispum*, which has excited the admiration of millions during the last few years. At the time of my journey, a certain number of more or less interesting Orchids were already in cultivation in Europe. They had been imported principally from the East Indies, Brazil, and Mexico, and their introduction was due to chance, rather than to careful search. . . . The Orchids once collected, difficulties began. It was necessary to bring them down from the mountains to the port of embarkation by roads which cannot be imagined by any who have not traversed them.

Phalaenopsis lindenii

At that time no steamboat had yet crossed the ocean, and the poor plants had to endure the sea-voyage at the bottom of the hold of a rough sailing vessel, after having waited, sometimes during more than a month, for a chance of carriage to a port near their destination. Packed like herring in a barrel, the heat and fermentation worked sad havoc, and but few of them arrived alive.

Altogether, ten years were spent in travels and botanical collecting, and in October 1845 Linden returned to the United States and Europe.

Linden later established himself as a nurseryman at Ghent but eventually returned to Brussels, where he founded the establishment known as Horticulture Internationale in conjunction with his son Lucien. In this nursery, which became a model for the profession, Linden's knowledge of plants and the localities in which they grew naturally proved invaluable. Direct competition with Messrs. Sander in England kept him alert in the search for new and desirable species, resulting in the exploration of many far-flung regions where orchids might be found. His uncanny memory of plant locations, plus his characteristic refusal to divulge these locations, enabled him to command lofty prices for particularly attractive species. Linden was expert at camouflaging information about his sources, which subsequently led to remarkable confusion concerning locations long after his decease. One of the trips he financed, an expedition to explore parts of the Amazon region and its most important tributaries—Tapajoz, Madeira, Rio Negro, Rio Branco, etc.—was recognized as one of the most important botanical ventures of the time.

Linden's recollections were so vivid that they served as the bases of directions followed by the numerous collectors he sent out on no less than seven expeditions to the various districts which he had himself explored years before. Many of the orchids which honor him—*Cattleyopsis lindenii, Maxillaria lindeniae, Odontoglossum lindenii, Phalaenopsis lindenii, Phragmipedium lindenii, Polyrrhiza lindenii* and *Scaphyglottis lindeniana*, to name a few—were discovered in those same regions.

Linden received a number of commendations and honors, from his own and several continental governments, for his contributions to horticultural literature. Among the illustrated works which he contributed to the expanding horticultural press were the *Illustration Horticole* and *Lindenia*, both of which were published continually for several years. In addition to the work of his pen and brush, Linden was also director of the Zoological Gardens at Brussels as well as consul for Luxembourg for some time.

He lived a long life, and though his death was not unexpected, when he died on 12 January 1898—at eighty-one years of age—his decease came as a shock and with much sorrow.

References

Garden, The. 1879. Linden's Illustration Horticole. Vol. 15, no. 378.
Gardeners' Chronicle. 1894. Jean Linden. Vol. 15, no. 379.
Gardeners' Chronicle. 1894. Jean Linden. Vol. 15, no. 385.
Gardeners' Chronicle. 1898. 23, no. 577.
Richter, Walter. 1965. *The Orchid World* (English Translation). New York: E. P. Dutton & Co.

Thomas Lobb (1820-1894)

VERY LITTLE IS KNOWN CONCERNING THE EARLY LIVES OF THE LOBB BROTH-ers. Beyond the fact that Thomas is recorded as having been born in 1820 at Cornwall, England, little else is known of their family connections and early youth. The first mention of Thomas in horticultural journals seems to refer to 1840, at which time he was engaged as a collector by James Veitch at Exeter. His brother William had been employed by the same establishment three years earlier. Both were sent on collecting trips in 1840, William selecting Brazil as his field of exploration and Thomas proceeding to India.

Thomas Lobb was fortunate, for much of the Indo-Malayan region was hitherto untouched by collectors and the virgin soil yielded a host of prized plants. Lobb was discriminate, though, selecting only plants he felt worthy of cultivation. He was, in fact, a retiring man of few words—so much so that it was even difficult to get him to describe a plant when speaking of his discoveries. If he ventured to speak of some particular species as "very pretty," however, it was quite sufficient for extra care to be given to it.

Desirous of obtaining rare plants from China, the Veitch firm dispatched Lobb for the job in 1843. Of interest is the agreement drawn up in this effect:

Thomas Lobb agrees to proceed to the British Settlement of Singapore, in the employ of James Veitch & Son as botanical collector, to make collections of living plants, seeds, and dried specimens of plants, and to collect for the said James Veitch & Son and for no other person. The understanding of this agreement is that the said Thomas Lobb's principal destination is to be China, should that country be open to admit a botanical collector, and in the absence of any definite instructions from James Veitch & Son, Thomas Lobb is to use his own discretion and be guided by existing circumstances as to what parts of China he proceeds to, and if on arrival at Singapore he finds circumstances are not favourable for his proceeding to China, he shall be at liberty to proceed to such of the oriental islands as may appear to him most desirable; but next to China the island of Java appearing to offer the greatest advantages to a botanical collector (if facilities offer for exploring the same with safety), he is directed to proceed thither, but it is left to his own discretion.

The Chinese were apparently not ready to receive English collectors, for Lobb adopted the alternative, visiting Java and the adjacent islands. In Java he collected many herbarium specimens, a list of which was given in Hooker's *London Journal of Botany* (1847–1848) with the following notice:

Mr. Heward, Young Street, Kensington, is charged with the distribution of the sets of the exquisitely beautiful and rare specimens of the mountains of Java, collected by Mr. Thomas Lobb. The number of sets is small, and the amount of species in each varies from 100 to 200, or nearly so. More perfect specimens have never been offered for sale.

By a later agreement Lobb went to India for three years, leaving England for Calcutta on 25 December 1848. Visiting the Khasia Hills, Assam, Moulmein, and lower and northeast Burma, he sent home most of the finest orchids found there, many of them previously known to science but all of them introduced by him into cultivation for the first time. Some of the most outstanding were *Vanda coerulea, Coelogyne (Pleione) lagenaria, Coelogyne maculata, Aerides fieldingii, Aerides multiflorum* var. *lobbi, Aerides multiflorum* var. *veitchii, Dendrobium infundibulum, Calanthe (Limatodes) rosea,* and *Paphiopedilum villosum.*

Later he visited the southern parts of the Malay Peninsula, North Borneo (Labuan and Sarawak), and other islands, discovering and introducing *Rhododendron javanicum, jasminiflorum, lobbii,* and *brookianum,* the ancestral forms of the later superb *javanico-jasminiflorum* hybrids. From these regions he also introduced some of the first nepenthes cultivated in England, including *Nepenthes rafflesiana, veitchii, sanguinea,* and *ampullaria.* Of the many orchids he sent home from the same regions were *Vanda tricolor* and its variety *suavis, Coelogyne speciosa, Calanthe vestita, Paphiopedilum barbatum, Bulbophyllum lobbii, Spathoglottis lobbii,* and many others.

Turning his collecting interests farther afield, Lobb subsequently went to the Philippine Islands, collecting in the neighborhood of Manila. Among the best orchids collected there was *Phalaenopsis intermedia,* the first natural orchid hybrid to be proven as such at a later date (see page 82). At this time there was much professional rivalry among horticultural firms and collectors, and information regarding the sources of discoveries was jealously retained. Thomas Lobb also maintained secrecy concerning his locations. In connection with his collections of living plants he prepared four duplicate dried specimens for distribution, but to protect his sources he labeled one set as being from Java, one from Borneo, one from the Malay Peninsula, and one from Luzon. This, of course, caused much consternation for years thereafter, because botanists working with the specimens were unable to make proper geographical designations and classifications.

The end of Lobb's collecting came as the result of an unfortunate loss of a leg due to exposure, a circumstance that induced him to retire at Devoran, in Cornwall. There he remained for the rest of his life except for a single visit to the home of his former employer, James Veitch, Jr., with whom he was staying on the occasion of that gentleman's sudden death in 1869. Lobb himself lived on for many years, dying at Cornwall on 30 April 1894.

References

Chronica Botanica. 1943. 7: 357.

Cottage Gardener. 1860. 13: 274.

Davis, Reginald S., and Steiner, Mona Lisa. 1952. *Philippine Orchids.* New York: William Frederick Press.

Gardeners' Chronicle. 1894. Obituary. Vol. 15, no. 386.

Irvin, R. 1960. The early orchid collectors. *The Orch. Rev.* 68, no. 803.

Journal of the Royal Horticultural Society. 1942. Vol. 62, no. 2.

Journal of the Royal Horticultural Society. 1948. Vol. 73, pt. 9.

Lemmon, Kenneth. 1962. *The Covered Garden.* London: Museum Press Ltd.

Merrill, E. D. 1945. The Philippines as a source of orchids. *Amer. Orch. Soc. Bull.* 13, no. 10.

Nature. 1942. 149: 438.

Orchid Review, The. 1894. Obituary. Vol. 2, no. 18.

van Steenis, C. G. G. J. 1950. Cyclopaedia of Collectors. *Flora Malesiana.* Vol. 1, ser. 1.

Veitch, James H. 1906. *Hortus Veitchii.* Chelsea, London: James Veitch & Sons Ltd.

Charles Samuel Pollock Parish (1822-1897)

THE LURE OF THE ORCHID BEGAN TO MOVE INCREASINGLY SOUTHEASTWARD in the 1850s. The orchids of India and Nepal had already fired the imaginations of English growers, but beyond those reaches little was known of other southeastern types. By coincidence a missionary in Burma became interested in native orchids as an adjunct to beautifying his home and mission. This hobby pursuit opened the door to yet another untapped mine of orchid treasures.

Charles Samuel Pollock Parish was born in Calcutta, India, on 26 January 1822. Educated at Oxford University, he took his B.A. in 1841. Eleven years later he was sent to Moulmein, Burma, in his newly appointed position as Indian Chaplain. Almost immediately, collecting orchids became a passion with him, though this pursuit indirectly stemmed from his interest in mosses. Parish related that *Porpax parishii* "was the first orchid I had ever gathered! When searching for mosses, I found this (to me then) singular plant, leafless and flowerless, and knew not that it was an Orchid. The naming of it by the great Lindley incited me to pay attention to the Order." Besides growing orchids in his garden, Parish thereafter sent plants to England, where Joseph Hooker and John Lindley received them gladly.

Rev. Parish wrote in later years that:

Cymbidium parishii was one of my earliest discoveries, having been found by me during my long journey in the distant jungles in 1859. On the same occasion I discovered *Dendrobium crassinode* and several other good things, but I was so bewildered then at the number of novelties of all kinds that I did not know what to choose. As I could not carry everything, I gathered then a fair quantity of *Cymbidium parishii* and *Dendrobium crassinode*; I sent them, with many other valuable things, to Mr. Low, the father, with one box meant for Kew; but all (six large cases full!) were sunk in the Ganges. It was a cruel dis-

Paphiopedilum parishii

appointment, as it was my first collection, a most valuable one; many of the plants I have never met again.

Near his home that same year he discovered *Paphiopedilum concolor* as well as *Paphiopedilum parishii*.

Lindley and Hooker spoke with great praise in behalf of Parish, forming high opinions of the plants he continued to send them with his own sketches. Meanwhile, Burmese orchids mysteriously began appearing in the sales rooms of England, *Phalaenopsis lowii* and numerous beautiful dendrobiums among them. The source of these introductions long remained undisclosed. Finally, it became known that the plants were sent by Parish and Colonel Robson Benson, an officer in the British forces in India.

During the 1860s a great number of Parish's plants were figured in the *Botanical Magazine*, including *Dendrobium parishii*. James Bateman commented therein:

A glance at the recent volumes of the *Botanical Magazine* will show the large number of new and beautiful orchids that have been secured to the collections of this country through the zeal and enterprise of Mr. Parish, whose eye seems to be ever ready to detect any new forms amid the striking vegetation of the rich country that is now the scene of his missionary labours.

A host of new plant discoveries was made by Parish between 1862 and 1867, including *Cymbidium tigrinum*, found in the Tenasserim Mountains. In addition to the phalaenopsis and dendrobium mentioned, species of *Coelogyne*, *Habenaria*, and *Vanda* are named in commemoration of Parish, as well as *Parishia*, a nonorchidaceous genus from Malaya.

Contributing to Mason's *Burma* (2: 148–202), Parish enumerated 350 of the indigenous orchids. Remarking on this large number of orchids from so small an area, he wrote in the same edition:

My opportunities of observation were almost unrivalled. Fixed at one station for upwards of twenty years, and having some 150 species growing in my garden, fresh supplies being continually brought in, it was my daily delight to watch their growth, and hardly a day passed on which I did not either draw or examine microscopically some one orchid or another.

Reports of Parish's observations appeared in other periodicals such as the *Journal of the Asiatic Society of Bengal*.

In 1871 Parish returned to England for a visit, bringing with him his large collection of analytical sketches and watercolor drawings, which he presented to the Royal Botanical Gardens at Kew. An account of this endowment was given by Reichenbach in the *Transactions of the Linnean Society*.

In 1878 Parish retired from his mission work and returned again to

England and Somerset, continuing his interest in orchids and botany in general. He died quietly in his sleep, at his home at Roughmoor, Somerset, on 18 October 1897, at the age of seventy-five.

References

Curtis' Botanical Magazine. 1931. *Dedications and Portraits 1827–1927.* Nelmes, Ernest, and Cuthbertson, Wm., comps. London: Bernard Quaritch Ltd.

Journal of Botany. 1897. Book-Notes, News, etc. 35:464.

Kline, Mary C. 1962. The Rev. Charles Samuel Parish. *Amer. Orch. Soc. Bull.* 31, no. 3.

Orchid Review, The. 1897. Obituary. Vol. 5, no. 58.

Heinrich Gustav Reichenbach (1823–1889)

AFTER JOHN LINDLEY'S DEATH IN 1865, HEINRICH GUSTAV REICHENBACH became the "Orchid King." Orchid specimens from all over the world were sent to him for identification, and these, together with his copious notes and drawings, formed an immense herbarium which rivaled that of Lindley's at Kew.

Heinrich Gustav Reichenbach was born at Leipzig, Germany, on 3 January 1823, the son of H. G. L. Reichenbach, author of the *Icones Florae Germanicae et Helveticae*. From the age of eighteen young Reichenbach took a great interest in orchids, often in association with John Lindley.

Though best known as an orchidologist, botanists in general owe him a debt of gratitude for his collaboration in his father's *Icones*. He edited and illustrated the latter volumes of this great work, contributing at least 1500 drawings of his own. The first volume of this extensive publication was, naturally enough, devoted to the orchids of Europe. It bears the title *Tentatem Orchidographiae Europeae* and is dated 1851.

His graduation essay, published in 1852, was on the origin and structure of orchid pollen. Separate publications included *Xenia Orchidaceae*, which appeared in occasional volumes from 1851, with about 900 of Reichenbach's pencil drawings, *Observations on the Orchids of Central America*, and the synopsis of orchid lore contained in the sixth volume of Walper's *Annales*.

In 1863 Reichenbach was appointed to the posts of professor of botany and director of the Botanic Gardens at Hamburg University. The duties connected with these posts occupied much of his time, as did the correspondence he carried on with orchid growers both amateur and professional.

Into the university herbarium were deposited all the clippings, notes, drawings, and scraps of information that reached his hand. Many of the herbarium sheets seemed messy and haphazardly done, without semblance of order. As they were later used in solving problems, however, the scrawly sketches used to clarify the accompanying dried sheets— many made with a few strokes of the pen—demonstrated a particular genius for catching the salient characteristics of the species in a botanically artful shorthand.

Though friendly and helpful, Reichenbach's letters were often tinged with wit and sarcasm. It was frequently inferred that he resented the intrusion of others into what he considered his domain. His herbarium was jealously guarded against too great familiarity on the part of his colleagues, and an aura of mystery surrounded its existence. Reichenbach himself, according to an obituary in the *Gardeners' Chronicle* for 18 May 1899,

... was possessed of remarkably distinct individuality, which was as remarkable as his curiously crabbed handwriting which few could decipher. Short and massive in stature till his recent illness, with a keen penetrating glance and aquiline nose, his features revealed something of the impetuous temper of the man, and his occasional biting sarcasms. His devotion to Orchids amounted to a consuming passion; not a scrap, nor a note, nor a sketch, however rough, came amiss to him if it related to an Orchid. To him meals and clothes were necessary evils, but his herbarium was a prime necessity of existence. The amount of his work was prodigious. Of its quality the botanists of the future will judge better than we.

He was a constant contributor to the *Gardeners' Chronicle*, sending that publication a weekly article on orchids from 1865 until the end of his life. He worked out the Orchidaceae for Seeman's two works, *Flora Vitiensis* and *Botany of the Voyage of H.M.S. Herald*. He also contributed descriptions of plants of the Orchid Family for the *Refugium Botanicum* from 1869 to 1872. One of his most excellent works, both from a descriptive and esthetic standpoint, was his *Reichenbachia*, a series of watercolor paintings of orchids issued from 1888 to 1894. The work was undertaken by Sanders' of St. Albans, illustrated largely by H. G. Moon, with plant descriptions by Reichenbach, after whom it was named.

Reichenbach's nearest approach to a synopsis of the Orchid Family was the sixth volume (1861–1864) of Walper's *Annales*, where he brought together on nearly 800 pages the species described between 1851 and 1855, with the addition of several new ones.

Reichenbach was emphatic about the correct identification of orchid species. He thus pronounced:

Authors should do more than secure to themselves the right of priority . . . by such incomplete diagnoses. Not only should a careful description be taken, but great care should be taken to help posterity in discriminating the species. Therefore the specimen, or those specimens, which furnished the evidence for the establishment of the species should be distinctly marked as "the type of my species!" I now always do this in my collection. I regard this as a *fidei commisum* for my lifetime that they will have to be distinctly kept within reach of the men of science after my death.

Reichenbach had occasionally spoken of having his herbarium deposited at Kew after his death, and when that tragic event occurred on 6 May 1889, at Hamburg, Germany, it was anticipated that the Kew Herbarium would soon thereafter be enriched with the Reichenbach collections. "It is greatly to be hoped," stated the *Gardeners' Chronicle* of 18 May 1889, "that his immense collections and notes will fall into competent hands (at Kew if possible), for collation and revision—a task that will, however, require years of concentration, for his publications are not only extremely numerous, but scattered through a wide range of publications in almost all European languages." It was enigmatic, therefore, that his will stated:

My herbarium and my botanical library, my instruments, collections of seeds, etc., accrue to the imperial Hof Museum in Vienna under the condition that the preserved Orchids and drawings of Orchids shall not be exhibited before twenty-five years from the date of my death have elapsed. Until this time my collection shall be preserved in sealed cases. In the event of the Vienna Institute declining to observe these conditions, the collection falls under the same conditions to the Botanical Garden of Upsala. Should the last-mentioned Institute decline the legacy, then to the Grayean Herbarium in Harvard University, Cambridge, Massachusetts. If declined by that Institute, then to the Jardin des Plantes at Paris, but always under the same conditions, viz., of being sealed up for twenty-five years, in order that the inevitable destruction of the costly collection, resulting from the present craze for Orchids, may be avoided.

Great consternation followed, for there seemed to be no reason to deprive the botanical world of his valuable type specimens for a quarter of a century. The terms of the will were respected, however, and the Hof Museum accepted the Reichenbach herbarium and library.

Professor Reichenbach was accorded great international recognition. He was elected a foreign member of the Linnean Society in 1879; was an honorary fellow of the Royal Horticultural Society; was awarded the Veitchian Medal in 1885 on occasion of the First Orchid Conference; and received a special medal struck in his honor at Ghent, presented by the king of the Belgians in 1888. Moreover, his merits were recognized by numerous orders and distinctions conferred on him by various other governments. He is additionally memorialized in the orchid genus *Reichenbachanthus*, as well as *Chondrorhyncha reichenbachiana*, *Kefersteinia reichenbachiana*, and *Sievekingia reichenbachiana*. Still, the practicality of the man is apparent in his statement alluding to these distinctions: "I cannot eat the honor."

References

Ames, Oakes. 1933. The Reichenbachian herbarium. *Amer. Orch. Soc. Bull.* 1, no. 4.

Ames, Oakes. 1941. Reichenbachia. *Amer. Orch. Soc. Bull.* 10, no. 5.

Curtis' Botanical Magazine. 1931. *Dedications and Portraits 1827–1927.* Nelmes, Ernest, and Cuthbertson, Wm. London: Bernard Quaritch Ltd.

Garden, The. 1905. Death of Prof. Reichenbach. Vol. 35, no. 913.

Gardeners' Chronicle. Prof. H. G. Reichenbach. No. 20. May 20, 1871.

Gardeners' Chronicle. 1889. The Late Professor Reichenbach. Vol. 5, no. 125.

Journal of Botany. Botanical News. Vols. 17–18. 1879–1880.

Journal of Botany. 1889–1890. Heinrich Gustav Reichenbach (1823–1889). Vols. 27–28.

Orchid Album, The. 1889. Vol. 8 (under pl. 377). London: B. S. Williams.

Orchid Review, The. 1913. The Reichenbachian Herbarium. Vol. 21, no. 249.

Orchid Review, The. 1917. Professor H. G. Reichenbach. Vol. 25.

White, C. T. 1940. A History of Australian Orchids. *Australian Orch. Rev.* 5, no. 4.

Benedict Roezl (1823-1885)

BENEDICT ROEZL IS KNOWN AS PERHAPS THE MOST INTREPID ORCHID COL-
lector who ever lived. Born in Prague, Bohemia, he became interested in
horticulture at twelve years of age.

I started in my horticulture career in my thirteenth year—in 1836. I was apprenticed in the gardens of the Count of Thun at Tötschen, in Bohemia, from
which, after three years, I went to the gardens of the Count Paulikowsy, at
Medica, Galicia. At that time these gardens contained the largest collection of
plants in Europe, and I was there enabled to gain most of my botanical knowledge of plants. After staying three years I went to the far-famed gardens of
Baron Von Hugel; from there I went to Telsch, in Moravia, to Count Lichten-
stein, and from there to Ghent, to M. Van Houtte, where I stayed five years.
I was *chef de culture* in the School of Horticulture of the Belgian Government. After this I served for two years, but I could no longer restrain my
ardent wish to see the tropics, and I proceeded via New Orleans to Mexico—
this was in 1854. In Mexico I started a nursery for European fruit trees; there
also I collected a large number of Mexican Pines.

Roezl, though a large, self-possessed man, was conspicuously noticeable because of an iron hook in place of his missing left hand. This
feature was a source of wonder to the many primitive tribes with whom
he spent a great portion of his life. Speculation existed for many years

as to how the hand was lost, for Roezl himself seldom mentioned it. In a rare interview he admitted:

I invented a machine for extracting and cleaning the fibre of Ramie and Hemp, and took out a patent for my machine from the Government of the United States on September 17, 1867. The Agricultural Exhibition awarded a diploma for it in February, 1868. This discovery was the cause in 1868 of the loss of one of my arms. Many people in Havana solicited me to exhibit my machine there, and I was asked by some gentlemen to try if the machine would extract the fibre from *Agave americana*. The result of the trial proved my assertion, that the fibre would come out green, was correct; but in endeavouring to show that they were right in their assertions they managed in some way or the other to fasten some screws tighter, so as to get the cylinders closer together, and I, not knowing this, in putting a leaf between the cylinders (making 360 revolutions per minute) lost my left arm.

Shortly afterward he began an incredible life of plant collecting. Employed by Messrs. Sander & Co., for forty years he criss-crossed the American continent, doing practically all his traveling by horse or on foot. A full account of his travels, adventures (he was robbed seventeen times), and plant discoveries would require volumes. In brief, his travels encompassed the following: from Mexico to Cuba; to California via New York, traversing the Rocky Mountains and the Sierra Nevada; to Panama and Colombia, from whence he forwarded 10,000 orchids to Europe; to Santa Martha and Río Hacha, where he collected 3000 odontoglossums; to Panama, San Francisco, and Washington Territory, collecting conifer seeds in the latter; back to Southern California, Panama and Buenaventura; through the state of Cauca to Antioquia, collecting large quantities of *Masdevallia*, *Miltonia vexillaria*, and *Cattleya warscewiczii*; thence down the Magdalena River to Colon and Panama; to North Peru and across the Andes; back to Payta and Buenaventura; then to Europe for four months to see his parents. On 3 August 1872, he went from Liverpool to New York and Colorado Territory; then to New Mexico and the Central American Sierra Madre, sending back 3500 more odontoglossums; again to Panama and into Venezuela, from whence he forwarded eight tons of orchids to London; from there to St. Thomas and to Havana and Vera Cruz, then to the Isthmus of Tehuantepec and into the state of Oaxaca, in Mexico, sending back, in all, ten tons of cacti, agave, and orchids; from Mexico City to Vera Cruz, and on to New York; back to Panama and Peru; across the Andes to Tarma and Chanchamayo, bringing back 10,000 various plants; thence back to Lima and southern Peru, to Morienda, Arigipa, and Lake Titicaca; across the Illimani Mountains to the province of Yungas; back to Lima and Payta, and again across the Andes to Guayaquil, Ecuador; down the Chimborazo; back to Guayaquil and the Valley of Cauca; and,

Miltonia roezlii

finally, back to London. He discovered about 800 species of flowering plants and trees entirely new to horticulture. Among the orchids named in his honor are *Selenipedium roezlii, Bletia roezlii, Pleurothallis roezlii, Masdevallia roezlii, Miltonia roezlii, Pescatorea roezlii,* and the genus *Roezliella,* besides many other valued hardy and greenhouse plants.

On his infrequent visits to London, Roezl particularly enjoyed stopping in at the auction rooms where his shipments were eagerly purchased by enthusiasts ever alert to obtain strange new offerings. A popular man with the wealthy estate owners and their growers, he relished discussing the various aspects of orchidology with them. His uncanny "sixth sense" about orchids delighted his employer; when a new orchid appeared in London during one of his visits, he and Mr. Sander would study it carefully and, if it had originated in an area where he had traveled, Roezl could usually deduce its place of origin. On his return to that particular area, more often than not he would relocate the plant in question.

During his last years he resided in his beloved Prague. There he died in October 1885. Among those eminent persons who attended the funeral was the kaiser himself. A statue was later erected to his memory in Prague—evidence of the high esteem accorded a native son.

References

Garden, The. 1885. Obituary. Vol. 28, no. 727.
Gardeners' Chronicle. 1885. Benedict Roezl. Vol. 24, no. 617.
Gardeners' Chronicle. 1892. Benedict Roezl. Vol. 11, no. 263.
Gardening World, The. 1885. October 24.
Kline, Mary C. 1963. Benedict Roezl—Famous orchid collectors. *Amer. Orch. Soc. Bull.* 32, no. 8.
Sander, F. 1952. Benedict Roezl and *Cattleya aurea. The Orch. Rev.* 60, no. 710.

Benjamin Samuel Williams (1824–1890)

ORCHIDS HAD BECOME WIDESPREAD IN POPULARITY BY THE MIDDLE 1800s—but almost exclusively among botanists and wealthy horticulturists. Prior to that time it had not even been considered that the middle classes could presume to learn the techniques necessary for growing the "Queen of Flowers," nor were prices sufficiently reasonable for the average person to take an interest in orchids as a hobby pursuit. Thanks to Benjamin S. Williams, however, through his articles on orchids and their cultural requirements, greater understanding of orchid culture was provided and orchids began to enjoy a new popularity as subjects for the average gardener.

Benjamin Samuel Williams was born at Hoddesdon, Hertfordshire, England, on 2 March 1824, the fourth son of Mr. James Williams, at that time gardener to Mr. John Warner, at The Woodlands. At the age of fourteen young Williams left school and began a career of gardening under the supervision of his father. At seventeen years of age he left the Hoddesdon garden for another position, where he remained for six years. During those early years his first interests were with pansies and ranunculus, and he often exhibited these plants at local exhibitions. From these he became interested in horticulture in general and became a formidable opponent in exhibiting fruits and vegetables in suburban London shows.

After a short term in the nurseries of Messrs. Adam Paul & Son at Chestnut, he returned to The Woodlands in the capacity of foreman under his father, in charge of the fruit and vegetable gardens. In this position he soon proved himself so capable that Mr. Warner appointed him orchid grower to the large and extensive collection being formed at the estate. His talents and energies expanded in this sphere, and shortly he gained the reputation of being one of the foremost and successful orchid cultivators of his day and generation. He continued in Mr. Warner's employ for several years, adding to his skill as a plantsman and during at least one year taking first prize for orchids in the London shows in competition with Mr. Hanbury, Mrs. Lawrence, and others who owned the leading orchid collections of England.

In 1856 Williams began business as a nurseryman with Mr. Robert Parker at Seven Sisters Road, Holloway. The partnership continued until 1861, when it was dissolved by mutual consent. Williams then moved the business to Upper Holloway, where it continued well past the turn of the century as the Victoria and Paradise Nurseries. The firm enjoyed a worldwide reputation for the excellence of their plants and seeds, and as a cultivator of orchids Williams always held his own both at home and abroad. He was a continuous exhibitor at all the principal shows: London, Manchester, on the Continent, and in the United States. In every instance he maintained his reputation honorably, winning numerous prizes and awards.

Williams first became a horticultural writer in 1851 when, at the suggestion of Dr. John Lindley, he wrote a series of articles for the *Gardeners' Chronicle* entitled "Orchids for the Millions." This series on orchid cultivation formed the basis of *The Orchid Growers' Manual*, which had passed through seven editions by 1894. His *Choice Stove and Greenhouse Plants*—in two volumes devoted to flowering and fine-foliaged plants—went through three printings, and his *Select Ferns and Lycopods* was also popular. He furnished the cultural notes for Mr. Robert Warner's *Select Orchidaceous Plants*, which was begun in 1862, and in 1881, in association with Mr. Warner again, he commenced the publication of *The Orchid Album*, a monthly illustrated periodical which gained great popular favor. Thus, through these many works, the fascination of the Orchid Family was widespread and popularized in every gardening circle.

Williams was an enthusiastic supporter of every movement for the welfare of horticulture or his fellow man. He supported the Gardeners' Royal Benevolent Institution for over forty years; served on the Floral

Committee of the Royal Horticultural Society; was a member of the committee that planned and carried out the memorable International Horticultural Exhibition of 1866; and, showing the warm interest he took in everything affecting the welfare of gardeners, was present at the inaugural meeting held for the proposed establishment of the Orphan Fund.

A capacity for suffering must also have been one of Williams' virtues, for, beginning in 1888, he was plagued by a steadily worsening internal disorder which was extremely painful. For two years he bore the agony stoically, but the death of his wife struck him a blow from which he never recovered; he died shortly afterward, on 24 June 1890.

References

Arnold, Ralph E. 1954. Other Days. *The Orch. Rev.* 62, no. 738.

Gardeners' Chronicle. 1890. Obituary—B. S. Williams. Vol. 7, no. 183.

Gardeners' Chronicle. 1890. The Late B. S. Williams. Vol. 8, No. 184.

Gardening World, The. 1890. 6 (1889–90). June 28.

Williams, H. 1891. Obituary. *The Orchid Album* 9. London: B. S. Williams & Son.

Hugh Low (1824–1905)

YOUTH AND THE LOVE OF ADVENTURE GO HAND AND HAND, AND BOTH HAVE appropriately found their places in various fields. Orchid discovery and cultivation, too, have been furthered to a great extent by the courage and daring of young men who followed their dreams. Of the many renowned travelers and botanical collectors in the nineteenth century, one of the most enterprising was a young Englishman named Hugh Low.

Coming from an established horticultural family, the Lows of Clapton, Hugh Low was born on 10 May 1824. His father, a Scot by birth, had established a nursery business (Hugh Low & Company) only four years previously eight miles from the heart of London. Choice greenhouse plants were grown in great profusion at the firm and a very high standard of cultivation became their hallmark.

Young Hugh was a lover of plants and a keen observer, and it is therefore not unusual that at an early age he eagerly grasped the opportunity for travel and exploration in the Far East. Numerous accounts are given concerning the circumstances of his departure. Some state that he obtained an appointment with the East India Company in 1840, 1843, 1844, or 1845 and met Mr. (subsequently Sir) James Brooke aboard ship, then on his way to Borneo. Other sources indicate that young Low was sent out to collect flora in the East Indies and that Brooke was already engaged all the while in Borneo. To date no substantial evidence has been found to indicate precisely when they first corresponded or met. In any case, whenever it was, Brooke was so impressed with young Low's bearing and abilities that he convinced the youth to join him as secretary and companion. Low subsequently spent nearly three years with Brooke in and near Borneo.

Early in 1845 Low sailed from Singapore to Sarawak. From there he returned to England where in 1848 he published his work entitled *Sarawak, its Inhabitants and Productions*, a compilation of notes made during his residence in that island. He remarked in his book that: "My object (the collection of plants and seeds) led me more into the country, and amongst the tribes of Aborigines, than any other Englishman who has yet visited the shores of this island."

The work contained a wealth of information on the natural history of the region, and his detailed descriptions of Bornean orchids gave further evidence of his abilities as an observant naturalist. The interior of Sarawak had not then previously been explored by other than the natives, and because very little of that part of the world was known botanically it was a thrill for Low to enter virgin territory and find a host of new and beautiful plants which he sent to the family firm in England. In Sarawak he discovered many rare plants. Several new species of *Nepenthes* were introduced as well as such distinctive orchids as *Coelogyne pandurata, Coelogyne asperata, Dendrobium lowii, Paphiopedilum lowii*, and *Arachnanthe lowii*.

Low's intellectual curiosity drew him into a study of the peoples of Sarawak as well as the country's economic potentialities and farming practices. He traveled extensively, sometimes with Brooke's officers and at other times alone, collecting plants, discoursing with the Malays and Dyaks in their remote settlements, and taking notes of everything he saw.

Brooke became acting governor of Labuan in 1848 and Hugh Low accompanied him and became colonial treasurer of the island. He also visited Lawas and Brunei and became the first climber to ascend Mt. Kinabalu, in 1851,* where he collected numerous fine plants to send to

* Thomas Lobb, the great Veitchian orchid collector, also reached Mt. Kinabalu in 1851, but, ironically, the natives would not allow him to climb its steep slopes.

England. So esteemed was he by the natives, and so well known as a collector of plants, that the indigenous "jewel" orchids, *Haemaria* and *Anoectochilus*, became known to the Malays as *Daun Lo* (Low's Leaf). *Boenga Lau* (from Low) became the common vernacular name for the many orchids he collected in West Borneo and the Anambas and Natoena Islands.

He had a winning personality and his knowledge of the Malay dialects was extensive. He had a keen empathy for the natives, their laws, and their customs—a faculty which was destined to build his future eminence.

In April 1876 Low was appointed chief resident of Perak following internal strife and struggle in the colonial government and the brutal murder of the previous resident. He was fifty-three years of age then, having spent nearly thirty years of his official life in the Labuan administration. He immediately introduced a reformed government—reestablishing good relations with the native chiefs, gaining their confidence, and reaffirming their functions in government policy. He also took a great interest in improving the agriculture of the colony. Among many improvements, he introduced high-class cattle—Jerseys, Alderneys, and

Paphiopedilum lowii

Nellore cattle from India—which were kept at Kuala Kangsa and on the Taiping Hills.

He was a fellow of the Linnean Society, the Zoological Society, and the Society of Antiquaries. He was created C.M.G. in 1879, K.C.M.G. in 1883, and G.C.M.G. in 1889. In the latter year he retired from his post after more than forty years' experience of colonial administration in the East Indies. During those years he enriched English orchidology immeasurably. A few of the orchids which commemorate his family name are *Houlletia lowiana, Sobralia lowii, Stanhopea lowii, Cymbidium lowianum,* and the hybrid orchid genus *Lowiara.*

Men like Sir Hugh Low were rare and valuable assets during those times. Their interests and accomplishments were varied and fruitful, and while orchidology may claim them for their halls of fame, their other endeavors, too, did establish the foundations of all further developments in their respective fields. Hugh Low was a pioneer of orchidology—and numerous other studies—in the Malay States.

He was married twice: in 1848 to Catherine Napier of Singapore and Labuan, who bore him a son and a daughter (Catherine died in 1851), and in 1885 to Anne Douglas of Carr House, Monkseaton, Northumberland.

He died at Alassio, Italy, on 18 April 1905, less than a month from his eighty-first birthday.

References

Agricultural Bulletin of the Straits and Federated Malay States. 1905. Vol. 4, no. 6.

Arnold, Ralph E. 1932. Sir Hugh Low in Sarawak. *The Orch. Rev.* 40, no. 468.

Blowers, J. W. 1958. Messrs. Stuart Low (Benenden), Ltd. *The Orch. Rev.* 66, no. 778.

Curtis, Charles H. 1955. Notes. *The Orch. Rev.* 63, no. 744.

Gardeners' Chronicle. 1905. Sir Hugh Low. Vol. 37, no. 957.

Journal of the Malayan Branch—Royal Asiatic Society. 1954. The Journal of Sir Hugh Low, Perak, 1877. Emily Sadka, ed. Vol. 27, pt. 4.

Lemmon, Kenneth. 1962. *The Covered Garden.* London: Museum Press, Ltd.

Orchid Review, The. 1893. Vol. 1, no. 10.

Orchid Review, The. 1905. Obituary. Vol. 13, no. 150.

van Steenis, C. G. G. J. 1950. Cyclopaedia of Collectors. *Flora Malesiana.* Vol. 1, ser. 1.

Ferdinand Jacob Heinrich Mueller (1825-1896)

DURING A PERIOD WHEN WIDESPREAD BOTANICAL EXPLORATION WAS FLOUR-ishing, one of the richest areas of the world was the Australian conti-nent. And one of those most instrumental in advancing the botanical knowledge of that region was Dr. Ferdinand Mueller.

Born at Rostock, Germany, on 30 June 1825, Mueller was educated for the medical profession, studying medicine and natural history at Kiel University. Botany was of great interest to him, and between 1840 and 1847 he botanized at Schleswig and Holstein, taking his Ph.D. in 1846 with a thesis on *Capsella bursa-pastoris*. During that year he also published a paper on the flora of Schleswig-Holstein.

In 1847 Mueller developed premonitory symptoms of tuberculosis.

Seeking a more genial climate, and having already lost both his parents, he left northern Germany that year and emigrated to Australia. The change of climate proved beneficial and he took a position as assistant to a chemist in Adelaide. Having sufficient means of his own, however, he left that position and for four years devoted his full time to the botanical and geographical exploration of South Australia. During that time he explored the then almost unknown Australian Alps, making extensive collections of plants and sending duplicates to botanists in Europe. Meanwhile his reputation grew as a naturalist of great promise and industry.

On the recommendation of Sir Joseph D. Hooker, director of the Kew Botanic Gardens, Mueller was appointed government botanist to the colony of Victoria in 1852. His first work on the botany of Australia appeared in *Linnaea*, volume XXV, 1852, under the title of "Diagnoses et Descriptiones Plantarum Novarum, quas in Nova Hollandia australi praecipue in regionibus interioribus detexit et investigavit." Then followed a series of papers on the botany of the same region in Hooker's *London Journal of Botany*, and in 1855, in the first volume of the *Transactions of the Philosophical Society of Victoria*, he published his descriptions of the novelties he discovered in the Australian Alps. From that time on not a month passed without some published account of his work on the flora of Australia.

In 1855–1856 he was attached to an expedition sent out to explore the Victoria River and other districts in central and northern Australia. On this expedition nearly twenty degrees of unexplored country were covered and Mueller collected many plants.

In 1857 he became director of the Melbourne Botanic Gardens, a post he held until 1873 when, much against his will, he was removed in consequence of his not meeting the popular requirements of the period. This action was taken as a personal affront and he never entered the gardens again. He was retained under his former salary as government botanist, however, and the herbarium and library remained under his control. He never got over his dismissal as director, though, and many of his subsequent letters contained biting references to it.

The first volume of his *Fragmenta Phytographiae Australiae* was published in 1858–1859. These were continued until about 1882, comprising eleven thin volumes and a fragment of a twelfth—probably the first work in Latin published in Australia. These volumes were critical observations of Australian plants and gave evidence of the progress of botanical discovery on that continent. Among others of his botanical works were *Systematic Census of Australian Plants* (1882), in which the distribution of all known Australian species was given; *Eucalyptographia*, published in 1884; a work on the *Myoporinous Plants of Australia* (1886); the *Iconography of Australian Species of Acacia and Cognate Genera* (1887–1888); and *Iconography of Australian Salsolaceous Plants* (1889–

1891). He was also the author of an important economic work on plants suitable for industrial culture or naturalization which was translated into several languages and passed through many editions.

Mueller's greatest ambition had been to prepare a flora of the whole of Australia; toward that end he had long been collecting materials. When the question of such a work arose in 1861, however, many botanists deemed it essential that the work be done by someone having access to the type specimens in Europe. Mueller cheerfully agreed and magnanimously and unselfishly sent his extensive herbarium to Kew, where George Bentham could study the specimens and at least partially form his bases of identification and classification for the seven volumes of *Flora Australiensis* that appeared from 1863 to 1877.

Ferdinand Mueller was a man of great energy and varied interests—despite a somewhat frail constitution—as may be shown by other of his interests. He was a keen geographer, having done exploratory work in Victoria, Tasmania, Northern Territory, and western Australia. He also helped in raising funds for explorations in New Guinea and Antarctica, and aided other well-known explorers in their labors. The esteem in which he was held by geographers is evidenced by the fact that a river in Queensland, a mountain in Spitzbergen, a range of mountains in New Guinea, a waterfall in Brazil, and a glacier in New Zealand all bear his name.

He named more Australian plants than any other botanist, and scarcely any Australian or European botanic garden failed to be enriched by his generosity. He was tireless in developing the resources of Australia and was directly or indirectly involved in many flourishing new industries. At his instigation, the camel was originally brought to central Australia for transport purposes. To orchidology he also contributed significantly, naming and describing about seventy species of Australian orchids. Well known among them are *Bulbophyllum minutissimum*, *Cymbidium hillii*, *Dendrobium dicuphum*, *Dendrobium gracilicaule*, and *Dendrobium smilliae*, as well as species of *Caladenia*, *Cryptostylis*, *Diuris*, *Prasophyllum*, *Pterostylis*, *Sarcochilus*, *Sturmia*, *Thelymitra*, and others. *Arachnis muelleri* and *Oberonia muelleriana* keep the memory of this energetic orchidologist alive still.

Mueller was inordinately proud of the honors and distinctions accorded him and delighted in adorning himself with his many titles and decorations. He was a corresponding member of over 150 scientific and political societies and was at the head or intimately associated with every movement for the promotion of intellectual culture. Though he gave his full enthusiasm to all that related to botanical and geographical exploration, he was nevertheless a strong supporter of the renowned Melbourne musical society and other social institutions. He was elected a fellow of the Linnean Society in 1859 and of the Royal Society in 1861. In 1871 he was made an hereditary baron by the King of Würtemberg and was one of the first to be appointed to the Order of St. Michael and St. George. Queen Victoria made him a knight commander of that order in 1879. In 1888 he was awarded a gold medal by the Royal Society.

It was conjectured that Mueller "denied himself the pleasures of matrimony partly from conscientious motives, but particularly in order to be free to give his time and his income to his favourite pursuits." Domestic comforts actually were few in his home, for all the rooms were blocked with specimens, so that sitting room and comfort were much lacking.

Mueller's insatiable appetite for titles and distinctions caused him to publish botanical contributions in every possible channel open to him. Occasionally this led to regrettable inconsistencies of botanical nomenclature. He needlessly added to the synonymy of Australian plants, publishing many of them under two generic names simultaneously, so that whichever generic view one might take, Mueller's name would still stand as authoritative! This practice, as well as other vagaries, were incomprehensible considering his botanical experience. Even so, the magnitude of his services to science is incredible and is considered of great value.

He died in Melbourne on 9 October 1896.

References

Gardeners' Chronicle. 1896. Sir Ferdinand Mueller. Vol. 20, no. 512.

Garden, The. 1896. Obituary. 50:322.

Journal of Botany. 1897. Ferdinand von Mueller. Vol. 35, no. 415.

Kerr, Ronald. 1966. The Tool that Moved the World. *Amer. Orch. Soc. Bull.* 35, no. 4.

White, C. T. 1940. A History of Australian Orchids. *Australian Orch. Rev.* 5, no. 4.

Gustave Wallis (1830–1878)

TRAVEL FACILITIES HAD IMPROVED TREMENDOUSLY WITH THE ESTABLISHment of new colonial outposts by the middle 1800s, and many were the advantages and opportunities available to the man adventurous enough to travel to foreign lands. Such a man was Gustave Wallis.

He was born 1 May 1830 at Lüneburg, near Hanover, Germany, where his father was a judiciary counselor. Young Wallis was born with a handicap; he was deaf and mute until six years of age, and it was 1836 before he could articulate. In fact, a speech defect persisted during his entire life. At about that time the father died, leaving Gustave's mother a widow with six children. With her means of support gone, she found it necessary to leave Lüneburg and move to Detmold, her native town. In that romantic and picturesque atmosphere, surrounded by mountains and forests, Wallis attended school and developed a love of nature and botany which in later years excited a desire in him to see foreign lands, above all, the tropics.

Wallis had great energy and an indomitable will even as a youth, and in spite of his speech impediment he acquired considerable proficiency in foreign languages, an accomplishment which stood him in good stead during the course of his career. At the age of sixteen he was apprenticed to a goldsmith but, disliking the work, he quit and became apprenticed to a gardener at Detmold. When his apprenticeship had ended he obtained employment in Munich, and during that period he frequently made excursions to the Alps where he collected and studied the plants of those craggy regions.

In 1856 Wallis was engaged by a famous German firm and went to southern Brazil to start a horticultural establishment. The parent firm went bankrupt, however. The branch establishment was abandoned and Wallis was left stranded, practically penniless. In 1858 he offered his services to Jean Linden of Brussels, who accepted them and sent Wallis to South America as a plant collector. He welcomed this opportunity and began a remarkable and hazardous journey, crossing the continent by starting at the mouth of the Amazon River and traversing the total length to its source, exploring that great river and many of its more important tributaries. In 1870 he was commissioned by James Veitch & Sons to explore the Philippines, his principal objective being to locate various species of *Phalaenopsis* indigenous to those islands. Though he was able to make enough finds to send a shipment back to England, the mission proved too expensive to be considered very successful, and Wallis had to be recalled. In 1872, however, he was sent to Colombia, a country already known to him. There he collected many fine tropical plants, including many valuable orchids.

Upon the termination of his contract with the Veitches he continued to collect plants in South America, commencing his last journey at the end of the summer of 1875, when he left to explore the northern and central regions of the land. He was next heard of at Panama, dangerously ill with fever. He recovered, though, and commenced work again. His second attack, combined with dysentery, proved fatal. Letters from the collector Edward Klaboch carried the news that Wallis died in the hospital at Cuenca, Ecuador, on 20 June 1878.

Many choice plants commemorate Wallis' services to orchidology: *Epidendrum wallisii*, *Epidendrum pseudo-wallisii*, *Houlletia wallisii*, *Masdevallia wallisii*, and many more.

References

Davis, Reginald S., and Steiner, Mona Lisa. 1952. *Philippine Orchids*. New York: The William Frederick Press.
Gardeners' Chronicle. 1878. 10, no. 241.
Irvin, R. 1960. The Early Orchid Collectors. *The Orch. Rev.* 68, no. 803.
Journal of the Royal Horticultural Society. 1948. Vol. 73, part 9.
Lemmon, Kenneth. 1962. *The Covered Garden*. London: Museum Press Ltd.
van Steenis, C. G. G. J. 1950. Cyclopaedia of Collectors. *Flora Malesiana*. Vol. 1, ser. 1.
Veitch, James H. 1906. *Hortus Veitchii*. Chelsea, London: James Veitch & Sons Ltd.

Robert David Fitzgerald
(1830-1892)

A CLUMP OF *Dendrobium speciosum* GREW ON A BOULDER JUST ABOVE THE high-water mark at Wallis Lake, near Sydney, Australia, in 1864. As observed by a young Irish-Australian ornithologist, Robert David Fitzgerald, the plant sparked in him an interest so consuming that the splendid work *Australian Orchids* culminated as a masterful contribution to orchidology and a monument to its originator.

Fitzgerald was born at Tralee, Ireland, on 30 November 1830. The son of a prominent banker and rigid supporter of the Church of England, young Robert was destined to break from the cultural mold established by an orthodox religious family. Sectarian dissension and strained relationships between the churches in the south of Ireland left Fitzgerald with a strong disbelief in any form of religion even at an early age. Instead, nature in all its forms appealed to him.

The instincts of a naturalist-scientist came to light soon because, concurrent with his studies in civil engineering at Queen's College, Cork, ornithology became his main hobby. At age fifteen he distinguished himself by completely copying a famous book on British birds in fine typescript, illustrating it perfectly with replicas of all the original figures. In addition, he formed a fine collection of British bird skins and eggs, including numerous type specimens. Many of the skins were expertly mounted, Fitzgerald having become in the course of his studies an accomplished taxidermist as well.

He and his family emigrated to Australia in 1856, settling in Balmain. That same year he joined the Lands Department of New South Wales.

Hunting and fishing were pursuits in which Fitzgerald delighted, and seldom did a holiday pass that he was not off camping at the Hawkesbury River or Brisbane Water. He was a splendid shot with an old double-barreled, muzzle-loading Manton brought over from Ireland, and it proved an invaluable tool for purposes of obtaining knowledge of Australian birds.

Late in 1864 Fitzgerald and Mr. L. S. Campbell (later to become a well-known botanist and director of agriculture) made an excursion to Wallis Lake to collect bird specimens. It was there that orchids entered into Fitzgerald's life. The two naturalists had shipped their sixteen-foot dinghy aboard a timber trader's ketch along the Wallamba River, to the lake. At the lake the dinghy was launched and the two men sailed off. At their very first landing they were amazed to see large clumps of "rock lilies" (*Dendrobium speciosum*) growing on rocks at the lake's edge. "One clump was remarkably fine," stated Campbell years later, "much better than anything we had seen previously. Mr. Fitzgerald longed to have this in his garden (at Glebe Point, Sydney), but considered it would be hopeless to take such a huge specimen off the rock to the steamer. I assured him that if we returned to that place he would get it all right. That clump of Dendrobium proved to be the origin of the remarkable publication by Mr. Fitzgerald, '*Australian Orchids*,' which made its appearance a few years later. . . ."

From the ornithological standpoint the trip proved barely worthwhile. Fish, however, were so plentiful that the sport was removed from angling, so the two turned their attentions to the botany of the area, particularly the epiphytic orchids. Many species were collected, some of them later identified at Sydney as *Dendrobium tetragonum, Dendrobium fairfaxii*, and *Dendrobium linguiforme*.

Gradually Fitzgerald's interest in orchids grew, and his knowledge of them increased steadily through observation and study. He particularly admired Charles Darwin, and for some time a steady correspondence was maintained between the two. References in Darwin's *Fertilisation of Orchids* (second edition) to Fitzgerald's observations bear witness to the serious thoughtfulness the young Irish-Australian gave to the Orchid Family, particularly to fertilization and pollination of Australian species. Most of his spare time was devoted to the study of orchids and ferns, though he yet remained relatively unknown in the botanical world. In 1869, however, he visited Lord Howe Island with Charles Moore of the Sydney Botanic Gardens. Previous to this visit almost all the endemic vegetable life of that isolated spot between New Zealand and Norfolk Island was unknown to science. Here and in numerous other Australian states Fitzgerald discovered many new orchids and other plants, and by his introductions he became publicly known to the "fraternity" of plant scientists.

In January 1873 he was appointed to the post of deputy surveyor-general of New South Wales, a position to which he applied himself with diligence and authority. Through his efforts in this office many natural wonders were preserved as public reservations—Katoomba, Leura, Wentworth Falls, Elizabeth Island, and numerous other scenic areas. A series of state visits resulted in a continuous stream of plant discoveries, one of which is among Australia's most beautiful orchids, *Sarcochilus fitzgeraldii*, named in his honor by Ferdinand Mueller, a close botanist-friend of his and a well-known authority on the Orchidaceae. Also in his honor, Mueller established the Australian orchid genus *Fitzgeraldia*.

Meanwhile Fitzgerald had moved from Balmain to Hunter's Hill, Sydney. There he built a remarkable fernery in which he carried on plant experimentation, besides continuing an avid interest in his work on Australian orchids. Rock by rock, the fernery was constructed entirely by his own hands. It consisted of an excavation measuring about thirty-one by fifteen feet in living sandstone rock, with a glass roof. Half the floor space was taken up by a deep tank, also carved from the rock and overlaid with stout beams an inch or so apart so as to form a strong floor. Rainwater was collected in an immense tank higher up in the garden, and through an ingenious system of plumbing was used and reused to provide the abundance of moisture necessary for the culture of the many rare and beautiful ferns and orchids never previously cultivated in any Australian city.

Not only was Robert Fitzgerald an accomplished surveyor, civil engineer, geologist, ornithologist, and botanist but he was also an excellent artist. In 1875 the first part of his great *Australian Orchids* was published, and all the monochrome illustrations appearing therein were drawn by Fitzgerald's own hand. In the second part they began to be colored. Living specimens were collected, from which each plate was carefully prepared. For the purpose of faithfully depicting each segment, Fitzgerald constructed a small microscope and forceps which held the flower or part thereof in a natural position. The first lithographs published were drawn on stones by Fitzgerald, and after printings he colored many by hand as a guide to those engaged in the work of coloring. Successive parts were issued at intervals, and the first volume, published in 1882, was dedicated to the memory of Charles Darwin.

As a busy public servant, Fitzgerald necessarily did his orchid work in limited spare time. Then in 1884 the Crown Lands Act caused the reorganization of his department, and as a consequence his own post was discontinued and he was forced to retire under a government pension in 1887. Relegated to the seclusion and relative inactivity of private life, Fitzgerald was thus enabled to devote much more study and attention to the delineation of the Australian orchids. The publication of *Australian Orchids* was enthusiastically proceeded with. The first government-subsidized volume was completed, and the second had already run into four parts, with material on hand for a fifth, when the author-artist died on 12 August 1892. Upon receiving the shocking news of his good friend's death, Ferdinand Mueller wrote:

It is indeed an irreparable loss, not only to our favourite science but to ourselves personally, who have learned to appreciate his sterling character in life. . . . So long as the lovely orchids of this part of the world embellish with singular and varied beauty the natural features of Australia, so long will the memory of our leading orchidologist be held dear in the study of God's works.

Fitzgerald's drawings and notes, which were to have completed the fifth part of the second volume, were carefully collected by Henry Deane and Mr. A. J. Stopps, Fitzgerald's lithographer. Working in cooperation they finished the last number in 1894.

Considering Fitzgerald's limited access to references, difficulties in transporting materials, and other disadvantages under which he worked, it was inevitable that he should occasionally be mistaken in his interpretations of species. His accuracy and botanical insight were, nevertheless, truly remarkable, and his errors were comparatively few. Apart from the approximately 200 plates prepared for his *Australian Orchids*, numerous unpublished plates were completed, as well as hundreds of exquisitely colored drawings of native flowers, all drawn from living specimens solely for Fitzgerald's amusement, without any intention of publication. He adamantly maintained that no accurate description of any orchid could be obtained from a dried and pressed specimen, despite the fact that his friend Mueller would never attempt to describe a new species until it had been thoroughly dried.

Fitzgerald was regarded as an amiable and versatile man. Though grave in manner, he possessed a kindly disposition with a winning manner and with his intimates he displayed a genuine Irish humor. He was frank and unpretentious, as easily approachable in official as in private life, and especially gifted, as it was ever noticed, to gain the respect and confidence of young people. He was married to Emily Hunt, by whom he had three sons and two daughters.

References

Britten, James, and Boulger, G. S. 1931. *A Biographical Index of Deceased British and Irish Botanists.* 2nd ed. London: Taylor & Francis.

Campbell, Walter S. 1924. Seeking Australian Orchids—R. D. Fitzgerald's Great Work—Reminiscences from Field and Study. *Daily Telegraph* (Sydney). May 10.

Daily Telegraph. 1892. Sydney. August 16.

Gardeners' Chronicle. 1892. Mr. R. D. Fitzgerald. Vol. 12, no. 301.

Journal of the Royal Society of New South Wales. 1878. Vol. 13, p. 102.

Messmer, Mrs. C. A. 1932. The Biography of Robert David Fitzgerald, F.L.S., and Arthur James Stopps, F.L.S. *Victorian Naturalist.* April.

Mueller, F. 1892. *Journ. Bot.* (Obituary note). Vol. 30, p. 320.

Rupp, Rev. H. M. R. 1944–45. A Critical Revision of R. D. Fitzgerald's "Australian Orchids." *Linnean Soc. of N.S.W. Proc.* 69, nos. 315–316.

Serle, Percival. 1949. *Dictionary of Australian Biography.* Sydney: Angus & Robertson.

Sydney Mail, The. 1892. The Late Robert David Fitzgerald, F.L.S. September 3.

Victorian Naturalist. 1892. Vol. 9: 75.

White, C. T. 1940. A History of Australian Orchids. *Australian Orch. Rev.* 5, no. 4.

Harry Bolus (1834–1911)

EIGHTEENTH-CENTURY DUTCH TRAVELERS AND OFFICIALS OF THE DUTCH East India Company were responsible for the initial introduction of South African orchids to European herbaria. They were followed by a succession of Swedish, German, and British collectors. Their orchid finds were described and catalogued by Thunberg and Swartz, Lindley, Reichenbach, and others. The data and specimens were widespread, however, and not fully comprehensive of South Africa's 500 endemic species. The first consolidation of this area's orchid plants was therefore a welcome contribution to the world's knowledge of South African orchids. This most significant work was done by Harry Bolus, a Cape Town stockbroker and amateur botanist.

Harry Bolus was born on 28 April 1834, at Nottingham, England. At the age of sixteen he went to South Africa as a poor apprentice and for fifteen years he lived at Graaff Reinet, in the center of the colony. His career was varied and interesting—first a boy with only a few shillings in his pocket; next, a stint of service as a volunteer in a Kaffir war; later, an insurance secretary; and still later he turned to sheep farming. In 1874 he became a broker in Cape Town in business with his brother. Twenty years later he retired, a wealthy man.

Bolus' interest in botany began in 1864 after the death of his first child. He fervently involved himself in the study of African flora, making excursions to the mountains in search of plants, describing them carefully with pencil and pen. Correspondence with Sir Joseph Hooker led to a large number of African succulents and bulbs being dispatched to the Royal Botanical Gardens at Kew, England.

Frequent trips to England, France, Switzerland, and Italy were an integral part of Bolus' life, and most of the major European herbaria were enriched by copies of the large fascicles of South African plants which he prepared with Professor MacOwen.

In 1876 he visited Kew, taking a large collection of plants for comparison with those in the Kew Herbarium. It was fortunate that he left duplicates behind, for on the return journey all his specimens were lost, along with much information gained on the visit, through the wreck of his ship, the *Windsor Castle*, in Table Bay.

After his retirement from business, the heaths and orchids of the Cape especially attracted Bolus. As a result, his *Orchids of the Cape Peninsula* appeared in 1888. His principal work was a book in two volumes, *Icones Orchidearum Austro-Africanum, Extra-Tropicarum*, published between 1893 and 1911. This work contained figures and descriptions of 200 South African orchids, drawn and described by himself from living plants. With the help of his friend, Dr. Guthrie, he monographed the genus Erica for the *Flora Capensis*, and in 1903, in collaboration with Major A. H. Wolley-Dod, he issued a *List of the Flowering Plants and Ferns of the Cape Peninsula*, with notes on the critical species. In later years Bolus was ably assisted by his devoted niece Miss Kensit in all his botanical work.

Bolus made numerous trips throughout the eastern and western provinces, collecting largely for his own herbarium. This collection and library, full of fine books which later became unprocurable, was the richest and most valuable assemblage of information on the flora of South Africa known at that time. His library included complete sets of the *Botanical Magazine, Botanical Register, Refugium Botanicum*, and the folios of Redoute, Jacquin, Bauer, and Masson.

Always interested in the furtherance of scientific and educational pursuits, Bolus founded the Bolus Professorship of Botany in the Cape University. He further bequeathed his herbarium and library to the

South African College, plus 27,000 pounds sterling, invested in government stocks, in trust for the upkeep and extension of the herbarium and library, and 21,000 pounds for the foundation of scholarships. In recognition of his scientific work and his liberality in endowing the professorship, the university conferred on him the honorary degree of doctor of science.

In 1873 he became a fellow of the Linnean Society, and he was one of the original members of the South African Philosophical Society.

Though possessed of an adventurous nature and inquiring intellect, Bolus was withal quiet and unassuming. Once, when giving evidence before a parliamentary commission, he was asked, "You are a botanist?" He replied, "I do not call myself a botanist, but I have studied botany in my leisure hours."

In May 1911 he and his niece landed at Southampton, England, where he suffered a severe heart attack, from which he never recovered. He died at Oxted, Surrey, on the twenty-fifth and was buried there in a quiet country churchyard on May twenty-seventh.

Dr. Bolus' name is commemorated in the orchid genera *Bolusiella* and *Neobolusia*, both of which were founded by Schlechter.

References

Curtis' Botanical Magazine. 1931. *Dedications and Portraits 1827–1927.* Nelmes, Ernest, and Cuthbertson, Wm. (comps.) London: Bernard Quaritch Ltd.

Gardeners' Chronicle. 1911. Obituary. Vol. 49, no. 1275.

Gardeners' Chronicle. 1911. The Late Dr. Bolus and the South African College. Vol. 50, no. 1281.

Journal of Botany. 1911. Harry Bolus (1834–1910). Vol. 49, no. 583.

Lantern. 1963. Kirstenbosch Jubilee issue. Vol. 13, no. 1.

John Seden (1840-1921)

To every lover of orchids the names of John Dominy and John Seden signify the dawn of orchid hybridization. Both worked together for many years in the employ of James Veitch & Sons, and both were pioneers in the field. The hundreds of new orchid hybrids created by them formed a great share of the world renown the Veitch firm enjoyed.

John Seden was born 10 July 1840, at Dedham, in Essex, England, and he began his career as a gardener early in life.

I first fell in love with orchids, etc., in 1859, when I lived in a private place next door to the late Dr. Butler, who had at that time a good selection of the best orchids in cultivation, and exhibited very successfully at Regent's Park and the Crystal Palace. The late Mr. Robert Bullen, late curator of the Botanic Gardens, Glasgow, was the grower. In 1860 Mr. Bullen went to Chelsea as orchid grower, and recommended me also to the late Mr. James Veitch. I started work there in January, 1861. . . .

In the fall of that year Mr. Veitch transferred Seden to the Exeter nursery, and it was under John Dominy's tutelage that he was first initiated into the practice of hybridization. Mr. Dominy's results in plant breeding had attracted wide attention and it was not surprising, therefore, that Seden should become interested in that line of work.

After the death of James Veitch in 1862, Seden was asked to return to the Chelsea branch to take charge of the orchids, stove plants, and nepenthes. There he continued further experiments in hybridization and cross-fertilization. Not only did he raise new orchid hybrids, but nepenthes, caladiums, begonias, alocasias, gloxinias, and amaryllis were crossed, and many notable hybrid progeny resulted.

His first orchid of hybrid origin, *Paphiopedilum* Sedenii, flowered in 1873, and from that time he raised 150 hybrid paphiopedilums, 140 laeliocattleyas, sixty-five cattleyas, forty dendrobiums, twenty-five laelias, sixteen phalaenopsis, twenty epidendrums, twelve masdevallias, nine calanthes, eight sophrocattleyas, five phaiocalanthes, six disas, four zygopetalums, and other miscellaneous hybrids such as *Chysis* Chelsoni, *Chysis* Sedeni, *Chysis* Langleyensis, *Thunia* Veitchii, *Sobralia*

Veitchii, *Cymbidium* Eburneolowianum, *Phaius* Amabilis, *Phaius* Maculato-grandifolius, *Epilaelia* Radico-purpurata, *Epilaelia* Eros, *Leptolaelia* Veitchii, *Angraecum* Veitchii, *Miltonia* Bleuana splendens, *Odontoglossum* Excellens, *Anguloa* Intermedia, and many others. His own name is commemorated—in addition to his hybrids—by the species *Cyrtorchis sedenii* and *Phragmipedium sedenii.*

In 1867 the younger James Veitch moved to Stanley House, next to the Chelsea nursery. He requested Seden to enter into his service in a private capacity, which he did.

So that he might have the advantage of some outside work, Sir Harry Veitch invited Seden to the firm's nursery at Langley in 1889. There it was that he expanded his hybridizing by raising various fruits, including strawberries, raspberries, apples, and gooseberries, all of which received awards from the Royal Horticultural Society's Fruit and Vegetable Committee. In all, Seden made over 490 crosses, the majority of which yielded plants, fruits, and flowers of great merit. In recognition of his contributions to horticulture, in 1897 he was chosen as one of the original recipients of the Victoria Medal of Honour by the Royal Horticultural Society.

In 1905, at the age of sixty-five, John Seden retired and went to live at Worthing where, due to the liberal beneficence of his former employers, he was able to spend the remainder of his life in leisure and happiness. He died there on 24 February 1921.

References

Gardeners' Chronicle. 1899. Hybrids and Their Raisers. Vol. 26, no. 655.
Gardeners' Chronicle. 1921. Obituary. Vol. 69, no. 1784.
Veitch, James H. 1906. *Hortus Veitchii.* Chelsea, London: James Veitch & Sons Ltd.

Harry James Veitch
(1840-1924)

IT IS ALMOST IMPOSSIBLE TO SPEAK OF HARRY J. VEITCH WITHOUT ALSO
referring to gardening and horticulture in general. For many years he
was regarded as the most outstanding figure in contemporary horticulture, and during the last fifty years of his life no one exercised so great
an influence on all things pertaining to gardening.

Harry James Veitch was the second of James Veitch's three sons
and was born on 24 June 1840, at Exeter, England. Like many notable
horticulturists, he was of Scottish descent, his great-grandfather having
crossed into England toward the close of the eighteenth century to take
up the offices of steward and bailiff to Sir Thomas Acland at Killerton,
Devon. Young Harry was educated at the Exeter Grammar School and
at Altona, near Hamburg, Germany. Afterward he attended the course

of botanical lectures given by Dr. John Lindley at the University College, London, by which he gained insight into the management of the seed business. Shortly thereafter he joined the staff of the famous French nursery firm, Vilmorin-Andrieux & Co., Paris, where he managed the seed department.

At the age of eighteen Harry Veitch returned to England to help his father in the management of the Chelsea nurseries, acquired five years previously from Messrs. Knight and Perry. His industry and business sense rapidly became apparent, and the firm of Messrs. James Veitch & Sons soon enjoyed the reputation of being the foremost nursery business in the world. Harry's influence in the business extended over almost the whole of his long and useful life.

When it was decided that the Great International Horticultural Exhibition of 1866 should be held in London, Veitch entered into the work with zest, becoming a member of the executive committee and of many of the subcommittees. With proceeds from the exhibition, the Lindley Library was purchased and vested in the Royal Horticultural Society. Veitch was intimately associated with this organization for many years and he, with others, was said to have laid the foundation for its popularity thereafter.

The Veitches sent numerous plant collectors to the various parts of the world and rendered a great service to botany and horticulture by their introductions of new species and hybrids. Sir Harry was particularly honored by the beautiful *Masdevallia harryana* and *Masdevallia veitchiana*, which were discovered by Veitchian collectors and named in his honor. Among their collectors were William and Thomas Lobb, Richard Pearce, John Gould Veitch, J. Henry Chesterton, Gustave Wallis, Guillermo Kalbreyer, Frederick W. Burbidge, Charles Curtis, and David Burke. In addition to developing many fine hybrids of *Begonia, Streptocarpus, Hippeastrum, Nepenthes,* and other genera, they had the distinction of raising the first hybrid orchid, *Calanthe* Dominii, hybridized and grown by their foreman, John Dominy.

Harry Veitch was a constant visitor at the continental horticultural gatherings for thirty or forty years. As early as 1869 he was among those present at the first international exhibition in Russia, which was held at St. Petersburg. Among those of his party also receiving cordial welcome from the czar were Sir Joseph Hooker, Dr. Robert Hogg, Dr. Moore of Glasnevin, and Mr. Robert Warner.

Because of the death of his father in 1869 and of his elder brother John in 1890, Harry Veitch became head of the firm. His responsibility, energy, enthusiasm, and keenness in business surprised even those who knew him best. The full responsibility of the extensive firm was taken well in stride: the nurseries at Coombe Wood—trees, shrubs, and herbaceous plants; Feltham—garden plants, florists' flowers, and seed production; and Langley—tree and bush fruits and, later, orchids. With the reins in his hands, the firm entered into the most prosperous period of its history.

Various publications were issued by Messrs. Veitch while Harry Veitch was head of the firm. *A Manual of the Coniferae* was published in 1888, with a second printing in 1900, and the ten parts of the two-volume *Manual of Orchidaceous Plants Cultivated Under Glass in Great Britain* were published between 1887 and 1894. A large number of Harry Veitch's own publications appeared in the *Journal of the Royal Horticultural Society*. These included *Orchids Past and Present* (1881), *Coniferae of Japan* (1892), and *Deciduous Trees and Shrubs of Japan* (1894). He also shared in the production of the history of the house of Veitch, entitled *Hortus Veitchii* (1906).

For nearly twenty-five years Harry Veitch was chairman of the Gardeners' Royal Benevolent Institution, ably conducting its affairs and contributing generously to its funds. He also supported the Royal Gardener's Orphan Fund and the United Horticultural Benefit and Provident Society. He was chairman and treasurer of the Horticultural Club for many years and additionally served as a member of the Board of Directors of the British Orphan Schools and on the committee of St.

*Odontoglossum
harryanum*

Anne's and of the City of London Missions. To all these organizations he gave his patronage freely and his financial assistance liberally.

The Second Great International Horticultural Exhibition was held in 1912, and Veitch again took a leading part. For his services in that regard, King George conferred the honor of knighthood upon him. He also received the Order of the Crown from the Belgian king, the French Legion of Honour, the French Isidore St. Hilaire Medal, and the United States' George R. White Gold Medal for eminent services to horticulture. Apart from knighthood, probably the greatest honor accorded Sir Harry Veitch was the award of the Victoria Medal of Honour in 1906, given by the Royal Horticultural Society, with which he had long been associated and of whose Orchid Committee he was chairman for many years. Even at the age of seventy-eight he undertook the onerous office of treasurer of the society.

Sir Harry Veitch retired from business in 1914. With his brothers John and Arthur both deceased, there was no successor in the family, and rather than risk losing the recognized reputation which the firm had acquired, he disposed of the nursery and sold the land for redevelopment.

Lady Veitch died in 1921, and soon afterward Sir Harry left off his horticultural activities and lived in complete retirement at his home in Kensington and East Burnham Park, Slough, though he still maintained a keen interest in the affairs and institutions with which he had been associated. He died at Slough, Buckinghamshire, on 6 July 1924, at the advanced age of eighty-four.

References

Curtis' Botanical Magazine. 1931. *Dedications and Portraits 1827–1927*. Nelmes, Ernest, and Cuthbertson, Wm., comps. London: Bernard Quaritch Ltd.

Gardeners' Chronicle. 1924. Harry J. Veitch, V.M.H. Vol. 76, no. 1, 1959.

Orchid Review, The. 1912. Mr. Harry J. Veitch, F.L.S., V.M.H. Vol. 20, no. 230.

Orchid Review, The. 1924. Notes. Vol. 32, no. 374.

van Steenis, C. G. G. J. 1950. Cyclopaedia of Collectors. *Flora Malesiana*. Vol. 1, ser. 1.

Veitch, James H. 1906. *Hortus Veitchii*. Chelsea, London: James Veitch & Sons Ltd.

Alfred Celestin Cogniaux
(1841–1916)

WHILE A LARGE NUMBER OF ORCHID COLLECTORS, BOTANISTS, AND HORTICUL-
turists made their contributions to orchidology by first-hand visits to
the natural orchid regions of the world, many others at home were left
with the painstaking tasks of classification and collation of the information collected. No less important were these tasks, and no less exacting
in diagnoses and detail. The known orchids of South America were yet
in a scrambled state by the late 1800s, and even though a great deal of
published and unpublished data existed, the orchids of Brazil, particularly, remained relatively unknown in European herbaria. It remained
for Alfred C. Cogniaux, a Belgian botanist, to organize and amplify
upon the orchid genera and species of this vast natural orchid region.
His comprehensive and critical systematization of the Brazilian orchids
stands as a monument to his achievements as a descriptive botanist. A
number of orchids, also, became his namesakes—*Dichaea cogniauxiana,*

Maxillaria cogniauxiana, Pleurothallis cogniauxiana, Miltonia cogniaux-iae, and the genus *Cogniauxiocharis.*

Alfred Celestin Cogniaux was born in Robechies, a little village south of Hainaut, Belgium, on 7 April 1841. Upon completion of his local primary schooling, he became a pupil at the Normal School at Nivelles in 1852. He became a teacher there in 1861 upon receiving his diploma as professor. He had scarcely finished his studies when, alone and without guidance, he gave himself enthusiastically over to botany. He occupied his attention first with indigenous plants and more particularly with mosses and hepaticas. His first botanical paper, on *Nitella tenuissima*, was published in 1863 in the *Bulletin of the Royal Botanical Society of Belgium*, in which many of his shorter papers on local botany were also subsequently published.

In 1872 he became the conservator of the Brussels Botanic Garden, where he was given the job of working on the family *Cucurbitaceae* in the great *Flora Brasiliensis* of Martius. His work on this family resulted in a volume with thirty-eight plates which appeared in 1878. After that he immediately undertook a general monograph of the same family, a work which won the Pyrame de Candolle Award in 1881 as the best botanical monograph to appear within the previous fifty years.

In 1880 he became professor of natural history in Jodoigne; four years later he went to Verviers. Meanwhile, his interest in the *Cucurbitaceae* and *Melastomaceae* led him to do several important papers on these families—further monographs and accounts which were incorporated in de Candolle's *Monographs* (1891) and Martius' *Flora Brasiliensis* (1883–1888).

While at Verviers, Cogniaux held the position of vice-consul to Brazil, and long before the *Flora Brasiliensis* was finished, he was put in charge of a general monograph of the Orchid Family. This work occupied thirteen years; it was begun in 1893, following the system proposed by Pfitzer. Based on J. Barbosa Rodrigues' earlier work on Brazilian orchids, *Genera et Species Orchidearum Novarum* (1877–1882), it was expanded by a folio of Rodrigues' unpublished original drawings. In this large undertaking Cogniaux was able to obtain the loan of Rodrigues' type drawings and to send them on to Kew for comparison and copying. Cogniaux's work contained all the orchids then recorded from Brazil, including many species found in the Guianas, Venezuela, Colombia, Peru, and the adjacent regions. Many were new species, along with detailed descriptions and line drawings. With the completion of the third volume in 1906, this work became not only an indispensable guide to the then known Brazilian orchids, but a valuable reference to all the orchids of northern South America as well.

Cogniaux retired from his chair at Verviers in 1901 with a pension which enabled him to settle at Genappe and devote most of his time to botany. From 1896 he had collaborated with A. Goossens in jointly authoring the *Dictionnaire iconographique des Orchidées*, a work in which a large number of cultivated orchids were illustrated by chromolithography, from watercolor paintings by Goossens. Published in parts and treating of species important to horticulturists, it was completed in 1907. And even while working on this complex and time-consuming task, Cogniaux labored on his *Chronique Orchidéenne, Supplément mensuelle*, begun in 1897. He was also a contributor to later volumes of *Lindenia* and the *Journal des Orchidées*.

In May 1900 he was elected foreign member of the Linnean Society and in 1903 received the diploma of doctor from the University of Heidelberg.

Despite the magnitude of his work in the Orchid Family, he still found time to work in other botanical fields. A *Flora of Belgium* was issued as well as a number of articles and descriptions of new plants published in Belgian, French, English, German, Swiss, Portuguese, and American scientific journals.

In the orchids, Cogniaux next worked out a monograph of the orchids of the West Indies. Though small, and without the valued inclusion of illustrations, this work proved valuable. Begun in 1909, it was published in the sixth volume of Urban's *Symbolae Antillana* in 1910. In it, over 500 species were enumerated from over ninety-six genera. It readily became a standard and leading reference on the orchids of the West Indies, from the Bahamas to Trinidad.

Following his extensive orchid work and despite declining health, Cogniaux returned to his first interest, the *Cucurbitaceae*, and had completed the first volume of his revision of the family when death overtook him on 15 April 1916.

References

Journal des Orchidees. 1896. Galerie des Orchidophiles—M. Alfred Cogniaux. Vol. 6.
Orchid Review, The. 1893. Vol. 1, no. 9.
Orchid Review, The. 1917. Obituary. Vol 25, no. 291.
Orchis. 1916. Gartenflora 55. 10: 145–148.
Proceedings of the Linnean Society of London. London. 1916. Obituary Notices. 129th Session.
Schweinfurth, Charles. 1959. Classification of Orchids. Ch. 2 of *The Orchids— A Scientific Survey*. Carl L. Withner, ed. New York: The Ronald Press Co.

William Boxall (1844-1910)

BY THE TURN OF THE CENTURY, PLANT HUNTERS HAD LITERALLY COMBED the forest and mountains of the world in their quest for rare and desirable orchid novelties. Only the most resourceful and knowledgeable collector could yet make a comfortable living in the trade. For a few, however, the adventure and satisfaction of exploration satisfied inner desires. Among such venturous souls, William Boxall was perhaps the best known and beloved of a singularly unique class of veteran orchidists.

Little is known of Boxall's early life beyond the year of his birth—1844. In the early 1860s he was employed by the Veitch firm at Chelsea and worked also in the gardens of Leigh Park, Havant, and at Earl Radnor's garden at Highwood. Later he was hired as foreman of the orchid department at Messrs. Hugh Low & Co., at Clapton.

Boxall's knowledge of orchids together with his great love for plants were quickly recognized by his employers as the qualities desirable in a good collector. Thus he was sent to Burma to try his luck at procuring rare and worthy orchids. Both Reverend Charles Parish and Colonel Benson had already shown the world that numerous showy species could be found there, and it was not long before Boxall began showing the results of searches so extensive that they reached even to the borders of China. *Dendrobium boxallii* was one of his earliest orchid discoveries, so named in his honor by Reichenbach in 1874. *Dendrobium wardianum* was one of his special finds; some of the plants sold in Stevens' sales rooms for as much as 100 guineas each. Other striking finds sent to England by Boxall in 1877 included *Cymbidium lowianum, Paphiopedilum boxallii, Vanda coerulescens* var. *boxallii*, and *Vanda lamellata* var. *boxallii* in 1880.

Subsequent quests in the Philippines resulted in large quantities of *Phalaenopsis amabilis* and *Phalaenopsis schilleriana* being dispatched to England. At a time when the difficulties of transportation and plant losses were still great, Boxall's ingenuity was remarkable. Preparing special cases glazed with ground oyster shells, he was able to transport the plants successfully in much greater quantity than most other professionals, thus becoming known as one of the world's most successful collectors.

Borneo, Java, Brazil, and Central America became further territories from which thousands of living plants were collected. Among his most worthy introductions, the following are cited: *Paphiopedilum bellatulum*, *Paphiopedilum ciliolare*, *Phalaenopsis brymeriana*, *Phalaenopsis stuartiana*, *Masdevallia bella*, *Cattleya schofieldiana*, *Laelia leeana*, *Vanda boxallii*, *Vanda roeblingiana*, *Vanda amesiana*, *Vanda kimballiana*, *Saccolabium bellinum*, and many others.

In conversation Boxall easily enraptured his audience, particularly children. His knowledge of orchids and their habitats was very great, but especially intriguing were the tales he recounted of things seen and heard in the countries he had traveled through.

Like many of that adventurous breed who had preceded him, the professional orchid collector Boxall undertook many difficult journeys in climates hazardous to his well-being. His health had been failing for some years because of diabetes, and this, coupled with a paralytic stroke in 1907, caused him to retire permanently to his home at Clapton. Though he recovered only partially from the stroke, he nevertheless frequently attended meetings of the Royal Horticultural Society and was a member of some years' standing on the Orchid Committee. In addition, he was one of the first recipients of the Victoria Medal of Honour in horticulture.

After struggling against poor health for many years, he passed away on 28 August 1910 at his Clapton home, leaving only his widow.

References

Davis, Reginald S., and Steiner, Mona Lisa. 1952. *Philippine Orchids*. New York: The William Frederick Press.

Gardeners' Chronicle. 1910. Obituary. Vol. 48, no. 1236.

Orchid Review, The. 1910. Vol. 18, no. 215.

Orchid World, The. 1910. Obituary. Vol. 1, no. 3.

van Steenis, C. G. G. J. 1950. Cyclopaedia of Collectors. *Flora Malesiana*. Vol. 1, ser. 1.

Ernst Hugo Heinrich Pfitzer (1846-1906)

THE SCIENTIFIC AND TECHNICAL ASPECTS OF ORCHIDOLOGY HAD ACTUALLY only been touched upon by the late 1800s. Evolutionary development in the Orchid Family, particularly as it pertained to the morphology and importance of vegetative peculiarities, had received small attention insofar as classification was concerned. Years earlier Sir Joseph Hooker had advocated that the study of botany was in serious need of revision, but few workers in the field distinguished themselves in orchid research and study until Ernst Hugo Heinrich Pfitzer, professor of botany and director of the Botanic Garden in the University of Heidelberg, developed a widely accepted system of classification based on morphological and vegetative characteristics.

Pfitzer was born on 26 March 1846, at Königsberg, Prussia, and from the beginning he was trained by distinguished educators in the field of biology—Sanio, von Caspary, and Wilhelm Hofmeister, among others. Thus, with a sound background of preparation for scientific research, in

1872—at the age of twenty-six—Pfitzer was appointed professor of botany and director of the Botanic Garden.

The Botanic Garden contained a large collection of orchids, giving Pfitzer ample opportunity to study a diversity of floral and vegetative structures. The natural arrangement of orchids was not quite settled at that time, and Pfitzer became increasingly convinced that relationships based on these structures—almost entirely neglected by earlier botanists—did exist. John Lindley's system of orchid classification was still in use at the time, and though Lindley was a pioneer who made substantial progress in this respect, his system fell short of later expanded needs. Pfitzer agreed that the floral characteristics were essential guides to a natural system of classification, but he insisted that leaf and stem characteristics were equally important in the indication of evolutionary trends. Preliminary studies and papers supporting his views were published from time to time in German botanical journals and elsewhere, and by 1880 he had received widespread recognition as a leading orchidologist.

The main results of his studies were published in outline form in the 11 December 1880 issue of the *Gardeners' Chronicle*. He was also assigned the orchids in the compilation of Engler and Prantl's *Die natürlichen Pflanzenfamilien*. In 1882 his *Grundlage einer vergleichenden Morphologie der Orchideen* appeared, a large quarto volume 194 pages long. This was the forerunner of several important following works and was quickly recognized as a scholarly and instructive book. This was followed in 1886 by *Morphologische Studien über die Orchideenblüthe*, an octavo volume of 139 pages and sixty-five figures, and a similar work in 1887, *Entwurf einer natürlichen Anordnung der Orchideen*. His contribution to Engler and Prantl's work was published in 1889, and in 1895 he wrote a paper entitled "Beitrage zur Systematik der Orchideen" for the nineteenth volume of Engler's *Pflanzenreich*. In connection with this work he paid several visits to the herbarium and libraries at Kew and the British Museum, where he was much respected and well received. In many respects his good-natured bearing and congeniality won people over to him. Engaging in manner and bright in conversation, Pfitzer was of a most cheerful disposition, seeming always to be enjoying what he was involved in, whether it be work or recreation.

Pfitzer's philosophical work on the morphology and classification of the Orchidaceae became well known and his system of arrangement of genera, in which he abandoned the importance given by Lindley to the character of the reproductive parts and took into account the vegetative development of the plants, was considered remarkable. He accepted the traditional division of the orchids into two subfamilies: the Diandrae (*Cypripedium* tribe) and the Monandrae (all others than *Cypripedium*), but opened up new vistas in his treatment of the latter. In disposing of the ophyridian genera by varying characteristics in the anthers and pollen masses, he recognized about twenty-eight additional groups of genera that depended almost entirely on vegetative structures. He further proposed and designated two dominant sections as sympodial and monopodial. In sympodial vegetative development, according to this system, each new growth matures fully in one growing season, continuous development being made by lateral buds that repeat the cycle of the original growth. The monopodials develop in such a way that the terminal growing point continues to extend indefinitely, the flower spikes emerging laterally.

Having laid the foundations of his system, in 1886 he undertook the preparation of a monograph of the paphiopedilums which was published in 1903. It was adopted in a more restricted sense than first proposed, however, because Pfitzer had also included the tropical American species, later agreeing to their separation.

In the summer of 1906 he was invited to speak at the International Conference on Hybridization and Cross-breeding, convened by the Royal Horticultural Society in London. In his talk, "Hybridisation as a Proof of Natural Affinity Among Orchids," he pointed out differences of classification based on both floral and vegetative characteristics, also the significance of recognizing genera that interhybridize. Though the natural arrangement of the Orchid Family remained yet unsettled, Pfitzer maintained that genera which could be hybridized together were certainly closely related. Several instances were cited, however, in which inexplicable results occurred. The possibility of parthogenesis was suggested in several such cases, but orchid hybridization was yet such a new practice that further experimentation was indicated.

While attending the conference he did some study and work at Kew; later he attended the Berlin Association meetings. By his increasing interest and masterly accomplishments, it was fully expected that a whole series of monographs might follow, but this was not to be, for he suddenly and unexpectedly died of heart failure on 3 December 1906, leaving a widow and daughter—and a whole scientific field—to mourn his loss.

References

Ames, Oakes. 1934. Ernst Hugo Heinrich Pfitzer—1846–1906. *Amer. Orch. Soc. Bull.* 2, no. 4.

Dillon, Gordon W. 1957. Development of a System of Orchid Classification. Understanding the Orchid Family—II. *Amer. Orch. Soc. Bull.* 26, no. 4.

Journal of Botany. 1907. Book-Notes, News, etc. Vol. 45, no. 529.

Kew Bulletin, 1907. Miscellaneous Notes—Ernest Pfitzer. No. 2.

Orchid Review, The. 1907. Obituary. Vol. 15, no. 169.

Orchid Review, The. 1956. Notes. Vol. 44, no. 758.

Frederick William Burbidge (1847–1905)

Borneo in the 1800s lay waiting for the intrepid collector, offering its vast assortment of botanical riches and beckoning enticingly. One of the pioneer orchid collectors who answered the siren call was Frederick W. Burbidge, gardener, writer, artist, and traveler.

Frederick William Burbidge was born at Wymeswold, Leicestershire, England, on 21 March 1847. His father was a farmer and fruit grower, and in childhood the son gained that love for horticulture that sustained him throughout a useful and active life. He was educated by home study and at the village schools and, after some experience in private gardens, he went to the Chiswick gardens of the Royal Horticultural Society. There, in 1868, he won numerous awards and certificates in his examinations. He also gained high honors in examinations at the Society of Arts in 1874, using his training there as background when he left Chiswick and went to the Royal Gardens at Kew. Here, among other duties, he gave considerable time to the art of botanical illustration. While at Kew he became increasingly involved in the plant studies then being conducted, and his thoughts and activities centered on the acquisition of horticultural and botanical learning.

From 1873 to 1877 Burbidge was a member of the staff of *The Garden* and became a frequent contributor to the gardening press. His book on *Cultivated Plants* (1877) was especially noted as one of the most useful horticultural texts of the period.

In 1877 Burbidge undertook a collecting expedition to Borneo in the employ of Messrs. James Veitch & Sons. The main purpose of the trip was to obtain and introduce new plants to horticulture, as well as birds, insects, and other objects of scientific interest. In particular, he was urged to search for certain nepenthes known to inhabit the island. These plants had previously been discovered by Sir Hugh Low in 1851, but his attempts to introduce specimens into European gardening had failed. Thomas Lobb searched for the plants in 1856, and though he actually reached the foot of the mountain upon which they grew, the hostility of the natives prevented him from collecting. Burbidge, however, was successful on both scores and was later able to introduce living plants and seeds. He also visited the three native courts of Jahore, Brunei, and Sulu, making extensive collections in the interior of the latter.

On his return from an extended trip through Australia and the Fiji Islands he met Peter C. M. Veitch, and together they formed the first expedition to Kina Balu, Borneo's Sugar Loaf Mountain. The journey was exhausting and endured with difficulty, for the entire route from Gaya Bay to the mountain and back to the coast through the villages of Kuong, Kalawat, and Bawang had to be covered entirely on foot. The expedition proved fruitful nevertheless, and on his return to England in 1879 Burbidge brought back many dried specimens and original drawings as well as numerous living plants. The following orchids were particularly well received and popularized in British glasshouses: *Paphiopedilum lawrenceanum* and *Paphiopedilum burbidgei*, *Dendrobium burbidgei* and *Dendrobium cerinum*, *Bulbophyllum leysianum* and *Bulbophyllum petreianum*, *Phalaenopsis mariae* and *Phalaenopsis grandiflora*, *Masdevallia burbidgei* and *Aerides burbidgei*. His account of the Bornean expedition was later recorded in his entertaining and enjoyable book, *The Gardens of the Sun*.

Upon his return home Burbidge was appointed curator of the Trinity College Botanic Gardens at Dublin, Ireland. His accomplishments in that capacity became known to all of horticulture and, in recognition of his work, in October 1897 the Victoria Medal in horticulture was conferred upon him. He was also highly pleased when the authorities at Trinity College conferred upon him the honor of master of arts *honoris causa*. Besides other degrees and awards, he was also a member of the Royal Irish Academy and a Veitch medalist.

For some time Burbidge had suffered from heart trouble, but it was with unexpected suddenness that a seizure killed him in his sleep on 24 December 1905, at his home in Dublin.

References

Gardeners' Chronicle. 1889. F. W. Burbidge, M.A. Vol. 6, no. 139.
Gardeners' Chronicle. 1905. Obituary. Vol. 38, no. 992.
Gardening World, The. 1906. Vol. 23.
Journal of Botany. 1906. Book-Notes, News, etc. Vol. 44, no. 518.
Orchid Review, The. 1906. Obituary. Vol. 14, no. 157.
van Steenis, C. G. G. J. 1950. Cyclopaedia of Collectors. *Flora Malesiana*. Vol. 1, ser. 1.
Veitch, James H. 1906. *Hortus Veitchii*. Chelsea, London: James Veitch & Sons Ltd.

Henry Frederick Conrad Sander (1847-1920)

IN HORTICULTURE, AND PARTICULARLY IN THE SPECIALIZED FIELD OF ORCHID growing, the name of Sander stands as a hallmark. The renown of that name is attributed largely to Henry F. C. Sander, of whom it is said that "no man contributed more to the forcefulness of high-class horticulture in Europe than he did."

Born in Hanover, Germany, in 1847, young Sander exhibited a love for plants that found fruitful expression throughout his life. At the age of twenty he entered the nurseries of James Carter and Company, seedsmen at Forest Hill. There it was that he met Benedict Roezl, the Bavarian explorer and plant collector with whom he decided to combine forces and interests. Roezl had been sending plants to England for years, but without a partner to receive and profitably dispose of the shipments, he had met with only small monetary success—just sufficient to enable him to continue his collecting and exploration.

Leaving Messrs. Carters, Sander commenced business as a seedsman in

George Street, St. Albans. Beginning modestly, the business soon took on great proportion, for Roezl's consignments of orchids and tropical plants became so extensive that a huge warehouse adjoining the seed shop was literally filled from floor to ceiling. Never before had orchids been received in England in such quantity, and Sander's systematic method of selling the plants was so profitable for both men that Roezl was able to retire comfortably in his native city, Prague.

Because of the number of plants hitherto received, Sander found it necessary to grow plants as well as import them. So, in 1873 he built his first greenhouse almost entirely with his own hands. This structure soon proved incapable of containing the growing collections and in 1881 a home and nursery covering four acres was built in the Camp district of St. Albans. The expanded facilities gave rise to Sander's business aptitude, and at one time as many as twenty-three paid collectors were searching the jungles and mountains of the earth for the firm of Sanders, St. Albans. The quantities of orchids received were enormous. Sixty greenhouses were stocked with thousands of plants and some of the finest species of orchids then known. Several of the houses were devoted to seed raising, and numerous hybrids were additionally tested and propagated.

For years orchid sales were held four days a week in London, with cattleyas selling in the greatest quantities. In February and March of 1886, 340 cases of this genus alone were received at the St. Albans nursery. With *Cattleya labiata, Dendrobium phalaenopsis, Cattleya schroderae,* and many other showy orchids, Sander did more to popularize orchids than nearly any other grower of the time, bringing them within financial reach of persons of modest means. Between one and two million plants were handled at the St. Albans establishment in the 1880s and 1890s, and some of the finest species changed hands for thousands of guineas. The firm became recognized as the showplace of horticulture in Europe, and kings and noblemen were frequent visitors.

As the orchid export business grew, it became obvious that far-reaching expansion would be necessary, so during the 1880s Sander established an orchid nursery at Summit, New Jersey, placing one of his collectors, Forsterman, in charge. As the nursery proved too distant from the home offices for convenient management, however, it was sold to John Lager and Henry Hurrell in 1896.

In 1894 Sander purchased a tract of land at St. André, just outside the city of Bruges, Belgium, where he established another orchid nursery. This establishment rapidly grew into an enormous firm with over 250 glasshouses devoted to orchids, azaleas, bay trees, palms, lilies, and begonias. The orchid section alone encompassed fifty houses, and great strides were made in growing and hybridizing odontoglossums. Meanwhile, Sander's collectors continued to penetrate all regions of the world.

When Sander decided on a thing, he was dauntless in his efforts to accomplish or obtain it. On one occasion he heard of a gigantic specimen of *Cattleya skinneri* and, determined to have it, he bargained with its native owner until it was finally acquired. The difficulties of packing and shipping were overcome, but on being unpacked the plant was found to be too large to pass through any of the doors of his greenhouses, and rather than divide or reduce it in any way, the doors and one end of a greenhouse were removed to facilitate entry. On another occasion the first consignment of *Dendrobium phalaenopsis* var. *schroderianum* collected by Micholitz was lost by the burning of the sampan carrying them. Upon notifying Mr. Sander of their sad fate, Micholitz at once received cabled instruction which stated simply, "Return, recollect."

Two plants he held in esteem above all others: *Sophronitis grandiflora* and the bay tree. The sophronitis color particularly appealed to him, and he often remarked that it was a shame to sell such plants for mere shillings, as their beauty entitled them to the guinea rank. At St. André he pointed with pride at the glossy-leaved bay trees, all personally selected and trimmed by his hand when he first built the nursery.

He enjoyed a wide circle of friends and was known for his pleasant manner in dealing with men. In business his reputation was built on adroitness and honesty. Tremendous energy was another outstanding characteristic. In building the St. André nursery he worked throughout the day, sleeping only while commuting by train or boat. Sander's reputation was further enhanced by his successes at the leading European and American horticultural exhibitions. The horticultural world never failed to look forward with the keenest interest to his exhibits of new plants at the Ghent Quinquennial exhibitions. Many Gold Medals and awards were won at the international exhibitions—at London, Edinburgh, Brussels, Antwerp, Paris, Petrograd, Moscow, Florence, Milan, New York, Chicago, and St. Louis. Besides the large numbers of hybrid orchids he exhibited, many new species were first shown by the House of Sander. *Vanda sanderiana, Aerides sanderiana, Cymbidium sanderi, Dendrobium sanderae, Paphiopedilum sanderiana, Anoectochilus sanderianus, Coelogyne sanderae, Macodes sanderiana, Maxillaria sanderiana, Odontoglossum sanderianum, Oncidium sanderae, Phalaenopsis sanderiana,* and *Sobralia sanderiana* were just a few of the admirable species that served to perpetuate the Sander name and fame.

Perhaps the greatest monument to Sander was the authoritative work, *Reichenbachia*, illustrated with life-sized colored paintings executed by the well-known painter, H. C. Moon, whom Sander hired for the work. Commenced in 1886, *Reichenbachia* became a treasured and valued series, and Sander personally supervised much of the work therein.

In recognition of his services to orchidology Sander gained numerous honors and distinctions. He was one of the original holders of the Royal Horticultural Society's Victoria Medal of Honour and held several foreign orders, including the Belgian Order of the Crown. As head of his firm, he was awarded the French President's Prix d'Honneur in Paris, the Veitchian Cup in 1906, the Coronation Challenge Cup in 1913, forty-one gold medals, twenty-four silver cups, and hundreds of trophies and diplomas. In addition, he was made a baron of the Russian Empire.

When World War I broke out in 1914 Sander and his family, as British subjects, fled to England from Bruges, retreating from the Germans at the last moment. The St. André nursery was held by the enemy, which caused the owner no end of concern and fear for both the firm and the employees. Compounded on his anxiety over the Belgian firm were other worries: the safety of his son and other members of the family in the British army, coal and labor shortages at St. Albans, and, above all, the grief caused by the impaired health of his wife. As a result, his own health suffered, bringing on the recurrence of an old illness.

He visited the Belgian nursery once after the war, in 1918, and went once again to that country for an operation advised by his physician. But a relapse occurred, and on 23 December 1920 he died at the age of seventy-four. His remains were interred at St. Albans.

A testimony by his dear friend, W. Watson, may perhaps give an idea of the esteem and admiration in which he was held:

. . . those who knew him intimately, as I did, will agree with me that he was indeed a noble fellow. Shrewd man of business as he was, he worked and schemed as few men are able to for success, which, when it comes, too often breeds ill will. In all his dealings Sander was an upright man. His generosity to Kew was quite exceptional. During his more prosperous times, say from 1880 to 1910, he freely gave plants of all kinds, many of them of considerable commercial value, to what he used to call "our great national garden." When he received a big importation of orchids or other plants from his collectors abroad, he would invite me to go to St. Albans and select a share for Kew. His knowledge of the habitats of plants was exceptional, and he was a skilled cultivator. As for enthusiasm, he was as full of it as a great schoolboy. I used to tell him he could turn a blacksmith into an orchid grower. The Bruges nurseries were his great pride. And how he did work there. He supervised the most trivial operations in the spirit of the Yorkshire farmer whose man said "The master's eyes do make the crops grow!" . . .

References

Garden, The. 1921. The Late Henry F. C. Sander, V.M.H. Vol. 85, no. 2564.
Gardeners' Chronicle. 1921. Obituary. Vol 69, no. 1775.
Orchid Review, The. 1921. Vol. 29, no. 338.
Orchid Review, The. 1962. Sander's Century of Orchid Growing. Vol. 70, no. 833.

Walter Davis (1847–1930)

FOR THOSE WHO REACH THE PEAK OF THEIR SKILLS AND ABILITIES JUST AS their era comes to an end, disappointment must be a bitter pill. Walter Davis, one of the last of the Veitchian collectors, was one of those to see the end of "that golden age of horticulture," the Victorian Era. The extent of his collections never had the time or opportunity to be extensive, but the excellence of the orchids he collected and introduced was undeniable, particularly those of the genus *Masdevallia*.

Walter Davis was born on 14 September 1847, at Amport, a small village in the County of Hampshire, Scotland. From his father he inherited a taste for natural history and outdoor pursuits, and at twelve years of age his interests turned to a love for gardening. Upon leaving school he entered the gardens of the marquis of Winchester. Thereafter he gained added experience in various other gardens until, in 1870, he entered the employ of Messrs. James Veitch at Chelsea, England. Serving under John Dominy in the New Plant Department, he eventually became foreman in charge of the nepenthes and fine foliage plants.

In 1873 an opportunity came to send a collector to South America. Davis was selected, his special object being to secure a quantity of *Masdevallia veitchiana*, which had already been introduced to English orchidists in 1867 but was still scarce. He sailed on 2 August 1873 and was successful not only in collecting *Masdevallia veitchiana* but several other species of the genus, including *Masdevallia ionocharis* and *Masdevallia davisii*, the latter named in his honor by H. G. Reichenbach. Twenty times he crossed the South American land mass, traveling like Gustave Wallis had done, by way of the Amazon Valley.

On his return to England Davis was selected to conduct the botanical analysis of herbage on the experimental plots at Rothamstead, and upon completion of the course he returned to the Chelsea nursery and continued under employment for the Veitches.

Plant propagation was one of his specialties, and, writing for the Exchange and Mart, he treated the subject for many years under the pseudonyms of Charles Benett (using his mother's maiden name) and Curiosus.

Upon dissolution of the Veitch firm Davis acted as temporary secretary to the Geological and Royal Geographical Societies, in that order. He also acted as secretary to a philanthropic society managed by American women in London.

Failing eyesight, caused by a paralytic stroke, forced Davis to spend the last ten years of his life in retirement, in the care of his eldest daughter, in Fulham. He died on 18 November 1930, and with his passing the world of orchidology bid farewell to one of the last reminders of an elegant and exciting period in orchid discovery and cultivation.

References

Irvin, R. 1960. The Early Orchid Collectors. *The Orch. Rev.* 68, no. 803.

Journal of Botany. 1931. Walter Davis. Vol. 69, no. 817.

Journal of the Royal Horticultural Society. 1948. Vol. 73, part 9.

Lemmon, Kenneth. 1962. *The Covered Garden.* London: Museum Press Ltd.

Orchid Review, The. 1931. Vol. 39, no. 451.

Veitch, James H. 1906. *Hortus Veitchii.* Chelsea, London: James Veitch & Sons Ltd.

Charles Curtis (1853-1928)

THE HOUSE OF VEITCH WAS PERHAPS THE MOST INFLUENTIAL IN THE IN-troduction of both species and hybrid orchids, and this no doubt was a result of the careful selection and training given to the gardeners and apprentices in their employ. It was not merely by chance that their collectors became famous, for by the acquired skill and intelligence of their training, they formed a highly capable retinue of plant experts. One of their most industrious collectors was Charles Curtis, who gathered plant material for them throughout the Malayan Archipelago.

Charles Curtis was a native of Devonshire, born in 1853 the youngest of four brothers who all began as garden boys at Bale's Nursery, North Devon, England. The paternal grandfather, a Norman by the name of Courtois, had settled at Barnstaple many years previously.

Equipped with a better education than his brothers, from Barnstaple young Curtis went to London, where he entered Messrs. James Veitch & Sons' nursery at Chelsea. For four years he worked in the New Plant Department, where he became acquainted with numerous travelers and studied hard to prepare himself for a post as plant collector. This opportunity came in 1878 when he was selected to undertake a mission to Mauritius and Madagascar to collect tropical plants for the firm. A great number of plants were gathered, among them the handsome *Angraecum sesquipedale* and *Nepenthes madagascariensis*. The trip lasted somewhat over a year. Unfortunately, the first consignment of plants collected was lost due to the treachery of a native servant who ran off with part of Curtis' supplies after cutting the rope which held the raft on which the plants were being floated downriver, so the work had to be repeated.

Curtis returned to England in 1879, and in 1880 he was sent to Borneo, Sumatra, Java, and the Moluccas, where he collected many interesting orchids, the collection consisting largely of *Paphiopedilum lowii*, *Paphiopedilum stonei*, and numerous vandas and rhododendrons. On the Bornean trip he was accompanied by David Burke, a young gardener who returned with the plants collected chiefly in Sarawak and who afterward became himself a plant collector.

After seeing Burke and the collection safely shipped at Singapore, Curtis proceeded to Dutch Borneo, his special object being to collect *Phalaenopsis violacea*, known in England but at that time still rare. Again he was successful, but once again he lost his first lot of plants, his clothes and instruments, and nearly his life as the result of another boating mishap. Once again he recouped, however. A few of the plants he discovered and by which he was commemorated were *Paphiopedilum curtisii*, *Nepenthes curtisii*, and *Rhododendron multicolor curtisii*.

Through his horticultural and botanical collections Curtis was brought into close contact with the authorities at Kew, by whom he obtained the appointment of superintendent of the Botanic Gardens at Penang in 1884. His skill in gardening was soon evidenced in the Botanic Gardens, for they became one of the most beautiful plantings in the East. On short leaves of absence he made collections of both living and herbarium specimens at Penang, Burma, the Lankawi Islands and neighboring coastal areas. On some of the trips he was accompanied by Mr. Henry N. Ridley. Both men were interested in the development of the rubber industry, and experiments they made in Penang proved exceedingly valuable to planters.

All the while Curtis continued to expand his herbarium, at the same time distributing duplicates to the Kew Herbarium and the British Museum. In further association with Ridley he published a catalog of the flowering plants and ferns of Penang, and a list of Malayan plant names. On his own he contributed many useful papers on the cultivation of bulbs, aroids, pot plants, ferns, roses, and orchids; instructions on drying plants; on the occurrence of gutta percha in Penang; and various other notes and papers published in the *Agricultural Bulletin of the Straits Settlements* from 1897 to 1902.

Owing to illness, in 1903 Curtis was compelled to give up his post at the gardens and retire, returning to his home at Barnstaple, England. His main herbarium was transferred to the Singapore Botanical Gardens. In Barnstaple he spent the rest of his life in horticultural enjoyment—tending his own collection of peach trees, carnations, orchids, sweet peas, streptocarpus, and neconopsis in a garden above the Great Western Station.

In the summer of 1928 a severe operation was necessary. For a while thereafter it appeared as though he might return to normal health, but five weeks after surgery, on 23 August, he died at his home at Barnstaple. To the end, his greatest regret was that, due to his poor health, he had never been able to visit again the scenes of his former labors.

References

Gardeners' Chronicle. 1928. Obituary. Vol. 84, no. 2174.
Irvin, R. 1960. The Early Orchid Collectors. *The Orch. Rev.* 68, no. 803.

Journal of Botany. 1928. Obituary—Charles Curtis (1853–1928). Vol. 66, no. 791.

Journal of the Royal Horticultural Society. 1948. Vol. 73, pt. 9.

Lemmon, Kenneth. 1962. *The Covered Garden*. London: Museum Press Ltd.

Orchid Review, The. 1928. Obituary. Vol. 36, No. 424.

Ridley, H. N. 1929. *Straits Settlement. The Gardens' Bulletin* 4, nos. 11, 12.

van Steenis, C. G. G. J. 1950. *Cyclopaedia of Collectors. Flora Malesiana*. Vol. 1, ser. 1.

Veitch, James H. 1906. *Hortus Veitchii*. Chelsea, London: James Veitch & Sons Ltd.

David Burke (1854–1897)

DAVID BURKE WAS ONE OF THE MOST WIDELY TRAVELED BOTANICAL COLLEC-
tors—and one of the last sent out by James Veitch & Sons to search for
orchids and rare tropical plants. Looked upon by many as an eccentric,
Burke was somewhat nonconformative, preferring the privations and
discomforts of living as a native over the civilized refinements of his
native England.

Born at Kent in 1854, he entered the Veitch firm at Chelsea as a young
gardener and, desiring to travel, was sent on a trial trip to Borneo with
Charles Curtis. His proclivity as a collector was thus proven, for he returned with a wonderful collection of orchids collected in Sarawak.

Burke's next mission was a solo trip to British Guiana in 1881, where
he rediscovered the curious insectivorous plant *Heliamphora nutans*,
which had not been seen since its discovery by the Schomburgk brothers on Mount Roraima in 1839. He also sent home the handsome *Ama-
sonia punicea* (*calycina*) and, among orchids, the rare *Zygopetalum
burkei*.

Subsequent journeys followed—two to the Philippines for phalaenopsis, two to New Guinea, and one to the newly annexed provinces of
upper Burma in 1891 in search of orchids. During 1894–1896 he made
three trips to Colombia for *Cattleya mendelii*, *Cattleya schroderae*, *Cattleya trianaei*, and *Odontoglossum crispum*.

Finally, having spent a short time in England, he left for the Moluccas
and Celebes Islands in 1896. Prior to departing for the tropics he seemed
to love so, he stated, "I'm off again, and if I make a good meal for someone I hope I shall give full satisfaction."

Burke was fully aware of the dangers involved in his expeditions, but
in spite of the differing mores and customs of the native peoples who
might at the slightest provocation rise against him, he had little love for
the refinements of society and gloried in the risks he was used to taking.
Yet, fate or the law of averages won out, for on 11 April 1897 David
Burke died at Amboina in a native hut far from any European settlement. Had it not been for information sent by a German traveler on that

part of the island at the time, history might never have known the fate of David Burke, one of orchidology's most adventurous plant collectors.

References

Curtis, Charles H. 1933. Men, Matters and Memories. *The Orch. Rev.* 41, no. 478.

Irvin, R. 1960. The Early Orchid Collectors. *The Orch. Rev.* 68, no. 803.

Journal of the Royal Horticultural Society. 1948. Vol. 73, pt. 9.

Lemmon, Kenneth. 1962. *The Covered Garden.* London: Museum Press Ltd.

van Steenis, C. G. G. J. 1950. Cyclopaedia of Collectors. *Flora Malesiana.* Vol. 1, ser. 1.

Veitch, James H. 1906. *Hortus Veitchii.* Chelsea, London: James Veitch & Sons Ltd.

Wilhelm Micholitz
(1854-1932)

COMPETITIVE SECRECY WAS ESSENTIAL FOR THE SUCCESS OF THE PROFES-
sional orchid collector. On the brink of discovering a long-sought prize,
particularly, he had to be extremely cautious with whom he conversed
lest the purpose of his presence in a vicinity be discovered. By the end of
the nineteenth century, desirable species could no longer be collected by
the thousands, and when a new area was found for collecting, it was of
utmost necessity that the location be kept secret. Competition had indeed
become keen, and on many occasions the collector found it necessary
even to remain hidden from the local populace of the town or village
used as his collecting headquarters. Among those bold and adventurous
plant seekers the name of Wilhelm Micholitz will long be chronicled
for his was a life of botanical intrigue and unceasing excitement.

A native of Germany by birth (born in Saxony in 1854), Micholitz
became a plant collector for Messrs. Sanders, St. Albans, England, at an
early age. Though only of medium size, he was strongly built yet of a
calm disposition and a clear mind. Micholitz understood people well,
particularly the Polynesian races among whom he often traveled. In
short, he possessed all the qualities that Messrs. Sanders desired in a
collector.

His travels were varied and too numerous to list here completely. A
sampling would include the Philippines (1884–1885), Aru Islands (1890),
Moluccas (1891), New Guinea and Sumatra (1891–1892), Ambon and
Natuna Islands (1892–1898), Burma and South America (1900). As
might be expected through such an itinerary of travel, Micholitz's plant
discoveries and introductions were numerous, and the many orchid species which bear his name testify to his immense energy and geographical
wanderings.

"Fearnley," reading through correspondence from Micholitz to his
employer, H. F. C. Sander, wrote in 1939:

Micholitz had to wait months in unsavory surroundings in the hope that one
of Colombia's many internal strifes would come to an end. On this occasion,
however, he waited in vain and no doubt he was happier when on the Aru

Isles in 1890 whence he wrote that money was unknown to the natives, and that a stock of handkerchiefs must be obtained for barter, "the people being rather savage."

Secretive! An Orchid hunter had to be so. Competition was then as great as ever it has been since. Micholitz cabled his employer from Singapore, immediately prior to his first search for *Vanda Sanderiana*—the King of Orchids: "E. not here, R. here. A. arriving next ship." Perhaps this extended his credit from the firm in England, for E., R. and A. were all on the same trail!

Phalaenopsis micholitzii

Competition! At Bhamo in the North West corner of Burma some two hundred miles from Mandalay, Micholitz wrote an amusing letter: "L.'s man has three men watching the approaches of the town. There are only a few plants (*Dendrobium nobile*) coming in and competition is very keen." Imagine his consternation! But he actually won through on that occasion as on most, and his firm landed many thousand "noble" Dendrobiums.

Micholitz's travels mainly involved the East—from Burma to the Philippines and the Eastern Archipelagos. His one trip to South America was the exception, one which was seemingly wrought with difficulty. On one occasion he had collected a large number of plants and had readied them for removal to the coast, when a revolution occurred. In recounting Micholitz's reactions, "Fearnley" (Fearnley Sander) continued:

... his boat was commandeered by first one party and then the other, until his plants had suffered considerably and, when speaking of the trip, Micholitz gave me a very definite opinion in English of revolutionaries and some Governments, and finished it in German—a lapse?—possibly much more expressive, but I did not ask for a translation.

One note by Micholitz to Sander, written on a hotel bill in Bogotá, Colombia, quite succinctly summarized his feelings about staying there:

I do not know what I would not give to be back in the well-ordered British or Dutch Colonies in the East, to be able to do work in peace and comparative comfort.

Also listed on the hotel bill was a charge for fifty-six glasses of beer. Might we speculate that Micholitz was attempting to drown his sorrows?

Micholitz made entomological as well as botanical collections, but his orchid finds are the real credit to his memory. One of his most famous discoveries was *Dendrobium phalaenopsis* var. *schroderianum*. Even in this find, however, he seemed plagued by misfortune, for the sampan on which the consignment was being transported caught fire and all the plants perished. On cabling the news to St. Albans, his return instructions were simply "Return, recollect." And so he did, and through his repeated labors, that beautiful species was finally introduced into the greenhouses of England.

Micholitz's name is perpetuated in many further of his finds—*Aerides micholitzii, Phalaenopsis micholitzii, Spathoglottis plicata* var. *micholitzii*, and *Coelogyne micholitzii*. His cymbidium introductions—the result of a journey to Annam—revolutionized the genus, with *Cymbidium insigne* (then called *Cymbidium Sanderi*), *Cymbidium erythrostylum, Cymbidium parishii* var. *sanderae, Cymbidium schroederianum*, and *Cymbidium cooperi* becoming popular cultivated members of the genus. Other large consignments included *Den-*

drobium atroviolaceum, Dendrobium dearei, Dendrobium johnsoniae, Dendrobium spectabilis, Dendrobium schutzei, Dendrobium speciosissimum, Anoectochilus sanderianus, Anoectochilus leopoldii II, Anoectochilus bohnhoffianum, and *Arachnanthe annamensis,* to mention merely a few.

After many years of service Micholitz retired to his native Saxony, comfortable with a well-earned retirement. Unfortunately, all his savings were lost as a result of monetary deflation in Germany following World War I, and from then until his death in December 1932, at seventy-eight years of age, he was forced to live in near poverty.

References

Fearnley. 1939. Orchid Hunters of the Past Century. *The Orch. Rev.* Vol. 47, no. 550.

Gardeners' Chronicle. 1932. Obituary. Vol. 92, no. 2401.

Sander, F. K. 1933. Obituary—Wilhelm Micholitz. *The Orch. Rev.* Vol. 41, no. 476.

van Steenis, C. G. G. J. 1950. Cyclopaedia of Collectors. *Flora Malesiana.* Vol. 1, ser. 1.

Robert Allen Rolfe
(1855-1921)

"HE WAS ESSENTIALLY A SELF-MADE AND SELF-TAUGHT MAN. HE ROSE from the ranks. His luck took him to Kew. He climbed into a position of scientific standing by sheer industry and perseverance." This quote by Otto Stapf simplifies yet essentially characterizes the orchidologist-journalist who for many years signed his herbarium notes with the initials R.A.R.

Forty years of service to Kew—the greater part of his professional career—typify the steady performance of Robert Allen Rolfe. His remarkable knowledge of orchids was gained through a keen eye and a good memory. He held his own against the formidable and jealous Reichenbach, stepping into the position of world master of orchidology when that renowned Hamburgian died. Recognizing the importance of garden hybrids, which the earliest botanists were inclined to ignore, he spared no effort to always keep in touch with all kinds of orchids in the horticultural field. His wonderful devotion to that particular family of plants undoubtedly led to the founding of *The Orchid Review*, a "general repertorium of orchid lore," as he loved to call it.

Robert Allen Rolfe was born on 12 May 1855 at Ruddington, a village near Nottingham, England. In 1879, after spending some time in the duke of Portland's famous gardens at Welbeck Abbey, Nottinghamshire, Rolfe entered Kew as an apprentice gardener. Though taken on as a horticulturist, his interest in botany and allied sciences led to his nomination as a candidate for a vacancy in the herbarium. Passing his competitive examinations at the head of the list, he commenced his career as government botanist in July 1880. Not long thereafter Sir Joseph Hooker, then director of the Royal Botanic Gardens, advised Rolfe to make orchids his specialty.

The Kew herbarium and library were an inexhaustible mine for young Rolfe and from it his academic knowledge grew, while the accumulation of plants in the gardens kept him in constant contact with the living material. Thus his authority as an expert developed gradually on a twofold basis.

During Rolfe's long term of service at Kew practically all orchid material passed through his hands. In his first few years he collaborated with Señor Don Sebastián Vidal in determining the large collections made by Hugh Cuming and Vidal himself in the Philippines. Rolfe later spent a great deal of time on the material which arrived in great profusion from these islands as well as on F. C. Lehmann's collection from Colombia and Ecuador. He founded the genera *Eulophiella* and *Neomoorea*, besides naming hundreds of species and reclassifying others. His first contribution to the literature of orchids was *A Revision of the Genus Phalaenopsis*, published in the *Gardeners' Chronicle* in 1886.

Before Rolfe's time the orchid specimens received at Kew were, for the most part, sent to Germany for determination by H. G. Reichenbach, because after John Lindley's death there remained no English authority on the Orchidaceae. Reichenbach resented Rolfe's "intrusion" into a field he felt was his private domain, but Rolfe had convictions of his own and generally stood by them. Thus, whatever enmity existed between the two masters sprang from their self-willed determination. Rolfe was known as "a hard nut to crack." Some even called him pigheaded. When he felt he was right about something, that was the end of it as far as he was concerned. When Reichenbach died in 1889, stipulating in his will that his herbarium be sealed for twenty-five years, it was a severe blow to Rolfe. Whether or not the action was directly intentional toward Rolfe, he felt badly about it, for in any case it deprived the orchid world of much valuable information for too long a time.

Rolfe's greatest interest was in keeping himself informed of everything possible that concerned orchids. He thought nothing of going on an extended journey by bicycle or train, in his own time and at his own expense, to see interesting collections or even a single specimen reported to be in flower. He regularly attended the meetings of the Royal Horticultural Society and was often wont to spend considerable time making notes on all the uncommon orchids exhibited. He became closely associated with the orchidists of England, lending his assistance to assure accurate naming of plants and, by his voluminous writing, setting forth the history of rare and desirable horticultural species. His great love for these flowers led him in 1893 to found *The Orchid Review*, a monthly journal which became the repository of a mass of information and critical notes from his pen. This periodical was almost the personification of its creator; for twenty-eight years it lived a remarkably regular, sober, and useful life. When Rolfe was forced by illness to give up his editorship, he did so unwillingly despite the hard work and personal financial loss incurred in its publication.

Though Rolfe was known chiefly for his work in connection with orchids, he also devoted considerable time to other plant groups, notably *Myoporineae, Selagineae*, and *Rosaceae*. His publications span forty years, beginning with a paper on oak galls in the *Entomologist* of 1881. Among his early important works was one in which he was engaged in dealing with the large collections of Señor Vidal in the production of *Phanerogamae Cumingianae Philippinarum* in 1885.

Many of the plants in the *Botanical Magazine* from 1905 to 1921 were described by Rolfe, especially orchids, and he also contributed to Hooker's *Icones Plantarum*. He monographed the Orchidaceae in the *Flora of Tropical Africa* and the *Flora Capensis*, excepting the genera *Brownleea* and *Disa*. Meanwhile, he contributed both popular and scientific articles to the *Kew Bulletin*, the *Gardeners' Chronicle*, the *Journal of the Linnean Society*, *Reichenbachia*, *Lindenia* and other journals. He was much interested in orchid hybridization and, with Charles C. Hurst in 1909, published *The Orchid Stud Book*, an enumeration of hybrid orchids of artificial origin.

Rolfe was of a shy, retiring nature, and this was deemed the result of an unfortunate deafness, a serious handicap to him. This defect, coupled with a natural modesty, kept him out of the limelight that makes for popularity. To some extent, however, he possibly profited from this disability, for he seemed able to proceed undisturbed with his work in circumstances that would have caused serious interruption to others. He was content the way he was, but occasionally sighed for more elbow room. All the same, he was a man of action, and, among the many eminent scientists developed at Kew, his work was worthy of high esteem.

Outward recognition of his accomplishments came through his election as an associate of the Linnean Society in 1885 and as an honorary fellow and member of the Scientific Committee of the Royal Horticultural Society in 1906. He was also a member of the latter society's Orchid Committee. He was awarded the Gold Medal of L'Academie

Internationale de Geographie Botanique a la Science in 1917, and shortly before his death he was honored with the Gold Medal of the Veitch Memorial Trust Fund and the Victoria Medal of Honour in Horticulture. Several species of orchids and other plants were named in his honor, as well as the natural orchid genus *Rolfea* and the hybrid orchid genus *Rolfeara.*

Rolfe had never traveled, and it was with keen anticipation, at the age of sixty-five, that he planned a trip to Central and South America to make up for the gap in his education as a botanist. But just when he was about to set out on his first tropical venture he was halted by the sudden occurrence of a brain tumor. His illness persisted, and on 13 April 1921, he died at his home at Kew.

References

Ames, Oakes. 1933. Robert Allen Rolfe–1855–1921. *Amer. Orch. Soc. Bull.* 2, no. 3.

Garden, The. 1921. Obituary. Vol. 85, no. 2579.

Gardeners' Chronicle. 1921. Mr. R. A Rolfe. Vol. 69, no. 1781.

Gardeners' Chronicle. 1921. Obituary. Vol. 69, no. 1791.

Kew Bulletin. 1921. Miscellaneous Notes. No. 3.

Orchid Review, The. 1933. Robert Allen Rolfe. Vol. 41, no. 475.

Stapf, O. 1921. The Late Robert Allen Rolfe. *The Orch. Rev.* 29, no. 337.

Henry Nicholas Ridley
(1855–1956)

BORNEO AND THE MALAY PENINSULA HAD ALREADY GIVEN UP AN ENORMOUS treasury of new and worthwhile plant materials by the latter part of the century, orchids being prominent among them. Through the efforts and introductions of plant collectors such as Sir Hugh Low, Charles Curtis, and David Burke, the botanic gardens and herbaria of Europe had been greatly enriched, but the end result—a complete flora of the area—remained to be done. This was accomplished by Henry Nicholas Ridley, a British botanist of exceptional capability. His orchid introductions, over 200 new species, seem almost incidental to his many other accomplishments in agriculture, zoology, horticulture, and other fields; a man of great versatility and seemingly unlimited energy, he became well known in all his fields of endeavor.

Son of the Rev. Oliver Matthew Ridley, he was born on 10 December 1855, at West Harling, Norfolk, England. An intense interest in nature, especially birds and insects, was evident even in his boyhood, and while still at school he wrote his first published paper on those subjects. At Exeter College, Oxford, he gained second-class honors in natural science in 1877, thereby obtaining a geological scholarship.

He received his M.A. from Oxford in 1882, meanwhile serving as assistant in the Botanical Department of the British Museum from 1880 to 1887, where he had charge of the Monocotyledons. Until that time he had viewed the field of botany with little interest, but in his new position he energetically threw himself into the work. In his leisure hours he studied the British flora and on holidays collected in southern Ireland, Norway, and Switzerland. During the years at the British Museum, he published a prodigious number of papers on the Monocotyledons and various notes on British plants and insects. His orchid works during that time included:

The Orchids of Madagascar (*Journ. Linn. Soc.*, Bot. 21, 1885).
A Monograph of the Genus Liparis (*Journ. Linn. Soc.*, Bot. 22, 1886).
Orchidaceae, Scitamineae et Cyperaceae Africanae (*Bot. da. So.*, Bot. Coimbra, 5, 1887).
Botany of the Roraima Expedition, Orchidaceae and Cyperaceae (*Trans. Linn. Soc.*, London, Bot. 2, 1887).
Notes on self fertilization and cleistogamy in Orchids (*Journ. Linn. Soc.* London, Bot. 24, 1888).
A Revision of the Genus Microstylis and Malaxis (*Journ. Linn. Soc.* London, Bot. 24, 1888).

With the Rev. T. S. Lea and Mr. G. Ramage, in 1887 he undertook an expedition to Fernando de Noronha, Brazil, collecting the flora, fauna, and minerals of that island and the flora of Pernambuco. These collections were deposited in the British Museum, and an account of them later appeared in the *Journal of the Linnean Society* in 1890.

He was well qualified by 1888, when he was appointed as first director of Gardens and Forests in the Straits Settlements, with headquarters in Singapore. The Singapore Botanic Gardens, founded in 1859, were 200 acres in extent, partly horticultural and partly used for raising economic crops. In addition, Ridley had under his control the Government House grounds and the Malacca and Penang Botanic Gardens.

Little was known of the Malayan flora at that time, so Ridley studied it intensively, exploring all parts of the peninsula as well as visiting Java, Sumatra, Borneo, and the Cocos and Christmas Islands, collecting large amounts of living and dried plants. Besides forming a good herbarium at Singapore, he distributed 2000 herbarium specimens a year to Kew, the British Museum, the Royal Botanic Garden at Calcutta, and else- ·

where. Living plants were cultivated at the Singapore Gardens, though many were also dispatched to Kew.

Ridley was kept hard at work; a great share of his time was taken by his labors with economic plants, herbarium work, publication of an agricultural bulletin, and writing articles on botany and general natural history for various publications (including the *Journal of the Straits Branch of the Royal Asiatic Society*, of which he was editor and Secretary for the Society). Nevertheless, he still managed to transform the gardens into one of the most picturesque and luxurious plantings of their kind in the world. Of the orchids collected by him and figured in the *Botanical Magazine*, the following were prominent: *Microstylis scottii, Paphiopedilum exul, Sarcochilus lilacinus,* and *Bulbophyllum galbinum.* Other of his orchid works included his "Orchidaceae of the Flora of Mt. Kinabalu" (*Trans. Linn. Soc.*, London, Bot. 4, 1894) and "The Orchideae and Apostasiaceae of the Malay Peninsula" (*Journ. Linn. Soc.*, Bot. 32, 1896).

One of the most significant and valuable accomplishments of Ridley's career was the development of a method of tapping Para rubber trees. This and his persistence in persuading the skeptical planters that they could profit by "growing" rubber, led to the gigantic development of the plantation rubber industry throughout the eastern tropics and the successful foundation of the industry.

After his retirement in 1912 Ridley devoted himself to writing and making further botanical expeditions. He had previously added to his travel experience by visits to Annam, Cambodia, Burma, Siam, Ceylon, Jamaica, and, in 1912, India. His botanical collections amounted to about 50,000 specimens, with some 3000 of them new to science.

His years of experience in the plant sciences gave him valuable preparation for the many outstanding works he subsequently produced. His *Flora of the Malay Peninsula*, which appeared in five volumes during the years 1922–1925, stands itself as a monument to the author. During much of the time in which it was written Ridley was seriously ill, even fearing that he would not live to complete it. After its completion, and his following work on plant dispersal, his health recovered, however. In addition to his *Dispersal of Plants throughout the World*, a work of 744 pages (1930), he contributed many papers on botany and other subjects to various scientific journals.*

He attended meetings of the Linnean Society with regularity, his erudition brilliantly showing despite his advanced age. In addition, he served as member of the council and as vice-president. In 1950, at the age of ninety-five, he was awarded the society's highest honor, the Linnean Medal.

* A full list of his publications is given in the *Gardens' Bulletin—Straits Settlements* 4, nos. 4, 5, 1935.

Ridley suffered a severe illness in 1953 which caused his eyesight to fail, but once again he recovered and greatly enjoyed celebrating his centenary on 10 December 1955. He died in his 101st year at his home at Kew, on 24 October 1956, remaining alert almost to the last.

Numerous plants and animals were named in his honor. Among the orchids, Schlechter named a genus of New Guinea orchid *Ridleyella*, and his name is further commemorated in *Acriopsis ridleyi, Eria ridleyi, Lecanorchis ridleyana, Coelogyne ridleyana, Dendrobium ridleyi, Sarcanthus ridleyi*, and *Dendrobium ridleyanum*.

References

Curtis' Botanical Magazine. 1931. *Dedications and Portraits 1827–1927.* Nelmes, Ernest, and Cuthbertson, Wm., comps. London: Bernard Quaritch Ltd.

Eaton, B. J. 1935. Mr. Ridley and Rubber in Malaya. *Gardens' Bulletin—Straits Settlements* 9, pt. 1.

Gardeners' Chronicle. 1928. Mr. H. N. Ridley, C.M.G., F.R.S. Vol. 83, no. 2159.

Holttum, R. E. 1957. Henry Nicholas Ridley, C.M.G., F.R.S.–1855–1956. *Taxon.* 6, no. 1.

Purseglove, J. W. 1955. Mr. H. N. Ridley's Hundredth Birthday. *Nature* 176.

South, F. W. 1935. Mr. Ridley's Work for Tropical Agriculture. *Gardens' Bulletin—Straits Settlements.* Vol. 9, nos. 4, 5.

van Slooten, D. F. 1935. Mr. H. N. Ridley and the Flora of the Netherlands Indies. *Gardens' Bulletin—Straits Settlements.* Vol. 9, nos. 4, 5.

Henry George Moon
(1857–1905)

EXCEPT FOR THEIR DRIED SPECIMENS AND PUBLISHED WORKS, FEW OF THE botanists, naturalists, and collectors connected with the history of orchids left behind tangible beauty or aesthetic evidence of their work. It seems ironic, therefore, that many of the finest and most beautiful paintings of orchids were executed by a man who had marital ties to the Sander family of St. Albans, England, but who was not really an orchidist himself. The outstanding set of orchid portraits in the famed *Reichenbachia* speaks eloquently for the orchidological contributions of Henry George Moon.

He was born on 18 February 1857, at Barnet, England. He was the eldest son of Henry Moon, a parliamentary agent of Westminster. Until the death of the father in 1866, the son's school days were spent at Dr. Bell's, at Barnet. Even as a young lad he revealed a love of art. After his Barnet schooling he was for some years a student at the Birkbeck and St. Martin's schools of art, where his talent and skill won him numerous prizes.

In 1878 Moon went to the law offices of Messrs. Cole and Jackson, solicitors of Exeter Street, where he worked as a clerk with a view to the profession of barrister. Law, however, could not hold his interest over art, and in 1880 he joined the art department of *The Garden*, a popular horticultural publication. From that time on most of the colored plates illustrated in the magazine, including many orchids, were painted by him, and in later years he performed similar services for *The English Flower Garden*, *Wild Garden*, and *Flora and Sylva*. Through the encouragement of Mr. William Robinson, who had been influential in obtaining for Moon the position on the staff of *The Garden*, he went to his friend's beautiful garden and woods at Gravetye Manor where he developed an intense love for the English landscape and conveyed his impressions to canvas. Much of his spare time was spent in the further study of landscape painting, often in the company of Mr. W. E. Norton, an American painter to whom Moon attributed much of his own success in art.

Moon first visited St. Albans in 1884, going to H. F. C. Sander's orchid nurseries to make drawings for Mr. Robinson, then publisher of *The English Flower Garden*. In 1885 Mr. Sander asked him to illustrate the *Reichenbachia*, a magnificent work on orchids that came out in 1886 and continued until 1890. Concerning the artist and his work, Sander's grandson David stated years later:

In the studio at St. Albans, . . . there would stand painting many days in the year a man, Harry Moon, who had, as with most artists, great individuality. He would be given some subject, usually a newly imported species flowering for the first time, and asked to paint it. One can readily imagine the resulting painting which would, whether good or bad, represent the plant *as seen by the artist*. What is much more interesting, however, is the thought that the man who paid for the painting would criticise it and demand that it reproduce a plant grown to perfection. This Harry Moon was rarely willing to do.

Harry Moon spent four years painting these glorious pictures for the *Reichenbachia* and supervised the printing of this magnificent work. The printing was all done by hand in our own printing shops in the Camp Road, St. Albans. Mr. Moon made the woodcut etchings and our expert printer and engraver Mr. Moffat, with the help of one or two boys, effected the printing.

In the fall of 1892 Moon decided to settle permanently at St. Albans with his mother and sister, making frequent excursions to the Hertfordshire lanes and woods, painting direct from nature, and discovering fresh beauty in sky, leaf, and glen as the knowledge of his art developed. Commentaries years later attest to his skill. From Mr. R. E. Arnold:

H. G. Moon was very close to nature, and primarily, for this reason he stands out as, perhaps, the greatest of all British flower painters. . . . His plants live, there is an atmosphere of reality about them, and instantly, when viewing one of his pictures, is the plant's natural surroundings, its natural environment, cast vividly upon one's mind. . . . Moon, from his studies, envisualised his plants in their natural surroundings, and he put his mind, his very soul, to the task of producing a living thing; his imagination was of the keenest and, moreover, was a specialized gift. He was always striving to produce something essentially natural, he was rarely guilty of overcolouring, he bestowed equal care upon the minutiae and the salient characters. His backgrounds lent not a little to the beauty of his pictures; his perfect relationship of background to subject is little short of marvellous; and from this, perhaps instructive gift, his pictures gain immeasurably . . .

William Robinson, of course, had been interested in Moon's work from the beginning—particularly the landscapes. "I often thought," he mused, "that if less of his work had been given to plant drawing, how much better it would have been for landscape art." Orchidists would probably disagree, however, because the outstanding *Reichenbachia* remains itself as a monument to the artist. Moon actually did paint delightful Turner-like landscapes, and though he never had the time to be prolific in that vein, the Sander family knew of some twenty or thirty completed paintings.

Other interesting facets of Moon's work on the *Reichenbachia* were given by David Sander.

. . . He married Mr. (Frederick) Sander's only daughter (in January, 1894) and spent twenty years of his life painting orchids. How he found time to illustrate "The Garden," "The Orchid World" and several other current periodicals is not told, and yet, like all artists, he was frightfully independent. . . . George Moon painted what he saw. This—need I stress it?—conflicted considerably, and I should imagine consistently, with my grandfather's idea of business! . . . Take— just to mention a few of these lovely plates—the first one of all, that of *Odontoglossum crispum* var. *alexandrae*. Surely an absolutely perfect picture of an orchid! Or the delightful soft pink spray of *Odontoglossum rossii* var. *majus*, in Plate 4, proceeding from the relatively small imported "piece" of a plant. Look at the *Dendrobium wardianum* in Plate 9. I was able to take this plate . . . and place it on an easel in an art gallery in London. Adjacent to it I staged a single specimen of the love flowering plant itself. The truthfulness of the picture was truly remarkable, every detail being correct.

And the next plate, of *Cattleya dowiana*, which even shows the typical yellowing of the leaves and sheath and mosaicing of the backbulbs, which so often precedes collapse of a plant and perhaps accounts for its contemporary rarity in cultivation. I can imagine the argument George Moon had with his then employer Mr. Sander! How provoked to anger by Sander's insistence on a bigger pseudobulb and better portrayal of the "size to which it can be grown," and the artist's probable refusal to go on with the picture, except as he saw it. Equally strongminded, he held the card which proved throughout the work to have been a trump!

As an art judge and critic, Moon's opinions were always valued, and he was frequently called upon to criticize at the London sketching clubs—the Langholm, the Gilbert Garrett, Polytechnic, Birkbeck, etc. He helped many young artists through their difficulties, and those with whom he was acquainted treasured his friendship.

For some years he had been in frail health, and his death at forty-eight years of age, on 6 October 1905, was accompanied by profound regret and grief in the world of both art and horticulture. He left a widow and two small sons.

References

Ames, Oakes. 1941. Reichenbachia. *Amer. Orch. Soc. Bull.* 10, no. 5.
Flora and Silva 3:341.

Garden, The. 1905. Death of H. G. Moon. Vol. 68, no. 1769.

Garden, The. 1905. The Late H. G. Moon. Vol. 68, no. 1771.

Gardeners' Chronicle. 1905. Obituary. Vol. 38, no. 981.

Journal of Botany. 1906. Book-Notes, News, etc. Vol. 44, no. 521.

Orchid Review, The. 1894. Notes. Vol. 2, no. 14.

Orchid Review, The. 1905. Obituary. Vol. 13, no. 156.

Sander, David. 1966. A Christmas Present for the Orchid Grower. *The Orch. Rev.* 74, no. 881.

Albert Cameron Burrage
(1859-1931)

THE POPULARIZATION OF ORCHIDS IN THE UNITED STATES CAME RELATIVELY later than in Europe, though a few individuals on the Atlantic Coast were growing them by the middle 1800s. By his enthusiasm and energy, Albert C. Burrage was one of those most influential in promulgating the rise of orchid cultivation in American horticulture. Few others have done more to encourage the study and cultivation of these plants.

Albert Cameron Burrage was born in Ashburnham, Massachusetts, on 21 November 1859, moving to California with his parents while still a child. When he was eighteen years old, after some months of study in Europe he returned to Massachusetts and entered Harvard College in 1879, from which he graduated *summa cum laude* in 1883. He next entered the Harvard Law School, graduating in 1884. Immediately thereafter he was admitted to the bar and began to practice law in Boston.

Considerable wealth and remarkable vigor contributed to Burrage's interests, and horticulture was one of the foremost. As a horticulturist he was internationally known, especially for his cultivation of orchids. His exhibits were always unusually beautiful, attracting great numbers of flower and garden lovers. Specific accomplishments that won him great distinctions included an exhibit of tropical orchids in 1920, a display of orchids every month during 1921, and an exhibit of native American orchids in the spring of 1921 which was viewed by 75,000 people.

Burrage went to extraordinary pains in exhibiting orchids in naturalistic settings. For a 1924 exhibit in Boston he brought in 100 tons of rockwork which were used in the construction of a cliff forty feet high, from the top of which water spilled over at the rate of 180 gallons per minute. Also included were forty-foot coconut palms weighing five tons each, shipped from a distance of 2000 miles. For further staging of some epiphytic orchids, he utilized a tree weighing four tons. In 1925 he won the Lindley Medal for his educational display of native North American cypripediums, exhibited at the Chelsea Show at London. Native soil was shipped with the plants—a full two tons of American loam—while pine and hemlock trees were additionally included to provide a realistic setting.

By 1922 he had assembled at his home in Beverly, Massachusetts, the greatest collection of tropical orchids the New World had yet seen, for which he was awarded America's highest horticultural award, the George R. White Medal of Honor.

In his interests as a horticulturist Burrage assembled a very large and complete library of botanical and horticultural literature. The section given to orchid publications was unusually comprehensive, for he rarely missed the opportunity of acquiring books and records of orchids and their culture. In addition to his experiments with the cultivation of orchids under electric light and various types of glass, he also invented a rotating greenhouse that could be made to face the sun at any hour of the day.

In 1921 Burrage was elected president of the Massachusetts Horticultural Society, and in the same year he was elected to the same office in the newly organized American Orchid Society, in which capacity he served until 1929, when he resigned because of ill health. In that year he gave the Massachusetts Horticultural Society $20,000, the interest from which was used in making the Albert C. Burrage Gold Vase, awarded at the end of each year for the most outstanding exhibit at any of the society's shows held during the year. In 1930 he donated another $50,000 to the society, the interest to be used for prizes and additions to the society's library.

He died on 28 June 1931 at his seaside home in Beverly. He was survived by his wife, two sons, and a daughter. At the time of his death he was a trustee of the American Orchid Society, an honorary fellow of the Royal Horticultural Society, a member of the Pennsylvania Horticultural Society, the New York Horticultural Society, and the Garden Club of America.

Albert Cameron Burrage was not only a horticulturist. He was always active in politics, and through his careful study of municipal affairs was recognized by his appointment by the governor in 1894 to the Boston Transit Commission, which built the Boston subway, one of the largest, most difficult, and most successful works undertaken in an American city. In 1896 he became president of the Allied Gas Companies of Boston. He was also greatly interested in minerals, and his private collection was known as one of the finest of its kind in the world. Copper mining subsequently attracted his attention, and in 1898 he organized the Amalgamated Copper Company and, later, the Chile Copper Company. He had keen ideas on the development of new processes for the treatment of low-grade copper ores and for many years devoted his time in that effort.

His name is commemorated in the hybrid orchid genus *Burrageara*, established by Black & Flory in 1927.

References

American Orchid Society Bulletin. 1932. In Memoriam. Vol. 1, no. 1.
American Orchid Society Bulletin. 1944. The Albert C. Burrage Gold Vase. Vol. 12, no. 8.
Orchid Review, The. 1924. Mr. Albert C. Burrage. Vol. 32, no. 373.
Orchid Review, The. 1931. Obituary: Albert C. Burrage. Vol. 39, no. 458.

Johann Jacob Smith (1867–1947)

HORTICULTURIST-TURNED-BOTANIST IS THE TITLE WE MIGHT APPLY TO Johann Jacob Smith, because a life-long interest in orchids led him to a serious taxonomic study of that plant family. His introductions and descriptions of Eastern orchids, plus his contributions to orchid literature, are surely justification for his being given a place of honor in the cultural history of orchids.

Born at Antwerp, Belgium, on 29 July 1867, Smith showed an early inclination toward natural history, which was encouraged by his aunt. His leisure time included activities of this sort—growing and sketching plants, tending animals (particularly mice), and making an aquarium and terrarium. At ten years of age he had already begun the formation of a private herbarium. His secondary education was obtained at the Higher Burger School in Amsterdam, where his talents were recognized by his teacher, Dr. J. C. Costerus, who advised him to take up the study of horticulture. There was no horticultural college at that time, so Smith entered the nurseries of Messrs. Groenewegen & Co. of Amsterdam. While working there he became interested in abnormal plant forms. For his own amusement he busied himself with sketching the species that came into bloom at the establishment.

Next came a year of service at Kew and two years at Brussels, first at the Linden orchid nursery and later at the Botanic Garden. Meanwhile, as his interest in plants grew, the commercial aspects of horticulture became less to his preference. At this time Dr. Costerus influenced Smith into going to the Dutch East Indies where, in 1891, he became an inspector on a coffee plantation. The lure of the virgin jungle adjacent to the plantation interested him more than coffee growing, and at the first opportunity he vacated his position. This opportunity was in the form of an invitation from Professor Treub, director of the Buitenzorg Botanic Gardens, to go there and serve as a temporary horticulturist while the curator was on a leave of absence in Holland. Upon the return of the curator, the position of chief gardener of the mountain gardens at Tjibodas was offered to Smith. Fate decreed otherwise, however, for the assistant curator became ill and died on the return trip to Holland; Smith became his successor. For nearly thirty-three years thereafter he was associated in various capacities with that institution.

All the while he became further absorbed with the Orchid Family and scientific questions attracted him more and more. At that time there was no one sufficiently knowledgeable to be of assistance; consequently, he described and illustrated many species himself. His field experience was broadened by a trip to the Moluccas in 1900; this aided in the groundwork of some of his later work.

In 1902 Smith went to Europe on a leave of absence, during which time he assembled the data for an orchid flora of Java for Dr. Treub, to be published in 1905. Upon his return to Buitenzorg he was offered a vacant position in the herbarium, which he accepted.

By 1910 Smith's contributions to science were prominently recognized and the University of Utrecht awarded him an honorary Ph.D. In 1913 he succeeded Dr. Valeton, taking over as chief of the Buitenzorg Herbarium, finally becoming acting director of the government Botanic Garden in 1922.

Influenced by ill health, Smith retired and returned to Holland, where he made his home at Hilversume, then at Utrecht—in close contact with the University of Utrecht Herbarium—and, finally, at Oegstgeest near Leyden, where he could work at his leisure in the National Herbarium at Leyden. As his health progressively declined, he necessarily stayed much at home, where he devoted his time and energies to his *Icones Orchidacearum Malayensium*. He also wrote articles and papers for the *Bulletin du Jardin Botanique de Buitenzorg*, in which he described numerous new species and added data to many previously described. Also from his pen came the eight-volume work on the orchids of Dutch New Guinea. His *Artificial Key to the Orchid Genera of the Netherland Indies, together with those of New Guinea, the Malay Peninsula and the Philippines* was published in *Blumea*. Orchid floras of Java, Sumatra, Amboina, and other areas followed, and an article entitled "Sarcanthus Lindl. und die Nächstverwandten Gattungen" was published in *Natuurkundig Tijdschrift voor Ned. Indië*, in which he clarified and segregated the genera bordering the genus *Sarcanthus*.

Smith's relaxation at home was in his garden. His small greenhouse was filled with orchids sent to him by friends all over the world, and this collection was the center of his interest. During the German occupation of Holland during World War II, lack of fuel prevented the heating of the greenhouse and, regrettably, he was forced to part with his collection.

On 14 January 1947, in his eightieth year, Smith died, his eminence as an authority on Eastern orchids remaining secure in the history of orchid achievements.

References

Orchid Review, The. 1934. Notes. Vol. 42, no. 495.

Schweinfurth, Charles. 1947. A Great Orchidologist Passes. *Amer. Orch. Soc. Bull.* 16, no. 3.

van Steenis, C. G. G. J. 1950. Cyclopaedia of Collectors. *Flora Malesiana.* Vol. 1, ser. 1.

Friedrich Richard Rudolf Schlechter (1872-1925)

"WITHOUT A GOOD MEMORY IT IS OF NO USE TRYING TO BE A BOTANIST; ONE had better give it up and be a merchant." Rather a discouraging and outspoken statement, by most standards, yet extremely characteristic of the egoistic self-confidence of the great orchidologist, Friedrich Richard Rudolf Schlechter—a man of driving ambition, great capacity for work, and a remarkable memory.

Schlechter was born in Berlin, Germany, on 16 October 1872. As a youth he served an apprenticeship as a horticulturist, and at nineteen years of age he left Europe for the beginning of botanical explorations that carried him to Africa in 1891 and later to Sumatra, Java, Celebes, Borneo, New Guinea, the Bismarck Archipelago, and Australia. For nineteen years thereafter he was continually in foreign lands, collecting botanical specimens and acquiring a constantly expanding knowledge of orchids in their native habitats.

Extensive trips were made to south tropical Africa (including the Yoruba country, the Cameroons and Togoland) in 1895–1898 as leader of an expedition for the German Colonial Department to investigate the caoutchouc industry. In the summer of 1895 he worked for several weeks in the Department of Botany at the British Museum, having just returned from South Africa. He had made extensive collections there, particularly asclepiads and orchids, and it was chiefly these that he studied during his stay in London. As a result of the expedition, the botanical appendix to his *Westafrikanische Kautschuk-Expedition* (1899–1900) contained the names of many new plant species.

In 1901–1902 he appeared in German New Guinea, and again visited there in 1906–1909. Though most of his time was absorbed by economic matters, he made it a point to find some for collecting and studying orchids, with the result that whereas ninety species belonging to thirty-two genera were known from the area in 1901, his collections brought the total up to the surprising figure of 1450 species (1102 of which were new) representing 116 genera. *Die Orchidaceen von Deutsch-Neu-Guinea*, the important work stemming from his introductions and discoveries, was published as a large volume of over 1100 pages in 1911–1914.

Schlechter also botanized in New Caledonia (1902–1903) and the results of his collections were published in Engler's *Bot. Jahrb.*, volumes 36 and 39, in which he again specialized in the Orchidaceae. A few years later *Die Orchideenfloren der südamerikanischen Kordilleranstaaten* made its appearance.

Between collecting trips Schlechter continued his visits to London, stopping in always at the herbarium at Kew and the British Museum. He was considered an interesting figure, but being no respector of persons or things, he was apt to trod on other people's feelings and sensibilities. He was dogmatic in his convictions, a characteristic which did not assist in making him popular; but on the basis of his achievements and experience, he was accorded great respect.

Throughout his career Schlechter was occupied with the publication of the results of his indefatigable research, and at an early period he set for himself the ambition of describing at least one new species each day. That ambition may have been achieved; it was estimated that he proposed in excess of 1000 new species of orchids alone. Simultaneous with the publication of the results of his findings, and beginning in 1893, his published contributions to systematic botany appeared with regularity each remaining year of his life. In those years he produced more than 300 individual papers. His contributions to *Orchis* and *Die Orchideen* represent valuable additions both to horticulture and orchidology.

Before World War I he married and settled in Berlin, where he took his Ph.D. and served as a curator in the Botanical Museum at Dahlem. There he continued his taxonomic work in a large, well-lighted room, surrounded by the cases of herbarium material he had brought with him in 1913. He devoted himself primarily to the orchids of both the Old and New World, including enumerations of those of the Chinese-Japanese regions and various parts of tropical America, and published as *Beihefte* of Fedde's *Repertorium*.

Schlechter died at only fifty-three years of age. His untimely death on 16 November 1925, at Berlin-Schöneberg, was thought to have been due to the lingering effects of diseases contracted in the eastern tropics. His name lived on, however, through the many species that bore his name, plus the genera *Schlecteria* of the *Cruciferae*, *Schlecterella* of the *Asclepiadaceae*, and *Schlecterina* of the *Passiflora*. The orchid genus *Schlecteriella* was named and dedicated to his memory by the Brazilian orchidologist F. Hoehne in 1944, and he is further commemorated by *Epidendrum schlechterianum*, *Gastrorchis schlechterii*, and *Goodyera schlechterii*.

The immense collections made by Schlechter were placed in the Botanical Museum at Dahlem, where they continued to grow, becoming one of the finest definitive herbaria of the world. Disaster struck in the form of World War II, however, when on the night of 1 March 1943 the museum was bombed and the thousands of critical specimens and notes destroyed. The following year Oakes Ames, another great orchidologist who had known Schlechter, wrote from Harvard University:

Now that the collection on which a large part of Schlechter's life work rested has been dissipated and now that the main groundwork of his prolific writings has been destroyed, it may be of interest to readers of the [*American Orchid Society*] *Bulletin* to know what evidence remains to interpret his conclusions and to measure the accuracy and dependableness of his deduction.

Nearly half a century ago my acquaintance with Schlechter began and toward the end of his life—he died in 1925—we were working together on a monographic treatment of the orchids of the world. As we did not meet until August, 1922, our association up to that time was through a copious correspondence and through the exchange of orchid specimens. Dr. Schlechter always made helpful analytical sketches of the species he studied and at my request an artist was employed to make for me not only copies of these sketches but tracings from the type specimens on which they were based. After his death his wife, Alexandra Schlechter, continued to have drawings made for me so that in time my herbarium contained a useful record of a large number of Schlechter's types with emphasis on the orchids of Middle America.

In the *Bulletin* from time to time, references have been made to the C. W. Powell orchid garden in the Canal Zone. Powell was deeply interested in the orchids of Panama and in his efforts to identify them he sent specimens to R. A. Rolfe at Kew. Rolfe was hesitant about supplying names because of his inability to interpret with certainty many of the Central American species which Reichenbach had described and at this time he was unable to consult the Reichenbach Herbarium in Vienna. Then Powell turned to Schlechter for aid and Schlechter published liberally the results of his research. Many new species were recognized and a very important paper devoted to Powell's orchids appeared in a German publication. Fortunately Powell had numbered the plants in his garden so that the types of Schlechter's new species were represented by living counterparts. At my request Powell made herbarium specimens for me from his numbered plates, so, with few exceptions, we have a complete series of the identical plants which Schlechter described. Furthermore, this representation of Powell's collection is re-inforced by sketches and tracings based on Schlechter's types.

We may say, then, that the loss of Schlechter's herbarium, while irreparable and tragic, is softened by the splendid record now available at Harvard University.

References

Ames, Oakes. 1944. Destruction of the Schlechter Herbarium by Bombing. *Amer. Orch. Soc. Bull.* 13, no. 4.

Ames, Oakes. 1933. Friedrich Richard Rudolf Schlechter—1872–1925. *Amer. Orch. Soc. Bull.* 2, no. 2.

Dillon, Gordon W. 1957. Development of a System of Orchid Classification. Understanding the Orchid Family—II. *Amer. Orch. Soc. Bull.* 26, no. 4.

Journal of Botany. 1926. Obituaries—Dr. Rudolf Schlechter (1872–1925). Vol. 64, no. 757.

Lantern. 1963. Kirstenbosch Jubilee Issue. Pretoria. Vol. 13, no. 1.

Orchid Review, The. 1925. Obituary. Vol. 33, no. 390.

Orchid Review, The. 1927. Notes. Vol. 35, no. 403.

van Steenis, C. G. G. J. 1950, Cyclopaedia of Collectors. *Flora Malesiana.* Vol. 1, ser. 1.

Oakes Ames (1874–1950)

"ONE OF THE OUTSTANDING BOTANICAL INSTITUTIONS OF THE WORLD IS THE Orchid Herbarium of Oakes Ames, at Harvard University in Cambridge, Massachusetts. It is the only herbarium in the United States and one of the few in the world which is devoted exclusively to orchids. . . .

"The Ames Herbarium, . . . represents the life work of Prof. Oakes Ames, once a leader in the botanical field in Harvard University, Director of the Botanical Museum and for many years the foremost American orchidologist. . . ."

These words of praise were published in the *Philippine Orchid Review* in 1955, written by Charles Schweinfurth, for thirty-five years an associate and close friend of Oakes Ames. They portray a short, but factual and unbiased, account of the ardor and diligence given by a remarkable man to his favorite plant family—the Orchidaceae.

Oakes Ames was born on 24 September 1874, in North Easton, Massachusetts. Grandson of Oakes Ames, the builder of the Union Pacific Railroad, and a son of Oliver Ames, later governor of Massachusetts, young Ames entered a heritage of culture, family wealth, and position. At an early age he became interested in orchids and formed a collection of his own.

Ames graduated from Harvard University in 1898, received his A.M. there in 1899, and joined the teaching faculty. Shortly thereafter he was chosen as director of the Harvard Botanical Garden. In 1926 he became professor of botany and chairman of the Division of Biology. In 1932 he was appointed Arnold Professor of Botany. From 1935 until his retirement in 1945 he served as director of the Botanical Museum and until his death was associate director and research professor of botany emeritus. All the while he upheld and contributed to the prestige of his alma mater.

All during his career Ames maintained an active interest in orchids, devoting most of his leisure time to the taxonomic study of that expansive plant family. His studies took him all over the world, and his work on orchids resulted in the publication of numerous papers on the orchids of various regions, plus seven volumes entitled *Orchidaceae: Illustrations and Studies of the Family Orchidaceae*. Ultimately, in the tradition of those great orchidologists who preceded him, Lindley and Reichenbach, he became the leading orchid authority in the world.

In the meantime he met Blanche Ames, a Smith College graduate who had taken top honors in her chosen field: art. They were married in 1900. Their combined accomplishments in orchidology left a most enduring impression on the botanical world; many of Ames' publications were embellished with the marvelous etchings and line drawings of his wife. In their North Easton home, Blanche Ames produced nearly infinite numbers of orchid illustrations under the guiding influence of her botanist husband. Much of her time was involved also in doing phylogenetic charts for Professor Ames' use in his course in economic botany at Harvard.

In connection with his teaching duties and research, Ames accumulated an extensive library pertinent to his studies and courses. An herbarium numbering over 14,000 sheets of dried economic plant materials was also formed, and during World War I Ames served on the Economic Research Council in Washington because of his eminent knowledge of plants useful to man. In this connection, his book, *Economic Annuals and Human Culture*, probably speaks most profoundly for his eminence in that field.

Though deeply involved in university studies which would have staggered even the most dedicated, Ames' zeal for orchid taxonomy remained at a high peak. For forty years he received specimens sent for identification and analysis from correspondents all over the world. As a result, an extensive orchid herbarium was formed. The initial work was first housed in the Ames residence at North Easton, then at the Bussey Institution in Jamaica Plain, and later at his home in Boston. In 1924 it was transferred to the Botanical Museum at Harvard. There it continued to grow, numbering 64,000 sheets, 4000 fresh orchid flowers preserved in alcohol, a collection of 20,000 glass slides of orchid flowers, and about 1200 volumes devoted mainly to the various phases of orchidology. Over 1000 pamphlets were also catalogued in that vast assemblage. In later years the collection became known as the most perfectly organized and complete herbarium of any plant group in any country in the world. Only the Lindley Herbarium at Kew and the Reichenbach Herbarium in Vienna approached the enormity and content of the Ames collection. In 1954 the entire herbarium was transferred to the new Harvard University Herbarium.

Oakes Ames is perhaps best known for his involvement with the orchids of the Philippines. Though interested in the flora of the Philippines since 1898, and despite his long association with Dr. Elmer D. Merrill, director of the Bureau of Science in Manila, he was reluctant to encroach upon a botanical area then being studied by various other botanists. In his own words:

Prior to 1898, there was a tendency among American botanists to leave to British, German and Dutch authorities the task of interpreting the orchids of Malaysia. These authorities had at their command the historic collections of the Old World and were well grounded in the intricacies of the Malaysian flora. Robert A. Rolfe, at Kew, had a definite interest in the flora of the Philippines; Rudolf Schlechter of the Berlin Museum, through his researches among Celebesian species, was turning his attention toward the Philippines; and J. J. Smith of the Buitenzorg Botanic Garden, the master of the Javan field, was actively engaged with the orchid flora of the outlying islands. And Fritz Kraenzlin was busy with his ponderous monographs of Eria and Dendrobium, genera comprising a host of Malaysian species. It seemed hardly wise or necessary for an American to enter a sphere of effort of which the materials were already in capable hands. Furthermore, in 1898, one might have counted on one's fingers and toes the number of Philippine orchids represented in the plant collections of the United States. Even had he wished to enter the field, an American botanist, if he had attempted to do so, would have merited being called rash, if not foolhardy.

Returning from a summer vacation in 1905, Ames was amazed, however, to learn from his assistant, Dr. Robert G. Leavitt, that the Bureau of Science at Manila had invited him to identify specimens accumulated through an intensive exploratory campaign—and that Dr. Leavitt had accepted on Ames' behalf, committing him to the research! Ames later commented:

. . . It was indeed a harrowing experience in view of my preparation for the job, because it soon became apparent that I lacked not only the specimens but the requisite knowledge to carry on critical identifications. It became apparent also that the Philippines possessed a richer orchid flora than had been revealed by the published records. Moreover, first and last, I was attempting to keep pace with the industry of over seventy collectors, several of them devoting their attention exclusively to the search for orchids.

. . . One morning in early September, 1905, the victim of perplexity and despair, I went to my laboratory and instructed my assistants, Dr. Leavitt and Mr. A. A. Eaton, to pack up the accumulation of specimens, to provide three microscopes, three cameras and a selected set of helpful books and to make themselves ready to accompany me abroad. I had decided that it was high time to visit the herbaria of Europe and to make a thorough examination of the available collections of orchids from the Malay Archipelago. It was planned to make analytical drawings of the flowers of significant types and to attempt to assemble a complete photographic record of herbarium specimens germane to the orchids of the Philippines. At midnight, on October 10, we steamed out of Boston Harbor on the Cunard liner, R. M. S. *Saxonia*, with an overwhelming burden of trunks.

As a result of his studies of the important collections of early Philippine types at Kew and the British Museum, and at Paris and Leyden, Ames became the world authority on Philippine orchids, describing hundreds of species new to science. Later trips to the jungles of Honduras and Brazil, plus a round trip of the world, served as addenda to his botanical versatility. Of his study of Philippine orchids he stated:

. . . My invasion of European herbaria to familiarize myself with Malaysian orchids was not only profitable in the line of my interests and ambitions but it proved to be the beginning of many influential friendships which were invaluable in subsequent research. It aroused intense curiosity because in a way it was indeed quixotic. At that time it must have disturbed the even tenor of such dignified institutions as the British Museum of Natural History and the Royal Botanic Gardens at Kew, where liberal concessions were made to enable me to keep outrageously early hours and where much space was needed to accommodate my cameras, microscopes, specimens and two active and earnest assistants. I learned how to enter the Kew Herbarium with the cleaners, before the staff arrived, through the basement and by way of the back stairs, and in retrospect it seems to me that I must have taxed to the point of alarm the kind hearts of my considerate British cousins. The memories of the helplessness I felt when I approached my task still linger vividly. As I have said above, the Malaysian region was formerly very much a special field of the British, German and Dutch botanists. But now the student of the Philippine orchid flora, to avoid pitfalls and to accomplish his purpose, must come to the United States, because nowhere else in the world is there a comparable assemblage of types and critically identified Philippine orchids.

Later, Ames wrote the orchid section in Merrill's *Enumeration of*

Philippine Flowering Plants. In March 1930 he and Mrs. Ames visited Manila, where he collaborated with the Philippine botanist, Dr. Eduardo Quisumbing, on a series of articles on Philippine orchids which appeared in the *Philippine Journal of Science* (1931–1937). Unfortunately, the manuscript of their fully illustrated ten-volume monograph was later lost in the liberation of Manila during World War II. Ames' visit also included meeting Ramos, Santos, and McGregor, the collectors who had for so many years furnished him with much of the material described and analyzed in his enumeration of Philippine orchids.

Numerous honors and awards were quite naturally accorded Professor Ames during his plenary career, among them the Gold Medal of the American Orchid Society, the Centennial Medal of the Massachusetts Horticultural Society, and the George Robert White Medal for eminent service to horticulture. In addition to being a fellow of many learned societies both in the United States and abroad, he was an honorary member of the American Orchid Society and served as a vice-president from its inception. Washington University awarded him the honorary degree of doctor of science, at St. Louis in 1938.

Fifty years of loyal service to botany and Harvard University terminated with Ames' death on 28 April 1950, at his Ormond, Florida, home, at the age of seventy-five. But his name lives on in the orchid genera *oakes-amesia* and *Amesia*, as well as in the charming Philippine *Vanda amesiana.*

References

American Orchid Society Bulletin. 1948. Orchids in Retrospect. Vol. 17, no. 7.

Ames, Oakes. 1945. Notes on the Orchid Flora of the Philippines. *Amer. Orch. Soc. Bull.* 13, no. 10.

Davis, Reginald S., and Steiner, Mona Lisa. 1952. *Philippine Orchids.* New York: The William-Frederick Press.

Philippine Orchid Review. In Memoriam. Vol. 3, no. 2, p. 16.

Proceedings of the Linnean Society of London. 1951. Obituaries. Session 162, 1949–50. Part 2.

Schweinfurth, Charles. 1955. Mrs. Oakes Ames as a Botanical Illustrator. *Philippine Orch. Rev.* 6, no. 1.

Schweinfurth, Charles. 1950. Oakes Ames. *Amer. Orch. Soc. Bull.* 19, no. 6.

Schweinfurth, Charles. 1956. Oakes Ames Orchid Herbarium. *Amer. Orch. Soc. Bull.* 25, no. 7.

Schweinfurth, Charles. 1955. The Oakes Ames Orchid Herbarium. *Philippine Orch. Rev.* 6, no. 1.

Lewis Knudson (1884-1958)

PRIOR TO FEDERAL QUARANTINE REGULATIONS WHICH PROHIBITED THE IM-
portation of orchid plants into the United States, large numbers were
collected and there was a constant supply of plants and blooms for a
flourishing industry. The Department of Agriculture's quarantine regulations sharply curtailed this seemingly unlimited supply of plants, however. In addition, growers were desirous of producing hybrids which
would give flowers of higher quality and which would permit flower
production throughout the year instead of during relatively short seasons. The problem of successfully germinating orchid seed was a limit-
ing factor, though. Noel Bernard had shown in 1909 that orchid seeds
in nature required mycorrhizal fungi for germination, and out of this

work a method was developed whereby a culture medium could be used and the fungus artificially introduced. A certain degree of success was attained, but failure with the method was nevertheless common. It remained for a young plant physiologist at Cornell University, Ithaca, New York, to become interested in the problem and to develop the asymbiotic method of orchid seed germination that revolutionized the commercial orchid industry. This man was Lewis Knudson.

Lewis Knudson was born in Milwaukee, Wisconsin, on 15 October 1884. After graduating from the University of Missouri in 1908 with the degree of B.S.A., he went to Cornell University as assistant in plant physiology and began teaching graduate students, all of whom were older than he. Liberty Hyde Bailey, then dean of the College of Agriculture, had told the head of the plant physiology department that he might engage an assistant who would be willing to do considerable rough work in addition to other duties, and who could be discharged at the end of the spring term if it seemed advisable. By the end of the term Knudson had been advanced to instructor status, however, receiving his doctorate and becoming assistant professor of plant physiology in 1911! His first major research was on tannic acid fermentation, and one of his two Ph.D. theses was written on that subject. Shortly afterward, he and his graduate students developed one of the first reliable cultures of nitrogen-fixing bacteria for inoculation of legumes.

Upon the resignation of Professor B. M. Duggar, whom Knudson had worked under, in 1912 he was made acting head of the Department of Plant Physiology, which in 1916 was incorporated into the newly created Department of Botany, and so Knudson gained another title: professor of botany.

One of Knudson's main interests was the organic nutrition of plants. In 1916 he began growing various plants in environments free from microorganisms. As a result of his investigations on the use of sugar by plants and his development of pure culture, in 1917 he adapted his techniques to the germination of orchid seeds.

In 1919 he was invited by the Spanish government to establish the study of plant physiology in Spain and to give courses in Madrid and Barcelona. Six months were spent in Spain and a year in France, where he carried out research at the Sorbonne and attended lectures in the Pasteur Institute. Here he was able to attend Madame Marie Curie's discussions on radium.

Continued interest in the pure culture growth of plants and his interest in the theories of Noel Bernard in France and Hans Burgeff in Germany led him to the hypothesis that orchid seeds could be germinated without the presence of the mycorrhizal fungi but with sugars and starches. European botanists were aroused to caustic comment by Knudson's early papers on these ideas. The hypothesis was verified when put to test, however. Eight years of investigation and experiments in seed germination enabled Knudson to prove conclusively that orchid seed could be successfully germinated on an artificial culture medium. This breakthrough brought about a revolution and a new awakening in orchid hybridization on both the amateur and commercial levels. Eventually Knudson published over twenty papers on the subject.

In 1938 the vanilla industry in Puerto Rico was threatened by a disease that caused continued root decomposition. A request for aid was sent to Cornell and Knudson responded. The solution appeared to be the development of hybrids resistant to root decay and of equal or better quality than that of *Vanilla fragrans*, then being cultivated for its flavoring. Knudson's experimentation in pollination and asymbiotic seed germination led to the development of two rot-resistant hybrids—the first *Vanilla* hybrids produced.

In 1941 Professor Knudson became head of the Department of Botany at Cornell. For twelve years he was consultant for the United Fruit Company and organized much of the research on bananas both in the tropics and in the United States, and his interest in the problems of tropical agriculture took him on many trips to the countries of Central America. His work there became a major contribution to the economy of those countries. His investigations dealt with a very destructive disease of bananas, with culture methods of producing bananas, and with the physiology of ripening of the fruit. The research involved resulted in better selection of farming land, increased productivity per acre, and the abandonment of replanting and cultivation by disc and harrow.

Less widely known but nevertheless noteworthy was his interest in the effects of radiation on chloroplast morphology in ferns. The pure culture technique was also used in this study, and through the use of X-ray on fern spores, many extraordinary permanent mutations were induced.

Knudson was an exceptionally effective teacher in both elementary and advanced courses of plant physiology and, when necessary, also lectured with marked success in the general botany courses. By his sympathetic and stimulating direction, twenty-five students completed the work necessary for the doctor's degree under him. Many of these students became widely known in plant physiology, horticulture, and related sciences.

During his period of active service Lewis Knudson was appointed to many of the most important committees of Cornell University, and memberships and honors were granted him by other organizations. He had been vice-president of the American Orchid Society, which in 1949 conferred on him its Gold Medal for distinguished service to orchidology. He was also an honorary member of the Orchid Societies of Caracas, Venezuela, and of Brazil; a fellow of the American Association for the Advancement of Science; a member of the Botanical Society of America; honorary member of the Real Sociedad Española de Historia

Natural; and member of the American Society of Naturalists, American Society of Plant Physiologists, Alpha Zeta, Gamma Alpha, Sigma Xi, and Phi Kappa Phi.

Knudson retired, after forty-five years of service to Cornell, on 30 June 1952. Even after retirement, however, his interests in science and plant physiology remained strong, and his emeritus activities in consultation and research continued without pause.

To honor him, the Federated Garden Clubs of New York State presented him its Gold Medal award in 1956 "for distinguished service in scientific research on the physiology and nutrition of plants," an honor conferred on only one other scientist, the famed Liberty Hyde Bailey. In 1957 he was awarded the degree of honorary doctor of science by his alma mater, the University of Missouri.

On 31 August 1958, at seventy-three years of age, he died in his home at Ithaca, New York. He had practically completed a monograph of the banana at the time of his death. He was survived by his widow, Caroline I. Knudson, and two sons.

References

American Orchid Society Bulletin. 1958. Necrology. Vol. 27, no. 10.

American Orchid Society Bulletin. 1950. Society Honors Two Scientists. Vol. 19, no. 8.

Nature. 1958. Vol. 182, p. 1640.

Miscellaneous papers provided by Cornell University, Ithaca, New York.

Index

Additions to a Chronological Guide to Descriptive and Taxonomic Orchid Literature

Timber Press thanks Merle A. Reinikka, Robert L. Dressler, and Gustavo A. Romero for their assistance in updating the Chronological Guide to Descriptive and Taxonomic Orchid Literature for this edition. Please see pages 97–108 for earlier literature references.

1968 J. Hutchinson and J. Dalziel. *Orchidaceae*. Flora of West Tropical Africa, Vol. III, Part I.

1968–84 V. S. Summerhayes and P. J. Cribb. *Orchidaceae*, Parts 1, 2. Flora of Tropical East Africa.

1969–70 E. Foldats. *Orchidaceae*. Flora of Venezuela, Vol. 15, Parts 1–5.

1970 J. Fowlie. *The Genus Lycaste*.

1970–94 F. G. Brieger, R. Maatsch, and K. Senghas. *Rudolf Schlechter's Die Orchideen*, Ed. 3.

1974 R. L. Dressler and G. E. Pollard. *The Genus Encyclia in Mexico*.

1974 L. A. Garay and H. R. Sweet. *Orchidaceae*. Flora of the Lesser Antilles, Vol I.

1974 L. A. Garay and H. R. Sweet. *Orchids of the Southern Ryukyu Islands*.

1974–81 F. Hamer. *Las Orquídeas de El Salvador*.

1975 C. A. Luer. *The Native Orchids of the United States and Canada Excluding Florida*.

1975 G. Pabst and F. Dungs. *Orchidaceae Brasilienses*, Books 1, 2.

1975 Horng-jye Su. *Taiwan Orchids*, Ed. 2.

1975–87 Tsian-piao Lin. *Native Orchids of Taiwan*, Vols. 1–3.

1975–88 G. Seidenfaden. *Orchid Genera in Thailand*, I–XIV. Dansk Botanisk Arkiv, Vols. 29, 31–34; Opera Botanica, Vols. 62, 72, 83, 89, 95.

1976–79 U. Pradhan. *Indian Orchids: Guide to Identification and Culture*, Vols. I, II.

1977   Assoçiacão Orchidiofilia de São Paulo. *Native Orchids of Brasil.*
1977   G. C. K. Dunsterville and L. A. Garay. *Venezuelan Orchids Illustrated,* Vol. VI.
1977   J. Fowlie. *The Brazilian Bifoliate Cattleyas and Their Color Varieties.*
1977   G. Williamson. *The Orchids of South Central Africa.*
1977–94   J. Arditti, ed. *Orchid Biology: Reviews and Perspectives,* Vols. I–VI.
1978   L. A. Garay. *Orchidaceae.* Flora of Ecuador, No. 9.
1978   Tang-shui Liu. *Orchidaceae.* Flora of Taiwan, No. 5.
1978   A. Millar. *Orchids of Papua New Guinea: An Introduction.*
1979   G. C. K. Dunsterville and L. A. Garay. *Venezuelan Orchids: An Illustrated Field Guide,* A–G, H–O, P–Z.
1979   E. Gentry and P. Foreman. *Native Orchids of South Australia.*
1980   T. Bose and S. Bhattacharjee. *Orchids of India.*
1980   H. R. Sweet. *The Genus Phalaenopsis.*
1980   P. van Royen. *The Orchids of the High Mountains of New Guinea.*
1980–89   C. H. Dodson and P. de Dodson. *Orchids of Ecuador,* 1–5, [6–8]. Icones Plantarum Tropicarum, Fasc. 1–5, 10; Ser. II, Fasc. 5, 6.
1981   R. L. Dressler. *The Orchids: Natural History and Classification.*
1981   J. Stewart and E. F. Hennessy. *Orchids of Africa.*
1981–85   G. Seidenfaden. *Contributions to the Orchid Flora of Thailand.* Nordic Journal of Botany, Vols. 1, 2, 5.
1982   L. A. Garay. *A Generic Revision of the Spiranthinae.* Botanical Museum Leaflets, Vol. 28.
1982   J. Stewart, H. Linder, E. Schelpe, and A. Hall. *Wild Orchids of Southern Africa.*
1982–85   F. Hamer. *Orchids of Nicaragua,* 1–6. Icones Plantarum Tropicarum, Fasc. 7–9, 11–13.
1982–89   C. H. Dodson and R. Vasquez. *Orchids of Bolivia,* 1–3. Icones Plantarum Tropicarum, Fasc. 6; Ser. II, Fasc. 3, 4.
1983   I. F. la Croix, E. la Croix, T. la Croix, J. A. Jutson, and N. Johnston-Stewart. *Malawi Orchids,* Vol. 1.
1983   L. Segerbäck. *Orchids of Nigeria.*
1983–86   P. J. Cribb. *A Revision of Dendrobium, sections Latouria, Spatulata.* Kew Bulletin, Vols. 38, 41.
1983–93   C. A. Luer. *Thesaurus Masdevalliarum,* Fasc. 1–18.
1984   M. Banerji and P. Pradhan. *The Orchids of Nepal Himalaya.*
1984   D. Geerinck. *Orchidaceae,* Part 1. Flore d'Afrique Centrale.
1984   H. Valmayor. *Orchidiana Philipiniana,* Vols. 1, 2.
1985   P. Lavarack and B. Gray. *Tropical Orchids of Australia.*
1985   R. McVaugh. *Orchidaceae.* Flora Novo-Galiciana, Vol. 16.
1986   G. J. Braem. *Cattleya: The Brazilian Bifoliate Cattleyas;* Band II, *The Unifoliate Cattleyas.*
1986   M. W. Chase. *A Monograph of Leochilus.* Systematic Botany Monographs, Vol. 14.
1986   S. Deva and H. Naithani. *Orchid Flora of North West Himalaya.*
1986   F. E. Hillerman and A. W. Holst. *An Introduction to the Cultivated Angraecoid Orchids of Madagascar.*

1986   R. L. Rodríguez Caballero et al. *Géneros de Orquídeas de Costa Rica.*
1986   M. C. M. Werkhoven. *Orchids of Suriname.*
1986–92 E. F. de Vogel. *Revisions in Coelogyninae,* II [includes material in I, published in 1983, Blumea, Vol. 28], III, IV. Orchid Monographs, Vols. 1, 3, 6.
1986–94 C. A. Luer. *Icones Pleurothallidinarum,* Fasc. I–XI.
1987   P. Cribb. *The Genus Paphiopedilum.*
1987   J. J. Vermeulen. *A Taxonomic Revision of the Continental African Bulbophyllinae.* Orchid Monographs, Vol. 2.
1987   L. Wiard. *An Introduction to the Orchids of Mexico.*
1988   G. A. Arosemena et al. *Orchids of the Coast of Ecuador.*
1988   G. J. Braem. *Paphiopedilum: A Monograph of All Tropical and Subtropical Asiatic Slipper-Orchids.*
1988   P. Cribb and I. Butterfield. *The Genus Pleione.*
1988   P. Davies, J. Davies, and A. Huxley. *Wild Orchids of Britain and Europe.*
1988   D. Du Puy and P. Cribb. *The Genus Cymbidium.*
1988   D. L. Jones. *Native Orchids of Australia.*
1988   J. Kenny. *Native Orchids of the Eastern Caribbean.*
1988–94 C. A. Luer and R. Escobar R. *Thesaurus Dracularum,* Fasc. 1–7.
1988–   C. L. Withner. *The Cattleyas and Their Relatives,* Vols. I–VI.
1989   L. Bockemühl. *Odontoglossum: A Monograph and Iconograph.*
1989   M. Clements. *Catalogue of Australian Orchidaceae.* Australian Orchid Research, Vol. 1.
1989   C. H. Dodson. *Orchids of Peru,* 1, 2. Icones Plantarum Tropicarum, Ser. II, Fasc. 1, 2.
1989   E. Hennessy and T. Hedge. *The Slipper Orchids.*
1989   B. Lewis and P. J. Cribb. *Orchids of Vanuatu.*
1989   H. W. Pritchard. *Modern Methods in Orchid Conservation.*
1989   T. Reeve and P. Woods. *A Revision of Dendrobium section Oxyglossum.* Notes from the Royal Botanic Garden, Edinburgh, Vol. 46.
1989   W. T. Upton. *Dendrobium Orchids of Australia.*
1989–93 J. Atwood et al. *Orchids of Costa Rica,* 1–3. Icones Plantarum Tropicarum, Fasc. 14–16.
1990   R. J. Bates and J. Z. Weber. *Orchids of South Australia.*
1990   J. B. Comber. *Orchids of Java.*
1990   S. Schelpe and J. Stewart. *Dendrobiums.*
1990–93 R. Escobar R. *Native Colombian Orchids,* Vols. 1–5.
1990–93 E. Hágsater and G. Salazar. *Orchids of Mexico.* Icones Orchidacearum, Fasc. 1, 2.
1991   C. Cash. *The Slipper Orchids.*
1991   I. F. la Croix, E. A. S. la Croix, and T. M. la Croix. *Orchids of Malawi.*
1991   B. A. Lewis and P. J. Cribb. *Orchids of the Solomon Islands and Bougainville.*
1991   A. C. Smith. *Orchidaceae.* Flora Vitiensis Nova, Vol. V.

1991   J. J. Vermeulen. *Orchids of Borneo: Bulbophyllum.* Vol. 2.

1992   J. Arditti. *Fundamentals of Orchid Biology.*

1992   H. Bechtel, P. Cribb, and E. Launert. *The Manual of Cultivated Orchid Species,* Ed. 3.

1992   N. Hoffman and A. Brown. *Orchids of South-West Australia,* Ed. 2.

1992   M. Mayda and J. Ackerman. *The Orchids of Puerto Rico and the Virgin Islands.*

1992   A. Pridgeon, ed. *The Illustrated Encyclopedia of Orchids.*

1992   L. B. Segerbäck. *Orchids of Malaya.*

1992   G. Seidenfaden. *The Orchids of Indochina.* Opera Botanica, Vol. 114.

1992   G. Seidenfaden and J. J. Wood. *The Orchids of Peninsular Malaysia and Singapore.*

1992   W. T. Upton. *Sarcochilus Orchids of Australia.*

1993   D. E. Bennett, Jr., and E. A. Christenson. *Icones Orchidacearum Peruviarum.*

1993   P. J. Cribb, J. J. Wood, M. W. Chase, and J. Stewart. *Thesaurus Woolwardiae,* Vols. 1–4.

1993   C. H. Dodson and R. Escobar R. *Native Ecuadorian Orchids,* Vol. I.

1993   R. L. Dressler. *Field Guide to the Orchids of Costa Rica and Panama.*

1993   R. L. Dressler. *Phylogeny and Classification of the Orchid Family.*

1993   G. Gerlach and R. Schill. *Die Gattung Coryanthes.* Tropische und Subtropische Pflanzenwelt, Vol. 83.

1993   M. A. Homoya. *Orchids of Indiana.*

1993   R. Jenny. *Monograph of the Genus Gongora.*

1993   R. Kaiser. *The Scent of Orchids.*

1993   W. R. Smith. *Orchids of Minnesota.*

1993   J. Stewart and W. T. Stearn. *The Orchid Paintings of Franz Bauer.*

1993   J. J. Vermeulen. *A Taxonomic Revision of Bulbophyllum.* Orchid Monographs, Vol. 7.

1993   J. J. Wood, R. S. Beaman, and J. H. Beaman. *Orchids.* Plants of Mount Kinabalu, Vol. 2.

1994   C. L. Chan et al. *Orchids of Borneo,* Part I.

1994   P. Delforge. *Guide des Orchidées d'Europe, d'Afrique du Nord et du Proche-Orient.*

1994   T. Sheehan and M. Sheehan. *An Illustrated Survey of Orchid Genera.*

Nomenclatural Update

by Gustavo A. Romero
Oakes Ames Orchid Herbarium, Harvard University Herbaria

MANY OF THE GENERA MENTIONED IN *A History of the Orchid* have been the subjects of floristic and monographic studies since the book was first published. Many of these studies are listed in the Additions to a Chronological Guide to Descriptive and Taxonomic Orchid Literature that begins on page 317. Some studies have resulted in changes in the generic and specific names used in the text and illustrations. The following list includes corrected names that are more likely to be found in the current literature. Simple orthographic variants, polynomials, and hybrid genera or species are not included in the update.

NAME USED IN *A History of the Orchid*	CURRENT NAME
Adactylus	*Apostasia*
Aeceolades	*Saccolabium*
Aerides fieldingi	*Aerides rosea*
Aerides micholitzii	*Aerides odorata*
Aerides sanderiana	*Aerides odorata*
Aerides wightianum	*Vanda testacea*
Apetalon	*Didymoplexis*
Bulbophyllum galbinum	*Bulbophyllum uniflorum*
Bulbophyllum leysianum	*Bulbophyllum antenniferum*
Bulbophyllum micholitzii	*Bulbophyllum retusiusculum*
Calanthe furcata	*Calanthe triplicata*
Calanthe masuca	*Calanthe sylvatica*
Calanthe veratriflora	*Calanthe triplicata*
Catasetum warscewiczii	*Clowesia warscewiczii*
Cirrhopetalum	*Bulbophyllum*
Coelia baueriana	*Coelia tryptera*

NAME USED IN *A History of the Orchid*	CURRENT NAME
Coelogyne lagenaria	*Pleione* ×*lagenaria*
Coelogyne wallichiana	*Pleione praecox*
Cogniauxiocharis	*Pteroglossa*
Corymbis	*Corymborkis*
Corymbis welwitschii	*Corymborkis corymbis*
Corysanthes	*Corybas*
Cullenia	*Durio* (Bombacaceae)
Cynosorchis	*Cynorkis*
Cynosorchis major	*Cynorkis major*
Cypripedilum	*Cypripedium*
Cypripedium spectabile	*Cypripedium reginae*
Cyrtopera	*Eulophia*
Cytheris	*Nephelaphyllum*
Dendrobium boxallii	*Dendrobium gratiosissimum*
Dendrobium calceolus	*Dendrobium roxburghii*
Dendrobium cambridgeanum	*Dendrobium ochreatum*
Dendrobium crassinode	*Dendrobium pendulum*
Dendrobium densiflorum	*Dendrobium farmeri*
Dendrobium dicuphum	*Dendrobium affine*
Dendrobium infundibulum	*Dendrobium formosum*
Dendrobium nobile	*Dendrobium primulinum*
Dendrobium paxtonii	*Dendrobium chrysanthum*
Dendrobium phalaenopsis	*Dendrobium bigibbum*
Dendrobium ridleyanum Kerr non Schltr.	*Dendrobium hendersonii*
Dendrobium superbum	*Dendrobium anosmum*
Dendrobium undulatum	*Dendrobium discolor*
Dendrobium wardianum	*Dendrobium pendulum*
Dendrolirium	*Eria*
Dienia	*Malaxis*
Diseris	*Disperis*
Doritis wightii	*Kingidium deliciosum*
Epidendrum alatum	*Encyclia alata*
Epidendrum aromaticum	*Encyclia aromatica*
Epidendrum cochleatum	*Encyclia cochleata*
Epidendrum crassifolium	*Encyclia vespa*
Epidendrum fragrans	*Encyclia fragrans*
Epidendrum lindleyanum (photograph p. 156)	*Barkeria lindleyana*
Epidendrum nodosum	*Brassavola nodosa*
Epidendrum pseudo-wallisii	*Oerstedella pseudowallisii*
Epidendrum raniferum	*Epidendrum cristatum*
Epidendrum vanilla	*Vanilla* spp.
Epidendrum violaceum	*Cattleya loddigesii*
Epidendrum wallisii	*Oerstedella wallisii*
Eria ridleyi	*Eria oblitterata*
Eulophia lindleyana	*Eulophia angolensis*
Euphrobosces	*Thelasis*

NAME USED IN *A History of the Orchid*	CURRENT NAME
Gastrorchis	*Gastrorkis*
Gastrorchis schlechterii	*Gastrorkis schlechterii*
Habenaria fimbriata	*Platanthera grandiflora*
Habenaria viridis	*Coeloglossum viride*
Haemaria	*Ludisia*
Hartwegia	*Nageliella*
Hartwegia purpurea	*Nageliella purpurea*
Josephia	*Sirhookera*
Lichinora	*Eria*
Limodorum tuberosum	*Calopogon tuberosus*
Lindleyella	*Rudolphiella*
Lissochilus	*Eulophia*
Lissochilus welwitschii	*Eulophia horsfallii*
Lycaste virginalis	*Lycaste skinneri*
Masdevallia bella	*Dracula bella*
Masdevallia burbidgei	*Dracula erythrochaete*
Masdevallia harryana	*Masdevallia coccinea*
Masdevallia roezlii	*Dracula roezlii*
Masdevallia wallisii	*Dracula chimaera*
Microstylis	*Malaxis*
Microstylis scottii	*Malaxis calophylla*
Miltonia roezlii	*Miltoniopsis roezlii*
Miltonia vexillaria	*Miltoniopsis vexillaria*
Miltonia warscewiczii	*Miltonioides warscewiczii*
Monochilus	*Zeuxine*
Mycaranthes	*Eria*
Myrobroma fragrans	*Vanilla planifolia*
Neottia australis	*Spiranthes sinensis*
Odontoglossum bictoniense	*Lemboglossum bictoniense*
Odontoglossum grande	*Rossioglossum grande*
Odontoglossum pulchellum	*Osmoglossum pulchellum*
Odontoglossum rossii var. *majus*	*Lemboglossum rossii*
Odontoglossum rubescens	*Lemboglossum rossii*
Odontoglossum sanderianum	*Odontoglossum constrictum*
Oncidium flexuosum	*Oncidium cimiciferum*
Oncidium papilio	*Psychopsis papilio*
Oncidium sanderae	*Psychopsis sanderae*
Ophrys aranifera	*Ophrys sphegodes*
Orchis latifolia	*Dactylorhiza* spp.
Orchis maculata	*Dactylorhiza maculata*
Orchis pyramidalis	*Anacamptis pyramidalis*
Orchis spectabilis	*Galearis spectabilis*
Oxysepala	*Bulbophyllum*
Paphiopedilum boxallii	*Paphiopedilum villosum*
Paphiopedilum caudatum var. *warscewiczianum*	*Phragmipedium caudatum*
Paphiopedilum curtisii	*Paphiopedilum superbiens*

NAME USED IN *A History of the Orchid*	CURRENT NAME
Paphiopedilum sanderiana	*Paphiopedilum sanderianum*
Pattonia	*Grammatophyllum*
Paxtonia	*Spathoglottis*
Pescatorea roezlii	*Pescatorea wallisii*
Phaius albus	*Thunia alba*
Phaius grandifolius	*Phaius tankervilliae*
Phaius wallichii	*Phaius tankervilliae*
Phalaenopsis grandiflora	*Phalaenopsis amabilis*
Phragmopedilum	*Phragmipedium*
Physosiphon lindleyi	*Pleurothallis tubata*
Podanthera	*Epipogium*
Polyrrhiza lindenii	*Polyradicion lindenii*
Rodriguezia secunda	*Rodriguezia lanceolata*
Roezliella	*Sigmatostalix*
Rolfea	*Palmorchis*
Saccolabium bellinum	*Gastrochilus bellinus*
Saccolabium blumei	*Rhynchostylis retusa*
Saccolabium calceolare sensu J. J. Smith	*Gastrochilus sororius*
Saccolabium denticulatum	*Gastrochilus acutifolius*
Saccolabium guttatum	*Rhynchostylis retusa*
Sarcanthus	*Cleisostoma*
Sarcanthus penisularis	*Cleisostoma tenuifolium*
Sarcochilus lilacinus	*Thrixpermum amplexicaulis*
Satyrium viride	*Coeloglossum viride*
Schlechteriella	*Rudolfiella*
Schomburgkia tibicinis	*Myrmecophila tibicinis*
Selenipedilum	*Selenipedium*
Selenipedium roezlii	*Phragmipedium longifolium*
Serapias rubra	*Cephalanthera rubra*
Sophronitis grandiflora	*Sophronites coccinea*
Spiranthes lindleyana	*Cyclopogon*
Sturmia	*Liparis*
Trichotosia	*Eria*
Vanda amesiana	*Holcoglossum amesianum*
Vanda hookeriana	*Papilionanthe hookeriana*
Vanda kimballiana	*Holcoglossum kimballianum*
Vanda sanderiana	*Euanthe sanderiana*
Vanda teres	*Papilionanthe teres*
Vanilla claviculata	*Vanilla bicolor*
Warszewiczella	*Cochleanthes*
Zygopetalum burkei	*Galeottia burkei*

CPSIA information can be obtained at www.ICGtesting.com
Printed in the USA
BVOW010624120113

310442BV00023B/782/P